MW01621043

JOE L. WEBSTER

To Billy Shore,
In my home church, we used to sing a gospel song, "Let the works I've done speak for me." Surely this can be said of you! Your commitment to the causes and public service you have undertaken is to be highly commended!
Thank you also for the confidance you have placed in my daughter, Briana.
With my best wishes,
Joe L. Webster

JOE L. WEBSTER

Dual Callings of Law and Ministry

GROUNDED IN FAITH, FAMILY, AND SERVICE

CHAPEL HILL

PRESS

Cover photo courtesy of Efren Renteria

PUBLISHED BY
The Chapel Hill Press, Inc., Chapel Hill, NC

ISBN 978-1-59715-277-8

First Printing
Printed in the United States of America

DEDICATION

This memoir is dedicated to my late brother, Rev. Dr. James A. Webster, who pastored First Baptist Church of Oak Ridge, Oak Ridge, North Carolina, for thirty-nine years. He dedicated all his heart, soul, and being to his pastoral responsibilities that for him were a labor of love. For seventy-six years he never forgot where he came from—the rural community called Goodwill—whose lessons learned established a firm foundation that served him well.

The Reverend Dr. James A. Webster Christian Family Life Center was dedicated at First Baptist Church, Oak Ridge on October 15, 2023
COURTESY OF CURTIS A. WEBSTER

A good man leaves an inheritance to his children's children.

—PROVERBS 3:22 (NKJV)

Command and teach these things. Don't let anyone look down on you because you are young, but set an example for the believers in speech, in conduct, in love, in faith and in purity. Until I come, devote yourself to the public reading of Scripture, to preaching and to teaching.

—1 TIMOTHY 4:11–15 (NIV)

Snow-covered Swan Range Mountains, part of the
Bob Marshall Wilderness, near Bigfork, Montana, June 1, 2024.
COURTESY OF THE HONORABLE DONALD W. MOLLOY

CONTENTS

FOREWORD

"History is the recorded part of the remembered part of the observed part of what happened." That definition, by Dr. George V. Taylor, University of North Carolina history professor in a "last lecture" many years ago, suggests that even at its best, history is fragmented and incomplete.

One reason for this absence of a preserved past is the paucity of personal memoirs. Memoirs as a genre of history date to ancient times. Yet the preserving and relating of select history, as seen through one person's eyes, is an unfortunate rarity. A few authors—among them Julius Caesar with his *Commentaries on the Gallic War* and Henry David Thoreau with his *Walden*—gain lasting remembrance and fame from memoirs. Most memoirists will not attain that exalted status, yet every human being has a story to tell.

The Joe Webster memoir that follows records a story that is significant on two accounts: (1) because of the era it covers, and (2) because of the man who relates it. The author was born in 1954, some three months before the US Court filed its *Brown v. Board of Education* opinion. Perhaps providentially, I am writing this Foreword on the seventieth anniversary of that decision. It is, without question, among the most impactful ones in the court's history, one that resonates profoundly through American life seventy years later. The era of history this narrative treats thus is one of deep and lasting significance.

The storyteller has lived through this period. He has been a significant actor in the life and events of a particular place as it, and its people, made their way through this fractious, often treacherous, time. As a youngster he integrated his community's previously all-white public schools. As an adult he chose the dual professions of law and ministry as vehicles for further social change. With accomplishments at both to his credit, he chose—or, more accurately, was chosen for—the judicial branch of government as a venue for giving all persons their due and striving to fulfill the biblical mandate to let "judgment run down as waters and righteousness as a mighty stream" (Amos 5:24).

The pervasive influences of family and faith drive the early stages of this narrative. "My parents were hardworking people who relied heavily on their faith in God," the author relates. They were not educated people, just good people. They cared deeply about their children and strove diligently to make them both educated and good.

The title of the first chapter, "A Community Called Goodwill," could have been the title of the book. The concept of "goodwill" pervaded the Webster family and the community in which it lived. Goodwill Baptist Church was at the heart of the community, and its influence on a young Joe Webster proved deep and durable.

So deep and durable, in fact, that when Webster chose the law as his profession, he could not disengage himself from the influence of the church. He thus became both a lawyer and a minister. When his father told him he could not be a Christian and a lawyer because a lawyer has to lie, Webster determined to prove him wrong. The reader thus will benefit not only from the author's depiction of an accomplished legal career but also from some of his well-crafted, inspirational sermons.

Rejection produces hurt and disappointment, intensely human experiences. Webster candidly acknowledges the hurt and disappointment he endured upon receiving negative responses to his law school applications to Duke University, the University of North Carolina, and Wake Forest University. Time and experience convinced him, however, that the Howard University Law School had been where he belonged. He grew to value the legal education he received there; to revere the teachers there who formed him, both as a lawyer and as a person; and to acknowledge that the ethical dimensions of his legal education had enhanced his humanity.

A confluence of this enhanced humanity with legal knowledge and skills shaped the young Webster as a lawyer. As the first African American to practice law in his hometown of Madison, North Carolina, he valued assisting people in need over earning significant money. Indigent civil clients received his able and caring efforts despite their inability to pay. He took his share of indigent criminal cases as well, and those clients, too, received able and caring representation. When practicing in Pittsboro, North Carolina, he represented a member of the Ku Klux Klan pursuant to an indigent-list appointment. For an African American lawyer, assigned to the case by an African American judge, that was the ultimate test of a firm belief that every citizen is entitled to legal representation.

The ethic instilled by family and church, and reinforced by legal education and life experience, remained firmly in place when Webster inserted his arms into the sleeves of a judicial robe. "Equal justice under the law is my motto," he said when installed in his present position, "and I will seek to live by that daily." In his courtroom every individual, however lowly and whatever the nature of the conduct alleged, is treated with the utmost dignity and respect. As a presiding judge he also does his part to preserve his country's democracy, as he brings schoolchildren into a friendly courtroom atmosphere and educates them on their nation's Constitution and creed.

Joe Webster has held many titles, among them son, brother, husband, father, grandfather, student, lawyer, minister, judge, biographer, friend, and public servant. He has patterned his life to fulfill the scriptural requirement "to do justly, and to love mercy, and to walk humbly with [his] God" (Micah 6:8). With this narrative he adds the title "memoirist." He performs well in this role, as he has in others. This Foreword barely touches the many facets of a life well and fully lived. For the parts and details necessarily omitted here, I commend the volume that follows to the reader's careful attention.

Willis P. Whichard
Associate Justice, Supreme Court of North Carolina
1986–1998

Billy Darnell Webster

My late brother Billy Darnell Webster, aka "Billy Jack," is the artist who painted the short tributes to God throughout this publication. I wish he were here so I could thank him for sharing them with me and allowing their use in this memoir. They will forever remind me of how talented, creative, and humorous Billy was. More importantly, Billy's art told the world who Jesus was to him. I mention him and some of his comments to friends and coworkers often. I miss him so much.

Gene Edward Threats

I got to know the late Gene Edward Threats over twenty-five years ago at the Cloister in Sea Island, Georgia. He was one of the people who photographed the Cloister guests during the dinner hours. I had no idea that he was also an artist of the first order. Many years later, after he had spent over a year in the hospital recovering from a kidney transplant, he mailed to me some of his art as a gift. In his letter to me, despite Gene's arduous journey during all of 2015 and part of 2016, he said, "God is still awesome and blessing." I was so happy that my wife, Diane, and I had the opportunity to visit with him in his home before his passing. Gene gifted to me several of his paintings, some of which are included in this publication. I also wish he was here so I could thank him for sharing his art with me and others.

An African proverb says, "They aren't dead so long as you keep calling their names." I will always call Billy's and Gene's names.

I also acknowledge **Shailyn Ramsey**, who visited my home during the 2023 holiday season. Somehow, I learned that she had an artistic talent that I had never heard about. I had been wondering who could assist me with some sketches I wanted to include in my memoir. She immediately said yes, and I immediately put her to work. She gave me one example of what I was hoping to receive, and I knew then that right in my extended family was an artist who loved to produce art, not so much for compensation, but as a labor of love. Thank you, Shay, for answering my call to help. Paraphrasing Proverbs 18:16, people's gift makes room for them before great men.

To my cousins **Addie "Shorty" Brown**, **Denise Smith**, and others from the community of Goodwill, whose names are too many to include herein, I owe a gift of gratitude, without whose assistance I could not have brought back to life the names and faces of ancestors and other residents of "A Community Called Goodwill." To those individuals who assisted me, I am deeply grateful.

I must give a special acknowledgment to **Pedra Denise Lee**, my career law clerk. Over the last twelve years she has freely given her insights about many of my writings and projects, and most importantly, through her words and prayers, reminded me not to forget my motto to dispense justice while offering hope, even to the many young men who come before me charged with very serious crimes.

I also must acknowledge **Marie Johnson**, an employee of the Mountain View Cemetery, the final resting place of my great-great-grandfather Rev. Samuel H. Gibson in Pueblo, Colorado. Marie helped me tremendously in securing photographs of Rev. Gibson's grave site, final residence, and the church where he was eulogized.

My consultation with and encouragement of the **Honorable Willis P. Whichard**, one of the giants of North Carolina history—the only person to serve in the North Carolina House of Representatives, North Carolina Senate, on the North Carolina Court of Appeals, and as an associate justice on the Supreme Court of North Carolina—has richly blessed me. Moreover, his willingness to write the Foreword to this memoir blessed and encouraged me in more ways than I can express in words.

Also, I acknowledge my family, especially my wife of forty-four years, **Diane Ramsey Webster**, and my children, **Briana**, **Camille** and **Evan**, whose computer skills and encouragement in pursuing this project helped me tremendously, especially in researching my family ancestry. Most of all, I acknowledge my **Lord and Savior Jesus Christ** for calling me twice, once as a lawyer with a conscience, and then as a preacher who believes and strives to be what I espouse from the pulpit. Despite the burdens of these dual callings, to use the title of the late Maya Angelou's *New York Times* bestselling book, "Wouldn't take nothing for my journey now."

INTRODUCTION

On February 12, 1954, I was born to Bettie Ester Moore Webster and James Edward Webster at the Annie Penn Hospital in Reidsville, North Carolina, the fourth of their eight children. My parents were hardworking persons who relied heavily on their faith in God. Like most persons of African descent of their day, they had married at an early age. They were mostly uneducated by today's standards, but were educated in life's experiences, which more than made up for what they missed in school. My earliest memory of my parents was seeing them kneeling in prayer in their bedroom at bedtime. There is no doubt that I am the fruit of the dedicated and continuous prayers and hard work ethic of my parents. I also believe that they prayed and worked their way out of poverty. They motivated all eight of their children to obtain a high school diploma, and several of them went on to obtain college or advanced degrees.

The year of my birth heralded one of the most significant and consequential decisions by the US Supreme Court when it unanimously ruled that the segregation of public schools based on race was unconstitutional, in violation of the Equal Protection Clause of the Fourteenth Amendment. The case was *Brown v. Board of Education of Topeka, Kansas*, 349 US 483 (1954). Most of the public schools, especially in the South, remained de facto segregated years after the *Brown* case was handed down. I was a product of those completely segregated schools, until under "freedom of choice" I chose to enter the then all-white Madison-Mayodan Junior High School in Madison, North Carolina, for my seventh-grade year in late August 1966. To this day, I do not know why I chose to help integrate the local schools. Two years later, in August 1968, the schools in my hometown were completely integrated.

One hundred forty-five years before my birth, on February 12, 1809, the sixteenth president of the United States, Abraham Lincoln, was born. History records that he, more than any other president, advanced the cause of freedom for black slaves in America by first issuing the Emancipation Proclamation. Also, significantly, on the day and month of Lincoln's and my birth, on February 12, 1909, the National Association for the Advancement of Colored People (NAACP) was founded in New York City. It would become the nation's largest and most widely recognized civil rights organization and played a role in much of the civil rights legislation a century later—for example, with the passing of the Civil Rights Act of 1964 and Voting Rights Act of 1965.

I have chosen to write this memoir as a testament to my children and children's children, my lineage that may come after them, and anyone who may desire to know my story. First, it is not a document whose purpose is to publicly boast of accomplishments, for I have absolutely nothing to boast about. Even when I was practicing law, in social settings I frequently did not tell others that I was an attorney. Those who have come to know me over the seven decades of my life know that boasting is not who I am. I'm hopeful that my example might encourage my children and children's children and others to also do what they can to make a difference in America and the world. I am especially hopeful that persons of color and those from humble beginnings will be encouraged not to give up, no matter what hardships or roadblocks come their way, but to move forward to accomplish whatever they desire in life. An African proverb says, "To stumble is not to fall, but to move forward faster." As a first-generation high school or college graduate of my memoir immediate family, I overcame many obstacles, some of which are revealed in this. I suspect that my IQ was only average, so I had to study longer hours than many others. But I never gave up on reaching my goals.

It is not the goal of my sermons and other spiritual writings in this memoir to be a theological guide to exegetical study of the scriptures, for my theological training is far too scarce for that. Perhaps it can be a training tool for how to remain grounded during sermon preparation. A sermon is not about the preacher/messenger, it's about the Message. What I have learned in over 25 years of preaching, is that it is how God speaks through the preacher in the pulpit that matters most. During the sermon if you are blessed to get out of the way, so that the audience can see and hear God and not see you, then your preaching will not be in vain. So, I hope that those that read my words will be able to see and hear God as I try to get out of the way in these sermons or other spiritual writings herein. I especially hope that someone will be encouraged by my words, to use the testimony of the old saints of Goodwill, "to run on and see what the end is gonna be."

Growing up in rural North Carolina on a farm in a large family was fun but challenging at times. The hot sun in the tobacco fields during the summer months in the northern Piedmont region of North Carolina seemed brutal at times. My first experience of working as a hired hand in tobacco came when I was around ten years old. During the tobacco harvesting season, I was hired to "hand leaves" to the person called a "stringer." During that first year of my working for a farmer, I earned sixty cents per hour. I will never forget that first day we worked for eight hours and at the end of the day, the farmer paid me with a five-dollar bill. The farmer commented that he owed me $4.80, but since he didn't have any change, he was paying me five dollars. I was so proud of that first payday that I went home and made a wallet out of plastic and paper to keep the five-dollar bill safe. I also recall showing it to my cousins when they visited our home. When I was twelve, my parents purchased a farm. On the deed, it said, ninety-eight acres +/– (more or less), and the farm had a two-acre tobacco allotment. In one or more years, my father leased additional tobacco acreage from other farmers. That first year we only had a mule named Kate to plow the fields and pull the slides or containers of tobacco. There was much about farm life that I didn't like, including working in the fields to do the all chores required to have a successful tobacco crop—including planting, hoeing, removing suckers from the plant, putting sucker oil to kill the suckers, topping the plants, priming, housing the tobacco in the barn, and removing it from the barn to house it in the packhouse until time to sell it at the warehouse.

With so many brothers and sisters, our home was adequate but with not much room to spare. We had four children sleeping in the same room, two in each bed in our modest home. My brother Floyd, or Ricky as we called him, and I slept together. Before we had become potty trained, we argued over which one of us had wet the bed the night before. I recently shared this with my adult son and told him that we would argue about which one of us was the guilty party and would try to determine whose half of the single bed the wet sheets were on. He responded, "That should have been easy to determine. All you had to do was see which one of you had wet underwear." My brother was two years younger than I was, and we often got into small skirmishes and my mother had to break us up. Having recalled these incidents, I wonder why I'm amazed to see my grandsons, who are couple of years apart, engaged in boyhood skirmishes one moment and hugging each a little bit later.

My parents had chickens running around in the yard at the home my parents owned from my birth to twelve years old. We had a milk cow, and my mother had a churn, so, we always had fresh milk and butter. We had chickens and hogs for meat. My parents planted large vegetable gardens, so we always had plenty to eat. My mother, as well as every mother I knew in my community, was an excellent cook. My family sat down at the table for meals, especially supper which is what we called the evening meal during my youth. However, my brother Floyd whose lifelong nickname was Ricky, and I had to stand at the table during our early youth because we didn't have enough chairs for my large family. I recall the time when I first gained the right to sit down at the table; it was when I cut my foot accidentally while walking barefoot one summer. I was taken to the doctor and received stitches to close the wound. I had to walk with crutches. I was able to sit at the table the rest of my childhood until I departed for college. I recall vividly relatives or others from the community dropping by unannounced while we were eating our evening meal. My parents would say, "Come on in and join us. We got plenty, such as it is." It may have been pinto beans, stewed corn, tomatoes, peas, or whatever we had in the garden at the time, or whatever my mother had canned or frozen during the summer months. We may have had fried fatback as the entrée, or no meat at all, but my parents invited whoever stopped by to "Come on in. We have plenty, such as it is." And before taking one bite of food, we'd say our blessing: "Dear Lord, we humbly thank you for this blessing that we are about to receive for the nourishment and strength of our bodies, for Christ's sake, Amen." I learned a valuable lesson about being obedient to my parents' directive to not start eating before everyone was seated at the table. One Sunday morning, my parents had not yet arrived at the kitchen table, and I—feeling hungry and impatient—poured my milk and cereal and had just begun to eat it, when my parents entered the room. I can hear my dad, "Boy, didn't I tell y'all to wait?" He began to give me a Sabbath-day lesson with his large workman's hands on my bottom. He never had to tell me to wait again.

As a young boy, I was very shy and quiet in the early years of my education. I was hesitant to answer questions in class because I was afraid that I would not get the answer right. All my teachers in elementary school were very kind and nurturing black women, although punishment in the form of being struck on the knuckles by one of those thick pencils was occasionally used if a student had to be disciplined for classroom disturbances. I personally was so quiet that some of my elementary teachers would call upon me to "take names" of those who had poor conduct if our teacher had to excuse herself from the classroom. My classmates referred to me as the "teacher's pet." My adult son told me recently that I was what modern-day students would call a "snitch." I never viewed myself as such, not as a child or now. In my early years of my education, I recall being sick with a cold or some other malady occasionally and staying at home from school. By the time I entered the first grade in late August 1960, my parents had four children in school, ages six, nine, eleven, and thirteen, and two others at home, so my mother was a stay-at-home mom at that time. She meticulously cared for me and nursed me back to good health. I later learned that it was difficult for my father to duplicate my mother's innate nurturing nature when it came time to comforting children. When I was almost ten years old, my mother had a medically difficult time after the birth of my youngest brother. All we heard was that she had a setback. My mother was in the hospital for more than a week. It seemed like a month to me. My father, being taught as a child that cooking was a woman's chore, and, also, not ever being welcome in the kitchen by my

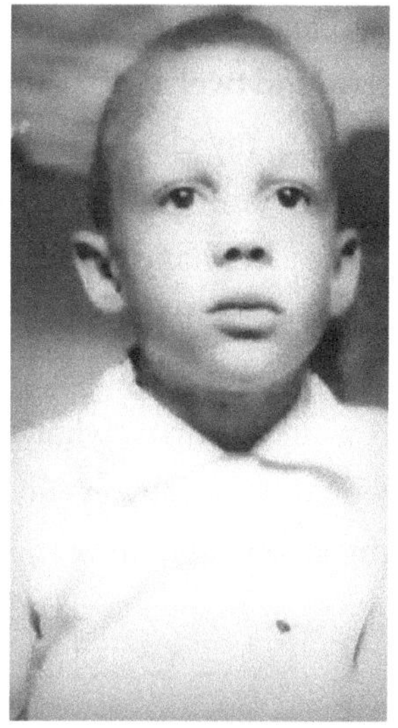

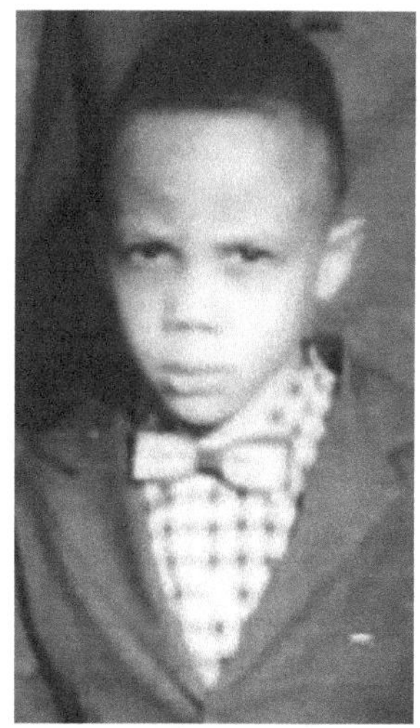

"Teacher's pet" in elementary school

mother, he couldn't cook. Also, my father didn't know how to respond to our simplest questions. I asked him, "When is Mama coming home?" His only response was, "I don't know." Our sadness was made worse by the fact that children couldn't go into the hospital room to visit our mother at that time. It was one of the happiest days of my childhood when my mother finally came home.

During my first-grade year at Charles R. Drew High School (grades 1–12), an event occurred that, if it happened today, would prompt the school administration to make child counselors available to the students in the class, and perhaps to others who heard about the death of my first-grade teacher. I recall being saddened by Ms. Hairston's death, and at the age of six, I wondered why she had died. Sixty-four years later, I still recall hearing someone, perhaps a classmate, say in first-grade terminology that her death was accidentally caused by a staple gun piercing a staple into her hand. At such a tender age, our minds were saddened and confused, so one could understand how one might have imagined such an unimaginable cause of death. I never learned what was the cause of Ms. Hairston's death. This may have been the first death I had ever heard about. My parents, grandparents, and even one of my great-grandparents were still living at the time. My parents took me to Ms. Hairston's home in the aftermath of her death. In the black community, families held visitations in the home of the deceased until late into the night. Those visitations were called "sitting ups." It was also custom in my early childhood for the body of the deceased to lie in the casket in the home where visitors could pay their respects. I recall having dreams about Ms. Hairston's death and don't recall speaking with my parents or anyone else about those experiences. Soon thereafter a much younger teacher, Ms. Fulton, arrived to replace Ms. Hairston for the remainder of my first-grade year. Another traumatic event occurred during my elementary school years. The father of one of my classmates who lived a short distance from my school committed suicide by hanging himself in his home. I have little memory of how this affected me if at all. I do not recall counseling being offered or mentioned by anyone. To this day I have not spoken to my classmate about this tragedy of his father's death for fear of him reliving it.

During my sixth-grade year of public school, toward the end of the 1965–1966 school term and twelve years after *Brown v. Board of Education* mandated desegregation of public schools, my classmates and I were offered the opportunity to become part of the initial stages of integration of the black and white schools to begin in late August 1966. I recall my teacher handing out forms, which I understand now were consent forms for our parents to sign. For some reason, I decided I wanted to be a part of this process, referred to as "freedom of choice." I don't recall having a conversation with my parents about what it would mean or what the pros and cons of leaving Charles Drew for the white school would be. In any event, I agreed to attend Madison-Mayodan Junior High School for my seventh-grade year, leaving behind most of my classmates attending Charles Drew High School. One moment is as clear in my mind today as it was in late August 1966: walking out my family's long graveled farm road to the bus stop and anxiously awaiting the bus to pick me up. I was the only black student entering at my bus stop onto a bus occupied by all white faces that I had never seen before. I recall gingerly walking down the aisle of the bus searching for an empty seat. Thankfully there were no incidents or even jeers that I recall that first day of school. On only one occasion during seventh grade did a white student say something to me that would be considered "bullying" today. Perhaps it was racially motivated, but there were no racial epithets stated during the incident, and I had no way of knowing what may have motivated the student to say something negative to me.

(TOP) Joe at basketball game and (BOTTOM) #30 in senior-year game, Madison-Mayodan Senior High School against North Surry High School

During my elementary, middle, and high school years, I made good grades and participated in extracurricular activities—especially my first love, basketball, which I learned to play on dirt courts from my older brothers and the many cousins who lived within walking distance of our home. I perfected my jump shot, and by my senior year in high school was the starting wing or two-guard. I had a reputation for my excellent defense, and I often was assigned to defend the best guard on the opposing team. I learned early that a basketball player can overcome deficiencies with hard work, hustle, and a willingness to take a charge by one's opponent. My senior year (1971–1972), our basketball team went 27-0 before losing in the semifinals of the North Carolina State 3A tournament. I believe I could have played college ball perhaps at a mid-level college, but knew I wanted to become a lawyer by the ninth or tenth grade. I also believed that college ball would have caused my grades to suffer. While I gave some fleeting thought to trying out as a walk-on my freshman year at Howard University, I did not pursue it, but played on intramural and frequent pickup games that fulfilled my continuing extreme first love of playing basketball.

By the late 1960s the civil rights struggle was in full throttle, and while neither my family nor anyone in my Goodwill community was directly engaged in this noble fight, I read about Thurgood Marshall, other leaders like Rev. Martin Luther King Jr., and Howard University Law School's role in civil rights litigation that was instrumental in aiding the struggle. By then, while the Civil Rights Act of 1964 and the Civil Rights Act of 1965 had been passed by Congress, those acts were not self-executing, and much litigation was taking place especially in the federal courts. As I stepped onto the main campus of Howard University in mid-August of 1972 as an eighteen-year-old freshman, the law school was also located on the main campus. I walked past it on many occasions going to and from classes. In ensuing years, I thought to myself numerous times that I had been graced with the great privilege of walking on the same plot of ground where other noted Howard Law School alumni had walked: Thurgood Marshall, Pauli Murray, Harold and Annie Brown Kennedy, Judges Damon Keith, Spottswood Robinson, Richard Erwin, Vernon Jordan, Governor Douglas Wilder, Reverend Dr. Charles Booth, and where many other noted legal luminaries had also walked. And the noted alumni from the undergraduate campus are great in number. Some examples are Ambassador Andrew Young, Roberta Flack, Chadwick Boseman, Kenneth Clark, Vice President Kamala Harris, Zora Neale Hurston, Toni Morrison, Jessye Norman, Phylicia Rashad, Debbie Allen, Ossie Davis, Letitia James, Congressman Elijah Cummins, Benjamin Chavis, and Congressman Gregory Meeks.

The story of my life and times is set forth in this memoir, through my sermons, speeches, and published newspaper and magazine articles. In this memoir I have chosen to include many photos of my family, friends, and newspaper and magazine clippings. In a familiar phrase, "A picture is worth a thousand words," so I have chosen to share what I have said and done through the many pictures to also tell who I am and what I believe, and about my dual callings of law and ministry. Images of my family illustrate the rich life that I have been blessed and privileged to live.

In 2017 I was favored to be able to publish *The Making and Measure of a Judge: Biography of the Honorable Sammie Chess Jr.* I dedicated that book to my late parents, my decades-long marriage to my wife, Diane, and our three children, Briana, Camille and Evan. I said then that my children were the greatest accomplishments of my life. That fact remains true today. The God-given gift of life is the most important gift of all.

As I have reviewed many sermons and speeches to determine which of them were worthy of publication, I was reminded that this memoir includes quotations from many learned scholars. Many of the quotes are from some of my mentors or those who have inspired me during my career in law and ministry. I have been motivated by many of those quoted, inspired by their words and example all my career to make a difference in this world. My appreciation for these many persons inspired me to include a chapter in this memoir titled "Some of My Mentors or Those Who Have Inspired Me." And of course, I quote from many of the authors of the Holy Bible.

I hope and pray that my memoir will be a testament of what God can do in the life of a person and his ancestry of humble beginnings, if one but attempts to follow the prophetic wisdom of my late mother, Bettie Ester Moore Webster. As I set off to Howard University in the eighteenth year of my life in mid-August 1972, she said, "If you put God first in your life and work hard, someone will see you trying, and someone will help you."

I have sought to be forthright in the words penned in this memoir, confessing at least some of my many faults and sins. I feel it important to impress upon my children and their children that I have been so very far from perfection in my life's journey—that the word "perfect" should never be considered, let alone mentioned when referring to their father and grandfather. Therefore, I have included a writing titled "Confessions from My Papa" in my memoir.

Also, I wanted my family and all who choose to consider me a mentor or role model to know that I have had a rewarding but arduous life's journey. Nothing has come easy for me. In fact, when I arrived on the campus of Howard University, I was required to enroll in a one-semester course in Remedial Reading, I'm guessing because of a low-test score. But as I often tell those whom I seek to mentor, it is not where you start, but where you end up that counts. So when I arrived in Washington, DC, from the Webster family farm, I hardly knew what a city block was. However, I went to work, "burned the midnight oil" (stayed up late at night studying, for today's youth and urban audience), went to class and participated in class discussions, and attended parties or other social events only on weekends. I was blessed to overcome my intellectual inadequacies and graduated May 8, 1976, from the Liberal Arts Honors Program, magna cum laude with a 3.51 grade point average, and earned a Phi Beta Kappa key.

I also write this memoir because I wanted my children and grandchildren to know many of my inner thoughts before my earthly mission is completed. I wanted them to know that much of their family history has been full of successes and failures, happiness and grief. I want my family and others to know how my family persevered through all the storms of life. It has been said that if you don't know where you came from, you won't know where you are going. I also wanted them to know that I am that turtle sitting on top of a fence post, which one of my mentors once told me about and I've seen depicted visually. I read that the vast majority of turtle species crawl upon the ground and cannot climb trees, and the few species that do, seldom do so. So, if one sees a turtle sitting on a fence post all alone, then more than likely the turtle couldn't have gotten there without some help.

ILLUSTRATION BY SHAILYN RAMSEY

Therefore, like the turtle, I have not become under my own power whatever I've been blessed to become in law, ministry, or any other endeavor. To use a familiar saying, I have not lifted myself up by own bootstraps. Indeed, my mother was correct when she told me that if I worked hard and put God first in my life, someone would see me trying and would help me. The "someone" she prophesized about has become "many," who are still helping me today. And the God I write and speak about in my sermons and speeches has undergirded me, encouraged my very soul, and ordered my steps in all that I have undertaken to do in my professional and personal life. I have been aided by too many to name in overcoming the many obstacles I have confronted. My journey has required me to humble myself, as encouraged by the words of Matthew 23:12 (NIV): "For those who exalt themselves will be humbled, and those who humble themselves will be exalted." The God I serve has lifted me above insurmountable obstacles, higher than I ever thought possible, and opened doors for me that I never even knew existed.

I also want my extended family from Goodwill, the community where I grew up, to see the names of their forefathers and mothers, and the name of my community and church in print. I recognized years ago that the oral history of our ancestors is good, but written history is even better. Beyond providing more lasting proof of what has taken place, why else did I want to write down Goodwill's history? It is because I am so very proud of how my ancestors persevered through the storms of life with faith and a hard work ethic unsurpassed by anyone. Also, when I was a child growing up, I was told that some of those who lived "in town"—a few miles away, with paved streets and indoor bathrooms—considered those from my rural Goodwill community to be "country," and less than because many of our roads were not paved, and wells and outdoor toilets were the norm. In this memoir I spend a whole chapter on my community and the great persons who came out of Goodwill. Years ago, I first noticed the scripture found at John 1:46 where Nathaniel, when he first heard of Jesus, posed the question of whether anything good could come out of Nazareth. Using this scripture, I first gave a speech at a Webster family reunion in Stoneville, North Carolina, in which I asked the rhetorical question "Can anything good come out of Goodwill?" Most recently, I posed the same question in a sermon for Providence Baptist Church located in Robersonville, North Carolina. The sermon highlighted the rural counties of Bertie and Martin in Eastern North Carolina. The answer to this question was easy because of the many success stories from these small communities. The chapter titled "A Community Called Goodwill" also answers that question clearly when I give a roll call of the many who have been successful among the lineage of the sons and daughters of poor and mostly uneducated farmers and sharecroppers, and later factory workers from the Goodwill community.

My memoir includes much research on my ancestry. I have found it helpful to my worldview to know who I am and where I came from. In the black community, our ancestors would often ask someone that they had not previously met, "Who your people?" I have long felt the need to know who all my people are, not just the "colored," Negro, black, or African American side of me. In just one visit to the community called Goodwill or Goodwill Baptist Church, one will immediately see many persons of light complexion like me, but in the same immediate family, much darker brothers and sisters as well as in the case of the eight children born to my parents. My cousin Addie "Shorty" Brown related to me that she recalls her relatives telling her they were successful in "passing" as they traveled back home from West Virginia by bus. This allowed them to sit anywhere on the bus, not only in the section for colored people. Another cousin of mine related to me that our Uncle Robert "Bud" Gibson, who was of very fair complexion, was traveling by train sitting in the colored section of the train with a dark-complexioned relative of his. An employee of the train approached him and said, "You don't have to sit back here." I was told he replied, "That's okay. I'm sitting back here with this little girl."

My own recent personal ancestry composition (DNA genetic testing profile) shows I am 57.6 percent sub-Saharan African, of which 53.6 percent is Nigerian with much smaller percentages of West African ancestry, including Ghanian, Liberian, and Sierra Leonean. My East African ancestry is approximately 7.5 percent. According to the DNA testing, I am 41.3 percent European, of which 40.3 percent is northwestern European, and that 36.7 percent of that is British and Irish ancestry. My genetic profile is not surprising. The early post-civil war Census list the race of the Webster, Gibson, and Strickland families as mulatto, meaning mixed race. The most current United States Census includes Black or African American as one of the seven racial or ethnic categories. Regardless of my own genetic profile, my life's work as an attorney, judge, minister, and in my individual capacity has been to uplift the marginalized and downtrodden members of our nation, especially persons of color who have suffered the most in America.

One's racial identity is a concept of human construction. During America's sad history of slavery and Jim Crow, in the case of African Americans, those in power of the majority race concluded that even "one drop" of "black blood" automatically made a person black or Negro. Regardless of my community's personal genetics, my Goodwill ancestry includes many great persons—hard workers gifted with various talents, and persons of unwavering faith, who testified on Sunday mornings about the goodness of God and how far our God had brought us, even out of slavery.

As I have done research and matured in age and wisdom, I cannot say with any degree of certainty whether my personal African ancestry during the years of slavery and Jim Crow was subjected to force by those who had the power to do so, or whether some of us were the product of natural human attraction, affection, and consent. Suffice it to say that personally, I know that I came into being by the grace of God, and as set forth in Psalms 13:14 I choose to praise Him because I am fearfully and wonderfully made; and I can proclaim like David did in this text about the Lord of Lords, "Your works are wonderful, (and) I know them full well." Also, I know that I know that I know with unquestionable certainty who I am and, even more importantly, whose I am. That is sufficient for me.

During my youth, a disabled man used to come to the Webster Reunion annually from Winston Salem. The planners would ask him to come forward and sing a song each year. As a child, I'd see him rise with his crutches, wobbling down the aisle with courage and conviction to the front of the church. Each year he'd sing the same song: "Be what you are and live the life. God knows your heart; you can't get by. He's coming back to judge the world. Be what you are and live the life." I encourage the generations after me to be what they are and live a Christian life. To do that, you must know who you are and, most importantly, whose you are and put your trust in a higher power than yourself.

This memoir also illustrates the intersection of law and ministry, which I consider to be my dual callings; both are guided by very similar ethical principles governing lawyer's and judge's conduct, and Bible scriptures that prescribe Christian living. To be called into the preaching ministry, even on a part-time basis, is a special calling, not to be taken lightly and requiring much soul searching. Many people, including many persons of faith, have asked me how it is possible to for me to be a lawyer-judge and preacher at the same time. I always answer with the same response: "Apparently you don't know the power of God."

For those who believe that one cannot be a lawyer-judge and minister at the same time, consider the similar standards of conduct required for each of them. Violation of these ethical standards does much harm to these professions and to society. Attorneys, judges, and those who seek to live Christian lives according to the Bible are all governed by many of the same prescriptions. Attorneys and judges must avoid even the appearance of impropriety. The American Bar Association's Model Code of Judicial Conduct, Rule 1.2, titled "Promoting Confidence in the Judiciary," states, "A judge shall act at all times in a manner that promotes public confidence in the independence, integrity and impartiality of the judiciary, and shall avoid impropriety and the appearance of impropriety." This rule applies to professional and personal conduct. As to attorneys, the Preamble of the Model Rule of Professional Conduct states, "A Lawyer should avoid even the appearance of impropriety" (CANON 9). In similar language, while some theologians debate the precise meaning of 1 Thessalonians 5:22, Christians are cautioned to "abstain from all appearances of evil."

Luke Chapter 18 speaks of an unjust judge who did not fear God; neither did he regard man. It seems the judge had no compassion for those who came before him seeking justice. Apparently, this unjust judge had not read Micah 6:8: "He hath showed thee, O man, what is good, and what doth the Lord require of thee, to do justly, and to love mercy, and to walk humbly with thy God." A widow persistently came before this unjust judge to beg for justice. She said, "Please grant me justice against my adversary." Bible commentaries suggest that the unjust judge finally gave into the widow's plea for justice because of her persistence in prayer. The wording of the scripture suggests that the judge finally gave in to the widow's request not because his moral compass or heart had changed, but because he was concerned about whether she might ruin his reputation among the community. Whatever the reason, the widow eventually received what she long sought—justice. Paramount in this text is the lesson that the widow's persistent prayer won the judge over to her cause.

My own oath as a federal judge, in pertinent part, states as follows:

> I, Joe L. Webster, do solemnly swear that I will administer justice without respect to person, and do equal right to the poor and to the rich, and that I will faithfully and impartially discharge and perform all the duties incumbent upon me as a United States magistrate judge under the Constitution and laws of the United States; and

> that I will support and defend the Constitution of the United States against all enemies, foreign and domestic; that I will bear true faith and allegiance to the same; that I take this obligation freely, without any mental reservation or purpose of evasion; and that I will well and faithfully discharge the duties of the office on which I am about to enter. So help me God. [28 USC. §453 and 5 USC. §3331]

Years ago, I applied for a judicial position. I had placed on my application that I was an ordained minister. I received an interview, and my minister status caught the eye of one of those on the interview committee. He asked, "What do you think a litigant who appeared before me would think if he or she knew you are a minister?" I responded that a litigant who knows that ministers are governed by principles of goodness, fair treatment, and other moral principles should also know that they would receive equal justice under law and that he or she would receive a fair trial, maybe even more so because I am a minister. Perhaps more so than most, I fully understand that in this very diverse nation, we have many religious beliefs. The First Amendment of the US Constitution does not favor one over the other; the Constitution guarantees freedom of all religions or to have no religion at all. As a judicial official I strongly believe that I cannot and should not take into consideration one's faith in the administration of justice. Neither do I have the desire to do so. To do so would be a violation of my judicial oath and my faith, which mandates fairness and impartiality as I administer justice based upon the facts and the law applicable in each case before me. I am hopeful that my memoir demonstrates that the life of a lawyer and judge can be above reproach and be guided by Christian principles and a moral compass that points toward doing what is just, fair, and the right thing. Another hope is my memoir also helps dispel a public misconception that has placed all lawyers and judges into the same dishonesty-and-distrust category as other vocations of low reputation. As attorneys, we have contributed to this reputation, as I described in my publication titled "Saving Our Profession: It's Up to Us," found here in chapter 7, "Contributions to the Legal Profession and Community."

My late father, James E. Webster, once asked me what I planned to do when I graduated from college. I responded that I planned to attend law school, and that I wanted to become an attorney. His response caught me off guard, as it was not grounded in firsthand knowledge or experience but total hearsay. My father said, "You know that you cannot be a lawyer and a Christian." I was puzzled as to why he said that to me, and I asked him why he thought that. My father first said, "You know." And I responded, "No, I don't know." He said, "Lawyers have to lie." I told him I didn't believe that. My father never mentioned that thought to me again. While I never considered inviting him to observe me try a case in court, I know that through the life and work I embarked upon in my hometown to advocate for those who could not speak for themselves and my community service; the advocacy I embraced beyond my hometown; and the service I rendered as a church trustee and later in the sermons I preached as an ordained minister, my father's impressions about one not being capable of serving as an attorney and Christian at the same time were dispelled. My father proudly told people, "My son Joe is a lawyer and a preacher." So I know he was very proud of me. Therefore, I know that my father, had he lived to see it, would have been overwhelmed with joy that his son had become a US magistrate judge, the first person of color to serve in this capacity on the federal court in the Middle District of North Carolina.

I am not alone in these dual callings of law and ministry. Numerous attorneys and judges have felt them. The Honorable Benjamin Hooks of Memphis, Tennessee, was a practicing attorney; pastored in Memphis, Tennessee, and Detroit, Michigan; was the executive director of the NAACP; and a judge on the criminal court in Memphis, Tennessee. The late Dr. Pauli Murray—civil rights activist, advocate, and author—became the first African American female Episcopal priest in the United States in 1977. One of my mentors, the Honorable Alexander Williams was a practicing attorney, law school professor, and later answered the call as an ordained minister, serving as interim pastor of Walker Memorial Baptist Church in Washington, DC. He became a US district court judge for the District of Maryland. Many others who are nationally known and more locally known in North Carolina have answered the call of ministry while simultaneously serving in the legal profession. Like mine, theirs is a call to make a difference in their communities.

In his interview of me for the *North Carolina State Bar Journal*, now-retired attorney John Gehring, who practiced in Walnut Cove, North Carolina, characterized my legal career as "a life of calm purpose." As a tribute to me during my induction into the Howard University Alumni Club of the Research Triangle Hall of Fame in 2018, the club commissioned a video created by Professor Bruce dePyssler, associate professor of communications at North Carolina Central University. It is titled *Judge Joe Webster: A Life of Calm Purpose*. I certainly returned to my native state after graduating from Howard University School of Law to make a difference, as I was encouraged to do by the old School of Religion professor on the main campus of Howard upon learning what I planned to do upon graduating. Over four and a half decades later, his words still ring in my ears. He said, "If you don't go down there and make a difference you might as well stay up here." I admit that my adherence to those words of wisdom has not always felt "calm."

In fact, many times in the forty-five years of my legal career, I've felt storms churning on the inside as I have sought to make a difference in my native state. Looking back on my career, I will say I have mostly remained calm to accomplish my purpose of making a difference. I repeated the words of that Howard professor six years after my law school graduation at the North Carolina Bar Association Convention in June 1985 in my acceptance speech as I was being awarded the Pro Bono Service Award. I was being honored for representing many clients for free or reduced fees in my hometown of Madison and Rockingham County, North Carolina. Whether as an attorney, judge, or minister, I have not wavered from the topic I was required to write about when I applied to sit for the July 1979 North Carolina bar exam. Each applicant had to write on the subject "Why I Want to Practice Law in North Carolina." I wrote,

> Since childhood I have been interested in the field of law. I have always thought that the study of law would lead to a fascinating, challenging, and rewarding career, one which would enable me to better myself, my state, and its citizens. Through the practice of law in the State of North Carolina, I feel certain that I will be able to realize this goal. Being a life-long citizen of North Carolina and realizing the acute scarcity of practicing attorneys in certain parts of the State, I hope to be able to go into some of those areas and provide legal services to individuals who might not otherwise be able to obtain such help. Hence, I sincerely believe that through the practice of law in the State of North Carolina, I can realize my full potential as an individual, and as an attorney, while also realizing my overwhelming desire to help others who are less fortunate than me. It is for these reasons that I have chosen to return to my home state of North Carolina to practice law.

My experiences as a legal aid attorney fresh out of law school as a Reginald Heber Smith Fellow ... then hanging my shingle to practice law in my hometown of Madison, North Carolina, for over six years; my short tenure as an associate attorney general for the North Carolina Department of Justice; my law practice with the law firm of Coleman and Bernholz in Chapel Hill; my board membership on the NC Board of Law Examiners; my service as deputy director of the Statewide Legal Services of North Carolina Program Inc.; and my unsuccessful campaign for a state district court judgeship for Orange and Chatham Counties all helped mold me into who I am today. Also, hanging my shingle to start a new law practice in Chatham County, Pittsboro, North Carolina, where I practiced for nearly twelve years—and amid this journey, accepting my calling as an ordained minister and my tenure as an adjunct professor of law at Campbell University's law school—helped prepare me for my judicial appointments that followed as an administrative law judge in the Office of Administrative Hearings for the State of North Carolina, and now as a US magistrate judge for the Middle District of North Carolina. These two positions have also contributed to my life's work. However, I write about all this humbly and with much grace, as I have nothing to boast about. I give all the praise to the one who woke me up this morning, my family and community that raised me, and of course my wife and children who have afforded me more grace than I deserve.

I have chosen to include in my memoir some of the most challenging cases I have experienced as an attorney and judge, including my representation of a member of the Ku Klux Klan (KKK); my representation of a defendant in a federal criminal case where one of the main witnesses died on the witness stand; as an administrative law judge presided in an environmental law case, where from the first day of litigation, I saw that politics was as much a part of the case as were the facts and applicable law. Of course, some of the most gut-wrenching cases I have experienced as a federal magistrate judge involve many young African American males who seemingly have done all they could to ensure they will be incarcerated for most of the productive years of their lives.

Highlights of my judicial career include the daily association I have had with some of the most incredible students of the law—including attorneys, judges, law clerks, and externs—that I have ever met. For their advice and counsel, I am truly grateful. It has been the great privilege of my life to serve our nation with them. Days ago, one of my term law clerks completed her time with me. Upon her departure, she left me the following thank you note on my desk:

> Judge Webster, It has been such a privilege to clerk in your chambers. You foster in your staff a sense of diligent hard work mixed with joy and levity, and I am honored to have played a small part in your lasting legacy. Thank you for always believing in me. I will fondly remember being serenaded by your gospel songs and educated on all the colloquialisms. Your faithful catbird, Ashley

There have been many outstanding days during my career. One of those was the day the late Vernon Jordan came to Durham to help dedicate the naming of the John Harvey

Wheeler United States Courthouse. It was an event of great magnitude and included members of congress, judicial, school, church pastors, city, and county officials, and family members of the honoree. Other highlights of my judicial career include the many CourtCares sessions where Durham Middle School students have been introduced to the federal courts, encouraged to stay on the right side of the law, stay drug and alcohol free, refrain from bullying and gun violence, and to never, ever give up, no matter how difficult their life's journey may seem. The promise I have seen in them has been greatly encouraging to me. I even saw promise in the little girl at one CourtCares session who said, "I can't be great because I am a mistake," in response to our guest speaker, a retired general's encouragement to the students that they could be great if they put their minds and hearts to it, and they worked hard.

I also include in my memoir a response to some who have asked me whether I have ever been discriminated against and whether I thought there was discrimination in our system of justice in America. Many among out nation look at the disproportionate number of African Americans one sees daily in court and serving disproportionately long prison sentences and conclude there must be discrimination. First, I saw discrimination as a child each time my parents dropped my siblings and me off at the Patovi movie theater in downtown Madison, North Carolina. We paid our admission fee to the movie theater personnel and walked upstairs to the balcony, which was the "colored" seating section. Whites paid their admission fee and walked toward the downstairs entrance for whites only. My siblings and I were shielded from racial discrimination at restaurants and places such as hotels and other public accommodations, because were never exposed to such places. For example, all our meals, except lunches at our segregated school, were consumed at home. My mother cooked every day, and with few exceptions, my family did not take family vacations. The few times when we did, we stayed with relatives up north or in the Midwest and never once stayed in a hotel during my youth. I don't ever recall staying overnight somewhere else when I was a child other than those few times we traveled to visit relatives in Baltimore, Maryland, and Cleveland, Ohio. I have included in my memoir an article entitled "Experiencing Racism and Disrespect Firsthand," citing two instances of what I believe was discrimination based upon my race. These took place after I moved into an all-white Chapel Hill, North Carolina, neighborhood in 2001 over twenty years after I became a licensed attorney at law.

As to whether I have personally observed individual judges making decisions based solely upon the race of the persons charged in criminal cases or litigants in civil cases, I cannot say with certainty that I have. I am very much aware of the racial disparities that exist in America relating to the proportions of black males in the state and federal prison systems. While I have not personally felt that my clients were treated differently because of race since I first entered the private practice of law in mid-August 1980, however, I have become increasingly alarmed by the many examples of cases that have received the national spotlight seemingly involving disproportionate treatment of African American persons by police officers. One cannot turn a blind eye to such cases in recent history as Brianna Taylor, Eric Garner, and George Floyd, just to name a few of the many whose names should not be forgotten. One can only guess at the multitude of black and brown men and women who were murdered before law enforcement wore cameras. I am also aware of the disparities of persons of color arrested for speeding tickets and other motor vehicle infractions. In years past I've heard young men of color complain of being stopped by police officers for no reason at all. Even if it was not true, the fact that there is a perception of injustice taking place based upon race is sufficient to cause great concern. Our system of justice will only work if those whom it seeks to serve have confidence in it.

Today, many of those being served—especially among the black, brown, and poor of our society—don't have confidence in the judicial system. This is very concerning. Early in my law practice, I traveled from my law office in Madison to a nearby county. As I sat there, I observed a white judge chew out a black detainee in his jumpsuit, seemingly for no reason at all. The judge's comments were demeaning in every manner. The incident occurred over forty years ago. I don't recall the judge's words, but they left an indelible impression on me. At the time, it had never crossed my mind to seek to become a judge one day. However, I recall vividly saying to myself, *If I ever become a judge, I will never treat anyone coming before me with such indignity and disrespect.* I cannot say whether the judge's comments were based upon the detainee's race, condition of poverty, or any other impermissible purpose. I do know that his comments were indefensible. I also know that not one attorney in the courtroom had the courage to challenge the judge's remarks, including me.

So today, I let each person coming before me in criminal cases know that "I see them." I refer to each of them by their name as I say good morning or good afternoon. While I cannot release most of them in detention hearings, using the standards of danger to the community and flight risk, and after considering any potential third-party custodian who may be proffered or offers testimony, I let them know why I have decided to keep them in jail pending trial or further proceedings in the case. No matter what decisions I make, I still seek to dispense justice while offering hope, which is one of the primary guiding principles of my judicial philosophy in criminal cases.

What I do see often in our America today—of which I have sometimes been a victim myself—is that persons of color still struggle to gain the respect of many in the white race. We all saw it in the disrespect that many, even some congresspersons, had for former president Barack Obama because of his race. America is still suffering from the anger built up among portions of the public who hated President Obama. I must say that I have had some incidents that I felt I was disrespected because certain persons could not get accustomed to my position of authority, even though my own conduct demonstrated respect for all I have been required to work with. I have observed this ugly disrespect even in my capacity as a federal judge. In America today, we are still a long way from the hope of Rev. Dr. Martin Luther King Jr. and millions of persons of color that one day our children would be judged by their character and not by their skin color. I contend that being disrespected when respect has been earned hurts as much as racial discrimination. I hope that my memoir in some way serves as a beacon for my children and children's children, and causes persons from all races, genders, faiths, and walks of life to become reconciled with one another. That is my hope and my prayer.

In conclusion of this lengthy introduction, I want to say a bit more about who I am and why it is that I am not far from the same little boy that grew up in the Goodwill Community beginning seven decades ago. During my youth, my family didn't have running water or an indoor toilet until I was twelve years old. We had a well, which was a tremendous advancement from what my parents had during their youth. I heard them speak of having to walk long distances to the nearest spring to carry back buckets of water for drinking, cooking, and bathing. Since they did not have electricity, they also placed containers of milk in the spring to keep it cool. All my life I have had electricity in our home but have lacked some modern-day necessities like air conditioning. Until I was twelve, my mother cooked on a woodstove. Despite my humble beginnings, I've been blessed to be in the presence of those who were born with a silver spoon in their mouths as well as those who, for lack of finances, had to brush their teeth with a toothbrush carved from a small tree limb. Whatever environment I've found myself in, I have always tried to be the same Joe who grew up in the Goodwill community outside Madison, North Carolina.

My late mother-in-law, Frances Glenn Ramsey, gave birth to fifteen children. She never had indoor running water or an indoor bathroom. Ms. Ramsey said to me once, "Joe, I used to think all lawyers and preachers were rich, but now that I have gotten to know you, I know that my coat tails are just as long as yours." Ms. Ramsey's comment to me is perhaps the greatest compliment I have ever received. Growing up as I did on a farm and part of a large family, there is no doubt that I have had an affinity toward those who grew up as I did, knowing the hardships that they endure. However, my education and positions have placed me with persons from all walks of life, and I am comfortable in any setting and afford the same respect to all.

My mind goes back to when I was practicing law in my hometown. I had been appointed by the court to represent a homeless man charged with larceny. It was alleged that he stole an item of clothing from a donation container in town. Although he was caught red-handed coming out of the donation container with the item of clothes in his hand, I pled him not guilty, tried the case as if he had been charged with a serious felony, and argued zealously to the judge that he should find him not guilty. I thought it ironic that he would be charged when he was the very kind of person for whom the donated clothes were intended. I also thought it was the kind of criminal offense that the police officer and prosecutor should have used their discretion not to charge and prosecute at all. Lest someone of financial means reads this and concludes that they should "judge shop" and avoid me as the judge in his or her case, I want to be clear. I took an oath to be fair and impartial and give justice to the rich and the poor equally. I have set aside any bias I may have (as all judges are required to do), and I will continue to do so long as I put on a black robe. To do otherwise would be to do great harm to our system of justice in America. I would also do harm to myself, my conscience, and reputation. Equal justice under law is indeed my motto, and I seek to live by that daily.

Despite the troubled times I've faced in my life's work, I've tried to find time to laugh and cause others to laugh. The late attorney B. B. Olive of Durham, North Carolina, once said to me that I "should never lose my sense of humor as a judge." I have not forgotten those words of advice from such a respected longtime member of the bar and Durham community. Although I take my work as a judge very seriously, I am known to occasionally bring laughter to the courtroom and in the pulpit. In short, I have always tried to be true to who I am, nothing more and nothing less. I hope that my children and my grandchildren and generations to come read this memoir and are able to discern this personal trait in me and see from my writings that I tried to help others less fortunate than I have been.

CHAPTER ONE

A Community Called Goodwill

The "DNA" of Goodwill"

"What became of the people of Sumer?" the old man asked. "Ah," the other replied, "They lost their history—so they died."

CHANCELLOR WILLIAMS

(quoted in the Strickland Family Reunion booklet titled The Genealogy of John Henry Strickland and Biddie Easter Taylor Strickland, July 2004 Family History)

At the outset, someone may ask, "I wonder why the author devoted an entire chapter to his community where he grew up?" For one thing, during the early years of that community's birth, most of my ancestors had little in the form of wealth, and I honor my church and community for persevering through the storms of life. But also, I dedicate a whole chapter to my community because I am them, and they are me. I cannot write about myself without writing about them. We are inextricably intertwined. Our DNA is the same whether we graduated fourth grade as my father did while achieving a PhD in life based upon hard work and prayer or went on to gain an undergraduate and law degree from Howard University, a master's degree in law from Duke University Law School, and later becoming a federal judge, as I did. We are all the same. In a familiar saying, "We put our pants on the same, one leg at a time." I wouldn't exchange my childhood experiences for that of a king or queen's son in England.

The Goodwill community, as I have come to know it since I was old enough to understand, is composed of several miles in all directions in the proximity of Goodwill Baptist Church, as many still refer to it today, or Goodwill First Baptist Church (since its incorporation). For my purposes of delineating, its unofficial boundaries begin near the intersection of Highway 311 and K-Fork Road in Rockingham County and extend several miles past the Stokes County line. Goodwill's residents, both pre- and post-slavery, originally contained mostly farmers, including a few landowners and mostly sharecroppers in the late 1800s until a few purchased their own land. There is no doubt that the center of the community is the church, where persons of faith joined together on Sunday mornings to praise God for getting them through another week. In my seventy years of life, I have not heard anyone speak about how the community and the church acquired their name, nor which came first: the church or the community. I can only guess that the community of believers in Jesus Christ came first, as there would be no church without persons of faith who saw the need to have a building where they could worship together. My paternal great-great-great grandfather, John H. Gibson deeded two and a half acres of land to the community to build its first dedicated church building. The deed dated November 8, 1902, from John H. Gibson to the "trustees of Colored Missionary Baptist Church" was recorded in the Rockingham County Register of Deeds Office on July 13, 1906, at 1 p.m. Deed Book 151, page 398.[1]

1902–1973

1974–present

Sadly, the population and vibrancy of the Goodwill community in years past is only a shadow of itself at the present time, and so is the membership of Goodwill Baptist Church, which has experienced a long but steady decline. Not unique to Goodwill is the declining birth rate, especially from two-parent homes. I heard a preacher say once, "If you don't hear any babies crying in the church, then you are looking at a dying church." Death has taken most of the generations born in the 1940s or before. And like most small rural communities and small towns across America, the lack of jobs in the area has caused many to move to larger cities such as Greensboro and Winston Salem.

1 The deed to the church lists the grantee as the Trustees of Colored Missionary Baptist Church. Goodwill Baptist Church was incorporated in the N.C. Secretary of State Office as Goodwill First Baptist Church on January 8, 2001 at 12:11 p.m.

Beginning 110 feet from the intersection of Bridge Street and Jay Street;thence with Jay Street N.57°15'E.55 feet;thence parallel with Bridge Street N.36°30'W.177 feet;thence parallel with Jay Street S.57°15'W.55 feet;thence parallel with Bridge Street,S.35°30'E. 177 feet to the beginning containing 9735 square feet more or less.

TO HAVE AND TO HOLD the aforesaid tract or parcel of land,and all privileges and appurtenances thereto belonging,to the said Charles N.Deshazo and his heirs and assigns,to their only use and behoof forever.

And the said Charles N.Deshazo his heirs and assigns,that they are seized of said premises in fee,and have right to convey in fee-simple;that the same are free and clear from all incumbrances,and that they will warrant and defend the said title to the same against the claims of all persons whomsoever.

In testimony whereof,the said James T.Barksdale and wife Roxie Boyd Barksdale have hereunto set their hands and seals,the day and year first above written.

James T.Barksdale (SEAL)
attest;[illegible] Roxie Boyd Barksdale. (SEAL)

STATE OF NORTH CAROLINA,ROCKINGHAM COUNTY.

I,J.W.Norman,a Notary Public for said County & State do hereby certify that James T. Barksdale and Roxie Boyd Barksdale,his wife,personally appeared before me this day and acknowledged the due execution of the annexed Deed of Conveyance,and the said Roxie Boyd Barksdale being by me privately examined separate and apart from her said husband,touching her voluntary execution of the same,doth state that she signed the same freely and voluntarily,without fear or compulsion of her said husband,or any other person,and that she doth still voluntarily assent thereto.

Witness my hand and Notorial seal,this 11th day of July A.D.1906.

(OFFICIAL) J.W.Norman Notary Public.
(SEAL) My commission expires Sep.13"-07.

STATE OF NORTH CAROLINA, ROCKINGHAM COUNTY.

The foregoing certificate of J.W.Norman a Notary Public of said County,is adjudged to be [illegible] the instrument.with the certificates be registered.

Witness my hand this 13 day of July A.D.1906.

Robt.P.Mitchell Dept.Blerk Superior Court.

Filed for registration at 1 o'clock P.M.July 13th,1906. J.A.Scales R.D.

TRUSTEES OF COLORED MISSIONERY BAPTIST CHURCH FROM JOHN H.GIBSON

STATE OF NORTH CAROLINA,ROCKINGHAM COUNTY.

THIS DEED maDe this the 8th day of November 1902 by John H.Gibson of Rockingham County and State of North Carolina of the first part,to Robt Webster,John Stultz & Dick Webster as Trustee for Colr'd Missionary Baptist Church State of North Carolina of the second part,WITNESSETH:

That said John H.Gibson in consideration of Ten Dollars,to him paid by said Trustee for said church,the receipt of which is hereby acknowledged,has bargained and sold,and by these presents does bargain,sell and convey to said Trustee of said Baptist Church and their successors a certain tract or parcel of land in madison Township Rockingham County State of North Carolina adjoining the lands of W.L.Fallis heirs & Jno.H.Gibson and bounded as follows,viz:

Beginning at and in the forks of the roas & about fifty yards west of Reed Welchès North west corner,thence west along the K.Fork & Madison Publis road to a stone Nine chains,thence South 5°East Six & one-half chains to a small white oak on the North side of a farm road,thence in a North-eastern direction following the said farm road Nine chains to the public road & beginning,containing two & one-half acres.

TO HAVE AND TO HOLD the aforesaid tract or parcel of land and all privileges and apthereto belonging,to the said Trustee and their successors to their only use and behoof forever.

And the said John H.Gibson covenant to and with the said Trustees of said Church & their successors that he is seized of said premises in fee,and has a right to convey the same in fee-simple;that the same are free from all incumbrances,and the he will warrant and defend the said title to the same against the claims of all persons whatsoever.

IN TESTIMONY WHEREOF,the said John H.Gibson has hereunto set his hand and seal the day and year first above written.

John H.Gibson. (SEAL)

ATTEST: Robt.P.McAnally.

NORTH CAROLINA,ROCKINGHAM COUNTY.

The foregoing instrument was this day acknowledged before,by John H.Gibson the grantor for the purpose therein expressed. Witness my hand & Notorial seal this 10th day of January 1903.

D.W.Busick Notary Public.

(OFFICIAL)
(SEAL)

NORTH CAROLINA,ROCKINGHAM COUNTY.

The foregoing certificate of D.W.Busick N.P.of said County,is adjudged to be correct and sufficient.Let the instrument,with the certificates be registered.

Witness my hand this 13 day of July 1906, Robt.P.Mitchell Dept Clerk Superior Court.

Filed for registration at 1 o'clock P.M.July 13th,1906. J.A.Scales R.D.

As shown above, the deed conveying land to the church, now officially known as the Goodwill First Baptist Church, was made November 8, 1902, by my paternal great-great-great-grandfather, John H. Gibson, to Robt. Webster, John Stultz, and Dick Webster, trustee for "Colr'd Missionary Baptist Church," State of North Carolina. The amount of land deeded was two and one half acres. The deed was recorded on July 13, 1906, at 1 p.m. Rockingham County Register Deeds, Deed Book 151, p. 398.

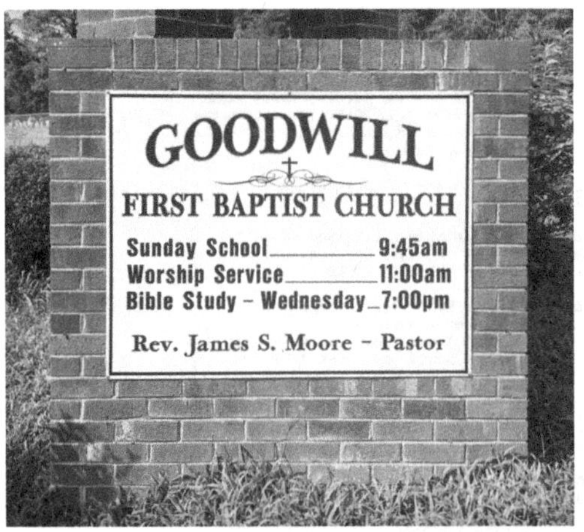

"The Cornerstone of Goodwill Baptist Church's Faith"—"This Jesus is the stone rejected by your builder, which has become the cornerstone."
ACTS 4:11–12; 1 PETER 2:1–10

Those who entered universities seldom come back to live or work in Goodwill or the nearby town of Madison. From the moment I entered law school at Howard University in mid-August 1976, I knew that I would return to my hometown to practice law for some amount of time. I always felt that God would have me to do so. Since its founding in 1818, no black attorney had ever had a law office in Madison. I am grateful I had the opportunity to do so and know that experience contributed greatly to my career accomplishments. I practiced law there for over six years from mid-August 1980 to the end of November 1986, representing thousands of clients, many of whom no other attorney would agree to represent.

Beginning in the latter half of the 1800s after the long, nearly 250 years of slavery in America when it was against the law for those of African ancestry to marry, marriages took hold, and in Goodwill, large numbers of children were birthed, as shown below. The growth of the Goodwill community and the pews of Goodwill Baptist Church increased through the early 1960s. Men and women of the Goodwill community—some of mixed heritage, or mulattoes, as the Census records described mixed-race families in the first censuses after the end of slavery—legally married and had babies every two years or so. The following list demonstrates the number of births of those living in or near the Goodwill community, including my own parents. One can surmise that farmers figured out that with large families, the more children they had, the more crops they could raise, and there would be free labor to work the fields.

Some of the Large Families in the Goodwill Community,
Second half of the 1800s through the 1960s[2]

Parents	Number of Children (3 or more)
James and Bettie Webster	8
Early and Sally Johnson	7
John and Bernice Moore	6
Howard and Lucy Oliver	6
Jesse and Mozelle Moore	5
Edward and Lillie Carter	9
Sonnie and Mabel Brown	10 *(includes a child who died as an infant)*
Fred and Annie Webster	14
Otis and Anna Kellam Ziglar	8
Oscar and Emma Jean Carter	6
James and Hortense Ziglar	7
Ezra "Ed" and Frances Kellam	7
Dewey and Josephine Webster	10
Herbert and Betty Moore	6
Walter and Lucy Ziglar	11
Nate and Ruth Johnson	11
George and Mildred Brown	6
Henry and Eddie Mae Moore	3
Benjamin and Savanna Brown	7
Isaac and Nealy Johnny	6
Vester and Alice Moore	5
Freddie and Lula Mae Webster	3
John H. and Lucy Johnson Gibson	4
William and Emma Jane Carter	13
Ferdinand and Frances Webster	4
Luther and Frances Scales	3
Noah and Hattie Kellam	12
Henry and Eddie Mae Moore	3
John "Jack" and Sallie Moore	7
Robert Watt Moore and Maggie Moore	5
Robert Watt and Ester Moore	11

2 The US Census Bureau defines a large family as a household containing five or more persons.

Samuel H. Gibson and Eddie Gibson	4
Johnny and Eddie Brown	7
Jessie and Lillie Carter	6
David and Beatrice Price	5
Roy "Barlow" and Ada Hairston	5
Richard and Margie Webster	4 *(1 child died as an infant)*
Freddie and Lula Mae Webster	3
Junior and Nellie Ann Hairston	3
Isaac Nowlin and Lizzie Nowlin	3
Sidney and Lizzie Oliver	5
Reid and Cosley Mitchell	5
Gilmer Henry and Sophia Mitchell Searcy	8
Rosevelt and Willie Galloway	8
Richard Sr. and Julia Gibson Webster	14
Mike and Beulah Mitchell	3
Otis and Marie Simmons	3
John and Virginia Welch	9
Wallace and Leola Price	7
Joe and Shirley Price	6
Arthur and Olivia Martin	15
Walter and Cleatus Troxler Ziglar	3
William Henry and Ruth Welch	3

As part of the annual Moore Family Reunion weekend on August 14, 2022, I delivered the 11 a.m. Sunday morning sermon at my home church, Goodwill First Baptist Church. My topic was "The DNA of Goodwill." In that sermon I gave a roll call of many of the early Goodwill pioneers and their offspring who have achieved great success in life in almost every imaginable field or endeavor. Here I repeat that roll call and include others from Goodwill whose DNA runs deep in the northern Piedmont Region of North Carolina soil. Beginning in the early 1960s, I suggest that those growing up in Goodwill or their offspring have achieved at a greater rate in science, ministry, law, public education, banking, government, postal service, athletics, and management at companies than communities of similar size in the United States. Goodwill has produced those who sacrificed so much on the battlefields of Korea and Vietnam. Yes, the DNA of Goodwill has produced good fruit. Pastors and preachers, like our present pastor James S. Moore, my brother Rev. Dr. James Webster, yours truly, Rev. Lillian Johnson, Rev. Lula Webster,

Rev. Henry Moore, Rev. Margie Webster, Rev. Linda Hairston, Rev. Isaac Johnson, and Rev. John H. Gibson. Rev. Samuel H. Gibson, and his son, Rev. Robert "Bud" Gibson.

The DNA of Goodwill has produced military veterans who have served with honor. Native son James Brown is buried in Arlington National Cemetery. June Webster, died on the battlefield during the war in Korea. During my youth I heard that he went to Korea and then got out of the army, only to return to Korea where he was killed on the battlefield. His remains lie in the Goodwill Baptist Church cemetery. Harvey Johnson, Willie Cain Webster, Wallace Ziglar, and Clarence "June" Smith sacrificed much in their service to our country in the Vietnam War. They did not get the recognition they had earned because of our divided country's opposition to our presence there. Consequently, these sons of Goodwill did not return home as the heroes that they were. Some suffered from undiagnosed illnesses after returning home. Harvey Johnson suffered for years prior to his death with illnesses from his service there, and Willie Cain Webster is still suffering. Many others, including Welbert Carter, Richard Webster, Rev. Henry Moore, Freddie Webster, Rev. James A. Webster, Roy Melvin Martin, James Elvin Martin, Clifton Moore, John T. Webster, Percy Carter, Wiliam "Louis" Moore, Horace Carter, Larry Moore, Floyd Webster, Curtis Webster, Charles Hairston, Reginald Searcy, Calvin Lewis "Tony" Kellam—who retired as a full-bird colonel—and Jerry Kellam all served their nation with honor. Cathy Price retired with the rank of commander, US Navy. Katina Paterson retired from the US Army after more than twenty-two years of service with the rank of sergeant first class (SFC; E-7). Daily we ought to remember to thank those military veterans who survive for their outstanding honorable service and sacrifice to our nation and never forget those veterans who have passed on.

In recent generations, beginning in the 1960s, many of those who have had successful careers entered well-known colleges and universities, mostly historically black colleges and universities (HBCUs) such as North Carolina A&T State University, Bennett College, North Carolina Central University, Winston Salem State University, Howard University, St. Augustine College, and Livingstone College. Arguably, these universities are some of the nation's finest institutions. They provide the foundation, courage, intellect, and patience needed to navigate and persevere in a still racially discriminatory society. Family members earned degrees from universities other than HBCUs, including Catawba College, the University of North Carolina at Chapel Hill, and Duke University. Many of the first college attendees from Goodwill entered HBCUs for good reasons. Many HBCUs welcomed hardworking, industrious students from the Goodwill community based upon the recommendation of teachers and counselors who had graduated mostly from HBCUs themselves. On a personal note, my own denial of admission to

Duke University Law School, Wake Forest University Law School, and the University of North Carolina Law School in 1976 caused me to work even harder, and I was welcomed into the entering class of 1976 at the Howard University School of Law. While the North Carolina law schools didn't know the Goodwill DNA that I was made of, nor were they award of my "How come I can't?" persevering spirit I inherited from my parents and my Goodwill Community, God placed me right where I belonged.

In 1963, Goodwill native, Benjamin "Ben" Johnson went to Africa as a member of the Peace Corps and later graduated from NC A&T State University (hereinafter A&T). Many others from Goodwill or with community roots have resumes full of accomplishments. Elder Perry Webster became the first African American chief of police in the history of the town of Madison. He presently pastors at Burning Bush Holiness Church in Stoneville, North Carolina. The son of Goodwill native Early Moore, Rev. Kenneth Moore, graduated from Apex School of Theology, received a master's degree from Wake Forest University and is pursuing a doctorate degree at Boston University. My brother, Rev. Dr. James A. Webster received a Bachelor of Arts in Religion and Philosophy, and a Master of Divinity degree from Shaw University. He was awarded the Honorary Doctorate of Humane Letters from Bethlehem Bible College. He pastored Oak Ridge First Baptist Church for 39 years.

Wanda Oliver Ziglar graduated from A&T. Larry Moore graduated from Livingstone College and earned his master's degree from Bowie State. He retired from the US Postal Service. Bernard Moore and his sister Dorothea Moore Russell retired from the US Secret Service. Their niece, Melanie Moore currently is employed with the U.S. Secret Service. Of his generation, my cousin Bernard Moore represents the DNA of the persevering, intestinal-fortitude spirit of Goodwill as much as anyone from the community. Bernard's his high school counselor told him that he was not smart enough to attend college. Rather than giving up, Bernard applied to work for the Federal Bureau of Investigation (FBI). It was the DNA of Goodwill in Bernard that said, "I will prove to you how smart I am." He retired from the Secret Service. Pearlis Eugene Johnson graduated from NC Central University (hereinafter NCCU) and became deputy regional administrator, Southern Region, of the FAA. Berna Dean Webster graduated from St. Augustine College and has had a successful career in the Washington, DC, area. Jerry Carter graduated from used his Livingston College and obtained his master's degree from UNC–Chapel Hill. He retired from the DC government.

Goodwill has produced great schoolteachers and teaching assistants: the late Rebecca Oliver (A&T), Joyce Carter Bivens, (Bennett College), Denise Smith (NCCU & Master's at A&T), Tami Martin Chapman (A&T), Yvette Martin (Winston Salem St. University

(WSSU) Vickie Searcy (A&T), Karen Price Scales (NCCU), Ivan Moore (Chowan College), Stacey Harris (A&T), and Tiffany Mitchell Galloway (A&T) come to mind.

Other Goodwill natives or their descendants became great athletes. All-State and All-American basketball player, Jerry Moore led his Madison-Mayodan team to the state tournament two years in a row, winning the championship in 1973. He played basketball at the University of Florida and Catawba College where he graduated. Donna Johnson Cummings was inducted into the WSSU Hall of Fame for her achievements in softball in 2016. Justin Johnson graduated from Appalachian State University, where he received three national championship rings as a member of the football team. Darrell Smith and his son, Samuel Kyler Smith played football and graduated from Elon University. Decarster Webster's grandson, James "Jim" Webster, played football at UNC Chapel Hill and coached at several universities including UNC Chapel Hill, East Carolina University, and was head coach at Tennessee State University. Bernard Moore's daughter Aubrey Moore played ice hockey at and graduated from Brown University and also voted MVP in 2012 and 2014.

George Brown has served as a supervisor in local industry for many years, and his late daughter, Crystal Brown graduated from A&T and received a master's degree from UNC-G. All of Joe and Shirley Price's six children, Cathy, Karen, Eric, Randy, Rodney, and Stacy Price graduated from NCCU. Calvin Kellam graduated from A&T. Patricia Wilson attended UNC-G and received an Honorary degree in Business Administration and Child Growth. Irvin Moore graduated from UNC-Charlotte and is presently working in Real Estate Financing with Bank of America. Carl Johnson, a Livingstone College graduate, has also had a successful banking career. Chanita Moore Scales graduated from Appalachian State, Tammy Ziglar graduated from A&T. Michaela Jones, PhD—whose father, Willie Cain Webster, serves as a deacon at Goodwill Baptist Church today—received her PhD at Meharry Medical College and a master's degree at UNC Chapel Hill. She has been very successful in her career and has been a true inspiration to many. Michaela's brother, Bradley Webster completed his undergraduate and graduate studies at NC State University. Currently he is a tenured professor at Wake Tech in Raliegh, North Carolina. Derrick Webster has served as the Minister of Music at Oak Ridge First Baptist Church since 1984; is a graduate of Shaw University, has a doctoral degree from Bethlehem Bible College and an honorary doctor of Humane Letters from Living Epistle College. Tony Mitchell is serves as head of the music department and music director of Galilee Missionary Baptist Church in Winston Salem. (Many others from the Goodwill community throughout many generations have had melodic voices that sing for the glory of God.) Caroline Moore graduated from Robert Morris University.

Benjamin Johnson, II graduated from George Mason University. Cheryl Mitchell graduated from Danville Community College and is a Registered Nurse. My oldest daughter, Briana Webster Campbell, a UNC-Chapel Hill School of Public Health graduate, is the managing director for the No Kid Hungry Center for Best Practices in Washington, DC. For more than twenty years, Briana has dedicated herself to making our nation a fairer, more just nation. Through her advocacy and innovative programming, she has worked to enhance access to health, education, and good systems, empowering families to overcome poverty and thrive. Briana has continued her education at the Georgetown University McCourt School of Public Policy.

Dylan Galloway is a NCCU graduate and presently serves as town administrator of Cheverly, Maryland. Battalion Chief Curtis Brown, recently retired as a fireman for the Greensboro, North Carolina, Fire Department. Captain Temeka Brown recently became the first African American female fire captain for City of Greensboro Fire Department. Stacey Moore, graduated from UNC-G and with a master's degree at Ashford University. Stacey is currently employed at Exelon Corporation in Baltimore as a senior project cost manager. My son Evan Webster is a manager at Trader Joe's in Chapel Hill, North Carolina, where he has the respect and admiration of all those above and beyond his level of responsibilities. Patricia Johnson graduated from WSSU, Tami Dalton graduated from A&T. Jaron Searcy graduated from Purdue University, Siera Davis, graduated from UNC-G. Lakeshia Scales graduated from UNC-G, Sherrod Simmons graduated from WSSU, Tyneesha Moore, graduated from A&T, Bethany Kendall graduated from NCSU, Gariel Kendall graduated from A&T. Tammy Ziglar graduated from A&T. Carinne Webster Lynch graduated from Hampton University and is fully committed to her church, family and community in northern California. Linda D. Addison, the granddaughter of Decarster and Murphy Webster, and daughter of Joyce and Janice Webster, is an author and poet living in Arizona.

My daughters and cousins with Juan Webster of Goodwill ancestry celebrating Juan's recent job promotion in Baltimore, Maryland, June 2024. (L–R) Camille J. Webster, Ryan Brown, Briana Webster Campbell, Honoree Juan Webster, Daryl Smith, and Dylan Galloway

Juan Webster has skyrocketed in the hospitality industry after graduating from UNC–Chapel Hill and continued his education with studies in the hospitality and Tourism Industry Department at North Carolina Central University. Until recently Juan was the general manager of the Pendry Hotel in Baltimore, Maryland. Juan is well respected not only in the hotel industry of Baltimore but throughout the city for his community service to help underserved communities. Just recently promoted, Juan now serves as senior director of social impact at Montage International. Juan and others mentioned here in their thirties and forties represent the younger generation of those whose ancestors go back two hundred years in the Goodwill community—attorneys, IT professionals, bankers, public health professionals, private industry managers, city officials, authors, coaches, the musically talented, and many others who represent the many positive qualities that were instilled in us by the early pioneers of Goodwill.

The branches of Goodwill DNA have spread far and wide since first taking root in the fertile soils of the community. Its borders have never been fully defined, but its influence has expanded by its heirs taking up refuge across the state, nation, and world. The late Helen White is an example of one whose blood is steeped in that persevering spirit of Goodwill. While she was not born in North Carolina and did not live in the Goodwill community, her mother, Alice Brown Penn Long, was born in and lived in Goodwill all her youth, and her remains were returned to be buried in the Goodwill Baptist Church cemetery. Alice was the sister of my great-grandmother Lucy Gibson Ziglar. Helen was the granddaughter of Johnny and Eddie Gibson Brown, who were residents of the Goodwill area. Helen was born in West Virginia after her mother moved there, and later moved to Chicago. She spent considerable time in the Goodwill Community when her mother returned annually to visit her family. I speak of Helen White as a daughter of Goodwill because of all the generations I chronicle in this memoir, no one overcame greater obstacles or achieved more greatly than she did. At age eight, she was stricken with spinal meningitis that caused her to be permanently blind, yet that didn't stop her from achieving much in life. She attended Bluefield College in West Virginia, where she received an associate in general studies degree. Helen later attended the Chicago Lighthouse for the Blind where she learned how to master reading and writing in braille, which allowed her to obtain a career as a medical transcriptionist at the University of Illinois Medical Center for thirty-five

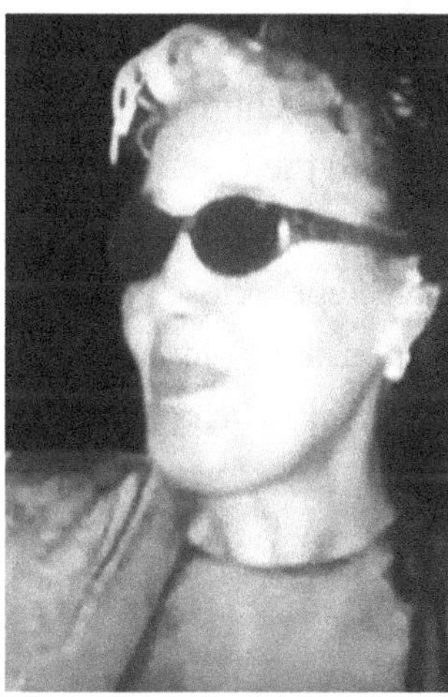

Helen White

years before retirement. She was beloved by many in her Chicago community where she lived for over sixty years. Like her mother and many of her cousins of her generation, she lived a long and selfless life. She recently succumbed to illness at age ninety-seven.

Timothy Maurice Webster, son of John and Mary Webster, moved some years ago to Johannesburg, South Africa. He has become a successful author, columnist, and leadership consultant. Patsy Webster Dalton and her daughter, Jasmine Scott, have achieved much since graduating from North Carolina A&T State University. Jasmine also earned her master's degree at Virginia Tech University and is now employed at Syngenta in the Washington, DC area. Five direct descendants of the Goodwill community have graduated from law school in the last twenty years. First, I am a very proud father of Attorney Camille Jordan Webster who followed in my footsteps to attend Howard University where she graduated Summa Cum Laude. She also graduated from the University of the District Columbia Law School's 4-year evening program while working full time. She is a member of the Maryland and D.C. Bars. After working as a law clerk for a United States District Court Judge, and an assistant state public defender, she now works in the Civil Division of the U.S. Department of Justice. Other law school graduates from my Goodwill Community extended family are: Nicole Webster of New York, who is the granddaughter of Goodwill native, Goyle Amos Webster, and daughter of John Webster and Diane Webster; Gerrod Marvin Webster, son of Betty Jean Webster Kendall and Gary Leon Kendall; Whitney Carpenter, great-great-granddaughter of Goodwill native, Decarster Webster; Allanah Wynn, great-granddaughter of Goodwill native, Alice Brown Long; and Markeshia Wilkins, daughter of Rosa Brown Wilkins and Mike Wilkins.[3]

In my roll call of achievers, I dare not leave out the majority who remained in the community to support their families and Goodwill. Those who stayed on the home front, the deacons, trustees, ushers, choir members, nurses, Sunday School teachers, those who toiled in the fields, factories for meager earnings, that they shared with the Goodwill church, more than any of those who went away to college and to work, have allowed the Goodwill Church and community to be a place that the rest of us could call home. For example, at least for the last decade, Tammy Dalton and Vonda Patterson have kept a close eye on the contributions and expenses of the church, an important responsibility in any church that goes unnoticed because it is done not in the open. Those of us who moved away can come home to a warm welcome and the comforts

3 I attempted to mention as many of the achievers of especially first- and second-generation college graduates that I thought of or as came to my attention. Based upon human experience, I am certain that some were not mentioned that should have been, and it was not intentional. I hope those persons will understand that I did the best I could with all the time constraints, including job, family, other responsibilities of life, my required reliance on oral history, and my and the faulty memories of others.

and love of this place we will forever fondly remember. Our younger ones need to know what God has done to mold the offspring of those who first named a church and a community. Our children and grandchildren need to know what they have in their DNA, but most important, what God did for our ancestors. God can do the same for them if they have that same faith, hard work ethic, and persevering spirit of their ancestors.

The DNA of Goodwill has not allowed us to forget where we came from, nor our obligations to our fellowmen and women. Many of us have been recognized for the work we have done and are still doing in the communities where we live. So the DNA of "community and public service" is one of the great traits that we learned right here in Goodwill—Love your neighbor as yourself and share with others less fortunate than you what you been blessed with. We are our brothers' keeper. Those of us who have more money than we need to pay our bills need to consider how blessed we are and need to pay it forward and reach back and help someone else climb up the ladder of success.

As I have studied the history of Goodwill Baptist Church, the Goodwill community, and those who made it what it is, I'm reminded that one must not neglect to recognize the greatest achievers among us. They are those who accepted Christ as their Lord and Savior and dedicated their lives to this cause. Most didn't receive any publicity, often were paid little or nothing, and garnered no titles or accolades. But one day, soon and very soon they will be recognized by the King of Kings and will receive their crown. Even while they suffered on life's perilous journeys, they found comfort in the fact that, one day, they would hear the voice of the Lord saying, "Well done, good and faithful servant. You have been faithful with a few things. I will make you ruler over many things: enter thou into the joy of thy Lord" (MATTHEW 25:23 KJV). A close walk of faith in God is the most important DNA trait of Goodwill's success.

I wish I could include every church leader in the history of the Goodwill Church or community, but I could spend many more hundreds of hours researching only to later determine that I have omitted someone. For those whose names are not mentioned, I pray that they will understand the impossibility of recognizing every deserving person in the roll call of early church leaders. Any omission was not intentional. Suffice it to say that God has richly blessed the heirs of those who first inhabited the Goodwill Community and built Goodwill Baptist Church.[4]

The names of the pastors of Goodwill Baptist Church and early church leaders and other members appear in the records of the church, beginning with the first pastor, Rev.

4 This listing of deacons, trustees, and pioneer men and women of Goodwill herein is not intended to be inclusive of all those who served, but only of those who are part of the written church record or within the present memory of the author and some of the few surviving members of the congregation and community who are old enough to recall some early members of the church and community.

Pastor of Goodwill Baptist Church, Rev. James S. Moore

Sandy Gilmore, followed by Rev. John H. Gibson, Rev. Pete Foye, Rev. R. Thurmond, Rev. Gus Silver, Rev. T. S. Station, Rev. H. A. White, Rev. James Parker, Rev. W. P. Park, Rev. B. H. Bonham, Rev. B. W. Mittman, Rev. John A. Jackson, and Rev. James S. Moore, who has served from 2012 to the time of this writing.

Among the early trustees of Goodwill Baptist Church were John H. Gibson, Richard Webster Sr., Bob Webster, and John Stultz, as shown on the deed conveying the two-and-a-half-acre tract of land to Goodwill Baptist Church in 1902. Other early church leaders included Sydney Oliver, Rev. Isaac Johnson, William Carter, Noah Kellam, and Richard Webster Jr. Later deacons of Goodwill included Roy "Jack" Webster, Welbert Carter, and Clarence Smith. From the 1960s through most of the late 1900s and early 2000s, included among the deacons and active men of the church members were Early Johnson, my father, James "Tom" Webster, Paul Carter, Rev. Henry Moore, Jesse Moore, George Brown, and Oscar Carter.

Early women leaders and active members of the church were Emma Carter and her sister, "Belle." In an interview with Addie Brown Martin ("Shorty"), she told me that Ms. Emma Carter, was the "mother of the church" during her youth, Ms. Emma had the assignment of preparing and bringing the Communion to church. Shorty says she remembers well seeing Ms. Emma Carter walking a long distance from her home once each month to church as she carried the Communion or Lord's Supper elements, the symbolic bread and grape juice. Other pioneer women church members included Ms. Nealy Johnson, Hattie Smith Kellam, Sallie Webster, Ethel Webster, Lillie Ziglar Carter, Lottie Ziglar Webster, Nannie Brown Boone, Anna Kellam Ziglar, Mabel Webster Brown, and Rev. Lillian Johnson Smith. After these active women of the Goodwill congregation came faithful church members such as Bernice Moore, Lucy Ziglar Oliver, Sally Moore Johnson, Mozelle Moore, Bettie Moore Webster, Eddie Mae Moore, Maggie Carter, Mildred Brown, Alice Ziglar Moore, Cleatus "Clea" Ziglar, Hortense Ziglar, Nellie Ann Hairston, Lula Mae Webster, Odessa Brown, Beatrice Price, Marie Webster, Lottie, Betty Ziglar Moore, Marie Ziglar Simmons, and others. Many of these devout women served in the choir and became ushers, missionaries, Sunday school teachers, and served other positions in the church. Until the recent death of Catherine Moore Baker on March 7, 2004, there were five women in the Goodwill Church who were first brought there as infants by their parents: Addie Brown Martin, Elsie Brown Hughes, Virginia Lee Oliver Smith, Shirley Oliver Price and Catherine Moore Baker.

All are close relatives of mine. They are all in their mid to latter eighties. Death has slowly but steadily decimated the membership of Goodwill in recent years. Among them are several of my father's sisters, my aunts, Emma Jean Payne, Lillie Bell Searcy, Louise Smith Joyce, and Sallie Ruth Lowe. Like many other congregations across the nation, the youth of the Goodwill community has declined in birth rate and church attendance. One can only wonders what God has in store for his people.

Under the leadership of the late Rev. B. H. Bonham, a new church building was begun in the early 1970s to replace the original structure. The new building was completed in 1974 and contained an indoor baptismal. Prior to that, baptisms took place in what was commonly referred to as the "baptizing hole," a small creek where those in the community went swimming during summer. It is located not far from the church near the Cardinal Road bridge.

During my youth, 11 a.m. worship services at Goodwill took place on the first and third Sundays of each month after 10 a.m. Sunday school. Goodwill began having worship services also on the second, fourth, and all fifth Sundays in 1975. Fifth Sundays were designated as Missionary Days. The 10 a.m. and 11 a.m. schedules for Sunday School and Worship service remain today. My recollection from my youth is that in the winter months, the stove that was located near the front of the church was the only source of heat. If you sat close to the stove you would become very hot, but it was cold in the back of the church. During the summer months, church leaders opened the windows, and you could see the church cemetery on one side of the church, and on the other side you could see the tall trees, and underneath were picnic tables. As a child I thought the worship services were far too long. The first pastors I recall were the late Rev. James Parker followed by the late Rev. W. P. Clark. Sometimes it seemed to me like Reverend Clark would preach twice, a second time between the main sermon and the benediction. In hindsight I know it was not a second sermon, but through the eyes of a fidgety, impatient child anxious to get outside and play, it may as well have been.

Every Sunday morning, no matter how late the sons of James "Tom" Webster and Bettie Ester Webster stayed out on Saturday night, getting out of bed early enough to attend Sunday school and worship service was the only option. We woke from what little sleep we had, listening to my parents' voices and gospel music on the radio. Soon after waking up, we ate breakfast and began to put on our Sunday best—suit, dress shirt, and necktie. I can still hear my father's voice as time for departure came near. He would not dare be late for Sunday school. My dad's voice rang out, "Y'all turn around here!" He meant finish getting dressed so that we wouldn't be late for church. On many occasions, as my father and I passed each other in the living room, or as he observed me sitting supposedly finished dressing, he'd look at me and say, "Bo Sholt [or Bo Shoat] Odie" (referring to his uncle Otis "Odie" Ziglar), "fix your collar on your coat and straighten up your necktie." He was comparing me to his uncle Odie, who I assumed frequently looked disheveled in his daily bib overalls, as was the case with most other farmers of his generation in the Goodwill community.

My earliest and longstanding memory of the 11 a.m. worship services at Goodwill Baptist Church was how often it was full of the spirit or holy ghost as we characterized it during my youth. It all began with an opening song and testimony service. I heard hundreds of times the following testimony of usually an elderly church member who boldly and with conviction stood before the congregation: "I thank God for waking me up this morning, clothed in my right mind, with a reasonable portion of health and strength." During church services over a half century later, I occasionally find myself quoting the same testimony of those old soldiers from Goodwill. Immersed with the testimony was singing to the glory of God. Sometimes at Goodwill, the word of the Lord was like that described in Jeremiah 20:9, when he said, "It was like fire shut up in my bones." Even as a young child, I felt the spirt of the Lord. During morning worship, one or more church members shouting in the aisles was not uncommon. I recall Deacon Paul Carter as a young man got his shout on regularly. At revival, held in the month of August, members of Goodwill and others from most communities in the county and counties nearby came to Goodwill to be revived. At revival the spirit was often high, and there might have been five or more shouting at the same time. Some of those filled with the spirit were to the point that those sitting beside them had to restrain their arms and bodies so they wouldn't harm themselves by falling against a pew or on the floor. I recall a powerful anointed man of God, Reverend Hall from Winston Salem, preaching at revival. I thought at the time that no one could out-preach him. But there were also others who came to preach at Goodwill during my youth from other communities who caught my attention. Reverend James W. France from Virginia, then pastor of Mount Carmel Holiness Church in Madison, and the late Reverend Willie B. Harbor, the former pastor of Burning Bush Holiness Church in Stoneville, were also spirit-filled preachers who preached through and by the power of God. It was obvious that their calling was real; it was not for show, and the spirit of the Lord was upon them. In my opinion, Goodwill's own pastors, the late Reverend B. H. Bonham and Reverend Benjamin Mittman, could "sho-nuff" preach. I thought Rev. Mittman knew the word as well as anyone I ever heard preach. My late brother Rev. Dr. James A. Webster, pastor of First Baptist Oak Ridge in Oak Ridge, North Carolina, for thirty-nine years—beginning with his initial sermon in the summer of 1975—came out preaching with remarkable anointed power. It seems that I recall portions of his initial sermon. I don't recall his subject or the title, but I seem to remember him quoting from Matthew and Luke: "Consider the lilies of the field, how they grow; they toll not, neither do they spin.... Be not therefore anxious for the morrow; for the morrow will be anxious for itself.... Look at the birds of the air; they neither sow nor reap nor gather into barns, and yet your heavenly father feeds them." Nearly forty-eight years later, not long before God called him home in May 2023, my brother was still preaching with an anointing power, sometimes despite illness when he didn't feel like preaching. It was evident he was being led by the spirit of an almighty God.

The closing of all sermons in the African American tradition, at least at Goodwill and other Baptist churches, included an invitation extended by the pastor, associate minister, or guest preacher to anyone in the congregation to come down the aisle and devote one's life to Christ if one hadn't done so, and an invitation to join the church. This was and still is referred to as "opening the doors of the church." The former pastor of Oberlin Baptist Church in Raleigh, North Carolina, Rev. Dr. Sherri Arnold Graham, offered an invitation that included the statement, "Everyone needs a church home, and every soul needs an address." At Goodwill, if anyone accepted the invitation to come, one of the deacons would come forward and ascertain why the person had come forward. Usually, it was to accept Christ as their savior and join the church to become a member. If the person had not been baptized, then the person would be informed that they would be baptized. In my youth, we didn't have an indoor baptismal, and so a person giving their life to Christ was baptized in the creek that flowed not far from the church. I first joined Goodwill Baptist Church at a revival when I was around twelve years old. In Goodwill Baptist Church and other churches' traditions of my youth, if one had not been faithful to his or her commitment to stay focused on one's spiritual life, or returned to sinful life—or "backslid," as church members referred to it—then it was common for that person to come forward at the invitation to reconnect to one's commitment to be faithful to God. In my late twenties or early thirties, after hearing a sermon by Rev. Benjamin Mittman titled "Rise and Shine," I came forward and, in my own mind and heart, confessed my sins and recommitted to follow Christ. I recall that moment just like it was yesterday. The pastor asked me whether I wanted to say anything? I could not say a word because I could not stop shedding tears. I know God knew my heart and knew that I, like David, was then and remain some forty years later a man after God's own heart. Since that day, I've tried to live a Christian life that is pleasing to God.

I joined the Goodwill Baptist Church at a revival service when I was about twelve years old. A half dozen or so of the boys and girls around my age were asked to come forward to sit on the front pew on the left side of the church during the revival service. No one told us that to join the church we then had to come forward to stand in front of the church when the "invitation" was extended by the guest preacher for the weeklong revival service. That night upon arriving home from revival, my mother explained that I needed to come forward when the "doors of the church" were opened for new members. So the next night at revival, I officially joined the church, and some weeks later I was baptized in a local creek in walking distance from my family's home. We called it the "baptizing hole," which also served as our summertime swimming pool. While I do not recall all the details of the occasion, however, as was the custom, those being baptized arrived at the site of baptizing surrounded by family and other members of the congregation. I recall people singing gospel songs on the banks of the creek. Those being baptized were taken into the water one by one; as the singing ceased, the pastor dipped each one of us into the cool water and said similar words as these: "Having accepted Jesus as your personal savior, because of your faith in Jesus and in obedience to His command, I baptize you, in the name of the Father, and of the Son, and of the Holy Spirit." And in the matter of a few seconds I had been baptized, publicly demonstrating my acceptance of Jesus Christ as my Lord and Savoir. After the baptizing we traveled to the church located nearby to dress into our Sunday church attire. I am certain that I along with the several others being baptized that early Sunday morning came to the front of the church at the end of Sunday morning worship service and were extended "the right hand of fellowship" by the deacons of the church first, followed by the other members of the church who shook our hands and wished us well on our Christian journey.

Original Goodwill Baptist Church Senior Choir

Goodwill Gospel Singers, Madison, NC—my father, James E. Webster, second from left

I also recall vividly the annual choir anniversaries of the early years of my life. Choirs came from local and distant communities—all dressed in beautiful robes. They sang from their hearts for the glory of God. The Goodwill choir would march in from the rear of the church, most members rhythmically swaying side to side as they came into the sanctuary. I can see them still today. At other times, one or more quartets would come to perform at Goodwill. We called the singing groups quartets even if they had more than four members. If there was a guitar player in the midst, it was a quartet. I have a photo of the singing group my father was in. James E. "Tom" Webster, with his cousins George Brown, Louis "Mush" Brown, and Paul Carter, along with Jimmy Vernon, Tom Hopkins, and Raymond Hopkins. They had organized a gospel singing group with Louis Brown as the guitarist. The group was called the Goodwill Gospel Singers. I regret not seeing my father and the other members of the Goodwill Gospel Singers perform, as their heyday preceded the age that I can remember. However, as a child, I saw scores of gospel groups perform at Goodwill Baptist Church, and I wanted to learn to play a guitar because I was so influenced and impressed with the talented men and women whom I saw perform.

Personally, the songs of my youth still resonate and sustain me when I'm experiencing low moments. None of us are exempt from valley moments. In the shower I sing those old songs I learned from my ancestors. I sing them as I ride down the highway, in my home, or even at my office. I remember so well someone's melodious voice would ring out during worship service, "I need Thee, oh I need Thee, every hour I need Thee, Oh bless me now my Savior, I come to Thee." And then somebody who has also had a hard week would call on the Lord, whom they knew specialized in whatever they needed and so they would sing, "Come by here, Lord, come by here. Oh Lord, come by here, I need your power. Lord, come by here." And then someone else who knew God and trusted Him like a lifelong friend would sing, "What a Friend We Have in Jesus, all our sins and griefs to bear, all because we do not carry everything to God in prayer." Our many hymns of praise and trust in a living God went on a long time as the Spirit was frequently there on Sabbath-day morning. "I will trust in the Lord, I will trust in the Lord until I die.... I'm gonna stay on the battlefield.... I'm gonna treat everybody right ... 'til I die." And the love for God was evident in that old wooden church during my youth. Somebody knew to sing, "I love the Lord, I love the Lord, down in my heart.... He's good to me.... He's good to me, down in my heart. I'm satisfied, I'm satisfied ... down in my heart"; "I don't know what I'd do without the Lord.... I couldn't even pray a prayer without the Lord.... I couldn't even sing a song without the Lord." And then somebody knew the scriptures about letting your light shine. They'd sing, "This little light of mine, I'm gonna let it shine, this little light of mine, I'm going let it shine, let it shine, Down in my heart, I'm gonna let it shine.... All in my home, I'm gonna let it shine, let it shine, let it shine, let it shine." I recall one of my mother's favorite songs, "If I live right ... I will overcome some day. If I walk right ... I will overcome some day." "I woke up this morning with my mind stayed on Jesus. I woke up this morning with my mind stayed on the Lord. Hallelujah, Hallelujah, Hallelujah!" I recall vividly, "I'm a soldier in the army of the Lord.... I don't mind dying in this army. I'm fighting for my rights in this army of the Lord ... in this army."

I loved hearing certain ones sing, "His eye is on the sparrow, and I know He watches over me." And at home, sometimes I go back to the songs of the slaves that lifted up their spirits—songs such as "I am climbing Jacob's ladder, soldiers of the cross. Do you think I'll make a good soldier, soldiers of the cross. Every round goes higher and higher.... Soldiers of the cross." And the song "Steal Away to Jesus" comes to mind. "My Lord calls me: He calls me by the thunder. The trumpet sounds within my soul, I ain't got long to stay here.... And then they sang, My Lord, He calls me. He calls me by the lightning. The trumpet sounds within my soul, I ain't got long to stay here."

The Goodwill Baptist Church cemetery contains many known and unknown members of the church and community. The names of many of those buried in the cemetery who passed in the early years are unknown as their grave markers have been lost to time. Like much of the early history of Goodwill Baptist Church and many other early congregations, records of births, baptisms, and burials were not meticulously recorded by writing them down and maintaining them in a secure place. Too much of the African American church and other history has depended upon oral history. Unfortunately, by the time of this writing, most all of those who could describe the exact details of the life of the Goodwill Church and community in the first half of the twentieth century have long since passed, including the names of those whose grave sites were only marked with a stone or a temporary funeral home placard. Nothing should be taken from these words as criticism of those who died or those family members left behind during the early years of Goodwill Baptist Church, as many suffered through the vestiges of slavery, Jim Crow, and a sharecropping system made worse by the Great Depression that left them financially debilitated, to say the least. Fortunately, however, as far back as anyone can recall, on Good Friday of each year, members of the church and community gathered and still gather to clean up the cemetery, removing limbs and other debris. From the existing marked grave sites, one can see the names of many of the large families that have made up the Goodwill community. The Moore, Webster, Ziglar, Johnson, and Brown family names predominate. Other families buried in the Goodwill cemetery include the Kellam, Martin, Smith, Price, Carter, and numerous others.

Sunday School attendance was very much a part of the agenda for most members of Goodwill Baptist Church during my youth. The late Deacon George Brown was superintendent for many years. During the 1960s and 1970s Sunday school attendance was great in numbers and was divided into adult and younger classes. Membership of the Sunday school was treated to three memorable events. One of was these was the Easter egg hunt on Easter Monday (the day after Easter Sunday). I recall my mother boiling many eggs, and we dyed them different colors. We then brought them to the church so that the adults could hide them. They must have allowed the children to keep all the eggs we found, because I vividly recall that I got very sick with a severe stomachache from eating at least a half dozen eggs from the Easter Egg hunt and vomited for much of the night.

In mid-August of each year, the young members of the church, especially looked forward to the Sunday school picnic, My recollection is that it was held at various parks such as High Point City Lake Park, Jamestown Park, Burlington Park, Winston Salem park, and the Salem Park in Salem, Virginia. Lunch baskets were packed by each family. Fried chicken, ham, potato salad, macaroni, green beans, sweet potato pies, cakes, you name it—the great cooks of Goodwill Baptist Church prepared a feast. The youth looked forward to going swimming in a real swimming pool rather than the creek we swam in and where church baptisms took place. The Sunday School picnic was the first time most of us had swam in a real swimming pool. During my early childhood, if there were public swimming pools, they were segregated and not open to blacks. Private ownership of pools by blacks or whites were unheard of in my community and nearby towns.

The Sunday School also held a Christmas Eve program, an exciting time of the year for all youth. It was exciting in part because we anticipated the bags of nuts, fruits, and candy that each person, young and old, would receive. Gifts were also passed out to members of the congregation. But for the youth, the promise of gifts under the Christmas tree from Santa Claus made Christmas Eve that much more suspenseful and exciting. The Christmas Eve program also included our youth being assigned a speech or recitation that we had to memorize and recite one by one in the front of the church. One of the highlights was when my great-aunt Mable Webster Brown came up to the front of the church and recited the same speech each year, which was followed with a chuckle from the audience. She recited with confidence the following words:

An Annual Christmas Eve Program Welcome

by Mable Webster Brown, and after her death, her daughter Elsie P. Hughes continues the tradition today

> Dear friends, you all are welcome to our exercise here, and we will do our hardest our smartest to appear, and if by chance we stumble, don't notice that at all. I'm sure you have stumbled too when you were very small. Oh yes you have sometimes I know, no use for you

My childhood memories also included the annual tradition of cleaning the Goodwill cemetery on each Good Friday. Many from the church and community came with their rakes, shovels, and it seems I recall brush brooms handmade from tree branches.

In the early days I recall seeing graves shaped into mounds. Some had headstones, some had funeral home placards with names on them, and some graves had a small rectangular cement block to mark the grave. Unfortunately, some had nothing to show who was buried in a grave by the early 1960s. However, like the other church and Sunday school sponsored activities, everyone had a great time just being together, and there was plenty of laughter, love displayed among participants, and keepsake memories. This Good Friday annual event continues today with many fewer members participating.

Goodwill had a men's baseball team in the 1960s. Its name was The Goodwill Tigers, and its home field was immediately behind the church building. An interview with my uncle Willie Cain Webster indicated that at some point, Wayne Flynt was the team manager. During the summer months, games were played against opposing teams during the late afternoon hours both on the home field and the away field within a thirty- or forty-minute drive from Goodwill. Away games were played in Ridgeway, Mayo, and Martinsville, Virginia, Walnut Cove, Hayes Chapel, and Stoneville, North Carolina.

I personally had a great deal of fun watching the games and the very talented players on Goodwill's team. My uncle Willie Cain "W.C." Webster was a superb pitcher. He had a pitch we all called a "drop." I always stood behind the screened fence behind the catcher. That pitch seemed to drop at least twelve inches across the middle of the plate. I always wondered how he learned to throw such a pitch. He also had a curveball. As I recall, James Searcy, Nate Johnson, and Samuel Tatum were powerful long-ball hitters. Other members of the team were James Joyce, Robert Searcy, Louis "Mush" Brown, Wesley Brown, Harvey Johnson, Cap Buster Searcy, Lorenzo Satterfield, James L. "Sonnie" Moore, Harvey Moore, and Roy Melvin Martin. Other memories of the baseball games were that the teams sometimes got off to a late start, maybe because the opposing team was late or some other reason. One of the Goodwill community residents, Ben Brown, who would drive up in a vehicle we often called a half car–half truck with a fox tail hanging from the back bumper, was always present at the home games. When it appeared to him the game would be starting later than normal, he would holler out, "Sun's going down, sun's going down." This was his way of telling the teams to start the game.

During the 1970s, while I was a student at Howard University for undergraduate and law school, the young women of Goodwill, had a softball team. Some of the players were Donna Johnson, Veronica "Bo" Tatum, Glenda Patterson, Tammy Satterfield, and Sherri Johnson. The team played squads from Madison, Walnut Cove, Stoneville, and Winston Salem. Donna Johnson informed me that Walnut Cove was Goodwill's main rival. My aunt Lillie Bell coached the team, and Gentry's Barber Shop of Madison was a sponsor.

Highlights of Two Ancestors: My Paternal Great-Great-Grandfather Samuel H. Gibson and My Maternal Great-Grandfather Robert Watt Moore

REV. SAMUEL H. GIBSON

I have chosen to feature here two of the older members of my family tree, both born in the mid-1860s. Both lived in the Goodwill and surrounding areas for all their childhoods, and in the case of Robert Watt Moore, all his life.

First, I detail what I have learned about my paternal great-great-grandfather Samuel H. Gibson. He was the son of John H. Gibson and Lucy Johnson Gibson. His father had been born in or around 1827. The 1860 and 1870 Censuses refer to John and Lucy Gibson's family as mulatto. I spent more time trying to discover as much as I could about Samuel H. Gibson because of his departure from the Goodwill community, never to return, according to my paternal grandmother, Annie Ziglar Webster. Despite never having met her grandfather, Samuel H. Gibson, my grandmother named one of her sons after him. His name was Sam Henry Webster and had a severe disability all his life. He was a child in a grown man's body.

All my childhood I wondered what had become of my paternal great-great-grandfather, Samuel H. Gibson, so I conducted an exhaustive search to find all I could about him. I had heard from my paternal grandmother Annie Ziglar Webster in the 1970s that her grandfather Samuel H. Gibson had left his wife and children behind and moved away from the Goodwill community many years before. His marriage certificate list his wife's name as Eddie Mitchell Gibson, and they married April 23, 1885, in Stokes County, North Carolina. I had wondered for years how he could have abandoned his wife and children, especially in an era when divorces were uncommon. We often judge before knowing the whole story. All my grandmother knew was that he had moved to Rock Island, Illinois, and that early in her life Samuel H. Gibson had sent a piano by train to Madison, and her family had gone to the station to pick it up. As a child, I personally saw that piano in the home of my great-grandmother Lucy Gibson Ziglar, her husband, John Ziglar. According to my grandmother, Annie, her grandfather Samuel H. Gibson never returned to the community where he grew up in the Goodwill community outside Madison, North Carolina. If in fact he never returned to his home in North Carolina, then what my grandmother, who was born in 1905, told me about her grandfather, would have had to come from what her mother or other relatives told her. Samuel H. Gibson left Madison in the late 1880s or early 1890s as he was living in Moline—Rock Island, Illinois—in 1891 according to the Moline, Illinois, City Directory.[5]

I had a conversation with two relatives who informed me that it was their understanding that Samuel H. Gibson had to flee the Goodwill area, leaving his family behind, because he had gotten into a fight with a white man and feared for his life. This was a plausible explanation, as many persons of African descent fled the south for the same reason. However, I can only speculate why my great-great grandfather never returned home.

During my research, I wondered how my great-great grandfather traveled the many miles to Illinois and other midwestern states at a time prior to the invention or availability of automobiles. Did he walk, ride a horse or horse and wagon, or go to a larger town such as Greensboro, North Carolina and ride a train the many miles to Illinois?[6] I wondered whether he had relatives living there in Illinois and nearby midwestern states such Iowa, Kansas and Missouri. It is probably the case that he chose the Midwest because of the many industries in that area. The area drew many other migrants from the South to the Midwest beginning two decades later after Samuel Gibson's departure from North Carolina.[7] It also remains a mystery how he ended up toward the latter part of his life in Pueblo, Colorado, which is over fifteen hundred miles from his birthplace in North Carolina. An attorney friend from my hometown, Eugene Russell, found online a picture

5 My research also found that Samuel H. Gibson married Kempie Robinson in Massac, Illinois, in 1904 pastored First Baptist Church, Colored in or near Mount Vernon, Illinois as late as 1907; lived in Lyons, Kansas as a minister in 1910; lived in Bloomington, Illinois in 1915 during which time he pastored Mt. Pisgah Baptist Church; lived in Rock Island, Illinois in 1920 and pastored Second Baptist Church, Colored, of Rock Island; lived in Livington, Missouri in 1930; and lived in Pueblo, Colorado in 1940, where he died.

6 on January 28, 1943. My great-great grandfather also served as the minister of the Masonic Lodge in Rock Island for a brief period.

Passenger train travel to Richmond, Virginia was possible from nearby Greensboro, North Carolina to Danville Virginia in February 19,1862 after the Confederate Congress and North Carolina State Legislature simultaneously approved the building of the rail line so that there could be train service to the Confederate Capital at Richmond. The rail line was completed in 1864. So, presumably my great-great grandfather could have quickly gotten out of harm's way by traveling the 25 miles from Madison, North Carolina to Greensboro in the late 1880s or early 1890s. See book "Images of Rail Greensboro Depot" Copyright ©2023 by David H. Steinberg and Kevin W. von der Lippe for the Greensboro Chapter of the National Railway Historical Society. Chapter One, 9.

7 Industries such as John Deere, located in Moline, Illinois, and other surrounding areas throughout the North and Midwest drew many migrants to work in manufacturing especially beginning around 1910. While Samuel H. Gibson's migration to the Midwest occurred by 1891, based upon his recorded residence in Illinois, he would have found many manufacturing jobs upon his arrival. Migration increased from the south increased steadily over the next 25 years. The period from about 1915 to 1970, became well known as the "Great Migration." See Isabel Wilkerson's The Warmth of Other Suns, The Epic Story of the Great Migration p. 9, © Copyright 2010. Some six million, mostly blacks left the south to escape the Jim Crow laws, racism, and the arduous labor of the tobacco, cotton and other agrarian economies of the south that made life miserable for them. The prospect of greater job opportunities and a better life incentivized them to migrate. The direction migrants traveled mostly depended on where they lived and the location of the rail lines. Samuel H. Gibson's primary motivating factor for migrating appears to be because he feared injury or death at the hands of a white man, which was not an unfounded fear in the late 1800s especially in the south.

of the burial site of Rev. S. H. Gibson in Pueblo, Colorado. I became very excited about this find. Later I called the Mountain View Cemetery and came to befriend an employee of the cemetery where my ancestor is buried. Her name is Marie Johnson, who in the last few years has placed flowers on my relative's grave. What a beautiful spirit she has. In addition, she made a financial donation to Goodwill Baptist Church, which sits upon land donated by my great-great-great grandfather, John H. Gibson. More importantly, Marie Johnson has attempted to help me learn more about Samuel H. Gibson's s sojourn in Pueblo from the 1930s until his death in 1943. His last home was 1544 East Orman, Pueblo, Colorado. His funeral was held at the Bethlehem Baptist Church. If I have any disappointment about my many hours of research about my paternal great-great grandfather, it would be that to date, I have not been able to locate a photograph of him. I have an idea of what he looked like, though. My cousin the late George Brown used to tell me that I looked like Samuel H. Gibson's son, Robert "Bud" Gibson. Also, another family member recalled hearing that Robert Gibson met his father at a church convention in Colorado. A man attending the convention approached Robert Gibson and told him that he looked just like a white minister that was attending the convention.

THE JONES MORTUARY
Routt at Summit
GIBSON—Rev. Samuel H., serves Tuesday 1 p. m., Bethlehem
aptist church. Body will lie in
ate at the residence, 1544 East
rman, from 10 a. m. Tuesday un-
l hour of service. Interment Mt.
iew.

Bethlehem Baptist Church, Pueblo, Colorado

My paternal great-great-grandfather Samuel H. Gibson is also buried in Pueblo, Colorado, with a stone marker shown here.

Last residence of Samuel H. Gibson at his death 1544 E. Orman, Pueblo, Colorado. Buried in Mountain View Cemetery, Pueblo. Church, gravestone, and residence.
IMAGES COURTESY OF MARIE JOHNSON

Although not conclusive proof, it is likely then that Rev. Samuel H. Gibson's portrait would look very similar to his son, similar to the many mixed-race persons of the late 1800s in the Goodwill community and nearby areas in Rockingham, Stokes, Surry, and Wilkes Counties in North Carolina and across the border into Virginia, in such places as Henry, Patrick, and Pittsylvania Counties, where some of my ancestors or distant relatives were born or living at the time.

It is still unknown why Samuel H. Gibson eventually moved so far away to Pueblo, Colorado, where his remains are buried. His presence there is supported by the telephone book references to him and his wife, Kempie Robinson Gibson. Samuel H. Gibson is listed in the 1940 Census as a minister, but no income is listed. Therefore, it is unlikely that my great-great-grandfather was the full-time or part-time pastor of a church there. Why he failed to return to his native state of North Carolina will likely never be known. His remarriage in Illinois may have played a part in his decision. Maybe he continued to be fearful of returning home. This is all speculation. It is also conjecture as to whether Samuel H. Gibson's failure to return home may be part of the reason that he is not listed in the will of his father, John H. Gibson. He left most of his property in Rockingham County to his daughter Julia Gibson Webster, who married Richard Webster Sr., a trustee at Goodwill Baptist Church in the early 1900s.

Robert Watt Moore

I was blessed to be very close to the youngest child of Robert Watt Moore and Ester Strickland Moore, my great uncle Early Narvell. Moore, a Goodwill native. He went home to be with the Lord on the Sabbath Day, November 12, 2017, at age eighty-five. I spoke with him numerous times about his father, Robert Watt Moore, who was born in 1863 according to his gravestone located in the Goodwill Baptist Church cemetery. (Census records place his date of birth in 1869.) Whatever the case, Early Moore comes as close to anyone whom I ever met who knew another person (his father) who had likely known a former slave: Early's grandfather John "Jack" Moore, who was born in or about 1825, according to Census records. Most likely Early's father knew his father well, and may have talked to him about slavery, although many former slaves and their heirs born during Jim Crow chose not to discuss their experiences. Perhaps they were just too painful. Robert Watt Moore and his wife, Ester Strickland Moore, also raised my mother, Bettie Ester Moore, the daughter of Ressie Moore Hairston and Charlie Hairston. I regret that I didn't talk more with my mother about her grandparents who raised her. She did volunteer a few things about her grandfather. She told me that one day she had a penny in her hand and her grandfather said, "Girl, give me that. You don't need all of that money." As was often the case with many of his generation, he drank fairly frequently, especially on weekends. They were hardworking people of their day. You couldn't be a sharecropper and have a dozen-plus children without being a hard worker. Apparently, men of that generation were not as concerned about cleanliness in the home. For example, my mother told me that her grandfather would sometimes clear his throat and spit on the fireplace hearth and scour it with his foot. She said that her grandmother would say, "Now, Watt!" And nothing else was said about it. She never spoke of him as being abusive in any way. She recalls when my father started coming around, sometimes Watt would say something like, "There comes Tom, with his tall ass." However, I didn't sense that he was being disrespectful in any way. I'm sure it was meant to be a term of endearment. After all, my great grandfather Watt must have given his blessings for my mother to marry my father when she was no more than sixteen years of age. I recall my mother telling me at some point she raised her age by a year. Soon after I became an attorney, I helped my mother secure a delayed birth certificate for the first time in her life.

Grave marker, my maternal great grand father and mother—Robert Watt Moore, 1863–1947 and Ester Strickland Moore, 1888–1950—buried in the Goodwill First Baptist Church Cemetery

My great-uncle Early Moore told me the following, which revealed the nature of the sharecropping system in the one-hundred years after slavery ended. Early and his brother George were preparing to walk to school one day, and they were outside talking to their father. The white owner of the farm they lived on approached his father. Early said the old man said, "Watt, them boys need to be in the field today." Rather than telling the man that his sons were prepared to go to school, Early's father bowed his head and said, "Yessah, yessah." Early said his father turned to him and his brother and said, "Y'all boys go in the house and change your clothes and get in the fields and go to work." Early told me that he was so angry he didn't know what to say or do. He said he was angry with the old man, and he was also angry with the way his father responded to him. Even though I had studied the institution of slavery and read about the institution of sharecropping that replaced slavery, this conversation with my great uncle caused me for the very first time to consider the fact that sharecropping was just a minor-upgrade form of slavery. I had never considered the fact that the white landowner could determine when the sharecropper and their families had to tend to the crops in the field. It is clear from my great-grandfather's response to the owner of the farm that his family lived on and worked that my great-grandfather felt subservient and feared what would happen if he failed to do as the owner of the farm demanded. His posture of bowing his head and saying, "Yessah, yessah," also is some indication that he had grown up around ancestors who reacted in the same manner. My maternal great-grandfather never owned land or a home, yet many of his offspring—including Early Moore, Jesse Moore, Sallie Moore Johnson, George Moore, Della Moore Johnson and others through marriage, hard work, and living a Christian life—became homeowners and successful in other ways, and whose offspring themselves achieved and did well also.

Despite all that our ancestors endured, we are still richly blessed, still persevering, and still pressing toward the mark of the high calling. Our ancestors left us with a tremendous work ethic, an enduring faith, and a Christian value system that includes loving and treating others like you want to be treated, a forgiving heart, honesty, fairness, integrity, and respect for and sharing with others. These core values making up one's moral compass need to be emulated and shared with our children and children's children, and with those who were not blessed to be raised in the small close-knit community called Goodwill.

Sayings of Goodwill Community Members

Our ancestors from Goodwill left an important legacy of meaningful favorite "sayings" that most of us remember years after the passing of our loved ones. Some demonstrate their faith walk, while others reflect the relative's humorous nature based on arduous life's experiences. Just a few of such sayings were recalled by the children and grandchildren of our ancestors:

- It will come out. After awhile! ALICE MOORE
- It's a scandal and shame before the Lord. ANNIE WEBSTER
- As you see the light, walk therein. JAMES EDWARD WEBSTER
- I don't know what I would do without the Lord. BETTY MOORE
- That's a sight and a scansion *[translated as scandal]* MOZELLE MOORE

- I am doing good. ED KELLAM
- God is able. FRANCES KELLAM
- Every dog has his day *and* You shot that shot right! EDDIE MAE MOORE
- You can lead a horse to the water, but you can't make him drink! COY JOYCE
- That's what I'm talking about. LOUISE JOYCE
- I am what I am, and that's all I am. FLOYD "PETE" WEBSTER
- Worrying ain't never solved no problem. OSCAR CARTER
- You don't ever wanna give a devil a hammer to hit you in your head. LULA MAE WEBSTER
- Dog if I know Walter. SONNIE BROWN
- My name is Bennet and I'm not in it. SALLIE BELLE JOHNSON
- The Lord will make a way somehow. MILDRED BROWN
- If someone comes by the house and says, "Let's," I'll say "Go." ADDIE "SHORTY" BROWN
- What don't kill you will make you stronger *and* God bless the child that has his own. MARIE WEBSTER
- Charity begins at home and spreads abroad *and* An idle mind is the Devil's workshop. BETTIE ESTER MOORE WEBSTER
- A heap sees but a few knows. MABLE WEBSTER BROWN
- If ifs and ands were pots and pans, the whole world would be a kitchen. BILLY "JACK" WEBSTER

Education in the Goodwill Community

The Goodwill community built a log cabin for its own school for the "colored" children (as they were referred to then). According to the church's records, during the early years it served as a church also. It was located on K-Fork Road not far from the church. During the early years, elementary and middle school age children of African American descendants attended this school from Goodwill and surrounding communities. I recall my mother telling me that even though she was four years younger than my father, they were in the same classroom.

During the early years, Professor Campt was the sole teacher at the school, and he drove his car from the town of Madison to teach all the pupils there. From the early years of my youth, many relatives who attended the school placed the building housing the school as being the now-renovated home of the heirs of Edward and Lillie Carter. My parents, James and Bettie Webster, attended school there until they quit school. My mother always told me she quit school because she did not feel she had adequate clothes to wear. In fact, my mother, raised by her grandparents, said she had one good dress that she liked. She said she often came home to wash it so she could wear it the next day. It must have been difficult to teach children, most of whom were the first generation of persons of color to attend school. This likely meant that the parents of the first students to attend that school could not read, or that their reading was very deficient. Years ago, it was told to me by a former student that one day when Professor Campt had the students reading from a book that he was very familiar, one of his students skipped an entire line. Professor Campt said to the student, "Skipped a line." Rather than the student returning to the line that had not been read, the student responded, "Skipped a line." I was also told that my father, James E. Webster, known to the entire community as "Tom," was being admonished by Professor Campt for something he had done. I was told that my father ran out of the school, followed by Professor Campt. Professor Campt supposedly hollered for my father to stop and said to him, "Come here, Tom." I'm told that my father looked around at him and said, "No, you come here." I can imagine that might have been my father's last day of school. Because of the circumstances under which these first Goodwill students experienced schooling—many having to walk many miles to attend school, having to stay out of school to work

Goodwill School for "Colored" Children Students.
COURTESY OF DR. MABLE DILLARD

Lowell Mason Campt, known as "Professor Campt."
COURTESY OF MIACHEL SCALES

in the fields, and overcome other obstacles, including poverty—it is a miracle that they were able to learn as well as they did.

There were several businesses located in Goodwill, including Minnie Sue's Place, owned and operated by Minnie Sue Hairston. She sold some of the best ham and bologna sandwiches to be found anywhere, going back to the first half of the twentieth century. She also sold my favorite childhood drink, Nehi Grape Soda. Minnie Sue's also sold something a little stronger. Minnie Sue's was a place of socializing in the community where many gathered for fun and laughter. In the early part of the twentieth century there was also a place of business located within walking distance beyond Goodwill Baptist Church off K-Fork Road that I'm told was owned and operated by members of the Roy "Jack" Webster family. And in the early 1960s my mother and father ran a local restaurant where my mother's specialties were hot dogs and hamburgers. They also sold assorted groceries in the store owned by community resident Henry Welch. Those businesses closed long ago.

During all my elementary and high school years, my best friends were all cousins who lived within walking distance from my family. We played together on dirt basketball courts at the edge of our parents' homes, played football in the Johnson's horse pasture, caught the bus together to school, went to the same church, and worked in the tobacco fields together. Our parents were also best friends, and we had the same upbringing. Because my closest friends were cousins and the sons of parents who had grown up together, went to church together, prayed together, and worked in the fields together, we were brought up and taught the same lessons of knowing right from wrong, the same Bible verses, and the same lessons about loving our neighbors. By example, we were all taught the same hard work ethic. Everyone worked back then.

I wish I had undertaken the writing of this historical document several decades earlier. Since that time, most of those whom I write about have passed on. People like my grandfather Fred Webster; his wife, Annie; Roy "Jack" Webster and his wife, Sallie; Sonny Brown and his wife, Mabel; and others born in the early 1900s would have been able to tell us much about the first decades of the twentieth century. How wonderful it would have been to ask them what they thought when they saw the first automobile or rode in one, saw the first plane in the sky or saw the first television. My great-uncle Early Moore told me he recalls the first time he rode in an automobile. Someone from the community came by his parents' home and gave him, his brother, and perhaps someone else and took them to downtown Madison, North Carolina. Upon arriving one of them looked up and saw a sign at a gas station that said Esso (now Exxon). One of the passengers in the car said, "We in Esso."

The generation that had spoken with the early pastors, trustees, and church members of Goodwill began dying out during my youth. I did speak with my paternal great-grandmother, Lucy Gibson Ziglar once about her ancestry. She lived to the ripe old age of 103, having been born in 1885 and died in 1989. I specifically asked her once whether either of her parents were white. She responded, "Not that knows of." The 1870 and 1880 Census records list her parents and grandparents as "mulatto." I was too young and didn't have sufficient knowledge to challenge her response. Even if I did, I had too much respect at the time for anyone in their mid- to upper eighties to do so. Fortunately, because of technology—especially Ancestry.com and the Census and other records made publicly available—information is more easily attained so that people can research family heritage.

While a small number of the early Goodwill community residents and those who attended Goodwill Church were landowners—for example, the John H. Gibson heirs (family of Richard Webster Sr., who married into the Gibson family—Julia Gibson, sister of Samuel H. Gibson), the Isaac Johnson heirs, the Sydney Oliver heirs, and the Noah Kellam heirs owned sizeable tracts of land—most others were sharecroppers in the years following the Civil War and into the early 1900s.

One need only look around throughout the length and breadth of the United States to see the many success stories resulting from the exemplary Christian teaching and prayers of the pioneers who grew up in Goodwill and Goodwill Baptist Church. With the help of an almighty God, our early Goodwill ancestors made a way out of no way. In just one generation, many families in the Goodwill community went from abject poverty to owning land, homes, and cars, mostly through hard work and faith in a living God. It is not debatable that central to that rise from poverty to the middle class was an unwavering faith in God that was at least the size of a grain of mustard seed. Consequently, those begat by the old farmers of the community of Goodwill have been successful and have reached heights that the pioneers of Goodwill Baptist Church and community would not have ever thought possible. Like my great-grandfather Robert "Watt" Moore, many of our other ancestors also turned the other cheek to racism, physical and mental abuse, humiliation, and dehumanization. Yes, they said, "Yessah," as they bowed their heads to those whom they were indebted as sharecroppers so that their children and children's children would have a chance to survive and prosper. I personally will always be indebted to my ancestors for all they sacrificed—and for their prayers. I personally saw my parents kneeling beside their beds as they prepared to go to sleep each night. For this and more I am grateful. I am grateful to such a faithful and merciful God whose mercies are new every morning, according to the Scriptures. I pray that

Goodwill Baptist Church and the goodwill community will continue to be beacons of hope and what it is possible to accomplish. To God be the glory!

The Three Goodwill Webster Families

An intriguing part of Goodwill history is that there are three distinct Webster families in the community, unrelated except by marriage. They are the families of my paternal grandfather Fred Webster, Richard Webster Sr., and Jesse "Jess" Webster. All three of these men married my Gibson ancestors. Fred Webster married Annie Ziglar Webster, whose mother was my paternal great-grandmother Lucy Gibson Ziglar. Richard Webster Sr. married Julia Gibson Webster, who was my paternal great-great-grandfather Rev. Samuel H. Gibson's sister; and Jesse "Jess" Webster married Lottie Ziglar Webster, who was my paternal great-grandmother Lucy Gibson Ziglar's daughter. It is also ironic that there have been no Gibson "sir names" (no male in the congregation whose last name was Gibson) for as long as anyone can remember. It is unknown where my paternal great-great-great-grandfather John H. Gibson or his wife, my paternal great-great-great grandmother Lucy Johnson Gibson, are buried. The same is true for others who were the earliest pioneers of the church. I am proud that my Gibson ancestors had charitable hearts. John H. Gibson donated 2 ½ acres of land to build the community church, and he or his son, also named John H. Gibson, was the second pastor of Goodwill Baptist Church from 1910 to 1917, according to church records. Possibly they are buried in Stokes County where John H. Gibson also owned land, or less likely, if buried in the Goodwill Church cemetery, their grave locations may be lost to time. In contrast to many others in the Goodwill community, the Gibson line of my ancestry owned land and could have afforded to purchase more expensive grave marker memorials that would last for hundreds of years. Such was the case with their daughter, Julia Gibson Webster who is buried in the Goodwill Church cemetery. The real estate records of Rockingham County, North Carolina show her father, John H. Gibson, owned 183 acres of land in 1886, and his Last Will and Testament list his daughter, Julia as the primary beneficiary. Julia Gibson Webster has a distinct upright grave marker.

Lest anyone get the impression that the Goodwill community and church have been a paradise without their own moles and warts, it is important for me to dispel that notion. Notwithstanding the current climate in America that tries to convince us that truth is unimportant, truth will always be important because, as is revealed in John 17:17, "Thy word is truth" (KJV). During my youth, a schism occurred among the members of Goodwill Baptist Church. The Goodwill church was clearly one made up

Goodwill Baptist Church Community Park located at intersection of Highway 311 (W. Academy St.) and K-Fork Road, Madison, NC. Recorded Rockingham County Register of Deeds Office, Deed Book 1092, p. 359.
PARK SIGNAGE COURTESY OF WILLIE CANE WEBSTER

of mostly relatives. There developed a disagreement about whether the church should part ways with the then pastor. It has been so long ago, more almost six decades since this first major schism in the Goodwill church family occurred that I can recall. Some members who had been best friends from their youth up until then became upset with each other for a time over this disagreement. It was sad to see this, and frankly, as a child, I didn't quite know what to make of it. As I recall, more than one vote by the membership occurred to remove the pastor. The second vote included members who had not attended church in years. I don't recall whether a vote ended the relationship with the pastor, or whether he decided to resign to settle the dispute. However, I do know that it took a while for forgiveness and unity to once again became the norm at Goodwill Baptist Church.

And many years later, during the second decade of the twenty-first century, an even more devastating event occurred at Goodwill Baptist Church. Church leadership determined that the pastor had been stealing the churches money for years. He was prosecuted and convicted of charges, sentenced to nine months in prison, and required to pay back thousands of dollars to the church as restitution. In my opinion that was the saddest chapter in the history of Goodwill Baptist Church and community. As many churches and other institutions have learned, it is very important to have checks and balances in place to ensure that no one person can write a check, withdraw money from the bank accounts, have access to credit or debit cards and have accountability for bank deposits. Additional systems that allow and encourage church membership to see all church financial records should be mandatory. Periodic meetings for church membership are critical. This is even more important when small church leaders are relatives. All churches should "trust but verify." The Bible at Romans 3:23 says that all have sinned and come short of the glory of God. No one is immune from the sickness called sin. Therefore, temptation often rears its ugly head that sometimes leads to tragedies like the one at Goodwill and churches around the world. No doubt many among the church leadership forgot about this truth and put too much faith in man, who has the capacity to disappoint every time. I say that this was the saddest moment in Goodwill church history because some members lost trust in the church as an institution; some left Goodwill and followed the pastor to another church, some lost trust in their faith, and some likely have not fully recovered years later. Splits among church membership are always a casualty. One of the worst casualties is when husband and wife go separate ways, but perhaps the worst casualty of all is the loss of "moral authority" of the church as an institution whose compass should always point toward truth, brotherly love, reconciliation, and, as in the case of the name of my home church, "goodwill" toward all people. Nevertheless, the good people of Goodwill who helped raise me have the capacity and a heart of forgiveness, and I'm confident that complete reconciliation will take place in due time.

I have wondered for many years why a pastor would fight to remain as pastor, especially in churches where the constitution, bylaws, and/or church covenant prescribes reconciliation when disputes occur. A provision in one such church covenant, reads as follows:

> In case of a difference of opinion in the church, we will strive to avoid a contentious spirit, and if we cannot unanimously agree, we will cheerfully recognize the right of the majority to govern.

In this divided nation where conflict is ever present, promoting reconciliation by agreeing in advance for the majority to govern seems to be completely reasonable—and the Christian solution to disagreements especially within the church.

Covenants, which are promises made to God and one another by the church membership, vary among churches. During my youth, Goodwill Baptist Church's covenant had a provision requiring members to "abstain from the sale and use of intoxicating drinks as a beverage." I didn't think of it at the time, but that provision appears to be more restrictive than the Bible scripture at Ephesians 5:18–20, which warns against drinking "too much wine." I preached a sermon once at Goodwill and told the congregation that, looking back, I wish that we had treated those with alcohol addictions kindlier and with far less disdain and judgment. As a child growing up in the Goodwill community, because of how addictions were viewed by my ancestors, I came to believe that being a "drunkard"—as those with addictions were called—was the worst sin of all. No doubt the feelings of church members about our neighbors with addictions caused many to stay away from the church and contributed to their low self-esteem. I believe a warm embrace by members of the church and community of those with alcohol or drug addictions would have had healing powers. I have learned, especially since becoming a husband and father, as the Bible teaches, that love does cover a multitude of sins. As bad as the damage to the church and community resulting from my home church's failure to value the lives of those with addictions, this paled in comparison to the damage done by pastors and members who fight over who owns the church, and specifically who will lead it.

I have never been a pastor of a church. However, since being brought to church by my parents seven decades ago, I have been a member, choir member, trustee, and an associate minister. As the Apostle Paul instructs in 2 Timothy 2:15 (KJV), I have also heeded his admonition to "Study to shew thyself approved unto God, a workman that needeth not be ashamed, rightly dividing the word of truth" Moreover, I have never been accused of lacking common sense or lacking good judgment. I cannot understand how a bitter fight among the pastor and church members could ever be in the church's best interest. I have preached on several occasions about an opinion I formed when I was in private law practice two decades ago. Two chairmen of the deacon boards of two different churches fifty miles apart called me to obtain legal advice within the same week. They asked me, "Is it legal for the church to put a lock on the church doors to keep the pastor from entering the church?" I concluded after deliberating on these two calls that both sides were feuding over who owns the church. Both sides were figuratively trying to take the deed out of the Lord's name. What a shame! That is why, to this very day, I find it difficult to be associated with a congregation that has church leaders and members who believe foolishly that they own the church. Psalm 24 makes clear that "The earth is the LORD's and the fullness thereof." And further, Psalm 50 says that cattle upon a thousand hills ... belong to God," and I heard an old preacher say one time, "and the hills belong to Him also." At best the Lord's church can succeed only if the pastor, deacons, trustees, or other church leaders and members work together. At least in the Baptist tradition, there is no room for dictatorships among the fold.

My opinion is that no one person has a monopoly on what saith the Lord. Varying viewpoints should be encouraged, heard, and considered. It is also my opinion that my late brother Rev. Dr. James A. Webster and my mentor and spiritual adviser, the late Rev.

Dr. Eliott J. Mason, possessed the kind of spiritual leadership and wisdom that allowed for very long pastorships at their respective churches, First Baptist Church Oak Ridge in Oak Ridge, North Carolina, and Trinity Baptist Church in Los Angeles, California. No one would ever mention their names and dictators in the same breath. They were humble servants, but confident in their purposes and visions. Their love of God and people caused them to be patient and loving in their pastorship responsibilities. That is where they found their strength. Obviously, this meant that they sometimes had to turn the other cheek, and perhaps at times, not have the last word. No doubt they believed in the words of that hit gospel song by Yolanda Adams, "The Battle is the Lord's, which is based upon 1 Samuel 17:47. These two pastors and others, past and present who possess humble spirits have known that the battle of church leadership is not theirs, but the Lord's. For this understanding of good pastoral leadership, my late brother James and Dr. Mason were respected far and wide, not only among their membership. The members highly respected their leadership, visions and goals for the church, and therefore their churches grew and prospered. Thus, disputes among the pastor, church leaders and membership, if any, were few and far between.

Regarding church disputes, churches should learn from what the legal system in North Carolina and across America has discovered over the last four decades. Mediations or settlement conferences are forms of conflict resolution that are powerful and effective tools to settle disputes of all kinds and have reduced civil lawsuits and trials tremendously across the nation. All sides of a church dispute should know by now that there are no winners in a pastor-congregation battle royale. Many churches have split and suffered. The church as an institution already faces enough competition, including sporting activities that take youth away from Sunday worship services, and perhaps worst of all, social media. Budgetary concerns brought on by the desire to look impressive to the world, also inflict much unnecessary strain upon many congregations today. Those churches that rely almost exclusively on a Sunday morning worship service model and do not have church programs for youth, seniors, and other disadvantaged populations outside of the brick-and-mortar walls are not likely to survive the first half of the twenty-first century. We need more "churches without walls!"

In conclusion, I hope that, before it is too late, human beings will come to our senses and recognize who owns the church and humbly and urgently beseech guidance from Him who owns and governs all things. The Apostle Paul, in his Letter to the Romans 15:5–7, encourages believers to live in harmony with one another and to be of one accord. In other words, as most of us learned from our parents during our youth in the Goodwill community, when we engaged in skirmishes, they often said, "Children y'all get along."

First Corinthians 12:25–27 (KJV) says, "That there should be no schism in the body, but that the members should have the same care one for another. And whether one member suffer, all the members suffer with it; or one member be honoured, all the members rejoice with it. Now ye are the body of Christ, and members in particular."

I will always be indebted to my parents and those examples in my community who helped encourage me, prayed for me, and welcomed me home the many years since I first departed from the community called Goodwill. I want them to know that if I never see them again, my heart rejoices that they stayed the course, kept their hands to the plow, and didn't give up on me or many others who sometimes strayed from the high calling of Jesus Christ. My character, my worldview, my understanding of who I am and whose I am, have been richly blessed by the Goodwill community and church that I will forever call home.

In the words of the old pastors and preachers of my youth, and the lyrics of a popular song by Andrae Crouch, "Let the Church Amen!"

CHAPTER TWO

Sermons and Writings by Our Papa

What It Means "to Be Called": My Perspective

NOVEMBER 20, 2023

Sometime during the spring of 1998, during the forty-fourth year of my life, I began to feel in earnest that God put me on this earth for an even greater purpose—not only as a lawyer to represent those who needed legal assistance, but also as one who was called to be an advocate for Christ.

I became restless and my sleep was disturbed at night. While attempting to sleep, I tossed and turned. As the lyrics to the gospel song of my youth say, "My soul couldn't rest contented until I found the Lord." It wasn't that I heard a thunderous voice calling out to me, telling me to go preach. I'm reminded of that old farmer who was walking in his fields when he looked up at the clouds and observed what he was certain were the letters "GP." He was also sure that those two letters meant, "Go preach"—that God had called him to preach the gospel. Thereafter he announced to all his friends and church members that God had called him to preach and soon after he undertook that calling. After several sermons, it was clear to listeners that he wasn't very good in the art of preaching. One of the farmer's best friends felt compelled to be honest with him and tell him that he didn't think the letters "GP" meant for him to go preach. Rather the

Joe with five of seven grandchildren, February 12, 2022

friend believed the letters he saw in the clouds meant for him to "Go plow." This also reminds me of words coming from one of my best friends, the Honorable Alexander Williams, now a retired federal district judge and an ordained minister, at my initial sermon. I had asked him to travel from his home in Maryland to have a few words during the program. Among other words that Alex stated in jest, he said, "Some are called, some are sent, and some came anyway." He then turned from the lectern and looked at me with a laugh.

Like the old farmer, over twenty-four years ago when I proclaimed to my family, friends, and church members that I had been called to preach, I was certain of my call. As I have told some of my friends, I did not seek this high calling. For one thing, I had always considered my legal career as a calling, not one that was just to make a living, but one that was suited for me to make a life, a life worth living. It was one where I thought I could make a difference in this world, being an advocate for the voiceless. At the time of my gospel ministry calling, I had been faithful to my calling as an attorney at law and had sacrificed financially because of my pro bono and other community service mostly in my rural hometown of Madison, North Carolina, and other nearby small communities. Having grown up in a rural community, I knew that the fees I charged couldn't be top dollar and my heart wouldn't allow me to overcharge anyway. Nevertheless, I felt strongly that God had placed upon me a new burden and that I had no choice but to accept it. The lyrics to a familiar hymn says, "Must Christ bare the cross alone and all the world go free, yes there's a cross for everyone and there is a cross for me." I knew that this new calling might create a schism between my wife and me. I recalled Diane's response as clearly as if it were yesterday. She felt our family's financial situation, already burdened, would be made even worse. I also knew Diane was not the traditional pastor's wife. She does not like to be in the limelight that traditional pastor's or preacher's spouses most often find themselves, whether they want to be or not. I had not conceived that my calling was necessarily a "pastor" calling, but I did not take the time to explain that to Diane. Neither did I take the time to explain that my calling would not require me to quit being a practicing lawyer and forfeit that source of income. I'm certain also that Diane felt that I would necessarily have to spend more time away from her and our children.

Why then would God call me to preach when he knew of my responsibilities as a lawyer, husband, and father, and that my dedication to community service was already quite burdensome? God knew that he gave me an abundance of common sense, and he knew that my love for my wife and children would not let me forsake them; I would carve out quality time for them, no matter how many callings I undertook. God also knew that

I had sense enough to understand that the traditional pastoral position would be too much for me to handle while I was a full-time practicing lawyer. I knew that preaching on Sundays was one thing, but that a pastoral position would require visiting the sick at home, in nursing homes, and in the hospital, along with counseling and other pastoral responsibilities that would be too much for me to handle. Moreover, even before my calling as a minister, I had settled in my own mind that I never wanted to make a living as a minister because I wanted it to be totally a calling from my heart and not at all at calling to make money. Certainly, I believe in the biblical text that a workman is worthy of his or her hire. However, my ministry calling is consistent with the biblical teaching that "to whom much is given, much is required." For me, that means some self-sacrifice is required. Early in my ministry, while I was still in private legal practice, I accepted honorariums for speaking engagements. Most church leaders felt very disappointed if I did not accept an honorarium for my services as a guest preacher. However, after becoming a federal judge I just explained to churches that my Rules of Judicial Conduct did not allow me to accept honorariums, and even if I could, I did not want to do so. My thought was that small churches especially could use the money for more important purposes.

But let me return to what a calling to preach means to me. Even though I have denied that God had called me earlier than during my forty-fourth year of life, I must admit that for some years prior to accepting my calling, I felt this compulsion to do more with the great blessings and unparalleled favor that God had mercifully granted me. Several years prior to my acceptance of the call to preach, I told my good friend Richard Scotton (a PK: preacher's kid) that sometimes I felt like God might be calling me to preach. I recall Rick's response in the backyard of my home at 316 Carlton Drive, Chapel Hill, North Carolina. He said, "Joe, if you are waiting for God to hit you in the head with a hammer to convince you that he has called you to preach, that will never happen."

I wish I had a more definitive answer to the question of how one knows for certain that he or she has been called to preach. However, I do believe that the Holy Spirit will give you the certainty that you need. Your calling won't be communicated by letters or abbreviations as you look up in the clouds as it was with the old farmer. But the spirit of the Lord will speak to you, sometimes with groanings that cannot be uttered. Romans 8:26 says, "Likewise the spirit also helps in our weaknesses, for we do not know what we should pray for as we ought, but the spirit itself makes intercessions for us with groanings which cannot be uttered." For the spirit to speak to you so that you can understand, you need to be living a righteous life, or at least be fully committed to one, which is different from a perfect life. On one occasion, Jesus himself, in Luke 4:18–19 (KJV), reading from a scroll that included the Book of Isaiah, said,

> Spirit of the Lord is upon me, because the Lord has anointed me to proclaim good news to the poor. He has sent me to heal the broken-hearted, to preach deliverance to the captives, and recovering of sight to the blind, to set at liberty them that are bruised, to preach the acceptable year of the Lord."

As a lawyer, judge, and minister of the gospel, these words from Luke also describe what I perceive to be my calling. Over the years I have resisted the temptation to pursue a traditional full-time pastoral ministry. Many who heard me preach approach me to say, "I believe you missed your calling." I strongly believe that just because one has one or more exceptional oratorical skills doesn't mean that God has called you into a traditional pastoral ministry. For twenty-six years my calling has been to reach a far larger audience—including those in my own legal profession and those who come before me in orange jumpsuits seeking justice.

In conclusion, I believe that for one to know with certainty the nature of his or her calling, one needs to be in constant prayer seeking God's guidance and direction. If a person is married, then he or she also needs to discuss and pray about a perceived calling with his or her spouse. Regrettably, I did not have such a discussion or pray with my spouse about making a final decision to accept God's calling. For many years now I have recognized my error. According to Mark 10:7–9, when you marry, you become one flesh. I believe that one called to ministry should at least attempt to be in accord with one's spouse concerning a calling that will affect the entire family. It is also an imperative that one believing he or she has been called should prepare themselves with much biblical and theological study, even more so than that prescribed in 2 Timothy 2:15 (KJV). That text says, "Study to shew yourself approved unto God, a workman that needed not to be ashamed, rightly dividing the word of truth." Much prayer and much study, plus faith at least the size of a grain of mustard seed, are necessary if one believes he or she has been called to preach. If your decision is to say, "Yes, Lord," come knowing that you will be engaging in a lifelong endeavor—that once you put your hands to the plow, there can be no turning back. Over the last twenty-four years, I have learned for myself that whether you are called, sent, or decided to come anyway to preach, to proclaim the good news, or whatever your calling might be, you need to come dressed in the full armor of God, King of Kings and Lord of Lords. If you do this, you will be all right. To God be the glory! Hallelujah!

Sermons from the Heart

DECEMBER 19, 2022

Recently, my thirty-three-year-old son, Evan, asked me how I come up with the sermons that I preach. He has heard many of them since he was a teenager. I responded that it happens in various ways. Sometimes a church or other organization has a theme, and if so, I try to gear my sermon or speech to the assigned topic. Sometimes, if you know the audience, the sermon seeks to target the needs of the audience. There may have been a death in the church family, so I try to comfort them and give them hope. Christians are not a people without hope. Sometimes I find myself needing to encourage myself. Pastors and preachers are like anyone else. I've thought to myself many times, *Who encourages the encourager?* The lyrics by Donald Lawrence and the Tri-City Singers proclaim, "Sometimes you need to encourage yourself in the Lord." So sometimes I preach sermons that encourage myself. Often, I get ideas from the very words of the scriptures. Sometimes I get subjects for sermons from scriptures I've heard other preachers preach. I've learned that there are many topics from the same scriptures because God speaks to preachers and gives preachers different thoughts about the scriptures. Sometimes the titles of my sermons come directly from the very words found in the Scriptures. For example, "Can Anything Come out of Nazareth" comes directly from John 1:44–46. "Is God Able" comes from the benediction found in Jude 24, which begins with, "Now unto Him that is able to keep you from falling" (KJV). "Learning to Suffer as We Labor with God" is from 1 Corinthians 3:9–11 (KJV). Sometimes, if you take the time to go into your secret closet or bedroom away from the hustle and bustle of life and the various sounds all around us, if you get quiet enough you might hear the voice of God speaking. Recently, He spoke to me from one of my daughter's beds in Washington, DC. The spirit brought Matthew 11:28–29 to my mind and said, "Come unto me all ye that are heavy laden, and I will you rest. Take my yoke upon me and learn of me" (KJV). Another time, in 2004, at one of the most financially insecure moments in my life, I was struggling mightily, tired of what I was doing and tired of what I wasn't doing. Then it came to me one day down in Pittsboro, North Carolina, as I sat in my car all alone. God spoke to me in unmistakable terms from Isaiah 40:23–32: that I should wait on the Lord and He would renew my strength. So my subject for the pastor's anniversary at Second Baptist Church in Chapel Hill, North Carolina, was "Wait on the Lord."

Some of my sermons originate from the old gospel songs going back to my youth that I heard at Goodwill Baptist Church. For example, my sermon "The Holy Spirit: What Is This?" comes from the lyrics to the song made popular by Walter Hawkins. It begins, "What is this that I feel deep inside? That keeps setting my soul afire. Whatever it is, it won't let me hold my peace." Some sermons also come from songs of the Motown era. Recently I preached, "Don't Let the Green Grass Fool You," one of the late Motown-era singer Wilson Pickett's hit singles. One day I was listening to a satellite radio station and heard that song. Immediately, the scripture found in Matthew 4:1–11 (also Luke 4:1–13) came to my spirit as being something I should preach about, and it was in line with, "Don't Let the Green Grass Fool You." These New Testament scriptures set forth that while in the wilderness alone, Jesus was tempted; one of the temptations took place after Satan had brought Jesus up on a high mountain and showed him all the kingdoms of the world. Satan told Jesus that if he would bow down and worship him, that Satan would give Jesus all of what he had shown him. Jesus responded, "Get the thence, Satan; for it is written thou shall worship the Lord thy God and him only shalt thou serve." It came to me within moments after hearing Wilson Pickett, his hit single had given me a relevant message for the members of the congregation during the COVID-19 pandemic. Simply stated, what I preached that day is that "the grass is not greener on the other side." And don't let Satan convince you to put God second to material things.

All in all, I know that all my sermons originate from God. Without God, I could not even think about, let alone compose a sermon acting under my own power. The source of all that we think or do comes from God, who is the Alpha and the Omega, the beginning and the ending of all things. I must admit that a few sermons have come to mind, and I've had the nerve to think that I've come up with something special. I felt kind of bold, wanting to pat myself on the shoulder. Just a few times I've said to myself with confidence, "Now, that will preach," as I heard an old preacher remark one time. But I have sense enough to know that if God ain't in it, you can find yourself in the pulpit all alone. I pray that in each sermon God will have me preach not for my own edification and glory but for the glory of God. I've been blessed that God has continued to give me sermons that have blessed my soul. As I prepare a manuscript, my hand is often led across the paper like a Ouija board. Tears often flow down my face as God speaks to me and tells me what to write. I thank God, for I admit that I feel I am not worthy of being one of his soldiers carrying the word of truth. I have not sufficiently prepared myself for this great calling that I did not seek. I admit that I have not done enough to follow the scripture found at 2 Timothy 2:15 that requires me to show myself approved unto God, a workman, that needed not to be ashamed, rightly dividing the word of truth. But for some reason, God has kept on giving me relevant sermons to preach. So yes, Evan and others who may read this—God does reveal to me sermons that are hopefully designed to encourage the faithful and hopeless at the same time.

Being a longtime lawyer and now a longtime judge, I can't separate my sermons from over forty years of seeking justice and civil rights for all people. Therefore, I try to make my sermons relevant to the events and circumstances of the times in which we live. Years ago, I spoke on the topic "God Can Level the Playing Field." I have preached periodically on "Love," on "Keeping Your Eyes on the Prize," and have sought to include, when possible, a shout-out to our youth, encouraging them not to give up; to persevere through whatever comes their way. I've found sermons in my work as a federal judge. When I'm on criminal duty, I see too many young black males who have seemingly given up on life. Some seem not to mind going to prison. On several occasions after presiding in court and observing how crack cocaine and even stronger street drugs have devastated the physical, mental, and human spirit of those coming before me, I have gone into chamber, my secret closet, and wept. Years ago, I preached at Goodwill Baptist Church from Ezekiel 37. The hand of the Lord brought Ezekiel out by the spirit of the Lord and set him in a valley full of dry bones. The spirit asked him, "Son of Man, Can these bones live?" So, I preached on this very subject: "Can These Bones Live?" I analogized the situation that Ezekiel spoke about with today's black youth and young adults who are often hooked on or selling drugs, and who engage in gun and other violence in the community. Among young American males, gun violence is the leading cause of death, and proportionately is even higher among African American males. "Can These Bones Live?" is a rhetorical question. I knew the answer before posing it. With God all things are possible, and yes, these bones, literally and figuratively, that come before me in my judicial capacity looking hopeless can live, but if only they allow God into their lives. None of us can change on our own. And last, with the deep racial and other divisions in our country, I have on several occasions preached about the gospel and reconciliation.

When invited to preach or speak, I like to know my audience. At churches, I know that I'm often preaching to the choir, as the saying goes. On other occasions, such as with the NAACP or other clubs or organizations, I feel like I need to remind them how our ancestors died seeking the right to vote and other civil rights. I know that I need to remind them that they must pay homage to our ancestors by being courageous themselves in their efforts to keep up the struggle. Sometimes such organizations and even church auxiliaries have themes for the program, and I try to speak on that theme.

In conclusion, whatever the occasion, I pray for God's guidance in each sermon I give. I do try hard to speak from my heart. I try to speak sincerely to the audience. Yes, I occasionally joke around to get everyone comfortable. But especially toward the end when it is time to bring the message to shore, I try to let God use me, hoping that He has gotten me enough out of the way so that He can get the glory. I heard the late esteemed pastor-preacher C. Gardner Taylor say that wherever you start (meaning no matter where your biblical sermon text comes from), you should end up at Golgotha, where Christ was crucified on the cross—where he shed his redeeming blood so that all who believe in him shall have the right to eternal life.

An Encouraging Word from the Late Rev. Dr. Charles Booth, Longtime Pastor of Mt. Olivet Baptist Church, Columbus, Ohio (1947–2019)

FEBRUARY 18, 2023

Early one morning, about six or seven years ago, I was feeling weary. I was in my court chambers, feeling a little down, mentally fatigued, and alone. I know that the Bible teaches, "Let us not be weary in well doing, for in due season we will reap if we faint not." (GALATIANS 6:9 KJV). The NIV puts it this way: that at the proper time you will reap a harvest if you don't give up. Nevertheless, I felt the need to call upon someone to talk to, perhaps to receive some encouragement. Over the years as I have often considered the plight of pastors-preachers and one of their primary job descriptions of encouraging the flock. I have often wondered, *Who is assigned by God to encourage the encourager?*

But that day, I needed the answer to another question at that moment when my faith was less than the size of a of mustard seed. (MATTHEW 17:20-21 NIV). I called upon one whom I had come to know just a little in the recent past. He had given me his personal cell phone number. I called Rev. Dr. Charles Booth, a Baltimore, Maryland, native, at that time pastor of the Mt. Olivet Baptist Church in Columbus, Ohio. He was a powerful, gifted, and God-sent preacher and, like me, was a Howard University graduate. Knowing that Dr. Booth had pastored for decades, I knew he had been through the fiery furnace and had on many occasions experienced what I was experiencing early that weekday morning. Dr. Booth answered his telephone. I asked him the following question: Besides prayer, what do you do when you get weary? His response was immediate. Dr. Booth said, "Go forward in the strength that remains and trust God for the power of resilience."

Praise God for those whom God has strategically placed in my life so that I might remain connected to the vine, faithful and persevering in all things, and so that I might have something of significance to share with others in whose lives I have been strategically placed.

An Encouraging Scripture

PSALM 27:1–6 (KJV)

1 The LORD is my light and my salvation; whom shall I fear? the LORD is the strength of my life; of whom shall I be afraid?

2 When the wicked, even mine enemies and my foes, came upon me to eat up my flesh, they stumbled and fell.

3 Though an host should encamp against me, my heart shall not fear: though war should rise against me, in this will I be confident.

4 One thing have I desired of the LORD, that will I seek after; that I may dwell in the house of the LORD all the days of my life, to behold the beauty of the LORD, and to enquire in his temple.

5 For in the time of trouble he shall hide me in his pavilion: in the secret of his tabernacle shall he hide me; he shall set me up upon a rock.

6 And now shall mine head be lifted up above mine enemies round about me: therefore, will I offer in his tabernacle sacrifices of joy; I will sing, yea, I will sing praises unto the LORD.

The Gospel and Reconciliation: "Drinking from the Same Well"

JOHN 4:4–14 (NIV)

Chapel Hill Bible Church Service in Commemoration of Dr. Martin Luther King Jr. Birthday and Life

JANUARY 18, 2004

> Jesus answered, "Everyone who drinks this water will be thirsty again, but whosoever drinks the water I give them will never thirst. Indeed, the water I give them will become in them a spring of water welling up to eternal life." JOHN 4:13–14

The other day I emailed a friend of mine, Judith Wegner, former dean and now professor of law at the University of North Carolina at Chapel Hill School of Law. Recently Dean Wegner has graciously assisted me as I have prepared to begin new duties to teach a course as an adjunct professor of law at the Campbell University Law School. I had e-mailed Judith to inform her of today's engagement and that I would be speaking on the gospel and racial reconciliation. As an aside I said to her that I was even more stressed out and stretched out than before. The pertinent part of her email response was, "I'm sure the gospel will uplift you and I know that racial reconciliation would if we could get closer to it. Hang in there."

ILLUSTRATION BY SHAILYN RAMSEY

Those words of wisdom coming from one whom I know to be such a thoughtful, caring, and dedicated person are so pertinent for all of us to remember. The gospel should and does uplift us, so I hope that I can be God's messenger today and a catalyst for helping lift our spirits and helping us to inch even closer to reconciliation as we remember and celebrate the birthday and life of Dr. Martin Luther King Jr. My allocated time today surely is not enough to do justice to a man whose name is synonymous with peace, one whom we all are indebted to, and who, in a short thirty-eight years, taught us what racial reconciliation is all about. But my charge also is to try to do justice to what sayeth the Lord about racial reconciliation. So, for this cause, I need your prayers. I know that Pastor Acuff could have looked around and found many more capable and able than me to stand here today. But we all must be ready when our name is called. Today I want to use as my text the Gospel of John, chapter 4, verses 4 to 13. And from this text I want to talk on the subject "Drinking from the Same Well."

I am so blessed to have met and gotten to know one of the great human treasures living in the Triangle area, Dr. John Hope Franklin, the James B. Duke Professor of History at Duke University, and well-renowned author of *From Slavery to Freedom* and many other books and publications. He is the former chair of the national advisory board for One America: President Clinton's Initiative on Race. In one of Dr. Franklin's books, *Race and History: Selected Essays, 1938–1988,* he writes so profoundly about an important factor in the reconciliation of mankind. In the relevant part of that book, Dr. Franklin writes,

> From the time that I taught at the Salzburg Seminar in American Studies in 1951, I have been a student and advocate of the view that the exchange of ideas is more healthy and constructive than the exchange of bullets. This was especially true during my tenure on the Fulbright Board, as a member for seven years and as the chairman for three years. In such experiences one learns much about the common ground that the peoples of the world share. When we also learn that this country and the western world have no monopoly of goodness and truth or of skills and scholarship, we begin to appreciate the ingredients that are indispensable to making a better world. In a life of learning, that is, perhaps, the greatest lesson of all.[8]

Our world leaders and all Americans would do well to take Dr. Franklin's words to heart as we consider racial reconciliation. For us to get even closer to reconciling with one another, I am of the opinion that blacks, whites, browns, and whatever skin tone or ethnic heritage we may be, we must go to the well and drink of the same water. My wife and I grew up on farms in North Carolina, and both of us had wells for most of our childhoods. These wells, like Jacob's well found in today's scripture, represented our source of water for drinking, cooking, and bathing. The water from those wells was indeed the very source of life. My family's well was located at the bottom of the hill in the backyard. But while my wife's well was also made of wood, and had a bucket and rope attached to a round log with an iron handle on the side, her family's well was located on the back

8 John Hope Franklin, *Race and History: Selected Essays, 1938–1988* (Baton Rouge: Louisiana State University Press, 1991), 291. Reprinted with permission.

porch. She had the Cadillac of wells in that it was located inside a screened back porch located right outside the kitchen. My wife's family didn't have to go out in the rain or snow to draw, or as we called it, to wind water. But these wells like Jacob's well in today's scripture represented a stopping-off point for the hot, tired, and weary after perhaps having spent many hours in the tobacco field or cornfield. We all drank from the same well, and even the same bucket, and even more amazing as I look back, from the same dipper. There was nothing better than that cool and refreshing water that we all took for granted. I learned as a child and even later as an adult that you must be careful when you are drawing water from the well. One day, as I was drawing water, the handle on the well at my wife's house suddenly slipped out of my hand and the iron handle hit my hand as the full bucket of water with great force fell back into the water, making the rope and iron handle spin around at a high speed. The iron handle struck my hand very hard, causing it to be bruised and quite sore. I learned the importance of being careful at the well. Likewise, we must be careful as we follow Jesus to Jacob's well of reconciliation.

In today's scripture, Jesus got word that the Pharisees had heard that he and his disciples were baptizing and winning more disciples than even John, so he quickly left Judea going north on his way to Galilee and passed directly though Samaria. For years, Jews before Jesus had traveled from Judea to Galilee. However, because of the animosity between the Jews and the Samaritans, Jews often traveled long distances out of the way so that they would not have go through Samaria. I am reminded how during America's recent history, that black families especially during travels from the North to the South, necessarily traveled out of the way so that they would not have to go through hostile territory where they might suffer harm and where they could not stay in white-owned hotels along the way. Today, because of fear, many whites won't travel through the black or low-income sides of town on the way to their side of town. But Jesus, in his encounter with the Samaritan woman, shows us the way to reconciliation among the races and cultures. He shows us the way to reconciliation between men and women.

Jesus demonstrates in today's scripture once again how he used ordinary people to accomplish his mission. In Jesus's time, custom dictated that theological conversations seldom took place between men and women. I believe we learn from today's scripture that to get a little closer to racial reconciliation, Christians must begin to follow Jesus through hostile territory and not avoid getting to know those who are different. But again, we must be careful. To make peace with one another, we can't act like we're all that—and then some. Dr. John Hope Franklin is right. America doesn't have a monopoly on goodness and truth or skills and scholarship. If we do follow Jesus to Samaria and the well, and upon arriving do act as if we are all that, then we may offend someone who is different racially or culturally, or of a different gender. If we do this, then we may miss our window of opportunity at making peace with those to whom we're trying to bring the good news. But at all costs, we must travel and meet up with Jesus at the well and begin to drink from the same water.

I believe today that we must change something about our methods of winning souls. When is the last time someone said to you as one of Christ's disciples, give me some of this water so that I might not thirst again? Church, many are thirsting for a way out of misery and lack of hope, and a way to reconcile with each other. God would have me say today that we as his disciples must first begin to drink from the same well.

We are going to make some mistakes on our journey toward reconciliation, but not to worry; God has a way of covering a multitude of sins and mistakes with His love. Sometimes I am so stubborn, I am learning that sometimes I must fall on my face before God can use me for His purpose. But we can't let fear of making mistakes keep us from meeting at the well. For there at the well we'll find the right spirit—not just any spirit, but the spirit of reconciliation.

We often try reconciling with each other solely on our own power without involving the Author and Prince of Peace. There is too much bitter history between blacks and whites for us to be able to get closer completely on our own. We refuse to discuss race relations openly. We don't want to drink from the same well. Some white people are saying, "Slavery ended almost 140 years ago. Why can't you people get over it?" Well, for many, slavery and its vestiges haven't ended—too many still working for minimum wages. Legally all can eat at the lunch counter, but still far too many can't afford it.

At lunch the other day, Dr. John Hope Franklin told me how his father, even though a lawyer in the early twentieth century in Oklahoma, was very poor mainly because the courts and judicial system didn't respect him and consequently his own people would not patronize him as they should. He told me that in 1921 thousands of armed whites attacked African Americans on the streets of Tulsa, Oklahoma, and burned every home and business in a thirty-five-block section of town. Many were killed in that riot. Some of the vestiges of slavery still exist today. I see some of it in my own law practice in Pittsboro. Many whites still don't want to drink from the same well. I've said before from this pulpit that racial reconciliation is a two-way street. Some black people are saying, "Why does the white group down there in Lee County still insist on flying the Confederate flag on January 19 of each year to commemorate the birthday of Confederate General Robert E. Lee?" Some blacks say, after all, the South lost the Civil War; it was over in 1865. Some black people are saying just get over the flag—it represents a time in history that is so painful, and it opens old wounds.

Man's attempt to drink from the same well of reconciliation hasn't been as successful as we desire. I strongly believe that for the races to reconcile, Christian people must take the lead, make haste, and go directly to Jacob's well—and there we will find living water that will uplift our spirits and give us insight that we can't figure out on our own. There at the well, we will find many races and all nationalities like on the day of Pentecost. There at the well will be Asians, Hispanics, and Indians, the Native Americans whom America will never be able to repay for all that was taken from them. There will be present blacks, browns, and whites. But there at the well we will find peace in the valley. Church, not to worry. One day there will be peace in the valley.

One day whites will be able to understand Ebonics, the language from the hood. Those from the hood will be able to understand and speak the Queen's English. Adults will be able to understand our teenagers when they shrug their shoulders, utter, "Yeah," or end a sentence by saying, "Holler," or just saying nothing and expecting us to read their minds. There at the well, after all of us adults get a dipper full of some of that living water, we may even be able to understand the words of rapper Jay-Z, or find some redeeming value in those jeans on our teenage boys that are still barely hanging on for dear life. There at the well, even Joe Webster will be able translate and find meaning in opera singing during a church worship service. There at the well, I might even be able to find spiritual guidance in Tim Conder's movie clips as he brings one of his messages here at the Bible Church. There at the well as we drink from the same water, I can imagine Pastor Mark Acuff with an earring singing gospel songs by the Brooklyn Tabernacle Choir. I can even imagine Jim Abrahamson, drunk on that living water like John in Revelation 1:10, being in the spirit on the Lord's Day.

Church, I'm sorry, but before I get to the well, every once in a while, I personally need to be uplifted with "Amazing grace, how sweet the sound that saved a wretch like me," or Thomas Dorsey's words, "Precious Lord, take my hand, lead me on let me stand, I am tired, I am weak, I am worn, through the storm through the night, lead me into the light, take my hand precious Lord and lead me on." Every once in a while, I need to hear the gospel so that I too can be uplifted and so that as my ancestors used to testify, I can run on and see what the end is going to be. I need some living water that moves and motivates me down on the inside and drastically changes me so that I can personally move a little closer to my white brothers and sisters.

All of us must begin to try to get a little closer to one another. I have never said it publicly, but I think I know why God sent my family and me to a place I sometimes refer to as my Nineveh—this place called Chapel Hill and the Chapel Hill Bible Church. As for me, I'm here because God knows my heart. He desires for me to grow to love those from a race some of whose ancestors may have subjected a whole race to slavery and unimaginable physical and mental abuse. And many Christians who didn't participate stood silently by while slavery was taking place. I am here because God wants me to fully forgive as I drink together from the same well.

God has already set forth a prescription for reconciliation. Jesus said to the disciples I give you a new commandment, that you should love one another. You must even love your enemies and those who despitefully use you. Church there is love in the living water. Rev. Dr. Martin Luther King Jr. and others have written about agape love. Marriam-Webster dictionary defines agape love as a selfless, spiritual love that is not sexual in nature. The word agape is of Greek origin and denotes a selfless and unconditional love. It is a love that expects nothing in return. Church, for there to be reconciliation we need to meet at the well so that our hearts can be transformed.

We do thirst for peace on earth and goodwill toward men as proclaimed by the angels when Christ was born. Luke 2:14. (KJV). You remember after Rodney King was mercilessly beaten by the Los Angeles police, he said, "Can't we all just get along?" I'm afraid we will never be able to get along, let alone love one another, unless we are filled with that living water found at the well, that well of water that wells up to eternal life. We must be filled with a dipper full of Jesus, who has reconciled us to Himself, the one who was sinless but took on our sins, the one who bled and suffered and died on Cavalry's cross.

So, the gospel encourages our efforts at reconciliation, but we must first go to the well and drink of the water that only Jesus can give. There we will find solace and the answer that we need. There at the well will be Samaritans, some from Iraq and Afghanistan and from around the world. There will be women, Jews, and Greeks. Paul said on one occasion in Galatians 3:28, "There is neither Jew nor Greek, there is neither bond nor free, there is neither male nor female, for ye all are one in Christ Jesus."

As I end, I am reminded of a 1967 speech Rev. Dr. Martin Luther King Jr. gave in a Christmas Eve sermon at Ebenezer Baptist Church in Atlanta, Georgia during the Vietnam War. It was a sermon promoting peace. Reconciliation requires us to love those that are of different races, nationalities, genders, those who speak different languages, those of different faiths or no faith at all, those who are poor and those who are rich, and as the Bible teaches in Matthew 5:43-44, to "love your enemies." This is the only way that there can be peace on earth. As we grow closer to God, may we grow closer to one another. As Jesus said in Matthew 11:15 (KJV) He that has ears to hear, let him hear.

Stopping by Bethesda on Your Way Home

JOHN 5:1–9

Homecoming Service, First Baptist Church, Chapel Hill, NC

SEPTEMBER 26, 1999

> Now there is in Jerusalem near the Sheep Gate a pool, which is in Aramaic is called Bethesda and which is surrounded by five covered colonnades. Here a great number of disabled people used to lie—the blind, the lame, the paralyzed. One who was there had been an invalid for thirty-eight years. When Jesus saw him lying there and learned that he had been in this condition for a long time, he asked him, "Do you want to be healed?" JOHN 5:2–6

Homecoming is a wonderful tradition in the African American church experience. As I prepared for this message, I inquired with a close minister friend about the origins of Homecomings in the church. It was suggested to me that perhaps Homecoming had its start in the first half of this century. At that time, many who had migrated north returned to their southern roots for a visit. I can imagine that as families moved long distances from their homes primarily in the US South to the Northeast and Midwest, families getting together for Homecoming every year was an important event.

ILLUSTRATION BY SHAILYN RAMSEY

As a child growing up in rural Madison, North Carolina, at Goodwill Baptist Church, from the eyes of a child, I remember the occasion as a time when my mother and the other women of the church prepared food to be consumed between the 11 a.m. and 3 p.m. services. I remember so well early in my childhood the food was served under the huge, shaded trees on large picnic tables in the church yard, and I remember that freshly made lemonade was prepared in large tubs. The Homecoming service at my home church took place the First Sunday in August of each year, which like here at First Baptist, was followed by a weeklong revival.

I remember so well how the church was filled that day, and even though we didn't have running water inside nor an inside bathroom during my early years, we had to open the windows to get some fresh air and pass out fans, and even though we didn't have a fellowship hall, everyone seemed to be happy and to have a joyous time. Most of all the spirit of the Lord and goodwill abided among those present. But for me as a small child, I just couldn't wait for the fried chicken and potato salad and lemonade. But as I grew older, I learned that Homecoming meant much more than good food. It was a time of reunion and getting to see relatives and friends who you had not seen in a long while. It was a time of thanksgiving and a time to praise God for all our blessings.

Today I know that some of you may have come from a long way to be here with parents, grandparents, aunts, uncles, and cousins. You have come here to Chapel Hill and First Baptist Church, a place where you will always call home, no matter how old you live to be. Somebody said, "Home is where the heart is." You have come home to where your heart is.

As we study today's text found in the fifth chapter of St. John, beginning at the first verse, I want to ask the question of not only those of you who have come from afar but also those of you who live here in the community, did you stop by Bethesda on your way home? I want to define home as not only this place where you have your roots, but home is also where I hope all of us will have as our final resting place, our heavenly home—that place that we often sing about in our gospel music, that place over yonder, that place where we will never grow old.

In our scripture today Jesus went up to Jerusalem from Galilee, to a feast of the Jews. Jesus had left Galilee, where our Bible teaches, he had performed two miracles: turning water into wine at a wedding (JOHN 2:1–11) and healing a nobleman's son who was near death (JOHN 4:46–54). While in Jerusalem, Jesus went by a sheep market, and located nearby was a pool called Bethesda.

Let me pause for a moment to tell you that although I attended college and law school at Howard University in Washington, DC, and knew of a city not too far away in suburban Maryland called Bethesda, I did not know until this summer that the city of Bethesda was named after the place referred to in our scripture today. I visited Bethesda, Maryland, and the National Institutes of Health this past summer as a chaperone for my seventeen-year-old daughter and nineteen other summer interns at the University of North Carolina at Chapel Hill. I learned that one of the reasons the federal government located the National Institutes of Health in Bethesda years ago was because of the scripture we are studying today. Indeed, Bethesda, which means "house of mercy," was descriptive of what the National Institutes of Health would come to represent. It would become a national facility, with some of the world's most learned doctors and scientists who take on the world's rarest and most difficult medical cases, those who are suffering and indeed need to get to the pool at Bethesda. You may remember that the former chancellor of the great university in this town, Michael Hooker, received treatment there during his last days.

And while there visiting the National Institutes of Health in Bethesda, we saw a few patients who, if they had been living in Jerusalem during the time of Jesus, would have probably been among those described in the text today: the impotent, blind, halt, and withered. We saw a few of them being taken through the common areas of the buildings in wheelchairs, and no doubt like those in our scripture today, they were waiting and hoping for the moving of the water. Church, I ask the question: did you stop by Bethesda on your way home today?

Verses 3 and 4 of today's text tell us the reason that the multitude of disabled were waiting by the pool: at a certain season, an angel went down and troubled the water, and whoever first stepped into the water after the angel troubled it, that person was made whole. He was healed of whatever disease or disability he was had.

Church, I don't know about you, but being honest with myself, I need Jesus to send one of His angels today to trouble the water. Church, I need Jesus to stop by. I need Jesus to stop by here at First Baptist Church today to make me whole. I need Jesus and His angels to stop by here just for a little while to pour out His spirit and anoint me. I realize I can do nothing without his spirit today. So, I need to feel his presence. I know that I have no power on my own, but that if God speaks through me, this message will have meaning. So, I need you to pray for his anointing upon me today.

I'm reminded of the story of the two preachers who were both guest speakers at a church at the same service. One of them was handsome, polished, educated, and well dressed. The other preacher was not so handsome, not well dressed, or well educated. The more educated and polished preacher began to preach first, and throughout his sermon there was no reaction from the audience. Then the other preacher stood up. He was not as well-spoken as the first one. But as he struggled with his words, the spirit of the Lord came upon him, and his sermon was much more effective than the first. So I need God to anoint me today with his Holy Spirit.

But who was this man camped out by the pool at Bethesda, a man who among the multitude dared to try and reach the water so he could be made whole? Who was this man who believed that there were certain healing powers in the pool called Bethesda? Who was the man who, even though he undoubtedly didn't have the full use of his limbs, thought he could be the first to get to step into the water when the angels troubled it?

We don't have a name for him. We can't look his telephone number or address up in the telephone directory or find his address on the internet. We don't really know what kind of infirmity or sickness he had. We don't know whether he was married or whether he had any children or other relatives. All we know about him from chapter 5 of St. John is that he had been sick for thirty-eight years.

But Church, I gain strength from this unnamed man, even though I know little about him. Church, sometimes if we lower our proud heads a little bit, we will learn something from the so-called little man, the person without a name or status. Because of how long he had suffered and endured, apparently without giving up hope, I'd like to think that he was a man of great faith—that he was a great man. Also, I believe that because he had probably been laying there by the pool at Bethesda a long time—in the public eye, at a sheep market where trade and commerce were taking place—he was not too proud to ask for help. I heard Dr. William Calhoun of Trinity Baptist Church in Baltimore recently say at a revival at the Alston Chapel United Holy Church down in Pittsboro, North Carolina, "that the greatest people in the world are those who have been through something." Church, how many of you have been through something in your life? How many of you have been sick and seemingly couldn't get well? How many of you have lost a loved one unexpectedly in the prime of life? Can you imagine what this man at the Bethesda pool had gone through the last thirty-eight years? He probably had been made fun of by many. However, apparently, he had made up his mind that no matter how long it took he was going to wait on the angel to trouble the water. Apparently, he still had not given up hope.

In contrast, many of us can't even stand having a cold, not to mention having an illness for thirty-eight years. But the man, whoever he was, along with a multitude of others, waited by the pool at Bethesda for the troubling of the water by the angel during a certain season. One thing we learn from today's lesson is that no matter how long we are sick, we need to persevere and never give up on being healed.

Church, on this Homecoming Day at First Baptist Church, one of the important lessons from this scripture for us is that there is a critical need for us who are called to do God's work to stop by the pool at Bethesda. There are many in our own community who are going through something today. Life is full of trials and tribulations. Just like the multitude of withered, halt, and disabled lying by the pool at Bethesda, there remain a multitude of disabled in our community and across the land suffering and needing a helping hand to get to the pool for healing. I've been thinking about and praying for the thousands who are suffering in Eastern North Carolina, the many who have lost all their possessions in the floods of Hurricane Floyd. But right here in our community there are many a young man and woman hooked on crack cocaine and alcohol, many a young man and woman who don't mind going to prison. As you know, one of my ministries is that of being a lawyer. I just celebrated my twentieth anniversary of graduating from law school and passing the bar exam. Over the years I have represented some of those who I am describing today who desperately need to get to the pool at Bethesda so that they can be healed.

Recently I was in court in Hillsborough. A lawyer there was pleading the case of this young black man who was hooked on drugs. You see, as a lawyer, you are called upon to plead the cause of justice even when the cause appears to be unjust. And the lawyer told the judge about his client's addiction to drugs. He went on to say that his client, who had an extensive criminal record, had become desperate and thought that the only way he could receive treatment was for him to commit another crime so that he could go back to jail. So, the young man went into a place of business and stole something. And after he got outside, he realized his goal of being caught hadn't been achieved, so he returned to the store and told the store clerk what he had done and pleaded with the clerk to call the police so he could be arrested.

Church, it's quite an indictment on a society when a person feels that committing a crime or sometimes even committing suicide is their only way out. So church, I hope you know by now what I mean when I ask the question "Did you stop by Bethesda on your way home?"

Church, many in our community are calling out, "What must I do to be saved and I need to be healed? But I just can't make it to the pool on my own—every time I try to make a step to get to the water, someone steps in my path or holds me back. Every time I try to straighten up and give up drugs, a member of such and such church or some other upstanding citizen seems to get in my path. Every time I make up my mind to do better, someone tells me I'm no good and that I'm worthless, though you tell me that God loves me also. Every time I try to get out of the ditch and reach up my hand for help, many pass by on the other side, even some with a clerical collar and some with a Bible in their hand."

Many of us are too quick to criticize those who are down on their luck and who have not yet found their way. We all need to be made whole. We are too quick to criticize the prostitute, drug addict, and those who have made mistakes in life. But for the grace of God, we too would be lying by the pool at Bethesda needing someone to help us.

Let's go back to our scripture for a moment. Consider the words of Jesus and the man in our text when Jesus passed by and saw him lying by the pool, knowing he had been in that condition a long time. Jesus asked him in verse 6, "Wilt thou be made whole?"

That seems a strange question to ask someone that Jesus knew had been in his condition for thirty-eight years. I'm sure that Jesus, being an all-wise God, knew that a big part of getting well is having a desire to get well. Ironically, not everyone wants to get well. Not everyone wants to be healed, because if they are healed, they'd have to go out and get a job, and they wouldn't have anything to complain about.

Rather than responding yes, I want to be healed, the man just focused on the only method by which he thought he could possibly be healed. He was like many of us today who focus on the medicine and not the Creator of the medicine. So the man responded to Jesus, "Sir, I have no man, when the water is troubled, to put me into the pool; but while I am coming, another steppeth down before me." But I draw strength from Jesus's response. Jesus simply says, "Rise, take up thy bed and walk" (JOHN 5:8).

Church, I have concluded that we must take off these suits and selfish attitudes of ours and begin to help somebody lying by the pool at Bethesda and the street corners of Chapel Hill and elsewhere on our way home. For you see, from Columbine High in Colorado to Los Angeles to more recently, teenagers worshiping in a church in Texas, and right here at home, our children are being shot down or subjected to violence in our communities. Crack cocaine and HIV/AIDS and drive-by shootings are robbing our youth of their health and their lives. We are living in critical times, but I am hopeful today. Man's adversity is God's opportunity to stir up the waters. So as Christian soldiers, we must stop by Bethesda on our way home. In 1 Corinthians 3:9, Paul says we are laborers together with God. Somebody said, God has no hands but our hands, no feet but our feet.

Since God called me to preach a little over a year ago, I've taken note, as I have traveled over the highways and been into a number of pulpits, that in each of them the carpet is too clean—it is not worn of use by those who need help most, those hooked on drugs and alcohol and those lying by the pools of Bethesda and Chapel Hill and across the land. I see too many churches whose lights are off all week long and whose doors are closed until maybe Wednesday evening and not again until Sunday morning. To some, church has become a members-only club, and I don't believe God is pleased with that. I'm afraid Jesus is going to come back and catch us with our work undone. I believe some of us think that the scripture that says that Jesus is coming back for a church without a spot or wrinkle to mean that He's coming back for a building with clean carpet and pews that are dust free. As the old gospel song lyrics of my youth proclaimed, "Church don't let him come and catch you with your work undone; he's coming again so soon." What we need to know today is that sometimes it doesn't take a lot of money to do God's work. Money won't cure the problem of the man lying by the pool at Bethesda or the man crying out for help in court in Hillsborough.

What those lying by the pool really need most is for someone to take them by the hand, spend some time with them, talk to them, and ask them the question, "Wilt thou be made whole?" And no matter what their response, we should not criticize them, but we need to let them know that we care and that we will help, and most of all that God is the answer for whatever their problem is.

I have been reading a book titled *Last Touch: Preparing for a Parent's Death* by Marilyn R. Becker, MSW. In that book, the author describes how her father fell ill with brain cancer, and she described the battery of tests he was subjected to and the many doctors they consulted about his condition. She described how the doctors only had a few minutes to spend with them and then their pager would go off. The doctors would be on their way because they could not afford to give more time to her father emotionally or financially. The author of the book described her father's doctors as being on an assembly line, only technicians doing their part. In our daily walk, we are too much of an assembly line. We don't take the time necessary to touch someone's life and thereby have an impact on them. The author says that what she was looking for was a healer, but all she could find were doctors.

I believe what the sick man's daughter was seeking, and what the man in the Hillsborough court and those on the streets of Chapel Hill and throughout the land are seeking, is spiritual healing. They can begin to get that if we who profess to be saved are willing to spend a few moments with them, say a kind word, do a good deed, say a prayer, and encourage them on the way.

Church, did you miss an opportunity to say a word of encouragement to someone on your way home today? Or did you become judgmental and say to yourself or maybe to the discouraged person that he or she ought to be in church this morning, and not out there washing a car or lying on the streets? Did you miss an opportunity to help some bruised and beaten brother or sister to get into the healing waters where God and His angels are waiting to move the water.

I want to briefly get across to you another message today. I recently saw a videotaped sermon by Dr. James Forbes Jr., pastor of Riverside Church in New York City, which was given when he visited Duke University during the last year. The text of his sermon also came from John (chapter 9, beginning at verse 1) and was yet another example of a miracle performed by Jesus—the story of the man who had been born blind. You may recall that Jesus passed by and saw the blind man. Jesus's disciples asked Him whether it was the man or his parents who had sinned. But after Jesus assured His disciples that it was neither, and after having pointed out that the man was born blind essentially so that the works of God could be made manifest in him, Jesus spat on the ground and made clay of the dust and spit and rubbed it on the blind man's eyes. Jesus then told the man to go wash in another pool, the pool of Siloam. The blind man did as he was told and gained his sight. One of the observations made by Dr. Forbes about the blind man was that he obviously needed someone to help him get into the pool of Siloam, and therefore it is likely someone had to lead him there. Then Dr. Forbes emphasized that if we would take someone by the hand and lead them to the pool, that some of the water will splash on us and heal us as well. Church, the fact of the matter is that all of us have sinned and fall short of the glory of God, so we need to stop by Bethesda on our way home.

Whenever I'm invited to preach, I find the need to give thanks for all God has done for me in my life. I want to give thanks today that God splashed water on me one day.

As one songwriter wrote,

> I was sinking deep in sin,
> far from the peaceful shore,
> very deeply stained within,
> sinking to rise no more,
> but the master of the sea
> heard my despairing cry,
> from the waters, lifted me,
> now safe am I.
> It was love that lifted me,
> love lifted me,
> when nothing else could help,
> love lifted me.[9]

I thank God today for His angels who trouble the water from time to time. All day and all night, as I go about my work, and then as I slumber and sleep, the angels keep watching over me. I have no choice but to stop by Bethesda on my way home.

Church, I know things look critical sometimes. You can't pay your bills on time. With age comes more sickness, aches, and pains. But the Bible teaches that if we as a body of believers—God's people who are called by His name—would just humble ourselves and pray and seek His face and turn away from our wicked ways, then He would hear from heaven and forgive our sins and heal our land. Not only will He forgive our

9 "Love Lifted Me" was first published in 1912 by lyricist James Rowe, with melody by organist Howard E. Smith.

sins and heal our land, but He will also get our sons and daughters off drugs and bring them back home and bring the family back together. (*See* 2 CHRONICLES 7:14.)

For me, the pool at Bethesda also represents something else. As I read the scripture repeatedly about the angel troubling the water, I can feel the presence of the Holy Spirit moving down on the inside. I thank God that, every now and again, I begin to feel God's presence burning deep down on the inside. The spirit of God helps me get through the tough times.

Church, sometimes, I too get down and out. Don't think that just because I am a lawyer and a preacher that I don't have needs and moments of hesitation and doubt. I get stressed out sometimes also. No one is immune from depression and illness. Sometimes I just get tired of hearing about other people's problems day in and day out while also dealing with my own issues. When I am at my lowest point, often some Christian soldier comes along and helps me with a word and helps me to get to the pool at Bethesda. But even when I just can't get there, and I am all alone, God is so powerful, in the middle of the night, the angels of the Lord begin to guide my mind and help me get to the pool. But when there is no pool around, when the pool is all dried up with despair and when it's polluted with the worries of this broken world, Jesus arrives and makes a way out of no way. He opens doors that I never knew existed.

Church, on your way to your eternal home, there are going to be many mountains to climb and hardships and disappointments and pain. No matter who you are; no matter how much money you have, nor how good you have been, there will be crosses to bear. No matter what happens to you, I want to encourage each of you, especially our young people, to never give up. Stay with the Lord. He has promised to fight our battles and supply our needs. And senior citizens, when you get to the point that you feel you can't go any further, when your steps get slow and your eyes grow dim, when you must go into the hospital or the nursing home, stay with the Lord. Jesus is still in the healing business.

Young mothers who are raising your children on your own, when you don't have money to pay your rent, stay with the Lord. If God has given you a husband who is abusive and won't give up alcohol, won't go to church with you, Jesus has promised to be by your side, and He will make a way out of no way. If your husband has left you for someone else, God knows your situation and will supply your needs. He has enough angels to trouble the water all over the world. Bethesda represents hardship and pain, but more importantly Bethesda represents healing and hope, hope for the hopeless.

In Genesis 21, in the middle of the wilderness of Beer-sheba—after being put out of her home by Abraham and Sarah, and after running out of water, and all but giving up—God heard the desperation of a mother named Hagar, and the cry of her son, Ishmael and God provided a well of water for Hagar and her son (GENESIS 21:14–20). Mothers, you may not know how you will pay your water bill, but as Jesus told the Samaritan woman at the well, if you drink the water that He gives, you will never get thirsty, and His water will be a well of water springing up into everlasting life. Young people, like Ishmael, your father may not be married to your mother, your father may not live with you in your home, you may not even know who your father is, but Jesus is a father to the fatherless.

Church, I know a God who fed five thousand with two fish and five loaves of bread and had twelve baskets left over. He healed the woman suffering with an issue of blood for twelve long years. He protected the three Hebrew boys in the fiery furnace. He will provide all your needs. Jesus is a way maker and a mind regulator. He is still a healer today.

Church, our forefathers had nothing, but made it through slavery and Jim Crow and the Depression and all the degradation that went along with those periods of our history. Like the man in our text who had been suffering for thirty-eight years, you may not be able to make it to the pool because of the burdens you bear. You may not be able to get anyone to help you. Even a priest may pass you on the other side of the road, but I know a God who will hear your cry and heal you wherever you are.

Some say Jesus is not performing miracles in these modern times, but I am a witness that He is still working miracles. I had a client who had a little boy born with his intestines on the outside of his abdominal wall. The doctors said he only had a 50 percent chance of surviving, but today he's healthy. My own brother was in a coma for several weeks after being in an accident, but God heard the prayers of the righteous at Goodwill Baptist Church and one day Billy woke up and God healed his body.

I know that many people today don't believe in miracles, but every day and every night, He keeps us alive and keeps oxygen in the air, and when He gets ready the rains come and quench our thirst. This summer there was a drought, but when God got ready, the rains came in abundance. And anyone who has thought about how a baby is first conceived, and then seen with your own eyes the birth of a child like I have, must know that God is still in our midst. While I find myself complaining like everyone does from time to time, I try to count my blessings and give thanks daily for all that he has given me and my family.

But to whom much is given, much is required. Jesus asks each of us to help the man and woman get to the pool at Bethesda. If we want to get home—that is, our heavenly home—we must take someone with us. As we climb the ladder to success we must stop by Bethesda and reach back and grab the hand of some man or woman waiting by the pool. You can't be selfish and try to get there alone. Jesus is asking us to stop by Bethesda on our way home. Must Jesus bear the cross alone and all the world go free? Yes, there's a cross for everyone and there's a cross for me. Church, to reach our heavenly home, we must stop by Bethesda. If we do, not only will we help somebody, but we will receive healing ourselves. You'll find healing at the pool at Bethesda. There's healing in the water. You will find strength there. You'll find confidence at Bethesda. You'll find peace and joy there. You'll find life itself at Bethesda. You'll find salvation there. You'll find everlasting life at Bethesda. You will find water like you can find no place else. There is balm in Gilead (JEREMIAH 8:22). Church, if you trust Him, God will meet you at the Bethesda pool and give you all you need for your journey home. Wilt thou be made whole? Take up thy bed and walk as you stop by Bethesda on your way home.

I'm looking forward to reaching my eternal home. Somebody said there won't be any crying there. No more heartache, no more pain, no more disappointment, no more doctors over yonder. There'll be joy over yonder. There'll be peace over yonder for those who stop by Bethesda on their way home.

A Promise You Can Count On: One That Will Never Be Broken

PHILIPPIANS 1:1–6

Triumphant One's Ministries, Pittsboro, NC,
Second Annual Carrie H. Bolton Youth Achievement Day

JUNE 15, 2008

> Being confident of this, that he who began a good work in you will carry it on to completion until the day of Christ Jesus. PHILIPPIANS 1:6

Like Paul in the first few verses of Philippians chapter 1, I have come to you here in Pittsboro with joy. The joy of the Lord is my strength. I bring you greetings from my Webster family.

Excluding weekends, I was here in Pittsboro, North Carolina, with you almost daily for nearly twelve years. There were some great days and difficult times, yet I count that experience of being a small-town lawyer and minister to be a memorable portion of my life, one that helped mold me and allow the potter to put the pieces of my life together. In hindsight I count it all joy, as Paul said on one occasion. Many of you here contributed to my ministry by referring clients, by praying for me when I was down, and even helping pay the financial costs of my stay here in Pittsboro. When I first came to Pittsboro, churches and pastors helped me find an office and prayed for my success.

While here in Pittsboro practicing law, God called home to glory one of my best friends, Elder Robert Siler, at such a young age, in his early fifties. And illness in the form of a stroke fell upon another great friend and companion in the ministry, Elder Carrie Bolton. And I, while preaching in the pulpit of my home church, became ill and entered the hospital with a heart condition requiring surgery.

But while I was here, in a place I sometimes referred to as Nineveh, I learned that God specializes in mending broken hearts and mending slurred speech, and yes, I learned that not even death can separate us from the love of God.

Also, while sojourning here in Pittsboro, the spirit of the Lord came upon me ten years ago this month and I was anointed to preach the gospel, the most important thing that has ever happened to me in my life.

Enough about me. I know you have come here to hear the word. So let me get into the scripture, just for a few moments.

In our scripture today Paul writes most likely from a prison in Rome. He writes a letter in the form of a prayer of thanksgiving. He gives thanks for the men and women at Philippi who had begun a faith journey. These were some of the early Christians who dared to believe that there had lived a man named Jesus. Some called him Jesus of Nazareth, others Jesus the Christ, one who lived a short life of thirty-three years.

Young people here today, you don't have to live a long life as long as you live a devoted life, one devoted to your faith in Christ. But these early Christians dared believe there lived a man who taught us to love one another, to even love our enemies. Honorees, I beg you to love one another as Christ loves us.

Young and old here today at Triumphant Ministries, you have confessed your belief in Jesus Christ. You have said in your confession that no matter what happens to you, you would hold out to the end.

There's a song that says, "You may be blind when it's over." But you have said even if my friends don't believe, even if my classmates laugh at me for having the nerve to believe in a God that allows sickness to consume me or death to take away my mother, that you still believe.

Paul gives thanks to those in Philippi who no doubt risked their lives for their faith. Those being honored today and all who are witnesses to this occasion, I give thanks to you for remaining steadfast in your belief and faith in Jesus Christ.

I recognize that in this day of twenty-four-hour TV—with cursing and naked men and women on television, advertisements that encourage you to try alcohol, try sex, and try everything—but Jesus seems to be the answer to all our problems. I know that remaining faithful is difficult.

But as Paul says in chapter 1 of Philippians, I pray for your partnership in the gospel, your partnership and your collaboration with God of the good news from the first day you believed until now.

Yes, I'm proud, so very proud of those who have other achievements, but I'm most proud of those of you here in Pittsboro and Chatham County who have confessed your faith and have remained faithful.

Paul says confidently in verse 6 that he who began a good work in you will carry it on to completion until the day of Christ Jesus.

The first thing you should remember is that this work you have undertaken (this spiritual work) is that God began the work in you.

When your life was turned from the streets of sin and all the wrong you were doing, God was who turned you around. In the lyrics of a well-known song, "This joy I have the world didn't give it to me, and the world can't take it away. This peace I have, the world didn't give it to me, and the world can't take it away." And Paul says that he who began a good work in you will carry it on to completion until the day of Christ Jesus. You can count on this promise. It is one that will never be broken.

This Christian journey and all that goes with it—the courage that God gave you to first believe in God's only begotten son, the one born to the Virgin Mary and who performed miracles, healed the blind, brought Lazarus from the dead, a belief in one who preached only a few years and then was betrayed by one of his own disciples, and who was crucified and died on Calvary's cross, so that we might have the right to eternal life and have it more abundantly. I give thanks today for the courage you have had from the beginning.

And so today I want to make my most important point with confidence and conviction: the same man who died two thousand years ago but who still lives—this "God of our weary years, our silent tears"; a God of hope that specializes in giving hope to those who have lost hope, those who have given up, those who have been abandoned, those who can't figure out what they want to do after graduation—is the God who woke me up this morning and let me open my eyes and gave me some food, the one who Paul spoke of over in Philippians, chapter 2. This man who made Himself of no reputation and took upon Him the form of a servant and made in the likeness of man, and being found in the fashion as a man, humbled himself and became obedient until death, even the death of the cross. And wherefore God hath highly exalted Him and given Him a name that is above all names, at the name of Jesus every knee should bow, of things in heaven and things on earth that every tongue should confess that Jesus Christ is Lord to the glory of God the Father. I heard Dr. Gardner Taylor say one time that he loves to call Jesus' name.

My main point is that what God began in you, some of you many years ago, He will complete it. He won't leave you alone. God will be with you even in your darkest hour. He won't abandon you. When you're feeling like you don't have a friend, remember you have a friend in Jesus. Do you remember, "What a friend we have in Jesus"?

This is a promise not from me but from God almighty. This faith that you began when you joined the church in that little wooden building and that faith that was confirmed when you were baptized in the cold waters of the creek, I want you to know that God will carry your good work on to completion even until Christ returns.

This is a promise you can count on, a promise that will never be broken.

I had a case recently, and the teenage girl who was a witness in the case said she had promised an adult that she would not tell anyone what someone had done to her. She said she had promised on her sister's life. And a few days later she broke her promise.

Sometimes in our marriages we promise to be faithful through sickness and in good health, but sometimes we break our promises. We sometimes promise our parents we are going to study hard in school and make good grades, but we break our promises. We enter into agreements to take care of certain things, but we break our promises.

But Paul says God will keep His promise to continue in us what He began. He says you can count on Jesus, the lily of the valley, the bright and morning star, Jesus the way maker, who makes a way out of no way, the mind regulator, Jesus the battle ax in the time of war. Church, no matter what the circumstance or problem, you can stand on the promises of Jesus. He said he'd never leave us nor forsake us. He will continue the work he began in us until Judgment Day. Be confident of this.

On this journey, some people will keep bringing up stuff that you did years ago but remember that you were given a clean slate. Christ has forgiven you. Over in Philippians 3:13, Paul said, "Brethren, I count not myself to have apprehended but this thing I do, forgetting those things I did, forgetting those things which are behind and reaching forth unto those things which are before," and verse 14 says, "I press toward the mark for the prize of the high calling of Christ Jesus."

Keep the faith, honorees, and all those present. The just shall live by faith. Over in Jeremiah 29:11, the prophet Jeremiah says, "For I know the plans I have for you, declared the Lord, plans to prosper you and not harm you, plans to give you hope and a future."

God has set you apart. Be proud of that. God has chosen you. He has called you before you were born, and you have accepted your call. God will continue the good work he began in you years ago.

I need to take a few minutes to personally appeal to our young men and women. I know I'm preaching to the choir this morning. If I could borrow a few lines from *Madea's Family Reunion,* a scene that took place at the family reunion. All had gathered at the family homeplace that was purchased from the former slave owners. Young and old were present. There at the reunion some of the teenagers and young adults were shooting crap and getting angry with one another. Young teenage women were there, some dressed inappropriately, and old men were looking at them in a lustful way. A mother and daughter fought one another in one scene at the family reunion.

And then they all gathered. And after a gospel song was rendered, the oldest member of the family posed the question that I must pose today. She said, "Is this what we've been praying for?" And then one of the young men spoke up. "What is she talking about?" And then all eyes are turned to Cicely Tyson as she began to speak and answer the question.

Cicely Tyson turned to the men and spoke to them sincerely. Paraphrasing, she was saying to the young men, I need for you to be men, to be leaders of your community, to give up alcohol and drugs, to marry and be fathers to your children. I would add today that there are too many going to prison, too many of you walking around looking like you are already dead with your pants falling off your bodies. You look bad, and even though your hearts are good, you look so bad. I join Cicely Tyson in her plea, "Young men, when are you going to stop killing each other? Don't get involved with gangs."

And then she addressed the young women. She told them, "You are more than hips and thighs. I need for you to take your place in society." She was trying to get across to them that they are more than sex objects for the pleasure of men. She encouraged them to take their place in society. Young women here today, often you are more mature in your thinking than young men your same age. You can help them. Tell them you're not a prostitute, that your body is the temple of the Holy Ghost, which is in you. (SEE 1 CORINTHIANS 6:19.)

Young men and women present today, don't be dismayed. I am confident that the God who began a good work in you will carry it on to completion until Christ's return.

ART BY BILLY D. WEBSTER

Don't Give Up

GALATIANS 6:9

Oberlin Baptist Church, Raleigh, NC

OCTOBER 5, 2014

> And let us not be weary in well doing for in due season we shall reap if we faint not. KJV

> Let us not become weary in doing good, for at the proper time we will reap a harvest if we do not give up. NIV

Paul's message today to the churches at Galatia is one of encouragement. The churches at Galatia at the time were beginning to impose strict rules for new converts based upon their Jewish understanding that the way to salvation was by circumcision and other rituals. In the Epistle to the Galatians, Paul gets them straight and lets them know that the way to salvation is by grace through faith in Jesus Christ. And then Paul went on in chapter 6 to teach them about the importance of a persevering faith. I want to talk today about persevering and not giving up.

We are reminded daily by the television, internet, newspaper, and other media about the tumultuous state of our nation and world, from wars around the world, heads being severed, shootings by police officers of persons who happen to be driving and walking while black or brown—to the most secure building in the world, yes, even the White House, being trespassed by a knife-wielding intruder. We are reminded daily about the state of the black community: senseless murder; black-on-black crime taking the lives of our young men, women, and even children in drive-by shootings. Whenever I have a chance to proclaim God's word, I'm led to try to leave my audience encouraged.

Eighteen months ago, I began an initiative in my court in Durham called CourtCares. My staff and I invite twelve-, thirteen, and fourteen-year-old middle school students to the US District Court for the Middle District of North Carolina, to introduce them to the federal court. We take that time to encourage our youth to stay on the right side of the law; to encourage them to be respectful of one another, their teachers, and others; and to recognize that every person needs to feel special, to be validated. We simply try to encourage them. We talk to them about bullying and how that can lead to suicide. We conduct a mock criminal trial and always have a guest speaker. This past spring, one of our guest speakers was giving a dynamic speech in which he was encouraging each student by telling them that each of them could be great. As he spoke, one little girl on the front row, loudly spoke out. "I can't be great because I was a mistake." My heart sank as I heard those words. What kind of parent or guardian or responsible person would teach a child that he or she was a mistake? Our guest speaker, a retired general and now working with state government, stopped talking to the students and began to speak to the little girl personally. I mention this because I wanted to illustrate the predicament that humanity finds us in today. You see what we as people and nation are up against and why I use my opportunities to encourage those under the sound of my voice. Giving hope to those who are seemingly ready to give up is a big part of my calling! So don't give up, Oberlin, never, ever give up!

Let me proceed to see if I can explain what I got out of the text today. Explaining the text is not always an easy thing to do. I talked with Rev. James Moore, one of my pastor cousins, on the telephone earlier in the week. He began to say that he wished he could explain things like he said he felt I could. And he said to me, "Some people are like parrots. They can talk, but they can't explain themselves." I hope that I'm not like a parrot today. That is one of the reasons I need God to step in and get me out of the picture. I need the spirit of God to come by Oberlin today. I'm going to put to a test what the old uneducated preachers in the pulpit used to say when I was a little boy growing up out in the country. They said that if you just open your mouth, God will speak for you. So let me get into the word.

Growing up on a farm in a community a little over one hundred miles from here, my parents always had a large garden. My parents planted the seeds in the early spring after my father had prepared the fields. Whether it was corn, green beans, peas, potatoes, tomatoes, or other vegetables, when prepared by my mother or others back then, they were just simply too good for me to take the time to really describe to you how good that food was. When my parents planted those seeds and plants, they had high hopes that they would flourish and there'd come a day when they could say that the garden "has come in." But before the garden came in, another way of saying when the green beans and peas were ready to be picked, often they had to take a hoe and dig the grass out of the garden. Sometimes, there would be a dry spell and it seems the garden would be slow to come in. And if the rains didn't come as hoped they would, sometimes some of our garden vegetables had to be replanted. Insects sometimes tried to destroy the garden vegetables. But in due season, at the appointed time the gardens would come in. The ancient Greek word "Kairos" describes what I mean when I say in due season. When God acts, when God gets ready, the garden would come in—sometimes it seemed like the gardens would come in overnight. I'm thankful today that as I look back on my upbringing, I can't ever remember a moment when my parents gave up. Oberlin, never, never give up! Keep on planting good seed! Keep on doing good! Don't give up.

Keep on striving, Oberlin. We've been promised a prize if we hold out and don't give up. I don't know about you, but one day I promised the Lord that I would hold out. There is a song that says when the battle of life is over, we will wear a crown. Hold on and hold out, Oberlin, God has proclaimed through Jeremiah 29:11: "For I know the plans I have you, declares the LORD, plans to prosper you and not harm you, plans to give you hope and a future." Church don't get weary in doing good, there is a harvest that will come if you just hold out. Don't lose heart in being a Christian. For in due time, in God's time—not your parents' time, not your brothers' or sisters' time, no, not even your time, but in God's time, your crop will come in. It's going to take perseverance, some patience to have a good harvest. We used to sing in my youth, "You can't hurry God, you just have to wait, you have to trust Him and give Him time, no matter how long it takes; He's a God that you can't hurry. He may not come when you want Him, but He's right on time." You know Dr. Ernesto Graham of Fayetteville; we stay in touch mostly by text and occasionally on the golf course. He recently sent me a text of a portion of scripture with the following words, "Rejoicing in hope, patient in tribulation, continuing in instant prayer."

My parents would always sow good seed. Church, not just any seed will do, but we must sow good seed for there to be a bountiful crop in due time. Unfortunately, some of us have taken up sowing bad seed. Some of us covet our neighbor's wife or husband, carry grudges, or judge others when we ought to be looking in the mirror at ourselves. We sow seeds of discontent and disharmony even in the church. Many of us don't even think about loving and forgiving those who trespass against us. We expect a blessing when we are sowing bad seed. Church, it's by the sowing of good seed that we can expect a good harvest in due time. Second Corinthians 9:6 says the point is this: whoever sows sparingly will also reap sparingly, and whoever sows bountifully will also reap bountifully. Our friend Job in 4:8 says, "As I have seen, those who plow iniquity and sow trouble reap the same." Proverbs 22:8 teaches us that "whoever sows injustice will reap calamity, and the rod of his fury will fail." What if I was a judge who ruled based upon favoritism, or because you were rich, or that you were poor, or based upon your ability to hire a good lawyer? What if I had a different set of rules for everyone who came before me? What if—what if—I was the kind of judge who didn't feed everyone out of the same spoon? If I don't sow justice in the courts of justice, then I know that I will reap what I sow. There are too many police officers who believe that their ability to carry a gun gives them a license to kill. I'm concerned about our young black men today, whether they are in the crossfire of the cops or the victim of senseless killings by those in their own communities.

This last incident that I first saw on the news and then on the internet took place in South Carolina, when a police officer stopped a young black man for not having a seatbelt on and then ended up shooting him; I must admit that that incident made me angry! I have a brown-skinned, six-foot-two-inch, twenty-five-year-old son whom I love dearly. He's working, supporting himself; like all here today, my son's not perfect, but I don't want anyone shooting him because of the color of his skin. Just the other day, the thought occurred to me that unless those of us who have something to lose, those who have good jobs and big homes, if we don't take a stand for justice, then we won't get justice. As you know, I have some limitations sitting as a federal judge. If I demonstrate in my actions and words that I've already made my mind up on a particular case, then I'd have to recuse myself. I want to be able to be on the bench to dispense justice. So I need for each of you who have something to lose to speak up and stand up for our youth. If our children are wrong, they are just wrong; justice must take place, but if they are right, then let the redeemed of the Lord say so! Church, it is true, you reap what you sow. Church don't give up. There is an award waiting for us if we make every effort to do good.

Oberlin, God would have us to demonstrate our love toward those who have disappointed you when they left Oberlin Baptist Church, some because they thought that the grass was greener on the other side, some who were just fed up with too much disharmony. Stay in the race, Oberlin. Fight on, Oberlin. Keep doing good. First Corinthians 15:58 says, "Beloved children [I'm glad to be one of God's children], be steadfast, unmovable [like a tree planted by the water], always abounding in the work of the Lord, for as much as you know your labor is not in vain in the Lord." Matthew 24:13 says he who "endures to the end shall be saved." Hold out, Oberlin; when you get weary and feel like you are about to faint and can't go on any longer, remember Isaiah in 40:28. He said in essence that we serve a God that doesn't get weary. He never faints, so you have someone to lean on. After we put our hands to the plow, as our ancestors taught us through example, if we follow God's commandments, and if we exercise perseverance, patience and hard work, our efforts will pay off after a while. Now, Church, after we have stayed prayed up, forgiven even our enemies; after we have fought the good fight, finished our course; after we have visited the sick and shut in, visited and prayed for those in nursing homes and hospitals, visited those in prisons and nursing homes; after we have gone the last mile of the way, in due season, when God gets ready for us; after we have taken up our cross daily and followed the one who sometimes seems to put us in harm's way in due season you will reap if you don't faint. After we have remembered that many of our ancestors one hundred years after slavery ended in America didn't have two rusty nickels to rub together (my mother told me that her grandfather saw her with a penny one day and said, "Give me that penny. You don't need all that money"). But in due season, after the rains come, and after justice had been delivered by the earthly judges, that Judge from on High, the God that brought us out of the ghetto and out of the hot sun on our farms and out of the misery and degradation and humiliation of Jim Crow, in due season—whether it's in our lifetime or on judgment day, when all the saints come gathering home, on the other side of Jordan, where those who have done good towards others—in that place, a home not made by man's hands, we who have kept the faith will have our reward.

Don't give up, Oberlin, no matter what your situation is. I've been trying to tell many of the young men who come before me that they should not give up! Seemingly they have lost all hope; no one will offer them a job; their lives seem less valuable to the world and even to themselves, so they sell drugs and carry guns, join gangs and sentence themselves to a lifetime of imprisonment. But they are our sons and daughters. Don't give up on them, Church. In due time, when God gets ready for them to change, they will change.

Oberlin, you have sown some good seed. Don't let it be in vain! I know that you are praying for a pastor. Help me to get the word out that we shouldn't quit coming to church because you are mad with the man or woman who spoke to you in a stupid manner the last time you were here. Yes, sometimes Christian folk can act and say stupid things.

But in due time, it might be in a nick of time, just before all hope is lost. I'm glad I didn't give up on law practice when the fees were slow to come in. My wife says my clients used to sometimes pay me with poke salad. I had a client that brought me some poke salad one day along with a piece of pork meat and cornbread when I was practicing down there in the small town of Pittsboro. One night at dinner, surrounded by my three children, I told my wife that an elderly lady, a former client, had brought me some "poke salad" for lunch. Immediately, my wife said, "Lord, children, your daddy's clients paying him with poke salad!" Sometimes to do good, as Paul exhorts us to do good in our text; we might have to work for poke salad or for nothing at all. I'm a witness today that if you humble yourselves, that in due time, God can move you from poke salad to the federal bench; he can move you from the outhouse to the White House! James 4:10 says to humble yourselves before the Lord and He will lift you up. Don't give up, Church, the word teaches that if you are faithful over a few things, He will make you ruler over many. God can elevate you and open doors where you thought there were no doors to open! Oberlin, in due time, in Kairos, God will bring you a pastor if you remain faithful and continue to do good toward others. Not only that, even though some of us have made enemies by how we treated them, in due time God will make your enemy your footstool if you don't give up (PSALM 110:1; LUKE 20:43). Proverbs 16:7 says when a man's ways please the Lord, He makes even his enemies to be at peace with him. God can and He will turn your situation around if you keep on doing good, keep on trying to please the Lord. Don't give up!

Stay in the game, Oberlin, cast your bread upon the water. I'm a witness that it will return many days later, many times tenfold. Keep on fighting, Oberlin, while you are able, while you have the use of your limbs, your eyesight, and while you have a good mind. Don't give up! When I moved to Chapel Hill there was a man who had no arms who I'd see often mowing the grass on the side of a major intersection off Highway 15-501 in Chapel Hill. He mowed barefooted. Young men and women, there are others who are blind and go to work every day.

And so, when a man came before me in criminal court the other day, I noticed he had seven children by seven different women and he had not worked in over twenty-five years, except some under-the-table work, although he was able bodied. There was no reason for him not to be working. As a judge I must separate church and state and couldn't say all that I would have liked to say to the young man. But I told him, my mother used to say that "an idle mind is the devil's workshop." Even though I had the power to let him out of jail pending trial, he's still in jail today because justice required him to remain there. Church, we are going to reap what we sow.

Persevere, Oberlin! Don't get discouraged. Don't lose heart in doing good toward others. Don't get weary. Don't get slack, nor fainthearted. Don't get depressed in doing for others. You are not on this Christian journey all alone. Somebody said, "If it's not one thing, it's two; if it's not one thing, it's another." Sickness and death, disappointment, and not getting the job you thought you should have gotten, not getting the grade you thought you should have, are just a small portion of what you can expect to experience in this journey called life. Don't throw up your hands Church! Some of us are so hardheaded and insist on doing it our way; drinking and drugging so much that we pass out; we faint and grow weary doing it our way. But even then, God continues to pursue us and give us a second chance and a third chance and a thousand chances to get it right.

I may not have another chance to come before you, as I turned sixty in February of this year. I reflected on the text found in James 4:14 that life is like a vapor; it appears but for a little while and then it vanishes. I want you to know that there's no reason to give up. I want you to know that a long time ago, I decided to follow Jesus. I know that when my legs get weak and my feet begin to swell, arthritis sits in, when my eyesight begins to grow dim, when I begin to have trouble getting around, and my mind begins to fade, and I begin to experience the realities of just living a long life, if that is my plight, I hope I can remember that God has an extra set of wings to share with me.. Isaiah in 40:31 said if you just wait on the Lord (if you don't give up, if you don't get weary as you are trying to serve Him), with God's help, you will renew your strength. God will mount some eagle wings on you, and then in due time, if you endure, you will again be able to run and not get weary, you will be able to walk and not faint. So, Church, don't get weary in well doing for in due time, when God gets ready, in the words of the text, we shall, we shall, we shall reap if you don't give up. Don't give up, Church.

Keep on pursuing God every day of your life, and just know that while you are struggling to pursue Him, He is pursuing you with His relentless grace. He would desire that all of us be one of His sheep, to know His voice. Keep on keeping on, as the old folk used to say. Our communities need you, every one of you is needed to help right the ship that is about to sink. Our young folk with their pants hanging down below their bottoms need for us present to not give up. Yes, many of them are hanging out on the street corner, not working, messing up their lives; they are on the brink of completely throwing in the towel. Our prisons have maxed out to the point that the government is contracting with private corporations to build more prisons.

Don't throw in the towel, young folk, no matter what happens to you. Man may not offer a job for you that will cause you to want to go to work every day, but I know a man from Galilee who can put you to work. Some of the great preachers today started off as drug users, dealers, pimps, and prostitutes. From my extended family come some strong Christians and preachers who were once hooked on alcohol and drugs. But God's grace gave them another chance, and one of them—Rev. Dr. Kenneth Moore from my hometown—is as gifted in the pulpit as any preacher to be found anywhere. Don't give up, Church! Don't give up! Don't give up. We shall reap if we faint not! Don't give up. Don't give up.

Can These Bones Live?

EZEKIEL 37:1–14 KJV

Black History Month Service, Goodwill First Baptist Church, Madison, NC

FEBRUARY 26, 2012

> The hand of the LORD was on me, and he brought me out by the Spirit of the LORD and set me in the middle of a valley; It was full of bones. He led me back and forth among them, and I saw a great many bones on the floor of the valley, bones that were very dry. He asked me, "Son of man, can these bones live?" I said, "Sovereign LORD, you alone know." EZEKIEL 37:1–3

Today, at this Black History Month Service here at my home church, Goodwill Baptist Church, I want you to know that the condition of our men, especially our young black men, continues to burden me as I go about my work as a judge and my work in the ministry. Two of the photos being displayed on the church program, snapshots of young mostly black prison inmates, are examples of a picture that is being duplicated daily thousands of times across the United States. I won't take too much time talking about the statistical data that has been collected. However, it is far more important that I use my time to speak about what God says about a solution. I will take a moment to tell you that at this junction of our black history, the data illustrate why many of us who care about our young men are so alarmed and are using every opportunity to enlist the faithful and others to help solve the problem of the disproportionate rate of African American men in prison today. It is a problem that I personally think about almost every day. Recent statistics show that while African American and Hispanic males make up 28 percent of the US population, they make up 62 percent of the prison population. Black males are six times more likely to be in prison than are white males. Not counting the number of black males who travel back and forth to college from their homes or who live off campus, more than three times as many black people live in prison cells than in a college dorm. And the black male dropout rate in college is causing there to be at some campuses at least twice as many black women on college campuses as there are black men.

Let me pause for a moment to say that since I was last here in the pulpit at Goodwill, I've come under the watch care of historic Oberlin Baptist Church in Raleigh and its learned and anointed pastor, Rev. Sherri Arnold-Graham. And I have become an associate minister there. Like Goodwill, Oberlin is also in transition. I hope that soon, the Goodwill congregation will be able to come worship with us in Raleigh as we pursue God's work of building an army. For one thing, I'm very proud of how you have made up the hedge and stood in the gap over the last months in the aftermath of the great tragedy and challenge that you have been confronted with here at Goodwill. I want you to know that I feel your pain and disappointment and pray that God will continue to bless Goodwill Baptist Church and this community. I know that you are familiar with the song made popular by gospel singer Yolanda Adams. You know that "the battle is not ours, it's the Lord's." I pray that God will reunite families and loved ones who have been scattered. But Church, I would be remiss if I didn't remind you that it is important and necessary for each of us in this community to reconcile or make peace with one another. Death can come as suddenly as Christ's return. Our ancestors sang a song with the lyrics, "Don't let Him [Christ] catch you with your work undone. Be ready, be ready, when He comes again. He's coming again so soon."

Let me move quickly to today's text. We find beginning at verse 1 that Ezekiel was in the spirit on the Lord's Day. I say the Lord's Day because every day is the Lord's Day. Ezekiel says the hand of the Lord was upon him and carried him out in the spirit, and the spirit set him down amid a valley. This vision is one of numerous visions you'll find in the Book of Ezekiel while Ezekiel is exiled with the children of Israel in Babylon. As you may know, ancient Babylon is where Iraq is located today. I've read that it gets very hot there, far over 100 degrees in the summertime in Iraq today. There is a place in California called Death Valley where the average July temperature is 115 degrees, and the annual rainfall is only 1.92 inches. I don't know whether this valley of dry bones in the thirty-seventh chapter of Ezekiel was like Death Valley or not, but the first and second verses let us know that in his vision, Ezekiel saw a valley full of dry bones.

In verse 3 of the text, the Spirit of God spoke to Ezekiel, saying, "Son of man, can these bones live?" And Ezekiel answered, "Sovereign God, only you know."

I stopped by Goodwill today to ask you a question. Can these bones live? Can our sons and grandsons, these mostly young African American men, be resurrected and brought back to life? Far too many have been locked up; many of their heads are so messed up that they seem to be happy and not have a care in the world. Can these bones live? Yes, I hate to say it, but in this part of our history in America, more are asking the question: can these bones live? From where I sit many, both young and old seemingly have given up hope for our youth. Many thousands of our youth and young adults seem to have given up on themselves and are in a state of depression and hopelessness. Let me momentarily jump over to verse 11 in today's text, where we learn that the whole house of Israel had given up hope, like what I see in America today. Chapter 37:11 (NIV) says in part, our bones are dried up and our hope is gone; we are cut off.

Church, if we have learned one thing from black history, whether we look at 350 years of slavery, Jim Crow, or segregation and all the lynchings and inhumane treatment that went along with these sad episodes of American history, we learned that giving up hope is a bad thing, and we cannot even think about giving up hope. Giving up hope is not an option. Right here in Goodwill, those who built this church didn't have hopelessness in their vocabulary. We've had some great soldiers here at Goodwill, men and women who are buried on these grounds. I won't take the time to have a roll call of all those who have contributed mightily to Goodwill Baptist Church and the community over the last hundred-plus years, but we do have a lot to celebrate here about this community's history.

But can these modern-day lifeless bones live? Can they become all that God desires them to become? Occasionally I ride the express bus from my home in Chapel Hill to my office in Raleigh to save on transportation costs. When I get on the bus in Chapel Hill, I see professional types, some wearing suits and ties, carrying laptop computers, and some students traveling to NC State University. When I arrive in Raleigh, I must then transfer to the local city bus to complete the trip to my office. That part of the trip is quite interesting and almost depressing at times. I see many of my people there waiting for the bus. Many youths can be found there hanging out using profanity, pants hanging down below their bottoms, having to hold their pants up as they try to walk. Church, do you know what a penguin looks like, that large animal that lives down there near the South Pole? Well, just recently I saw one somewhat short brother in his hoodie and baggy pants and big coat walking around looking just like a penguin as he walked around. The last time I rode the city bus, several young adult men were entertaining a couple of young women using language that is too harsh to utter in church or anywhere else for that matter. Not long ago there in Raleigh, I waited at a red traffic light that was about to turn green and I saw a young brother trying to beat the light trying to run across the street as he held up his pants. But can these bones live?

The conduct and disrespect of our sons and daughters toward their parents does make you pause when considering whether these bones can live. Just the other day I had a conversation with one of my law student interns who informed me that her twenty-two-year-old brother, who stays at home, said to their mother, "Shut up, you old hag." The student said that her mother was going to Court to try to get her son out of the house. Something is very wrong with this picture. Can any of you here over fifty years old imagine what kind of condition you would be in even today if you had told your mama, "Shut up, you old hag"? I know what kind of condition I'd be in if my father had heard me say that to my mother. I'd be standing up here trying to preach with both arms still in a sling with a neck brace on, still trying to figure out what happened to me forty years earlier. People would be asking me, "Joe, what in world happened to you?"

I'm glad today that the God of the Most High gave this vision to Ezekiel, a man whose steps were ordered by the Lord. So, when asked in verse 3 whether these dry bones could live, Ezekiel said, "Sovereign Lord, you alone know." Ezekiel may not have known or been certain of the answer to the question, but at least he knew and respected the one who knows all. There are those among us who claim to be Christians, but don't ever utter the words "Oh Lord God!" But Ezekiel knew Jehovah—Rapha, the Lord our healer. Ezekiel knew Jehovah Jireh; the Lord will provide. So Ezekiel confidently responded to God's question, "Lord God, you know all things!"

Church, there are things that we just don't know the answer to as Christians, things that will always be a mystery to us, but as long as we know that man from Galilee—the one who walked out on the water; the one who said, "Peace, be still," and the winds and raging seas obeyed; the one who spoke three words, "Lazarus come forth," four days after he died and had been buried, and Lazarus came out of his tomb; the one who some refer to as the lily of the valley, that bright and morning star—everything will be all right. But Church, in 2012 when things seem to be so dire, one must ask the question: can these bones live?

I don't want to just pick on our youth because it isn't their entire fault. Many of us older one's act like we don't have good sense. Some of us act as if we too may have raised ourselves. We haven't been the best examples. I attended a meeting in Pinehurst this past Friday and was speaking with one of the waiters there. In our conversation he told me about a man who used to work with an acquaintance I used to know in the area who worked in Pinehurst also. The man he spoke about was having some marital difficulties with his wife some years back. The waiter there at the hotel told me the wife had put her husband's obituary in the paper. The only problem was that the man was still living and working. We older ones are not very good examples for our youth to follow. I heard a retired professional basketball player say one time he was at a reception, and someone came in the room who was all dressed in a very fine, expensive suit of clothes. The man telling the story said to his friend that a "suit" just walked in. A suit is a person who is not about too much when it comes to standing up for something; a suit is someone who runs toward the exit when differences arise, someone who doesn't believe in helping anyone less fortunate unless he or she is getting some publicity or there is something in it for him- or herself. A suit can talk a big game but is missing courage and conviction. I wish we had more of those courageous men here at Goodwill like my father, the late

James "Tom" Webster, and others who spoke their minds, not always in a way that someone more educated would articulate it, but more importantly he and others spoke the truth. Goodwill, if you are just a suit, you are just as bad off as the young prison inmates that we speak about today.

But let me return to the text. Verse 4 reads, "Again he said unto me, Prophesy upon the bones, and say unto them, O ye dry bones, hear the word of the LORD." O Goodwill, while you are going through this difficult season in the church's history, hear the word of the Lord. Remember that what you are going through is just for a season. It's just another one of those times of disappointment and tumultuous winds of life that will surely come in all our lives. I read a sermon by one of my favorite preachers and theologians, Rev. Dr. Gardner C. Taylor. He said we need a "stormproof religion" to get through difficult times. A stormproof religion is one that is firm and unshakable when the winds of life come; a stormproof religion is one that allows you to stand still when that wayward husband leaves you for another woman. A stormproof religion is not sometime-y; it allows you to forgive when someone despitefully uses you, when your best friend lies to you or betrays you. A stormproof religion allows us to be steadfast in our faith—no matter what comes our way. If you have a stormproof religion, you will be able to say during the worst of times that for God I live and for God I'll die. If you have stormproof religion, you will be able to say like Job, even when affliction and death comes, that the Lord giveth and the Lord taketh away, blessed be the name of the Lord.

Church, can these bones live? It doesn't matter whether you are young or old, rich or poor, black, white, or brown, short or tall, if the most high God speaks, you can expect some action. God begins in verse 5 to speak to the dry bones. "Behold, I will cause breath to enter you and ye shall live": God says, "I will lay sinews upon you, and will bring up flesh upon you, and cover you with skin, and put breath into you and ye shall live." Church, I'm a witness that if God gets hold of you, you will be a changed person. The word says not only shall he put breath into you, but at the end of verse 6 it says that "ye shall know that I am the LORD."

Can these bones live? It is now Ezekiel's time to preach. Ezekiel began to prophesy as commanded, and there came up a noise and a shaking, and the bones came together, bone to bone. As a child, when a bad storm came during the summer, loud thunder and lightning sometimes shook the whole house. My parents used to say, "Chillun, y'all get in there and sit down and be quiet because the Lord is doing His work." In our text today God was doing His work. The text continues, And Ezekiel looked, I suspect in amazement, he saw "the sinews and the flesh came up upon them, and the skin covered them," but according to verse 8 he saw "no breath in them," just like we see no breath in many of our men and women today.

In reading this scripture, I'm reminded of how God first made man in God's own image. Genesis beginning at chapter 2, verse 7 says, then "the LORD God formed man of the dust of the ground and breathed into his nostrils the breath of life; and man became a living soul." I'm also reminded about how God created woman from Adam's rib and I was imagining what Adam must have seen when he came up out of surgery. History tells us that the Garden of Eden must have been somewhere over there in the Middle East or Africa perhaps. And so, I imagine that Adam, still groggy from the anesthesia, looked up and saw a beautiful sister who looked like Michelle Obama, CeCe Wyans, Beyoncé, Alicia Keys, Natalie Cole, or Yolanda Adams. And then my human imagination further clicked in, and I was thinking that if Adam had been like some of us men, his first words would have been, "God, do you need another rib?" But we know that man had not fallen at that point, and the Bible says when God brought Eve to Adam, his first words were, "This is now bone of bones, and flesh of my flesh: she shall be called Woman, because she was taken out of Man." Church, unless God breathes the breath of life into your nostrils, these bones cannot live.

Let me move on. In verse 9 of our text, God told Ezekiel to "Prophesy unto the wind, prophesy son of man, and say to the wind, Thus saith the Lord GOD; Come from the four winds, O breath, and breathe upon the slain, that they may live." Church, today we need some more volunteer soldiers to reach out and show some love to our youth and young adults and help breathe life into them. Time is growing short, and those of us who are in the valley working among the dry bones with Ezekiel are getting tired and weary. Several of my mentors across the country have died or retired due to age and poor health in the last few years. We need some fresh soldiers.

In verse 10 Ezekiel prophesied to the wind as commanded and "breath came into [the dry bones], and they lived, and stood upon their feet, an exceeding great army." I feel like proclaiming today what the Apostle Paul said in 1 Corinthians 15:55. He said, "O death, where is thy sting? O grave, where is thy victory?"

With my own spiritual eye, I can begin to see our youth come to life after God has used the wind to breathe life into the dry bones.

As I think about today's scripture and how God breathed life into the dry bones, I'm reminded of that old Negro spiritual that paints a clear picture of how the dry bones came together piece by piece. The song says,[10]

10 The melody of "Dem Bones" (also called "Dry Bones" and "Dem Dry Bones") was composed by author and songwriter James Weldon Johnson and his brother, J. Rosamond Johnson.

Ezekiel cried, "Dem dry bones,"
"Dem dry bones," "Dem dry bones,"
"Oh, hear the word of the Lord."
The toe bone connected to the heel bone,
The heel bone connected to the foot bone,
The foot bone connected to the leg bone....

Church, we who are yet walking around in our right minds can play a big role in the resurrection of our youth. I believe with all my heart, soul, and mind that we are going through this season in part because we have been disobedient. We haven't prayed without ceasing. It doesn't cost one penny to pray. The Bible even encourages us to go into our secret closet to pray. We don't have to put on a suit or go into the public. We've been dry bones ourselves. Second Chronicles 7:14 says, "If my people which are called by my name, shall humble themselves, and pray, and seek my face, and turn from their wicked ways," then we will hear from heaven and God will forgive our sins and heal our land. I believe that if we followed this commandment, if we were obedient to the Great Commission, that God would go into the ghettos, barrios, and country villages like Goodwill across the land and breathe life into the dry bones and raise up a great army from among our young men and women who have lost hope and direction in their lives. I believe our youth and young adults would not only come to life but would become soldiers in the army of the Lord.

In verse 11, God explains to Ezekiel, "These bones are the whole House of Israel" who are complaining about their bones being dry and their hope being lost, that they were cut off. Apparently as I mentioned earlier the House of Israel couldn't find their way out of bondage and the condition they were in. Have you ever felt like you couldn't find your way out? Have you ever felt you couldn't find your way out of debt; you couldn't find your way out of a relationship that you knew was bad for you? Have you ever been depressed and in despair, sick without a cure in sight? You couldn't find your way out. But we receive assurances not only in today's text but throughout the Bible. But verses 12–14 gives me much hope and assurance that what we are experiencing right now won't last always. God told Ezekiel to prophesy to the House of Israel that he was going to open their graves and bring them up from the graves. Tell them, Ezekiel, I will bring them "back to the land of Israel. Then you, my people, will know that I am the Lord. Not only that but I will put my spirit in you, and you will live, and I will settle you in your own land. Then you will know that I the Lord have spoken, and I have done it, declares the Lord."

Goodwill, do you believe these bones can live? To use the words of Andrae Crouch, in his hit song "Church," you may be in the valley of dry bones. Young people don't give up. Help is on the way. Isaiah 40:31 says but they that wait upon the Lord "shall renew their strength." I can see these young folk mounting up wings as eagles; When God breathes life into them and gives them new life, they will be able to run and not get weary; and they shall be able to walk again and not faint. The New Testament calls it the new birth. I'm glad that Jesus made it possible for us to be born again.

Yes, yes, our young men as exemplified by the dry bones can live! Yes, they can. I know this because in the darkest hours of our history during slavery, God made a way seemingly out of no way. But I personally know that our young men and women can be brought back to life because Christ's death on the cross, His shed blood, brought me back to life. And in the words of an old song of my youth, "One day when I was lost, Jesus died upon the cross. I know it was the blood that saved me." Young folk here today, just by believing and committing your lives to Jesus Christ, you can live. Some of our ancestors didn't have much education, but they had figured out what was important; they sang, "because He lives, I can face tomorrow, because he lives all fear is gone." Because He lives, these dry bones can live. Yes, I can see them get up from where they are, the jail cells and crack houses and prostitution houses, if we begin to pray and live the kind of life that God is calling for in these last days. If we do our part, Church, our young men will no longer be dry bones; God can, and He will, breathe life into them. I can see them shake off the shackles of imprisonment, hopelessness, joblessness, homelessness, and disrespect. I can envision our young men taking responsibility for their children—paying their child support and just as importantly, marrying the baby's mama before the baby is conceived. Whatever your situation, God can breathe life into you. Just ask Him for whatever you need. He's got it. He's got the whole world in His hands. Yes, these bones can live because Jesus sacrificed His life one day and He lives today.

I'm asking—no, I'm begging—as many of you that are present; I'm begging you to begin to offer a hand of hope and encouragement by wrapping your arm around as many young boys and girls as you can. We need to start when they are two or three years old, long before they get a rap sheet. Too many of our young men don't have a man around the house that they can call "Daddy" because Daddy is in prison or has given up and is satisfied with being one of the dry bones of our society. Young people, be encouraged. I've met people who didn't have a mama or a daddy like many of my generation had growing up, and they didn't let anything keep them from being successful. You may think of me as being somebody big, because God has blessed me with a few titles—lawyer, judge, preacher—but even today I too have insecurities and disappointments like anybody else. And so I've had to reach out at times for help, and people have continued to help me, pray for me, and encourage me along the way. Some of my encouragement has come from some who never even graduated from high school. Don't get so big that you ever think you know it all. So, if for no other reason, to honor my ancestors and show my appreciation for all their sacrifice, as my ancestors used to testify with confidence at the end of their testimony with much conviction, "I'm gonna run on and see what the end is gonna be."

Through their words and songs, but more importantly through the lives they lived, my ancestors here at Goodwill are still encouraging me today. They used to sing, "If I couldn't say a word, if I couldn't say a word, if I couldn't say a word, I'd just wave my hand."

ILLUSTRATION BY SHAILYN RAMSEY

Part of my brief theological education, spoken from the mouth of Rev. Dr. Gardner C. Taylor, lets me know that no matter where I took my text, as the generation of preachers before me used to say, no matter what book, chapter, and verse I read from, I must make my way to Golgotha or Calvary's cross as soon as I can. That's because that's where the dry bones will find life, even everlasting life. Golgotha is where the lame will be able get up and walk; that's where the blind will receive their sight. That's where the dry bones will be able to find the courage to never give up. As the old song from my youth goes, "It was there on the cross where I first saw the light and the burdens of my heart rolled away; it was there by faith that I received my sight and now I am happy all day." Jesus died for you and me. God so loved the world that He gave his only begotten son that whosoever believes in Him, even the dry bones of our society, they too can have eternal life.

Not only will these dry bones live, but because Christ came and sacrificed His life for the sins of humankind, these bones might have life, and they might have it more abundantly. (JOHN 10:10 KJV) Amen and Amen.

Standing Up for the Cause

LUKE 10:25–29 NIV

Christian Legal Society's Prayer Breakfast, North Carolina Central University Law School, Durham, NC

APRIL 2, 2016

On one occasion an expert in the law stood up to test Jesus. "Teacher, he asked, "what must I do to inherit eternal life?" LUKE 10:25 NIV

Today, I am so grateful to have been called to this stage with my preaching hat on rather than my black robe that I wear as US magistrate judge for the Middle District of North Carolina. Sometimes I have difficulty separating the two callings. For one thing, they are similar. Both call upon me to walk uprightly, avoid even the appearance of impropriety, to be ethical in all my dealings and to treat everyone respectfully and lovingly in my daily walk. Both callings also require me to stand up for the cause of justice, righteousness, and fairness. And as a part of my judicial duties, when possible, I try to encourage those who come before me as I dispense justice while offering hope. Many of those who come before me, by virtue of circumstances, often not completely the fault of their own, seemingly have given up on life. Too often I see young black and brown brothers come before me who seem to have drawn the short straw from the beginning of life. Most have no relationship with their fathers; some don't even know who their fathers are. You know their story without even hearing it. You know that most have quit school by the tenth or eleventh grade, thereby depriving themselves of an education and a pathway out of poverty. You know that many have turned to drugs, either consuming them to self-medicate and/or selling them to survive and support their families. Poverty has no respect of persons or racial or gender identity.

We learn from our text today that these young men and women that I have just referred to are our neighbors. I need for a good many of you to commit to standing up for this cause. What is this cause that I speak about today?

In today's text, a certain "lawyer" stood up, with an improper purpose in mind. He stood up to ask Jesus a question, but with an ulterior motive in mind. The text says the lawyer sought to tempt Christ, perhaps thinking that Christ would not know the answer and thereby be discredited. By now Christ had begun to gain followers and He preached with authority. That certain lawyer did not know who he was up against. I was taught at Howard University Law School, perhaps in my criminal justice clinic, that on cross-examination, one should not ask a witness a question that you don't already know the answer to. You might just get an answer that hurts your case. But what this lawyer who stood up didn't know is who Jesus was—that the one that he sought to tempt or put to a test was the one who could grant this "eternal life." He was the one who was the author and finisher of our faith and who knew all things. The question was, "Master, what shall I do to inherit eternal life?" Jesus answered the lawyer's question with a question. "What is written in the law?"

> "Thou shall love the Lord thy God with all thy heart, and with all thy soul, and with all thy strength, and with all thy mind, and thy neighbor as thyself."
>
> That certain lawyer, still thinking that he knew more than Jesus, asked, "And who is my neighbor?"

Your neighbor is the Durham middle school boy in the back of the courtroom who could not stay awake at yet another CourtCares program. Our guest speaker, a retired college head football coach, not knowing the students' circumstances, made him stand up so that he could stay awake. After the program was over, I inquired with the counselor who accompanied the students to that session if she knew why the boy couldn't stay awake; what was that student's circumstances? The counselor responded that the young man was essentially homeless; his father was in prison, and his mother was on drugs. Those under the sound of my voice today, I ask you, Who is your neighbor? And what are you doing to help them?

I know that many of you here today would love to know what job you will have upon graduation and whether the bar exam will be a stumbling block to your future success. Yes, you have worked so hard during undergraduate and law school and so you might be thinking that ought to be enough to ensure success in life. But what is success? Is success passing the bar exam, getting the title "attorney at law" and beginning a successful law practice, or making a lot of money? Money can help you do some things, but "money ain't everything." The Bible says the love of money is the root of all evil. The word also says at Mark 8:36, "What shalt it profit a man to gain the whole world and lose his soul?"

Almost ten years ago, I sat down for lunch with esteemed 1958 North Carolina Central Law School graduate, the Honorable Sammie Chess Jr. I first met him early in my law career in the 1980s. What a great man! With the help of too many to mention, I recently finished writing a biography at Duke University Law School, *The Making and*

Measure of a Judge: The Biography of the Honorable Sammie Chess Jr. He is a retired civil rights lawyer and judge. On that day ten years ago, I don't recall what we were talking about, but Judge Chess said, What shall it profit a man to gain the whole world and lose his soul? He spoke to me about his career of service; that of representing many who could not afford his services in High Point. He lived a life of sacrifice and danger. I'm sure many hated him because he was willing to give his life for the cause. Judge Chess paraphrased another scripture from Ecclesiastes 11:1 when he said to me, "Bread cast in the water will return fourfold."

Judge Chess went on to tell me how he had hung his shingle in High Point in 1960, two years after graduating from Central's law school and spending two years in the army. In High Point he took up the cause of justice for black women who could not even give birth to babies in dignity in a High Point hospital. Yes, they would allow black women to have a child in the maternity ward, but as soon as the child was born, they would roll the mother and her baby out of the birthing room and station them out in the hallway, solely because of the color of their skin. Chess filed a lawsuit to end this discriminatory practice. Many were being locked up for demonstrating the segregated lunch counters, segregated movie theaters, and segregated public schools. High Point had even passed an ordinance that prohibited blacks and whites from being buried in the same cemetery. During the 1960s and '70s, Chess, former civil rights attorney Julius Chambers, and others fought these laws with all their mind and strength. They knew that those affected by these discriminatory laws were their neighbors. Don't you know that it takes courage to be a good lawyer? Also, you can't be a good lawyer if you are selfish or don't care about helping others, and you can't be a good lawyer unless you are committed to the cause of justice.

So, especially to the soon-to-be-graduates of this great law school, I pose the question, as Jesus was asked by that certain lawyer in our text: who is your neighbor and what is your responsibility toward them? And I ask those present nearing graduation, are you willing and ready to stand up for the cause? Are Michael Brown in Ferguson, Missouri; Freddie Gray in Baltimore; Walter Scott in South Carolina; Eric Garner in New York; the list goes on and on—are they your neighbors and shall their deaths be in vain? During my childhood during the Vietnam War, the army had a large poster out in front of the post office in my hometown that said, "We need a few good men." Today we need a few good lawyers, who, at least early in your careers, don't care about driving a Lexus or Mercedes or living in a big house.

I can tell you a little something about personal sacrifice. My wife accuses me of having worked for poke salad in my law practice. I'm sure she would say that early in my law practice there in my hometown of Madison, North Carolina—as the first and only black lawyer in that town's almost two hundred years of existence—and later in Pittsboro, North Carolina, she felt discouraged. Many times, I too felt discouraged! But I knew that I had been called to return to my hometown and later to Pittsboro where I was needed. I knew that there were many there who did not have a voice and needed me. So I returned home and I, stood up for justice even when many clients couldn't afford to pay me. But I'm a witness today; that bread cast in the water will return not only fourfold but tenfold. I'm standing before you today, not on my own power, but I'm standing on the shoulders of Sammie Chess Jr. and Julius Chambers, Annie Brown Kennedy, Henry Frye and so many others. I'm standing before you today on the power of prayer of many who are not known and will never be written about.

I need for some of you in the audience to stand up and stand out, not to tempt Jesus as the lawyer in our text today or to stand for any other nefarious purpose, but to stand up for the cause of justice and the cause of fairness and equality. "Equal justice under law" should guide you as attorney advocates as you begin your journeys.

May I tell you a little bit about how I got here today? My story is not unique. My late mother, Bettie Ester Webster, in mid-August of 1972, as I was leaving for Howard University, said, "Joe, if you put God first in your life, and work hard, somebody will see you trying, and somebody would help." I don't know how she knew that because she had told me once that she only had one good dress to wear to school and she would come home and wash it out and hang it up to dry. My mother quit school in the tenth grade and my father quit in the fourth grade. My mother was raised by her grandparents during the Great Depression, and I'm sure they did the best they could.

I've found that my mother knew what she was talking about, when she said that I needed to put God first in my life and work hard. I've found that someone has seen me trying and someone has helped me at each fork in the road of my life. I'd get to those forks in the road; I didn't know which way to go. But God would order my steps and keep me from making the wrong turn and going in the wrong direction. I went about my practicing law and living my life with a clear purpose of just doing good. Six years after graduating from law school, I received the prestigious NC Bar Association's Pro Bono Service Award in 1985 for representing many poor people who couldn't afford a lawyer. And four years later I became only the second African American on the NC Board of Law Examiners, where I later became chairman. In between and even after, I experienced many difficult days. I remember driving home one day, thinking about the fact that on that day I had less than a total of a hundred dollars in my business and personal accounts.

One day, down there in Pittsboro, North Carolina, I was feeling sorry for myself as money wasn't coming in as I thought it should; I had many times over more bills than I had money; I was stressed out seemingly worse than I had ever been. I didn't know how I could continue. Have you ever been completely stressed out? I was exhausted but couldn't afford a vacation. But I recalled the many times when I was a little boy, one of eight brothers and sisters, that I looked in my parents' bedroom at night and saw them down on their knees praying at bedtime. Sometimes you need to just get down on your knees as if to get closer to God in humble submission. So, I locked my office door and got down on my knees and began to pray. As I was praying, tears rolling down, God began to speak to me:

> What are you all stressed out about? Haven't I supplied all your needs? Have you and wife and your children ever had to miss a meal? Don't you remember when I woke you up a few years ago to hear and see your son experiencing a terrible seizure, didn't I answer your prayers and heal him? In September of 1996 when Hurricane Fran brought the trees down upon your house destroying two cars and doing great damage to your home, didn't I keep your young family safe without even one scratch? Didn't I answer your prayers? When your wife had surgery and the doctors couldn't figure out why her fever was still running high, and she couldn't come home because of that. Don't you remember how I led you to gather around her hospital bedside with your children and began to pray? Don't you remember that at that very moment, her fever lifted, and she soon went home from the hospital?

And I want you to know that God answered my prayers regarding my career. Frankly, all I ever wanted to do was to hang my shingle and be of service to humankind. Ten years ago, I became an administrative law judge for the state of North Carolina, some twenty-seven years after becoming a lawyer, really the first time that I had made a good salary, and then three and a half years ago, I became a US magistrate judge for the Middle District of North Carolina, the first African American to hold that position in the Middle District of North Carolina. So, this has been my journey over the last thirty-seven years. I want you to know that I'm still seeking Him and standing up for justice and trying to make a difference in our profession, our judiciary, and our community.

I'm here today to encourage you. I hope that you don't have to experience the hardship that I've had to experience, but bread cast in the water will return fourfold. The

Bible also says be not weary in well-doing, for in due season, in God's time (Kairos) we shall reap if we don't give up (GALATIANS 6:9). I sense that many of your generation are feeling that opportunities are lacking because of the job market. You are worrying about many things—the huge amount of school loans you have had to borrow. You are worrying about getting a job that will afford you the lifestyle to which you have been accustomed. But can you imagine what few opportunities were like thirty-five or forty years ago, or the generation before that. When I returned to North Carolina in the spring of 1979, I was told that there was only one black partner in a majority firm in the state. North Carolina Central Law School has well prepared you to hang your own shingle if you must. You are well prepared to stand up not for self-gain, but for the cause of justice and fairness, and the dignity and respect that those less fortunate believe are missing in their lives today.

The Good Samaritan in our text today could have passed by on the other side just like the Levite and the priest did when they saw but ignored the bruised and beaten-down brother lying by the wayside. They passed by on the other side. The Samaritan people and the Jewish people had no dealings with each other at the time of Christ, but the Good Samaritan stood up and declared, "I am my brother's keeper." Those demonstrations we have seen on television and making the headlines about the mostly unarmed black men who have been gunned down by police officers have been proclaiming that black lives matter. We learn through our text today that all lives matter. If you've been to law school, you have been given much and much is required of you!

I am a witness today that God can make a way out of no way. I suppose when I hung my shingle, I didn't have sense enough to know that I was engaging in a stressful endeavor, that it would be stressful on my marriage and stressful on my family. But we never missed a meal; we didn't run out of gas for lack of money. No one came to repossess our cars. Don't be discouraged, for if you stand up for the cause, God will be by your side.

Stand up, young men and women, those of you who will need to have courage as lawyers in the days ahead. Many of you need to go back to your hometowns, especially if strong advocates for justice are missing there. I know you want to live where the bright lights are located and where you can go to the theater and shop at Nordstrom's and Neiman Marcus. What about Filene's Basement? You may have decided that the Walmart brand doesn't suit your taste. I'm a witness that God will meet you wherever you end up. You may be feeling inadequate. God needs you to spend some time in those places where no one else wants to go. I heard a preacher say one time that "God has no hands except our hands, no feet except our feet." I suspect that most of the law students present here today would say that you went to law school so that you could be prepared to help somebody and make a difference in this world. Great things can happen if you go back to your hometowns or other more rural communities. Jesus went back to his hometown; the Bible says that "He came unto his own and his own received him not," but Jesus became the savior of the world. I went back to Madison and became a US magistrate judge. These members of the Oberlin Baptist Church Youth Choir and thousands of others are looking to us for leadership and direction. Don't let them down. With a law school education and law license, you will be able to practice law in all hundred counties in the state of North Carolina. You will be able to right many wrongs, solve many problems, and encourage many people not to give up. But if you give up, others will give up as well. So, I want to leave you today encouraged. The old members of my church used to say, "I believe I'll run on and see what the end is gonna be."

And then there is, even more importantly than standing up for the cause of justice, the need of us fair-weather Christians to stand up for the cause of Christ. In the words of the late Rev. Dr. Gardner Taylor, more of us Christians need to have a "stormproof" religion, one that is not based upon whether things are going well or badly for you. You need to be deeply anchored in the Lord. As gospel singer Douglas Miller sings with great conviction,

> Though the storms keep on raging in my life, … But if the storms don't cease and if the winds keep on blowing in my life, my soul has been anchored in the Lord!

As believers in Christ, we have so many examples to stand upon. So lean on them. The trial lawyer in me causes me to want to call up a few witnesses every now and again. I know my time has run, but Chelsea, can I call up a few witnesses that we can lean on? When you get weary—I've had many weary many times over the last years since I entered Howard Law. Stand up, lawyers, lean on Daniel in the lion's den. Stand up and lean on the Apostle Paul. God can and will change your heart on the road to Damascus and lead you to a higher calling. What about the woman with the issue of blood? God can give you faith; just ask Him. Just tell Him that if you just can touch the hem of his garment, you know you would be made whole. You may have an issue of blood or another illness. Stand up and lean on Jesus, the lily of the valley; the bright and morning star; lean on the "I am," He won't let you fall. Some of us are so hardheaded that we insist on falling anyway, but the God that I've gotten to know all these years—He will pick you up, dust you off, stand you on your feet and shine a light in the dark places and straighten out and order your steps and allow someone to see that you are trying.

I'm about to close, but years from now let it be said that certain law school graduates from North Carolina Central University, with courage and conviction, stood up and asked the right questions:

> Why is it that courtrooms are full of black and brown people, and why does the school-to-prison pipeline exist? Why is it that there is a disparity in health care for black and brown people? Why is it that there is better education taking place in the wealthy communities, far better than in the poor communities? Why are so many young black men being murdered, some by police officers and many others by our own people involved in gangs? Why aren't all these tragic circumstances being designated national crises deserving of the billions of dollars we are devoting to ISIS and the war on terror?

There is plenty of work but not enough workers. So, I implore you, new lawyers, to stand up and be counted. God will fight your battles! Don't be afraid, for if God be for you, then who can be against you? I'm a witness that God will help you to stand tall and keep you on your feet when you are too tired to continue standing. Stand up, Central graduates, for the cause of justice, and stand up for the cause of Christ. I hope I have convinced you today that these two pillars are the same cause! Keep on standing; keep on struggling; keep on persevering. Never, ever give up! You will receive a great reward in knowing that you have helped some bruised and battered brother or sister to a higher place. But there is an even greater reward, and that reward is eternal life for those who believe and put their faith and trust in Christ alone. So, I'm going to keep on standing, keep on sharing, and keep on loving. Be encouraged! Keep on standing up for the cause of justice and the cause of Christ. Those that have ears to hear let them hear!

A GIFT FROM AND BY GENE THREATS

God Is Light

1 JOHN 1:5–7

Barbee's Chapel Baptist Church, Durham, NC

JUNE 23, 2002

> This is the message we have heard from him and declare to you: God is light and in him there is no darkness at all. 1 JOHN 1:5

As a fellow Mason, I feel blessed that you have invited me here today to bring the St. John's Day Message. My sermon is about light, but first I want to talk about darkness.

It seems to the natural eye that we are living in times of darkness. Every day I turn on the television and see that during the darkness of the night, someone was murdered. A short while ago, it was an eighty-nine-year-old lady in Durham who was senselessly murdered by five young folk barely having reached their teenage and young adult years. In the Holy Lands, bombs go off seemingly every day, killing many innocent people, including babies being held by their mothers. Even within our churches we are hearing about pedophiles—priests who take advantage of our youth in a manner that you simply cannot comprehend. It alarms all of us that there is so much violence and loss of innocent life. Especially for we Masons, there is an alarm at the outer door and many who recognize the knock aren't answering the alarm. The alarm is a warning that our youth are overdosing on drugs and dying because of violence and darkness in their lives. It seems that there is a constant battle between light and darkness.

There are many symbols in Masonry, and today darkness is symbolic of sin. It seems sin in all forms is all around us. There is the seamy side of life. We Masons aren't immune from the seamy side of life. Galatians 5:17 (KJV) says, "For the flesh lusteth against the Spirit, and the Spirit against the flesh; and these are contrary the one to the other: so that ye cannot do the things that ye would." John 3:19 (KJV) says "that light is come into the world, and men loved darkness rather than light, because their deeds were evil."

As Masons, we learn that there are three great lights in Masonry: the Holy Bible, Square, and Compass. For most of you here, I don't have to remind you that the Holy Bible is the Masons' rule and guide of faith. The square is to square our actions. And the compass circumscribes and keeps us within due bounds with all mankind, and more especially with our Masonic brothers. You would think that especially Masons would remember these symbols, but darkness seems to be controlling our lives also. Many of us have some dark secrets we don't want anyone to know about. Many of us believe that what we do in the dark will never come to light. But God is light.

There is yet another side of darkness that all of us will encounter one day, and that is the seemingly dark side of sickness and death. As a sometimes chaplain at the hospital here in Chapel Hill, I recently have seen more sickness than I have time to talk about today. Darkness in the form of sickness sometimes comes into our lives suddenly and without warning, not based necessarily upon anything we have done. Whether you are young or old, one day you can be walking around a picture of good health, and before the end of the day, you can be in the intensive care unit of the hospital on life support. The older I get, the more that I recognize just how precious and how fragile life really is. The Book of James records that life is like a vapor; it appears for a little while and then it vanishes (4:14). So, Masons, hug your parents, your wife, your sons, and your daughters.

I recently saw a man in his thirties in the hospital with a hole in his stomach as big as a basketball. Another man and his son were in a plane crash, and they were burned over most of their bodies. They were there in the hospital with their bodies wrapped like mummies in thin cloths hanging on for dear life. Many there in the hospital have terminal cancer. Evidence of excruciating pain gripped the remaining portion of one man's face as tubes ran from his throat. So, for many, it seems that darkness overshadows and is larger than light.

Yes, to the human eye it seems that darkness sometimes overshadows light, but I am here today to let my brothers and sisters and all others know that God is light and in Him is no darkness at all. We learn first in Genesis 1:2–3, thanks be to God, "In the beginning when the earth was without form, and void and darkness was upon the face of the deep, and the spirit of God moved upon the face of the waters, and God said, let there be light; and there was light."

Generations later, Jesus was bringing light into the world while Mary was still carrying Him in her womb. Luke 1 records that Mary went to visit Elizabeth, who was also pregnant—with John the Baptist. Upon hearing Mary's voice, Elizabeth's unborn child leaped in his mother's womb, and Elizabeth was filled with the Holy Ghost. Light began to shine even before Christ was born (LUKE 1:41). Light then became flesh as light was born in a manger. "Shepherds were abiding in the fields, keeping watch over their flock by night" (LUKE 2:8), "and the glory of the Lord shone round about them, and they were so afraid" (v. 9). Wise men followed the star in the east that lit up the sky (MATTHEW 2:1, 9). And while Christ was yet walking in the flesh, he brought light into the lives of many.

As Masons, we have a secret password that we dare not disclose, but today, I bring you a word that I cannot keep secret, a word that has been locked up in my bones, and that word is that God is light and in him is no darkness at all.

As a lawyer, over the past twenty-three years I've gotten good at calling up witnesses. If you don't believe God is light, just call up blind Bartimaeus over there in Jericho; ask him about how his whole life was filled with darkness. Just ask him how Jesus came along and gave him his sight. Can I get another witness? Lazarus, Lazarus, just testify about how you had been dead for four days and how Christ raised you up from the dark tomb. Testify about how you heard Christ's voice say, "Loose him and let him go." And you saw light once again. Can I get another witness? Just ask the woman with the issue of blood, about how for twelve long years she had suffered and how long a cure for her condition had remained a mystery to her doctors and how they had remained in the dark. She had faith and touched the hem of His garment and was made whole. God is light.

I don't have to go back two thousand years to see that God is light. Less than two years ago, my little nephew was run over by a car on Weaver Dairy Road in Chapel Hill, North Carolina. His head and brain were swollen, and he was fighting for life. Things looked bleak there in the UNC Hospital. I went by to see little Eric Ramsey and his family. One morning while his father was there all alone, I heard the doctor tell him that they may have to put his son into an even deeper coma, that this might help the healing process. I saw the despair on my brother-in-law's face, so I went into the hospital room and sent up a silent prayer amid those taking care of little Eric. I then went out and saw the child's father and he told me later that he went and saw that the doctors were preparing to take some drastic action. So, he left the hospital room, and shortly thereafter the doctor came out and said, "I don't know what happened, but suddenly without explanation, your son has begun to get better." While the doctor didn't have an explanation, I believe that I know what happened. Fellow Masons, light came into the room and said, I am still in the healing business, and the effectual fervent prayers of the righteous still availeth much. God is still light.

A year later, over there in the hospital, I saw the results of the power of light once again. A woman from Gastonia had received a new liver a week earlier. She was in her room all alone sitting on her bed praising the Lord for she had been granted new light and new life. She told me the story about how she had been suffering for many years, about how she was near death. She had been waiting for a new liver to become available for a long time. When her organs began to fail and all hope was almost gone, one old woman of great faith in her community called her on the telephone. The old woman had been praying day and night. Fellow Masons, never stop praying. She told the patient one afternoon that she should not be dismayed, that before the end of the day she would get what she had been praying for. The patient went on to tell me that at eleven-thirty that evening she got a call telling her to come up to Chapel Hill because they had found her a new liver. Fellow Masons, after all these years, God is still light. So as I sat down on the bed beside her in the hospital room, she was crying and laughing for joy at the same time. God had shown her firsthand that He is still light.

A few weeks later, I saw the power of light once again. A woman suffering with cancer told me the story about while she was in the hospital, she had a dream. While she was experiencing the dream, she saw the feet of Jesus and heard His mighty voice. She told Jesus in the dream that she didn't like being where she was. In the dream, Jesus said to the woman, I'm going to take you back to your home. And suddenly she woke up and she saw a frightened nurse standing by her bedside. The nurse told the woman, "You had been in a coma, and I just disconnected your life support." The doctors didn't know what happened; they couldn't explain it, for they had declared her to be legally dead. But I believe I know what happened. Light came into the room and said, "I am the light of the world." Light came into the room and said, "I will decide when my faithful servant goes to her heavenly home." God is still light and him is no darkness at all.

And I don't have to even tell the story of anyone else. One day I was preaching at Goodwill Baptist Church and became very sick. I didn't know it, but my heart began to beat too fast. I didn't know that I'd had this condition from birth. Later that evening I became even sicker and so dizzy I couldn't walk. The rescue squad had to pick me up from my home. I could hardly breathe. I arrived at the hospital by ambulance, and they had to shock my heart twice to get it back in rhythm. I became well immediately. Light came into the hospital room and said, "Webster, you're in good hands." So I'm a witness today that God is still light.

I don't have to talk about others' experiences. One day I was walking in sin and in darkness, and God showed me the light. In some ways I am like John, not in the sense of being all that holy nor having a personal relationship with the physical Jesus. But I am a witness to that light. I have seen Him with my spiritual eye, and I have felt the power of the light with my own hands. And every now and again, light fills up my heart with joy—unspeakable joy. In Jeremiah 20:9, Jeremiah says it's like fire shut up in my bones. So, like John, I guess you could say that I am qualified to speak about that light—to testify about how he has kept me all these years and continues to bless me.

I must take a few moments to talk to the Masons here today. Some of us Masons are proud of the fact that we know the password, but we haven't studied God's word and so we are not walking in the light. We know the right words to get into the lodge; can come into the lodge on our due guard with our shiny shoes and new suits. We know how to make the right turns and face the three great lights. But still, some of us are not walking toward that one greatest light.

I stopped by Barbee's Chapel to let all Masons and visitors know that there is a light greater than the three great lights in Masonry. Amid all our imperfections, our warts, our impatience, our intolerance, our prejudices, and our many sins, Jesus is light. Amid many uncertainties after September 11, 2001, when we saw the airplanes crash into the Twin Towers buildings and that then fall to the ground in New York City, killing nearly 3,000 people, Jesus is still light.

I'm happy today that in my darkest hour, when my mind is overwhelmed with worry—for I too worry from time to time about paying my mortgage, about my children and other loved ones—I'm so glad that trouble don't last always, and that the God I serve is light in dark places. When the sun goes down and the storms of life come around, when the thunder and lightning come near, Jesus is light. He is a light unto my feet and a lamp unto my path (PSALM 119:105).

When things seem to be going wrong, Light reminds me, "Webster, I'll be with you," and "in addition to being light, before Abraham was, I am." This light is a precious cornerstone, the dew of Hermon (PSALM 133), a bright and morning star.

When Hurricane Fran came by my house in September 1996, when the trees began to fall on my family's house, when all the lights went out and as my children screamed out in fear, we could still see light amid darkness and tragedy. Jesus is still light. Light continues to remind all of us that our crooked edges are being made straight and the bumpy roads level. He's giving us insight and knowledge. Don't you remember, Masons, that light has brought us out of darkness into the marvelous light—that Jesus is the light of the world?

Today, I know that we Masons have three great lights, but I want you to know that there is one greater light. He is Jesus Christ. I must tell you today that Jesus is light, but He invites us to let our lights shine also. Romans 13:12 says, "The night is far spent; the day is at hand: let us therefore cast off the works of darkness and let us put on the armor of light."

There is an old African proverb about a man who worked for a railroad company. His job was to warn the train conductor of danger on the track ahead. One night he got a call from the station that the track crossing a deep ravine had been damaged. So when the train came by, he stood outside and waved the lantern and waved the lantern. But the train just kept going; it plunged into the deep ravine below and everyone on board was killed. The authorities, believing the man had done something wrong charged him with a crime and took him to court. The employee testified about how he had waved the lantern to warn the train conductor, but he didn't stop. The jury found him not guilty. But as the man left the court, he thought to himself, *But my lamp wasn't lit.*

Fellow Masons and friends, our lamps must be lit. Fellow Masons, yes, Jesus is light, but the Bible teaches us in Matthew 5:16 that we also must also let our lights shine. "Let your lights shine before men, that they may see your good works and glorify your Father which is in Heaven." Are your lamps lit today or are you walking in darkness? As an old song goes, do you have "oil in your vessels" and are "your lamps trimmed and burning?" Fellow Masons, Jesus is light. He is the light of the world.

Senior citizens, be not afraid; that light will continue to shine upon you also. When your arthritis flairs up, remember Jesus is light. He will provide when your steps began to get short, and your memory isn't what it ought to be. Jesus is light.

Young people, Jesus is light. You will be confronted with opportunities to do drugs and alcohol and many other temptations. Your future may look dark, and it may seem that you can't figure your way out. But Jesus is the light at the end of the tunnel. Just remember God is light.

Young and old, when you go into the hospital, and your fever won't go down, remember Jesus is light. When you get tired of being tired of being sick, remember that the light has His hands stretched out saying, "Come unto me all ye that labor and are heavy laden, and I will give you rest. Take my yoke upon me and learn of me for my yoke is easy and my burden is light." God is light.

I'm about to conclude. But, Church, while light walked upon the earth, He had some enemies who sought to put the light out, but they couldn't. The devil tried to starve the light in the wilderness for forty days and forty nights, but the light just kept on burning (MATTHEW 4:1–11). Many talked about the light and lied on Him, but the light just kept on shining. The rulers tried Him without a lawyer and tried to dim the light by getting Him to confess. Somebody said, but Jesus never said a mumbling word (MARK 15:2–3). But amid the so-called trial, the light just kept on shining. They thought they could put the light on low beam and thereby lessen His effectiveness, but the light shined even brighter. Amid cries of "Crucify him, crucify him," enemies of the light tried to put the light out by trying to make Him look like a common criminal. They hung Him on the cross between two thieves. While hanging on the cross, the light even saved a thief. Jesus said, "This day you shall be with me in paradise" (LUKE 23:43). And to those who crucified Him, the light said, "Father, forgive them for they know not what they do" (LUKE 23:34). The crowd ridiculed and made fun of him. If you are the Son of God, they said, come down from the cross and save yourself. But the light just kept on shining. While hanging on the cross, they pierced Him in the side until blood began to stream down, but the light just kept on shining.

The Bible says at the ninth hour, darkness covered the whole land (Mark 15:34). A songwriter said, "The sun refused to shine, that Jesus Christ was dying. Oh, my Lord, oh my Lord, what shall I do?" But the light just kept on shining. Even though we know that Christ died a physical death, the light just kept on shining. For on the third day, Jesus got up from the grave, proclaiming all power is in His hand. "O death, where is your sting, O grave, where is thy victory?" And today the light is still shining brightly, for Jesus is light and in him there is no darkness at all.

ART BY BILLY D. WEBSTER

Iron Sharpens Iron in the Community

1 PETER 4:10 NIV

Oberlin Baptist Church Men's Retreat, at the Home of Rev. John Leaston, Louisburg, NC

JUNE 25, 2016

> Each of you should use whatever gift you have received to serve others, as faithful stewards of God's grace in its various forms. 1 PETER 4:10, NIV

This has been an amazing week. This past Sunday was Father's Day. My almost twenty-seven-year-old son and his fiancé went to church with my wife and me and then came to our home for lunch. As soon as they arrived, my two daughters from Washington, DC, joined us via FaceTime. Soon after they joined us, I was presented with Father's Day cards and gifts. First, I opened my son's and then my middle child's, my daughter's, card and gift. Both gave me beautiful casual shirts. And then I opened my oldest daughter's card and then the card of my grand dog named Polo, a Teacup Yorkie. Polo's card said," Grandpa, I know we have some issues, but I love you. And then the card read, "and I am looking forward to having a big brother." I then opened my oldest daughter's gift, and it was a gift of life: a copy of a sonogram showing my first grandchild in the making. So, it was a great Father's Day for me. And then on Monday, I was interviewed on the live radio program on NPR called *The State of Things*, where I was able to tell part of my life's story. Within moments after I returned to my office, I began to get emails from persons who had listened in—emails of encouragement and praise. Within a day or two, I received an email from someone who no doubt was concerned about the publicity I was receiving. The person's message was a friendly reminder to me that my goal of helping the community was laudable, but everyone would not appreciate me bringing so much attention to myself.

I tell you these events of this past week, and especially the latter one about the responses I received, because I need to prepare you for your journey into the hedges and highways of community service. I'd like to be able to say that I, on my own, came up with this text found in 1 Peter, but it came about because I had shared with a confidant how I was feeling about the words I had received, cautioning me—a child of the Lord of Lords and King of Kings—that I needed to consider reducing my community involvement. For some reason, while I was telling the story, a few tears began to flow down, I suppose in part because of disappointment. As you venture out to use the gifts that God has uniquely given all of us present here, some of those who should understand you best—family, friends, and colleagues, and yes, even other soldiers of the cross—won't understand you. Despite your sacrifice and being led by the spirit, they will send you a message that you need to be careful in your public pronouncements. I have no reason to doubt the genuineness of such cautions I sometimes receive. I know that there are those who are hoping that I won't be successful as a federal judge. I know some comments are prompted by jealousy, a human condition that has been around since the beginning of humankind. But my Bible tells me in Psalm 23 that "even though I walk through the valley of the shadow of death, I will fear no evil for thou art with me." I'm not afraid of losing my job for speaking truth, even truth to power.

The very next morning, the first thing that I saw on my desk, all neatly typed out, were the words from 1 Peter 4:10: "As each has received a gift, use it to serve one another, as good stewards of God's varied grace." And then about the middle of the page were the words "Never stop being who God called you to be.... The world is a better place because of your courageous spirit." My law clerk, Pedra D. Lee, had left me this encouraging reminder. I'm happy today because God has surrounded me with great persons of faith, who have studied and have coveted deep in their hearts the word of God. When I get discouraged, one of God's chosen ones has the right words to lift my spirits. So, as you prepare to go out into the community, you will need to know God for yourself, and as the Bible teaches, you need to study the word to show yourself approved unto God, a workman who needed not be ashamed. You also need to have some Christian friends who also know the Lord, so they can help lift your spirits and, just as importantly, can help hold you accountable. Indeed, iron does sharpen iron.

I had received so many positive compliments about how well they felt I had done on the radio show that I almost had forgotten that not everybody was pleased that I had "spoken truth to power." I guess I had almost forgotten that Satan doesn't like success. Satan doesn't like the fact that God has elevated me to the federal bench. Satan doesn't like that I had the audience of the nation and, because of the internet, the audience of the whole world. As you proceed out into the community to try to make a difference, know that not everyone will love what you are saying or representing. Know that jealously or envy creeps in from sources that you would not expect.

Perhaps the person who sent me the message suggesting that I should reduce my public engagements because of my position as a federal judge didn't understand the power of God. Perhaps that person didn't understand that once called, as a true Christian, your steps are ordered by the Lord; that once you put your hands to the plow, there's no turning back. Yes, I know even some judges are of the opinion that we need to lower our profile since we sit in lofty places—so high that we don't call our workplace an office, but rather it is called a "chamber." Apparently, the word "office" isn't good enough to describe this workspace that is big enough for several judges. Many of us have paneled walls and hardwood floors; we have our own bathroom that no one else can use. My desk is big enough for two judges. It is pretentious enough that if you are not well grounded in the word, one could, as one of my white lawyer friends said to me one time describing some wealthy people we observed as we were standing out front of the Grove Park Inn in Asheville, say, "Joe, these folk here even hold their mouths differently." I need for you to hit me upside the head if you ever see me holding my mouth differently. I have tried to remain the same humble, unpretentious little boy who grew up on the farm in the community called Goodwill, outside Madison, North Carolina. I'm of the opinion that those of us sitting in positions of respect should speak more publicly and not less.

I know some judges who are so guarded and afraid of speaking the truth, they fear that someone might try to use their truthful words against them—afraid that his or her spoken truth will show bias, and a litigant might argue for their recusal in a particular case. Many judges are even afraid to admit that the court system is more favorable for persons who are wealthy. And the various rules of evidence and civil procedure don't favor the poor who cannot afford a lawyer to speak for them. Some judges are afraid to even argue for improvement in our system of justice which we are encouraged to do. I believe God has ordained me for this purpose, and so I have no fear.

Christians should expect to receive criticism, some positive and some negative, as we do work in the community. Not everyone's steps are ordered by the Lord. Not everyone knows the scripture that proclaims that if God be for you, then who can be against you? God is truth and justice. He is the architect of fairness and second chances and third chances. And yes, He is a shelter in a storm.

I'm here this morning to tell you that now is not the time to reduce your community involvement. Over there in 2 Timothy 1:6–7, Paul said to Timothy, "Therefore, I remind you to stir up the gift of God which is in you through the laying on of my hands. For God has not given us a spirit of fear, but of power and of love and of sound mind." So, men gathered here today, I want you to know that I have no intention of reducing my community involvement. I'm here this morning to tell you that now is not the time for that at all. My hope is that I can continue to feel the fire burning for years to come. I believe that God would want us to know that as long we frequently stir up the gift of God—whatever gift He has given each of us by going into the hedges and highways with the love of God—then we stay grounded ourselves and will be able to do some good. But if we go out into the community infrequently, and under our own power, not filled with the spirit that only God can give, then we will not bear fruit and our labor will be in vain. The gifts that God has given us need to be cultivated, not just occasionally, but 365 days a year. We are called upon to be in the community while forsaking ungodly living. Only then will we be able to hear the words, "Well done, good and faithful servants; thou hast been faithful over a few things, I will make you ruler over many things: enter thou into the joy of thy lord. (MATTHEW 2:23 KJV)

Many of us are fearful of going out into the community. But God has not given us the spirit of fear. God will take care of you. As the old song goes, "His eye is on the sparrow, and I know he watches me."[11]

The persons who believe that judges should only be heard in the courtroom making rulings and not speaking up for right and wrong in the community don't have the same understanding of a judge's obligations as I have. I am not persuaded to forsake the gifts that God has so graciously given me. While others may be concerned about me losing a highly coveted, good-paying job as a federal judge, I have no such fear. Perhaps what others don't understand is that the scriptures say that "the cattle on a thousand hills belongs to God." And so, I know that my judicial position belongs to God also. What evil people do against you and me, as we go into the community to serve—whether it is as a mentor at a school, being involved in a prison ministry, being a coach of a youth sports team, or whatever you are doing to better your community—just know that what evil people do to you can turn out to be for your good.

Three years ago, my staff and I started a program in my court called CourtCares not to bring attention to ourselves, but because I wanted Durham middle school students to know that we care about them. I felt that those who come before judges especially in criminal court don't think judges and others in the system of justice care about them. I wanted the middle school students who visited to participate in the CourtCares program to be reminded to stay on the right side of the law, to stay away from alcohol and drugs, to refrain from gun and other violence, to stay out of gangs and refrain from bullying, to otherwise be respectful of their fellow students and teachers, and to learn about our Constitution.

This is my sermon today. As my law clerk reminded me, "you should never stop being who God called you to be." As the text says, "Serve one another." If you do so, our communities will become better places. Iron does sharpen iron in the community.

11 Gospel song written in 1905, lyricist Civilla D. Martin and composer Charles H. Gabriel.

Giving All

MARK 12:41–44

Oberlin Baptist Church, 131st Homecoming Service, Raleigh, NC

OCTOBER 16, 2011

> Jesus sat down opposite the place where the offerings were put and watched the crowd putting their money into the temple treasury. Many rich people threw in large amounts. But a poor widow came and put in two very small copper coins, worth only a few cents. Calling his disciples to him, Jesus said, "Truly I tell you; this poor widow has put more into the treasury than all the others. They all gave out of their wealth, but she, out her poverty, put in everything—all she had to live on." MARK 12:41, NIV

From these four verses, I want to speak on the subject "Giving All." Join me in a word of prayer....

At the outset I want to say that I am thankful to God for waking me up this morning, clothed in my right mind, with a determination to live so that God can use me. The Bible says that if you humble yourself before the Lord, He will lift you up. I am thankful today that God has lifted me up higher than I ever thought I could be lifted.

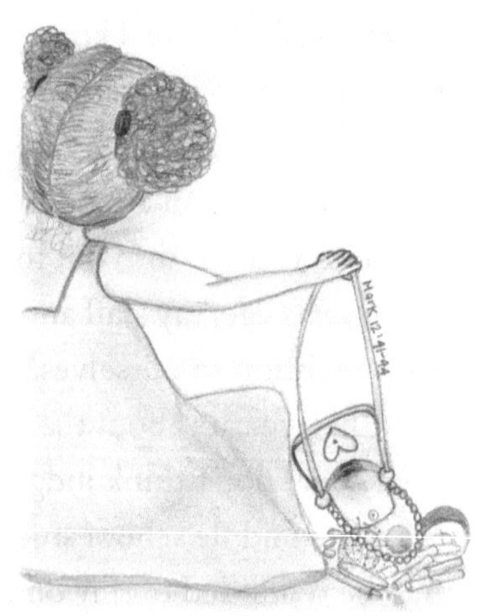

ILLUSTRATION BY SHAILYN RAMSEY

I feel extremely blessed to have been afforded this great opportunity to share with you on the occasion of the 131st Homecoming Service of the historic Oberlin Baptist Church. Being a student of history, I feel even more privileged to have been asked by your pastor to be your speaker for this occasion. I hardly feel up to the task. For one thing, this pulpit is still vibrating from the three-day revival where Rev. Dr. H. Beecher Hicks Jr. brought down the house. I have heard some great preaching in my life, and what I heard on Monday and Tuesday nights almost two weeks has me still rejoicing about what God did here at Oberlin during revival.

I hardly feel worthy of having this opportunity to be with you as your guest speaker. It is the great ancestors of Oberlin Village and elsewhere in America who sacrificed so much—those who endured the cruel, inhumane institution of slavery and the Reconstruction and Jim Crow eras of our history whose shoulders I stand on today. Their voices are still crying out, that God can keep you if you work together and trust in God. So I honor those brave men and women who had the courage to build a church and to build a community less than a decade and a half after slavery officially ended in America, thirteen years after the founding of the Ku Klux Klan and the rise of lynching of African Americans in the South. Twenty years after the founding of Oberlin Baptist Church, North Carolina passed legislation establishing a literacy test that was used to disenfranchise or keep black people from being able to vote. So, on this Homecoming Day at Oberlin, we honor the men and women of the Oberlin community who overcame tremendous obstacles.

Before taking my text, I must also say that this thing called preaching is not an easy task. Maybe that's what's behind the fair number of Christians who have asked me over the last thirteen years, "How is possible for you to be a lawyer, judge, and preacher at the same time?" It seems I recall one man asking me whether isn't being a preacher and a lawyer at the same time an oxymoron. Without hesitation, my answer to those people who ask me such questions is that apparently you don't know the power of God! But preaching is a challenge. For one thing, I find it difficult to get Joe Webster out of the way so that God can do His thing. Yes, even after many sermons since July 1998 when I did my initial sermon at Goodwill Baptist Church in Madison, North Carolina, I am still seeking personal perfection in the pulpit. Even though I know better, I'm still worrying about crossing every "*t*" and dotting every "*i*". I've learned that this thing called preaching requires you to abandon success in the sense that the world looks at it. The late Rev. Dr. William Augustus Jones of Brooklyn, New York, taking his text from the scripture 1 Corinthians 4:1–2, offered a sermon titled "Stewards of the Mysteries":

> "We are the stewards of God's mysteries." He preached about the danger of striving for success as a preacher and as a pastor. Dr. Jones said that "the only way out of this sickening syndrome is to keep one's feet on the ground—to enter daily the inner sanction of self-security where we stand naked before the Holy Presence and let God check us out." Dr. Jones concluded by saying that "when we get quiet long enough to listen to God, He says in unmistakable terms, 'I didn't tell you to be successful, I told you to be faithful—Be thou faithful unto death.'"[12]

12 Rhinold Ponder and Michele Tuck-Ponder, eds., *The Wisdom of the Word Faith: Great African American Sermons* (New York: Crown, 1996), 75–76.

Oberlin, I needed this time to tell you that sometimes I must remind myself what is important as I stand before a congregation. As I speak from the pulpit, sometimes, in the words of the title to the gospel hit song, "Encourage Yourself,"[13] I need to encourage myself, but more importantly I need be encouraged by your prayers and amens to truth. I ask for your prayers that, despite what I have written down on paper today, the Spirit of the Lord would reveal to me what God would have me to say on your 131st Homecoming Anniversary service.

On Tuesday night, October 4, 2011, I sat in the pews on the right side of this congregation beside my judicial colleague Julian Mann and his wife, Diane, who happen to be members of a nearby church, Holy Trinity Lutheran. Having heard Rev. H. Beecher Hicks Jr. on the Monday night revival service here at Oberlin, I had invited Julian to accompany me to Tuesday night's service. Immediately to the other side of me in the pew was a young girl probably no more than eight years old. She sat with an older sister and three other siblings along with a man and woman whom I took to be their parents. When the offering plate was being passed around, it became our turn to place our offering into the plate. When the plate was passed to the little girl, she hurriedly reached into her purse to give her offering. She began getting out one penny after the other. And then I observed her turn her purse upside down and shake the little purse, making sure that she had given all she had.

I was so moved by what I observed. I was so encouraged, not only by that one act of the little girl giving all she had, but as the smallest of the children returned from the restroom, he accidentally bumped into one of my guests, and the little boy turned to say, "Excuse me." I hesitate to tell you what my response was, but I was moved to do something intended to encourage all five children. I thought about what I might do during service and near the end of the service. I passed a note to the oldest child inquiring about their mother's name. Observing what I had in my hand, she wrote the mother's name on the piece of paper and beside her name she wrote, "Thank you." Church notwithstanding what we see on the six o'clock news every day, many families are still teaching their children right from wrong and the need to be respectful of others. I'm convinced that there are many more respectful young folks in our community than those who are running around out of control. We need to be about encouraging our youth every day.

So, the little child whose name regrettably I don't know brings me to this message today found in the twelfth chapter of Mark, and it can also be found in twenty-first chapter of Luke. In our scripture today, we have Jesus along with his disciples in the temple.

13 Song written by Donald Lawrence and performed by Donald Lawrence and the Tri-City Singers.

According to Mark 12:41, Jesus sat down opposite—maybe meaning across the room—from where the offerings were being placed into the temple treasury. He watched as many rich people threw in large amounts of money. But Jesus also observed a poor widow put in two small copper coins, worth only a fraction of a penny. I find it a bit ironic that the rich threw in their offerings while the poor widow put hers in. I wonder whether the wealthy considered this act of benevolence to be just one of the commandments or Jewish laws, customs, or rituals that they had to follow. In preparing for this sermon, I learned that Jews have 613 commandments they must follow (248 commandments of what to do and 365 commandments of what not to do). Included among these commandments or Mitzvot are three relevant to the text today: to separate the tithe for the poor, to give charity, and not to withhold charity from the poor. These three are found in the fourteenth and fifteenth chapters of Deuteronomy. For the wealthy there in the temple, money probably was no big deal. I'm glad to see the wealthy in the temple, though, because they needed to be there. Rich folk don't always see the need to go to church. In contrast, the poor widow put her offering in guided by a humble and giving heart. Her giving seems to have been more heartfelt. I have met in my life a couple of people that it was said of them, they had the first dollar they ever earned. Lord, forever spare me from such foolish obsession with money!

Oberlin, this event found in our text became a teachable moment for Christ and an educational opportunity for his disciples. So Jesus called them to himself. I can hear Jesus with my spiritual ear as he said, "I tell you the truth, this poor widow has put more in the treasury than all the others. The wealthy gave out of their wealth, but the poor widow gave out of poverty, put in everything—all she had to live on." If I might take some liberty with this scripture, depending on how long her husband had been dead, she could have still been bereaving her husband's death. We don't know from the scripture, but she might have even been suffering from depression. She may even have been wrestling with loneliness and depression. When my father died in 2003, my mother's health began a long decline; she had waited upon my father and their eight children for almost the last fifty-seven years of her life, and I am sure she missed him greatly. My mother seemed depressed to the family, and we believe my father's death hastened the onset of Alzheimer's disease. But the scripture just refers to the woman in the text as a poor widow. But she was in line with those who had much, and she had so little. She even gave what she would live on. My, my, what faith she had!

I'm sure some will say, "Well, that was foolish of the poor woman to give all she had." Some will say, why would anyone try to help someone else if it would leave you destitute and perhaps a ward of the state yourself? Church, maybe, just maybe, she had heard Jesus speak. "Then Jesus said to his disciples, 'Therefore, I tell you, do not worry about your life, what you will eat, about your body, what you will wear. Life is more than food, and the body more than clothes. Consider the ravens; they do not sow or reap; they have no storeroom or barn; yet God fees them. And how much more valuable you are than the birds.... Consider how the lilies grow. They do not labor or spin; yet I tell you, not even Solomon in all his splendor was dressed like one of these' (LUKE 12:22–27).

Maybe just maybe she had heard Jesus speak, "Give and it will be given to you. A good measure pressed down, shaken together, and running over, will be poured into your life. For with the measure you use, it will be measured to you" (LUKE 6:38). Maybe the poor widow had heard Jesus speak—that it is more blessed to give than to receive (ACTS 20:35).

Many of us at revival gave a little pinch of the extra that we had, while the little girl sitting beside me in the pew gave all she had. I will forever remember the picture indelibly etched in my mind of her shaking the pocketbook to dislodge the last penny that may have been stuck in the corner.

But Jesus observed from the opposite side saw the rich put in large amounts of money into the collection for the poor and the poor widow put in two pieces of copper, which Jesus teaches had more value than all the others. I stopped by Oberlin to remind you that those who built that first church here on this location in 1880 were not long out of slavery. But God has proven repeatedly that He can take a little and make much out of it if it is given by a cheerful giver. The Lord loves a cheerful giver.

Church, pray with me, I'm talking about giving all. I know that many may be here today who aren't making it from paycheck to paycheck or one Social Security check to another. Those who built this church didn't have Social Security, didn't have a pension, didn't have Medicare or Medicaid; some made ten cents an hour, yet the God we serve provided all that they needed. My mother was raised by her grandparents. Her grandfather was born in 1863 and her grandmother, 1888. I used to listen in amazement when my mother told me when she was a little girl that she found a penny and her grandfather saw her with it, and he took it from her and said, "Girl, you don't need that money!" That lets me know there was a time in our history when a penny was worth something.

Church, I'm here today to remind you that we all need to do better, that this is a critical time in the lives of many across the country and the world. We need to give our all. Giving all is not just about giving money. I've told my three children many times that "money ain't everything." God calls upon us to give the best of our service. He calls upon us to help one another. I heard an old preacher say one time that "God has no hands without our hands, no feet without our feet."

Church, we can't be like the poor widow operating under our own power. We are going to need the Lord to give us attributes that many of us weren't born with. Giving all requires courage. Lord, grant us courage. Giving all requires commitment. Are you committed, Church? Giving all requires perseverance; endure to the end, Church. The race isn't given to the swift, neither to the strong, but to the one who endures to the end. What if the former Oberlin slaves had given up? What if they had depended on Congress or the president? Sometimes I'm sure they gave out, but there's a difference between giving up and giving out. Giving all requires faithfulness—not only our faithfulness, but God's faithfulness as well, for Great is thy faithfulness. It is new every morning. Great is thy faithfulness. Giving all requires patience. I'm short on patience at times, so I must ask God for patience. I'm glad God is not through with me yet. Giving all requires us to even forgive our enemies; that's a hard thing to do, but what if the former slaves of the Oberlin community and throughout the South had not forgiven their slave masters? Giving all requires that you give without the expectation you will receive something in return.

Giving all requires us to give of ourselves. It requires sacrifice. It sometimes requires us to be in strange places, worshiping in places where we'd rather not be—places where we are not comfortable, spending time with those who we think we are not like, eating with those who we don't normally eat with. I heard a sermon at the Chapel Hill Bible Church in Chapel Hill, North Carolina, where the guest preacher, Rev. Emmanuel Katongole from Uganda, said,

> Christian life is about learning to eat and drink together in my father's house. In my father's house there are many rooms, he said. And then the preacher said, unless we eat and drink with the poor, you won't be able to hear them chew their food and you won't be able to feel their pain and hear their cries.

Reverend Katongole also said that there is an African proverb which says that if you want to walk fast, walk alone, but if you want to walk far, walk with others.

To tell you the truth, as I reached out to friends to invite them to this special occasion, I was made to realize that here in the Triangle I do not have that many friends who are like the poor widow in today's scripture. Therefore, I could not invite those to church today who need to be blessed by a word of encouragement and who need a warm meal afterward. The Bible teaches us that we should invite the poor to our luncheons and dinners rather than our friends and relatives who will later repay us by inviting us to their receptions. Few among us invite those we are commanded to invite: the poor, the crippled, the lame, the blind. Only by inviting them will be blessed (Luke 14:12–14). Giving all includes giving of ourselves, and so, Church, we are not honoring the founders of this church by forgetting those who are less fortunate. For those of us here who are on way up the ladder of success, we must reach back and take the hand of others and help them up the ladder also.

Today I am also preaching to myself, and in every sermon, I try to encourage our youth. I know you feel like giving up at times. Society tries to convince you that you need to be selfish to get ahead, that you need ten pair of Nikes and all the other expensive clothing that makes you look "fresh," a word I've heard my son use. The youth of today feel like you need the latest iPod, iPad, and iPhone and any other hi-tech equipment that comes out. I hear the iPhone 4S came out this week and folk were lined up to buy it. I bought a newer phone not many months ago. The man at the store said to me, do you want to purchase a "smart phone"? I didn't know what he was talking about, and I responded, no, this one is smart enough. Do you have anything like my old phone?" A little later I bought one of those little side things to hold your phone in, one of the knock-off brands from Walmart or the Dollar Store that you put your phone in and hook it to your belt. My son came that weekend and saw me wearing the side holder, checked it out, and said, "Daddy's got an upgrade."

Young folk, based upon my own personal experience, giving all will make you much happier than buying a new iPhone. I must confess that giving all has been difficult for me. What happened to me is the same thing that happened to many of my generation. I got all messed up when I got into this sickening madness of buying new cars when a used one would have made more sense. And I bought big houses so I could live comfortably, but once I get through servicing the debt, there is little left over. I too am guilty of investing in what Dr. Gardner Taylor calls "things that perish." I encourage the young among us here to learn from we older ones that we need to give all, give all, but not to give all to the creditors. I read recently somewhere that we should "live simply so that others may simply live." I thought of this when Hurricane Irene devastated many along the East Coast recently. My heart said give, give all, but reality set in as I concluded that I had spent it already on bills and hardly had anything to give, so that others could simply live. But I also realize that I, like many of you, lack the kind of faith that is the size of a grain of mustard seed. Lord, increase our faith so that we can give all in order that others may simply live.

We can learn so much from the poor widow and the young child who recently graced Oberlin at revival. Neither of them sought fame but, in their own way, gave all. Today, in this time of great uncertainty, when the greatest minds are trying to figure out how to create jobs here at home and around the world, when many have not had a decent job in two or more years, when our college and professional school graduates get a degree and sometimes find that their education is not living up to its promise, the answer is to give all. Like my wife and I, you too probably can't get one more stitch of clothing in your closets. Your shoes are gathering dust and mold, causing you to have allergies. You can first begin to give that away. Then give of your treasure. It all belongs to God anyway. Some people in our society have so much money that if they lived a thousand years they wouldn't be able to spend it all. Just as importantly, give of your service, not just any service, but as the song goes, "the best of your service."

Oberlin, God is requiring more of us. Give all, Church. I continue to come back to the text. The comparable text in Luke says Jesus looked up at those giving into the treasury. I don't know whether this means he had been in prayer or just what. But Jesus says give all. You can't give all unless you first have faith—faith that God will supply your needs. Be encouraged, Church; look toward the hills from which cometh your help.

I'm about to conclude this message, but Dr. Gardner Taylor, who graced this church with his appearance at the Tuesday night revival service, has had such an influence on my preaching. He has preached for seventy years. I have no doubt that many preachers will be quoting him for the next five hundred years. He has said that no matter where you start—in other words, the preacher might begin his or her text at Genesis or Romans or Mark or wherever he chooses, but the preacher needs to make their way to Golgotha as soon as he can. We need to do this, Church, because that is where Christ shed His redemptive blood for you and for me. Golgotha is where they hung him high; crucifixion is a terrible and painful death. Church, when you think about giving all, you need to make your way to Golgotha as soon as you can, because that is where the blind receive their sight; that is where the lame walk again. We used to sing when I was growing up, "There's power in the blood, wonder working power, in the blood of the lamb." We all need to make our way to Golgotha as quickly as we can, because we can find courage there; we can find faith to give all; we can find the power to forgive and the grace to be forgiven at the cross. The old soldiers at Oberlin had it figured out and I agree with them. They sang, "Down at the cross where I first saw the light and the burden of my heart rolled away." Oberlin, you can find peace at Golgotha. We need to run to Golgotha, for that is where we can receive our pardon. The pardon says you are forgiven, no matter what you have done. If you'll go to Golgotha, you can receive your manumission papers; a freedom that nobody can take away. It was at Golgotha, where some forty-five to fifty years ago, God first found me, and He started running after me. I ran as fast I could, but I found that I could not outrun God. I need to make my way to Golgotha so that I can give all, so I can have the blind faith of the poor widow and the young girl here at Oberlin who emptied her pocketbook, giving all she had.

Give all, Church; give of your treasure; give of your time; give of yourselves. If you do so, you'll keep making progress. Church, the words of an old gospel song written by Lucie Eddie Campbell sum up my sermon today.

> If when you give the best of your service,
> Telling the world that the Savior has come,
> Be not dismayed when men don't believe.
> He'll understand and say, "Well done."
>
> When I come to the end of my journey,
> weary of life and the battle is won,
> Carrying the staff and the cross of redemption,
> He'll understand and say, "Well done."
>
> Misunderstood, the savior of sinners,
> hung on the cross he was God's only son.
> Oh, hear Him call to His father in heaven,
> Let not my will but Thine be done.
>
> If, when you've tried and failed in your trying,
> hands sore and scarred from the work you've begun.
> Take up your cross and come quickly to Jesus,
> He'll understand and say, "Well done."

Give all, Church. Give all. Give all.

Love Is the Answer

1 CORINTHIANS 13:1–13

Hayes Memorial Holy Church, on the Occasion of Family and Friends Day, Greensboro, NC

OCTOBER 30, 2005

> And now these three remain, faith, hope, and love. But the greatest of these is love. 1 CORINTHIANS 13:13, NIV

It seems that many people today are talking about love, but many are just talking and not living a life of love. In 1965 Hal David wrote the lyrics and Burt Bacharach composed the music to, "What the world needs now is love sweet love, that's the only thing that there's just too little of. What the world needs now is love sweet love." Then there was "Love Train," written by Kenny Gamble and Leon Huff and made popular by the O'Jays in the early '70s, and well-known love ballad singer Lionel Ritchie wrote a hit song, "Endless Love." He said in that song, "It's only you in my life. You're every breath that I breathe, every step that I take. You will always be my endless love." Many others, gospel, contemporary, and non-spiritual singers, are proclaiming the benefits of love. For our youth, too often, the rappers of today are equating love with only sexuality, leaving our youth to believe that going to bed with anybody and everybody defines what love is for them.

ART BY BILLY D. WEBSTER

I want to place today's text in proper context. In chapter 12 of 1 Corinthians, Paul had been teaching about the many spiritual gifts within the church body. Some have wisdom, some have the gift of healing, and some can work miracles; some even have the gift of prophecy, some can speak in tongues. And then in chapter 13, Paul is dealing with the problem of lovelessness in the Corinthian church. The Corinthian church, like many of our churches today, struggled with the abuse of spiritual gifts, divisions within the church, envy of other people's gifts, and the same kind of problems that face our churches today. In today's scripture, Paul's message is loud and clear: no matter how beautiful you can sing, you may even sprout up wings as angels, and sing like you have been singing with the angels in the heavenly choir, but if don't have love, it won't do you any good.

You might even be a prophet, understand all mysteries and have all knowledge, and even have enough faith to move mountains, but if you don't have love in your heart, then you are nothing. Verse 3 says that even if you give all your goods and worldly possessions to the poor and even give up your body to be burned—that is, you can have the kind of faith that would cause you to make a public display by sacrificing your body by being burned to demonstrate your faith—yet you don't have love, then it profits you nothing.

God is not interested in big public displays to show the world how great a Christian you are. I recall being invited to a choir anniversary in Sanford several years ago. The anniversary took place in the civic center or auditorium there. In anticipation of the anniversary choir making their entrance, the congregation got quiet and then the choir marched in swaying all in unison, all dressed up in their coordinated suits and dresses. When they got to the stage, they kept on marching around in a circle and went out the way they came and moments later started marching in again wearing their expensive-looking robes. I wasn't too impressed, and now I know that if love wasn't present, then all of that profited them nothing.

What is this love I'm speaking about today? First, you must love God. The Bible states in Deuteronomy 6:5 that we are commanded to "love the Lord thy God with all our heart and with all our soul and with all our strength, and all our mind." So, all love begins with loving God. To love Him as we are commanded, then, we must be fully committed to Him. How many of us love God only part of the time—when He blesses us with a good job, a new car, and a big home? Then we walk around proclaiming God is good, but when trouble comes, when sickness comes, Lord have mercy!

What else do we know about love? Today's scripture says in verse 4 says that love is not puffed up. I hate to hear folk walking around bragging about what they have given in church or to one cause or another. Many give to be recognized, but if love is missing you might as well have kept your money. Verse 4 also says that love suffereth long. Long-suffering is a good quality to have. Church, somehow some church leaders have been teaching a prosperity ministry, that suffering isn't a part of this journey through here. You're going to need to suffer in this world we live in. To make it through this messed-up world, you need to be longsuffering. You're going to need to be longsuffering in order to love your neighbors, your enemies, and those who despitefully use you. Folk will use you today if they can, but God is calling upon each of us to be used. It is not easy to love everyone, sometimes even those like your children or spouse whom we are called upon to love. Love hurts: we get hurt sometimes by following God's commandment to love. We must be tolerant of others so that we can deal properly with others' shortcomings. We must be patient with others. Some of you, young and old, have fallen in love and thought that he or she was the one, only to find out that he or she was not faithful and not committed to you. Love hurts.

I've learned over the years that in addition to loving God, you must love yourself. Young folk here today, I want you to know that if you don't care about yourself, then you will use drugs and alcohol and abuse your own bodies. So love yourself. God only gives you one body, so love yourself, take care of yourself, and young folk, stay away from drugs and alcohol. Death and destruction will follow if you stay out there too long.

After you love yourself, then you must love those who are in need: the poor, the uneducated, and the infirm. We must have compassion and be sensitive to those who have less than we do. For the most part, we are a nation of great wealth. Some of us have three or four cars in our yards. Some of us are finding that we can't drive them about now because of the high gas prices. Just down the street from my family in Chapel Hill are five-thousand and six-thousand-square-foot houses, which are completely separated from those we are called upon to love: the poor and other marginalized people in our society.

Church, we must begin to walk with others like we used to in the earlier days. In the earlier days, I remember as a child, out in the country where we lived on the farm, people would come by sometimes at suppertime, and my parents would say, "Come on in and sit down and have some supper. We have plenty, such as it is." It may have been pinto beans, corn bread, and buttermilk, but my parents always offered what we had to others, even if they were alcoholics who might have stopped by. We must begin to walk with others once again, no matter who they are.

I must pause here for a minute to tell you that recently America showed as a government that it is lacking in the kind of love that I'm talking about today, when thousands were allowed to wallow in filth and the dirty floodwaters of New Orleans for days in the aftermath of Hurricane Katrina, before our government could figure out what to do to help them. It is no doubt that the black and brown faces and their poverty contributed to the government officials' inaction. I am ashamed of their slow response. I'm ashamed that many in the nursing homes couldn't get out in time because of a slow and inadequate response. Many referred to our people as "refugees." I looked up the word "refugee," and the dictionary defines the word as a person who flees from his home or country to seek refuge elsewhere, as in a time of war, persecution. The last time I checked, black and poor American citizens were not fleeing from a foreign country seeking refuge in our own country. Well, at least they got a small portion of it right: the dictionary does define a refugee as a "person." At least we have come a little distance in this country.

Several years ago, I was telling someone that I tried to trace my ancestry back using the official documents in a state government office and was not able to get anywhere with my research. The woman said, "You were looking in the wrong place." She said, "You should have looked under the livestock records. That's where they kept the records of slaves, in the livestock records." So, as I saw what was taking place especially in New Orleans when they said they couldn't get through to help them, and when I saw news reporters there from the beginning bringing live pictures, I knew then that while we've made progress in this country, we as a race are still viewed by some as livestock and are not to be loved like God is calling upon all of us to do today.

I am reminded of what Jesus said in his own words, in Matthew, chapter 25.

> On the last day, Jesus will say to those on His right hand, "Come enter the Kingdom. For I was hungry and you gave me food, I was thirsty and you gave me drink, I was sick and you visited me." Then Jesus will turn to those on his left and say, "Depart from me because I was hungry and you did not feed me, I was thirsty and you did not give me to drink, I was sick and you did not visit me." Then they will ask Him, "When did we see You hungry, or thirsty or sick and did not come to Your help?" And Jesus will answer them, "Whatever you neglected to do unto one of the least of these, you neglected to do unto me!"

America still has not fully come to grips with its history of slavery and racism. America as a country has on its money "In God We Trust," but this country still has not learned what it means to love. So we must love those who are different, those who can't speak for themselves, the poor, the aged, and the disabled.

You recall the response of the Good Samaritan in Luke 10:25 who helped the beaten and abused man lying on the side of the road, while the priest and Levite looked upon and then passed by the man lying there. The Good Samaritan didn't ask, "I wonder if he is a Jew," as you know the Jews didn't have any dealings with the Samaritans. They were not reconciled with one another. I'll speak more about reconciliation in a moment. But you can be a priest, the pope, a lawyer, judge, doctor, or even have several PhDs, but if you don't have love, you are nothing.

What else does today's scripture say about love? Verse 5 says that "love does not behave itself unseemly, seeketh not her own, is not easily provoked, thinketh no evil. We must behave with good will toward all men."

Church, love causes you to forget about the things of old that happened to you; it causes you to forgive those who have trespassed against you. The Lord's Prayer in

Matthew 6:12 says, "Forgive us our debts as we forgive our debtors." And verse 14 says, "For if we forgive men their trespasses, your heavenly father will forgive you." So, we are compelled to forgive no matter what someone did to us or said about us, no matter how bad, in order to have the kind of love Paul is speaking about in today's text. Love requires us to forget that it even happened. What if God hadn't forgotten about what you did when you were in the world, not thinking about anybody but yourself? What if he had said, "Joe, do you remember what you did when you thought no one was looking and listening? Do you remember how you treated that fellow back in 1995?"

So, love not only requires us to forgive those who have trespassed against us but also requires us to forget. We must be like God and totally forget. I've heard some say, "I will forgive, but I won't forget!" I stopped by Hayes Memorial today to tell you that you have not forgiven unless you have also forgotten.

Church, the love I'm speaking about today requires us to forgive and forget. Love means forgiving and forgetting. Let go of it, forget about the mean things that church members said to you here when you were undergoing difficult times. Forget about what others said in the heat of passion—those angry words that seem to do so much harm. Reconcile or make peace with your brother or sister. None of us has all the answers. None of us are right all the time. All of us have sinned and fall short of the glory of God. Remember that Christ loved us so much that he voluntarily went to the cross; he said in essence, "Here am I. If you need somebody to hang on the cross so that the members of Hayes Memorial can know what it means to love your enemies, I will go to the cross. If you need somebody to be crucified so that members of this church can know what it means to forgive those that you might have said hateful words to over the years, then I will go to the cross."

Church, it's time—past time—to reconcile with our white brothers and sisters. Sometimes I wonder what God thinks of the fact that, for the most part, black folk have their own churches and white folk have theirs. It is time for us to reconcile with one another. We all prejudge one another. Some whites are not the only ones who are prejudiced. Many of us have not forgotten how an entire race was treated during slavery and for more than one hundred years after slavery ended. Rosa Parks is lying in state this very day in the Capitol in Washington, DC. If she were able to speak, she would say, "Yes, I still remember how me and my entire race were humiliated, insulted, and relegated to the lowest-paying jobs, jobs white folk wouldn't do." But Rosa Parks, because she had love in her heart, would also say that we must love those who despitefully use us. She is crying out from her casket that love is the answer! So blacks and whites and Indians and Jews and Hindus and Muslims must begin to love one another unconditionally. I went with a group to London, England, in March 2003 to minister to and learn from Muslims, Sikhs, and Hindus. I learned all over again that we as Americans don't know everything, that to reconcile with our brothers and sisters around the world we must first love them unconditionally.

I must say a word or two here about loving and making peace with your own family members. It is hard to love those who you believe should know better—who do the awful things that we sometimes do that often hurt so much. God would have us to try harder to keep our marriages together and our children together. There needs to be reconciliation among our families. But love is the answer. Love is the answer. If there ever was a time that families need to love another, the time is now. Love is the answer.

Verse 8 in today's scripture says love never fails; you can count on love, but gifts of prophecy shall fail; speaking in tongues is all right, but it too shall cease; I heard on the radio that Albert Einstein was so smart, so brilliant, that after he died his brain was kept and preserved. But his knowledge vanished. And then in verse 13 the scripture says, "And now abideth faith, hope, love, these three, but the greatest of these is love." I often struggle with ups and downs in my own life. I often say if I just had a little more faith, that's all I need. But after studying today's scripture, now I know that what I really need is a little more love.

Church, the scripture says that God is love. Church love is the answer. The scripture says that love cures a multitude of sins. Whatever the problem is, love is the answer. Love never fails. When I have fallen, love picked me up and dusted me off and said, "I forgive you." There was a song we used to sing at Goodwill Baptist Church which went something like this: "Love lifted me, love lifted me, when nothing else could help, love lifted me. I was sinking deep in sin far from the distant shore. I was sinking—sinking never to rise no more. But the master of the sea [thank God, the master of the sea is love]; love heard my despairing cry, now safe and I. Love lifted me, love lifted me. When nothing else could help, love lifted me."[14]

Young folk, I want you to know that love has lifted me up higher than I ever thought I could rise. Love has been opening doors for me—doors that I didn't even know existed—and opportunities I never asked for were presented to me. Love is the answer, not sex or drugs or alcohol or big cars or houses or any material thing, but love is the answer, love is the answer.

It's time to bring this message to shore, but I want to tell you that it's time we start telling our youth to put down their guns—too many are dying, too many are going to prison. We need to teach them that love is the answer. Love is the answer.

14 "Love Lifted Me" first published in 1912, lyricist James Rowe, melody Howard E. Smith.

The Verdict Is In

JOHN 3:19

Oberlin Baptist Church, Raleigh, NC

APRIL 15, 2018

> This is the verdict. Light has come into the world, but people loved darkness despite light because their deeds were evil. JOHN 3:19, NIV

I just returned from New Orleans, Louisiana, Friday evening. I'd been there for a training for federal judges. While I love to travel occasionally, I've learned that there is no place like home. I spent part of my trip on well-known Bourbon Street, where everything seems to be acceptable. I ate well there, got some good seafood and African food. Two of my judicial colleagues kept on trying to get me to eat some oysters, both cooked and raw (oysters on the half shell). *Yuck!* After continuing to push oysters on me, I finally told them that there was a verse in the Bible that says: If you resist the devil, he will flee from you. I guess they finally figured out that you can take the man out of the country, but you can't take the country out of the man. And last there was a casino next door to my hotel. I'd not been one to try to win any money, so I told my family I was going to go in there and put a quarter in the machine and see what happens. Well, on my last day there I went in and asked an attendant what the least amount was you could put in the machine, and she said this one is fifty cents. I went to the machine and couldn't even figure where you put the money in, so I immediately left out.

This morning, I want to take my text at John 3:19, the NIV, and it reads as follows: "This is the verdict. Light has come into the world, but people loved darkness despite light because their deeds were evil." I want to engage you for a short while on the subject "The Verdict Is In."

In the fall of 1976, as a first-year law student at Howard University in Washington, DC, I learned that the word verdict means "to speak the truth." There have been a lot of verdicts arising out of several famous trials in the United States—a few of them referred to from a historical perspective as "trials of the century." One such trial began in late 1994 and concluded in 1995—the trial of O. J. Simpson. He had been charged with murdering his wife, Nicole Simpson, and Ronald Goldman. Johnny Cochran and others represented Mr. Simpson. You may recall, Mr. Cochran argued to the jury a now-famous statement concerning a pair of tight-fitting gloves found at or near the scene of the murder. He said, "If it doesn't fit, then you must acquit." You may recall that. The jury deliberated for less than four hours and gave their verdict of "not guilty." You also may recall that many African Americans rejoiced about the verdict while you probably couldn't find a white person who believed that Mr. Simpson was innocent. To the contrary, many believe he got away with murder. I don't have the time right now to explain the ramifications of the two views, but you should know that the words "not guilty" and "innocent" are not synonymous. In the criminal law context, they are not the same thing. So the verdict that was rendered that day by a jury in 1995 in Mr. Simpson's case remains controversial to this day.

Let me fast-forward to the verdict in today's text in John 3:19. In the earlier verses of chapter 3, Nicodemus, a member of the Jews' ruling council, came to Jesus by night. It appears he heard about and maybe had even seen some of the miracles that Jesus had performed. Nicodemus knew that Jesus was someone special and had some-connection to God. In fact, John wrote that Nicodemus recognized Jesus as someone who was God-sent. But Jesus told Nicodemus that no one could see the kingdom unless they were born again. (I've told some of you that when I was a little boy, my mother had a conversation with me and told me that she knew that I was a morally good boy, but she said that being morally good is not enough, that I must be born again in order to go to heaven.) Nicodemus didn't understand what Jesus was telling him, and I didn't understand what my mother was saying. I just knew that if my mother told me, then I believed it to be true. In a later verse, John 3:16, is perhaps the most important verse in the whole gospel: "God so loved the world that He gave his only begotten son, that whoever believeth in him should not perish but have everlasting life." So this pronouncement, this verdict, this truth spoken by Jesus is the one that matters most on judgment day. Oberlin, this is the verdict, and it is true. Our text says that Light has come into the world, but people loved darkness despite light because their deeds were evil.

What is this new birth? Ten or fifteen years ago, I asked one of my mentors who was like a second father to me, the late Reverend Dr. Elliot Mason, pastor emeritus of Trinity Baptist Church in Los Angeles,[15] what does it mean to be born again? He wrote me a letter in response:

> Being born again is the result of the total surrender and submission of one's heart to our Lord and Savior, Jesus Christ, and it involves the confession of that belief with our mouths. Romans 10:10 says,

15 Dr. Mason's son, Wayne Mason, was my best friend at Howard University School of Law, and Dr. Mason became my spiritual adviser over the next three decades.

> "For with the heart man believeth unto righteousness; and with the mouth confession is made unto salvation."

I want to make it clear that being born again is not something that can be achieved by human effort or design, but it comes about when God gives you a new beginning and a new heart, a pure heart. Matthew 5:8 says, "Blessed are the pure in heart: for they shall see God." It is a transformation from what you once were to something new. Paul says in 2 Corinthians 5:17 that "if any man be in Christ, he is a new creature; old things have passed away, behold all things are become new." Being born again involves a renewal of your mind, a cleansing of all filthiness, a regeneration or spiritual makeover. Being born again is the result of an unwavering and deep-hearted commitment to undertake a new direction and new purpose for your life. This new heart that I speak about today can only be obtained as a gift from the almighty for committing one's life to take up the cross. It is a gift for one's undying faith and belief in Jesus Christ. In our scripture today, Jesus told Nicodemus that "God so loved the world that he gave his only begotten son that whosoever believeth in him should not perish but have eternal life" (JOHN 3:16). So today I have concluded that you cannot be born again from above without believing and having faith in Jesus Christ. Church, I can't find the precise words, and maybe I have failed in my efforts to fully describe what it means to be born again. There's a song made popular by Walter Hawkins that says, "What is this? That I feel deep inside, That keeps setting my soul afire, Whatever it is, It won't let me hold my peace."

Oberlin, the verdict is in: Jesus has made clear the path to salvation. This desire of many of us to live in darkness—many of us have indeed decided that we love darkness better than light; we continue to love evil deeds. We sneak around, wait until it gets dark in hopes that no one will see us. As a young trial lawyer one time, I recall arguing to a jury that what's done in the dark will come to light. The verdict is in: Jesus is the truth, the way, and the life. No one can come to the Father except through Jesus. The verdict is in. No more deliberations, no need to consider any more evidence or consider the exhibits; no need to try to figure out who's telling the truth or who is lying. The verdict is in: The final arguments have been made and considered. The Judge and jury, Judge Jesus has spoken. In every case, Jesus has the last word. One of the last seven words as Jesus hung on Calvary's cross was: It is finished.

Church, the verdict is in. Light has come into the world to give us a second chance and a third chance and a tenth chance to believe so we can have a heart change. God can change your heart. We forget sometimes that He has all power in his hands. The president of the United States, whoever he or she might be at any period in history, has a lot of power, including the power to pardon someone convicted of a federal crime, but the president doesn't have the power to restore us to new life that is brought about by being born again.

The verdict is in. If you accept Him as your Lord and savior, He will turn your life around, no matter what you have done. The Bible says to draw near to Him, and He will draw near to you. The old quartets used to sing, "Just a closer walk." The verdict is in. Mercy is everlasting. What we call Article 3 federal judges get lifetime appointments for just a select few, according to the Constitution, but a Judge named Jesus appoints his believers for eternal life. God's love for us is so great that nothing can separate us from the love of God. Romans 8:38. The verdict is in: If you accept Christ, one day there will be no more trials, no more tribulation, no more crying, no more disappointment, and no more pain.

The verdict is in: The trial of Jesus by Pontius Pilate was unsuccessful in silencing Christ. Yes, he and the crowd who chose Jesus over a murderer named Barrabas to sacrifice had a few moments of exhilaration as they beat Jesus and spat on him and then crucified him on Calvary's cross. But they couldn't silence him. I heard former ambassador Andrew Young of Atlanta say recently, speaking of Dr. Martin Luther King Jr. on the fiftieth anniversary of his death, that the Africans have a saying that "as long as someone calls your name, you are not dead."

I can see Jesus hanging there on the cross, all bruised and beaten, blood streaming down. I don't know why he sacrificed his life for me and you, but as the song goes, I'm glad, so glad he did. The verdict is in: On the third day, he got up from the grave. Oh death, where is thy sting? Oh grave, where is thy victory?

The verdict is in, Reverend Leaston. I recall the Apostle Paul saying that he just tries to preach Christ crucified. If we, all preachers, could just preach Christ crucified and His resurrection, our communities would be better off. The verdict is in, Deacons and Trustees: Jesus's truth endures for all generations. You too must be born again. You can't be leaders of the church unless you have surrendered your life to Christ. The verdict is in, Choir: keep on singing to the glory of God. For some reason, I can't remember the contemporary songs well. I remember mostly those lyrics that my ancestors were singing during my youth that didn't require a hymn book to sing from, or even a piano player to sing by; back when Goodwill Baptist Church had an outdoor toilet and a water cooler, an oil stove, and no air conditioner. They opened the windows. Passersby on foot could hear the praises of our ancestors gathered there.

For those of you who are still undecided whether you should give your life to Jesus, the verdict is in. Long life is not promised. While blood is still running warm in your veins, consider my Savior, Jesus the Christ. He died for you and for me. If you really think about it, He doesn't ask much of us. Only believe.

Church, the verdict is in. All you got to do is accept Jesus as your Lord and Savior. Romans 10:8 says, "If thou shalt confess with thy mouth the Lord Jesus, and shalt believe in thine heart that God hath raised him from the dead, thou shalt be saved."

In your confessions, you must mean it, really mean it. You have to mean it from your heart. God loves a sincere confession, a humble spirit. God knows our hearts; he knows everything about us. John says in 4:24 that God is spirit, and his worshipers must worship in spirit and in truth. Since light came into the world, we can no longer hide from God, so we must give all of ourselves to God, confessing that we all are sinners saved by grace. Surrender, Church, trust Him to order your steps. Single women present today, put your trust in Jesus to keep your boyfriend around if you surrender your life to Jesus. Those who have lost a loved one, the verdict is in. My older daughter's brother-in-law in his forties passed after heart surgery.

I just attended a seminar in New Orleans that was on restorative justice. Such programs are popping up around the country. It is a recognition that our criminal and civil justice system does not and cannot solve all the problems that especially crime brings upon victims and their families. There was a woman there who, within a period of two years, her two sons were murdered in Boston. They remain unsolved crimes. She gave her statement about how God had allowed her to forgive those who took life from her sons. She had yet a third tragedy fall upon her family. Her sister shot and killed her brother in their mother's home. I'm glad that the woman recognized that the verdict is in. She testified on a panel that God had transformed her life; the restorative justice program had given her a new reason to live after losing her two sons.

Church, there is power in the blood of Jesus. There is deliverance in the love of Jesus. Don't you want to surrender today? Surrender all. The verdict is in. Your choice is to remain in darkness and reject the verdict of light, or you can accept Jesus today and be transformed; you can be made brand-new. You may not fully understand it, but the old folks sang, "You'll understand it by and by." I can't tell you that if you surrender to Him today, you won't have disappointments, that everything will be easy for you. Look to Jesus, and you won't have to bear your burdens alone. The verdict is in. In John 8:12 Jesus said, "I am the light of the world." In 1 John 1:5–9, the writer says that "This is the message we heard from him and declare unto you: God is light and in Him there is no darkness at all." The verdict is in. I can tell you that in your darkest hours, He will lift you up and turn you around and place your feet on solid ground. I am a witness today. See where He brought me from. In 1 Peter the word says that God brought me out of darkness into a marvelous light. Today I can testify of his goodness, of his mercy. The Lord is my light and my salvation. The Lord is the strength of my life of whom shall I be afraid. Oberlin and guests here today. I'm concluding—I'm approaching my twentieth anniversary in the ministry, having been called in the spring of 1998 when I was burdened down practicing law there in Pittsboro, North Carolina. The weight of the world seemed to be upon me. The verdict was already in. I had some tough cases; many of clients couldn't pay me, and yet I was called to continue practicing law there in Pittsboro for another eight years. I am a witness that God will comfort you if you surrender your life to Him.

I will now open the doors of the church. I invite you to come forward to indicate that you accept Christ as your savior. I used to hear the old preachers say that if you make the first step, God will make two. But I believe that if you step out on faith, before you have completed your first step, God will meet you there and accept you as you are. Will you come?

My Brother's Keeper: Just Keep Him

Theme: Extending the Compassion of Jesus to Our Local Communities

MATTHEW 25:34–36

Chapel Hill Bible Church, Chapel Hill, NC

FEBRUARY 23, 2003

> Then the King will say to those on his right, "Come, you who are blessed by my Father; take your inheritance, the kingdom prepared for you since the creation of the world. For I was hungry and you gave me something to eat, I was thirsty and you gave me something to drink, I was a stranger and you invited me in, I needed clothes and you clothed me. I was sick and you looked after me, I was in prison and you came to visit me." (MATTHEW 25:34–36, NIV)

Today amid the celebrations across the country of Black History Month, I want to first acknowledge and honor the legacy of the many persons of African descent who have given so much to America and the world, especially those men and women who humbled themselves like Christ, and turned the other cheek, and persevered through unimaginable circumstances. For those brave soldiers, we give thanks and acknowledge their contributions today.

"My Brother's Keeper"

In Matthew chapter 27, verse 32, we learn there was an African, Simon of Cyrene, a city in North Africa, who the Roman authorities found among those present at Christ's death march to the gallows of Golgotha, carrying the cross of Jesus. We know from Genesis that while Father Abraham and Sarah had a son named Isaac, we cannot place less importance on the fact that there lived an Egyptian named Hagar, who with Abraham had a son named Ishmael, from whom God promised to make a great nation. So, we honor these persons for their sacrifice also.

For almost a quarter of a century, I have worn my lawyer hat and used the law both as a sword and as a shield in the communities in which I have worked. Today, with my minister's hat on, I want to talk about what we as individuals and the church ought to be doing to extend Christ's compassion to our local communities and to demonstrate that we are our brother's keeper.

Christian responsibility in the local community being my focus today, it is ironic that in less than two weeks, on March 7, several of us from this church and the InterVarsity Christian Fellowship at the University of North Carolina and Duke University will be leaving for eight days on a journey to London, England, to minister mostly to a large and primarily Hindu, Sikh, and Muslim community from India, Pakistan, and East Africa. And while with great enthusiasm I look forward to this foreign mission trip, I have pondered how much could be accomplished locally if we spent an equal amount of time, energy, and resources as we will spend on our trip to London. Those of us who will be making this journey ask for your prayers as we cross the Atlantic to do God's work.

There is seemingly so much need right here in the Chapel Hill and Durham area. There is a great deal of poverty, sickness, and inadequate education and housing, evil and injustice right here. Crime is running rampant with no end in sight.

Since 1979, I have had the privilege of visiting our brothers and sisters in prisons across the state of North Carolina from Ahoskie in the northeast corner of the state to the Avery/Mitchell State Prison in the far west. In some ways it is an indictment on our society that the prison industry is one of the leading employers in many counties in North Carolina and America. Especially for many persons of color, it seems to be a lifelong place of residence. I visited the youth prison in Butner, North Carolina, recently and observed long lines of our brothers going to breakfast. It seemed to me that at least three out of every four were African American young men. That seems to be typical in many prisons across the land. I can't describe for you how that makes me feel when I go to visit a prison or when I go to court and see a sea of black and brown faces. I know that many of you here aren't feeling connected to what I'm saying right now, but just bear with me for a moment.

Church, are you your brother's keeper? With the burden of keeping your brother comes great responsibility. Educator Booker T. Washington is credited with saying "The highest test of civilization of any race is its willingness to extend a helping hand to the less fortunate. A race, like an individual, lifts itself up by lifting others." To fulfill this church's goal of extending Christ's compassion in the local community, we must begin to lift those who feel marginalized in our community. As a child, I heard a preacher say that God has no hands without our hands, no feet without our feet.

I suspect that some of you still may be wondering what you have in common with those in prison who have been convicted of robbery and murder. I first want to say that many of them may not be there because of anything wrong they have done, for recent technology proves what many of us already knew, and that is, some are there because they have been wrongfully convicted and have been years later exonerated by DNA or other evidence. As Christians, we should feel the pain of others, no matter where they are. Our love must be unconditional. I like what Pastor Mark Acuff said in a sermon two weeks ago. Preaching from the thirteenth chapter of John, he said, "We must possess a washing-feet love." That scripture requires us to wash the feet also of those who have committed trespasses against our society. In this society, we are doing a good job of putting many out of sight, but they cannot be out of our minds and hearts.

Those of us here in the Bible Church and those at First Baptist, University Methodist, the Catholic churches, the mosques, and synagogues are inextricably and irrevocably intertwined with one another whether we want to be or not. The late James Baldwin, a great American writer and civil rights activist, wrote,

> Each of us, helplessly and forever, contains the other—male in female, female in male, white in black, black in white. We are a part of each other. Many of our countrymen appear to find this fact exceedingly inconvenient and even unfair, and so, very often, do I. But none of us can do anything about it.[16]

I'm convinced that there are many among us here who are very compassionate, but too many of us possess an attitude of, "I've got mine, you'll just have to get yours like I did." The local community isn't seeing our compassion enough. Also, they are not seeing our faith enough. In the fourteenth chapter of Matthew, Jesus departed by ship and went into the desert, and a great multitude followed him. Upon seeing them, Jesus was moved with compassion toward them, and he healed their sick and fed all five thousand of them. In other words, seeing great need among the multitude, Jesus was moved to action. Church, for this church to extend the compassion of Jesus to our local communities, like Christ in the desert and on many other occasions, we must be moved to action. We are our brother's keeper.

The extent to which this church and others continue to be relevant in its impact depends on how we reach out to others, especially those who are in need and who

16 Permission of James Baldwin, excerpt from Here Be Dragons: from The Price of the Ticket: Collected Nonfiction 1948-1985. Copyright © 1965 by James Baldwiin, renewed © 1991 by The James Baldwin Estate. Reprinted with the permission of the Permissions Company LLC on behalf of the James Baldwin Estate.

are different from us. For several years here at the Bible Church, some of us have been grappling with the need for the church's congregation to be more diverse and inclusive. Racial reconciliation in our churches and communities still seems a long way off. Reconciliation is a two-way street. I invite all of you to occasionally go worship at churches of other racial and ethnic backgrounds. There you may find the answer that you need for many of life's most pressing problems. There are many old soldiers of great faith there who have weathered the storms of life for over three-fourths of a century. Our faith will be greatly tested as we go about our mission of being our brother's keeper.

My mother told me the other day about how my oldest brother wanted a suit for graduation from high school. Accomplishing this would not be a big deal for most of you here today—but my family had no extra money. Mama told me how she had faith and told the store owner downtown of her situation, and he allowed her to buy the suit on time. Also, I have told the story several times about my conversation with my mother-in-law. I asked her how she and her disabled husband were able to feed their fifteen children. She said, "Sometimes I would go to the cupboard and the cupboard would be bare, but there was always food on the table." Church, the same faith that purchased a graduation suit and that put food on the table for fifteen children will allow us to overcome the monumental task of reconciling with one another. But if you segregate yourselves and wait on others to respond to your invitation to come here to the Bible Church, then reconciliation will never take place. These walls must come down for reconciliation to take place.

As we are aware, Sunday morning at eleven o'clock is the most segregated hour in the United States. Throughout this land, it is as if we think there will be two heavens. But I read about a place over there in Revelation 7:9 and 10, where it said,

> After this I looked, and there before me was a great multitude that no one could count, from every nation, tribe, people and language, standing before the throne and before the Lamb. They were wearing white robes and were holding palm branches in their hands. And they cried out in a loud voice: "Salvation belongs to our God, who sits on the throne, and to the Lamb." (NIV)

Church, I want to be in the number described in Revelation. But I know that the only way I can be in that number is if I've been to the wilderness like Jesus. When I go before the eternal Judge sitting on the throne in today's scripture, I want to be able to say that I just came out of the wilderness. There is an old Negro spiritual which says, "If you want to find Jesus, go in the wilderness." Church, we are our brother's keeper, especially those in the wilderness. There are many sick, poor, and downtrodden in the wilderness. Here in Chapel Hill and Durham, some of the wealthiest communities in our state, the homeless shelters are bulging at their seams. The price of housing and medical care is out of reach for many of our brothers and sisters of all colors and nationalities. Whether our brothers and sisters are in the prisons, hospitals, nursing homes, or no home at all, they are often in the wilderness of despair. We must be about creating hope for all, no matter who they are.

There are so many sick among us who need those of us who are strong. The last time I was in the pulpit here in December of last year, my father was present, but since that time he has fallen ill and suddenly without warning cannot walk without the aid of a walker. Just this past Wednesday Daddy was admitted to the hospital and diagnosed with bone cancer. Amy Peng, who I had gone to see in the hospital and who had been on the prayer chain here at the Bible Church for a long time, died recently. Her family is standing in the need of the prayers of the faithful. Jean Lesesne's doing much better, but I'm sure her husband, Hank, would say she has come this far by the power of prayer. We need to keep on praying without ceasing. Church, we must be about keeping our brothers and sisters if we want the vision of this church to be realized—that of extending Christ's compassion to the local communities. We who are of the household of faith can learn from Paul in his message to the faithful about their fellow believers. Romans 15:1 says, "We then that are strong ought to bear the infirmities of the weak and not please ourselves. We must be in constant prayer for those who are sick whether we know them or not."

Church, take a moment to look around you at this beautiful structure. No doubt many of the church leaders and members are pleased with what the Lord has done in making this possible, the largest church structure in Chapel Hill. But Church, it may just be that God needs for us to also build on this property a shelter for the homeless, a nursing home for the infirm, and a complex for senior citizens who are healthy but too poor to live elsewhere, a refuge for those with HIV/AIDS, and a counseling center for troubled youth. God is calling on the Bible Church, First Baptist, the Catholic, Episcopal, and churches everywhere to care for the homeless, sick, and spiritually dead. They too are our brothers and sisters. We are our brother's keeper.

It seems to me that from a spiritual and morality point of view, America is in declining health. To reverse this decline, the Bible Church may need to work shoulder-to-shoulder with other congregations, the private sector, and our governments. Land is becoming very scarce in the Chapel Hill area, so churches should come together and buy up some land and work with Habitat for Humanity and others to build homes for those who cannot afford to live here. If we don't do so, we will lose our strength of diversity in the very near future. Chapel Hill will be just another place for the rich and politically connected.

And since there are several persons of color in our audience today, some of the privileged few to be able to go to some of our great universities, first I want to say to you that today is a time of forgiveness. Viewing our history in this country, that is a hard thing to do. I also want to say that while you are so very blessed, and on your way up the ladder of success, I beg you to reach back and take someone with you. In God's kingdom, there is ample room at the top. Dr. Marian Wright Edelman of the Children's Defense Fund said, "All of our Mercedes-Benzes and Halston frocks will not hide our essential failures as a generation of black 'haves,' who did not protect the black future during our watch." My oldest daughter, Briana, is a junior at Carolina majoring in health policy and administration. I will be disappointed if she doesn't figure out a way to use her knowledge from Carolina and upbringing in the church to help those who have no health insurance and those without a voice in the healthcare system. Somehow, we must do what we can to close the gap between the haves and the have-nots. All of us bear some responsibility for the predicament we find ourselves in today.

Those of you attend this church regularly must know that this church's vision of inclusiveness and extending the compassion of Jesus to our local communities won't be cheap in financial resources, time, or commitment. But for the skeptics, my response to you is the same one I make to the many who have had the nerve to ask me, "How in the world can you be a lawyer and preacher at the same time?" My answer is always the same: "Apparently you don't know the power of God." Daily, as a body of believers, we underestimate God's power. On a personal basis, I am like Paul when he said in 1 Corinthians 15:31, "I die daily." But I am also an example of how God can take a little bit and make more. When I was a child, I was very quiet and shy, scared to speak up for what was right. For our youth and young adults today, I want you to know that if you devote yourself to the service of mankind, God will continue to shape and mold you and create something good and wonderful in His eyes.

Chapel Hill Bible Church has undertaken a commendable and exemplary goal of reaching out to those who have not traditionally been among the congregation here. In essence, the church leaders and congregation have proclaimed, "I am my brother's keeper." However, historian John Henrik Clarke has stated, "In Africa you never say, 'I am my brother's keeper,' you just keep him." Church, we've got a lot of "keeping" to do before we can make the vision a reality. Ultimately, we will all be judged by how we treat the least of these, as the scripture teaches. We say we want the poor to come to church here at the Bible Church or other churches on Sunday. I'm afraid we won't be successful in this endeavor if we don't get to know the faces and hearts of those living on the edges of society on Monday through Saturday. We cannot know their needs unless we walk in their shoes just for a moment. We may just need to let those in need to spend the night with us or pick our brothers and sisters up and take them to breakfast before bringing them to church so they won't be hungry during service. I know this church is on a tight budget, but two fish and five loaves of bread can feed a multitude when God is in the mix.

Church, as I conclude today, as we begin to carry out the vision in our local communities, be prepared for sacrifice, and be prepared to be rejected. For even as John says in chapter 1:11, "Christ came unto His own and his own received Him not." But the Apostle Paul, in his letter to the Galatians, at 6:9, says, "Let us not be weary in well doing: for in due season, we shall reap, if we faint not. Church, as the songwriter proclaimed, "Nobody told us that the way would be easy." But if we put our hope in Jesus Christ, we won't faint, but we will be able to accomplish the goal of extending the compassion of Jesus to our local community. I have confident assurance that in a couple of years, we will be able to look around and see where the Lord has brought us. Church, we are our brothers' keeper. We need to be about keeping them, so that on that day of judgment, on that great getting-up morning, on that day when reconciliation will be complete, we will be able to hear the great King say as in verse 40 of today's text, "I tell you the truth, whatever you did for one of the least of these brothers of mine, you did for me." I want to hear Him say, "Well done, well done, good and faithful servant. Now, come on into a place where every day will be Sunday, a place where there will be no more crying, no more poverty, no more war, and no more disappointment."

A Church without Spot or Wrinkle

EPHESIANS 5:25–27, 32

Walker Memorial Baptist Church, 114th Anniversary, Washington, DC

MAY 15, 2005

> Husbands, love your wives, just as Christ loved the church and gave himself for it; That he might sanctify and cleanse it by the washing of water by the word, That He might present it to Himself a glorious church, not having spot, or wrinkle or any such thing; but that it should be holy and without wrinkle. This is a great mystery; but I speak concerning Christ and the church. (EPHESIANS 5:25–27, 32, NIV)

I am so grateful to once again be in your presence at Walker Memorial Baptist Church, here in the nation's capital, my second home where I did my undergraduate and graduate studies at Howard University and the Howard University School of Law. I am truly humbled when I think of the many preachers or other speakers that you could have asked to come to help you celebrate your 114th anniversary, yet you chose me.

Looking back 114 years ago to the year 1891, we find that some brave, faithful, and dedicated brothers and sisters from Shiloh Baptist Church were guided to found Walker Memorial Baptist Church at an organizational meeting on April 23, 1891. In that year of 1891, not all that transpired in our nation was being led by the Holy Spirit. For that same year, 112 lynchings were recorded. And just a stone's throw from here over there in Congress, after passing the House of Representatives, Representative Henry Cabot Lodge's bill calling for federal supervision of elections was killed in the Senate by a southern filibuster.

Notwithstanding the bleakness of the times in 1891, Agricultural and Mechanical College for the Colored Race (1891–1915) now North Carolina Agricultural and Technical State University and commonly referred to as North Carolina A&T State University, or for short, A&T was founded in Greensboro. That same year, West Virginia Colored Institute (1891–1915), now West Virginia State University was founded in Institute, West Virginia, to educate sons and daughters of ex-slaves.

But nothing surpassed what happened here in Washington, DC, in 1891 with the founding of this great institution, Walker Memorial Baptist Church. So today I want to congratulate those of you whose ancestors played a role in starting this church and just as importantly those of you who have stayed on the battlefield to ensure this church's survival and effectiveness for 114 years.

During this past winter, this subject of "A Church without Spot or Wrinkle" came to me one day while I was taking a shower. Perhaps it came as a result as I was thinking about getting all washed and cleaned up. But I know that getting cleaned up on the outside is just part of the solution for preparing to meet God. There is a song we used to sing, "Nothing can wash away my sins.... Nothing but the blood of Jesus." So the soap and water in my shower didn't give me this sermon.

I first want to say that here in the nation's capital, I hope that my message today can be heard down at the White House, a place that is full of spots and wrinkles, where the president's thinking is apparently all messed up with spots and wrinkles. It seems that he who would rather spend tax money on bombs and bullets than Medicaid for the very poor, a president that seems to be more worried about his own future legacy than the day-to-day livelihood of the disheartened, dispossessed, and disinherited. It was President Franklin D. Roosevelt who said years ago that "the measure of our progress is not whether we add more to the abundance of those who have much, but whether we provide enough for those who have too little." So, I hope today that the sound waves can somehow take my message down to 1600 Pennsylvania Avenue. And I hope that the halls of Congress—all filled with representatives, senators, and the lobbyists for big business who have too many spots and wrinkles to speak of—will somehow hear my message today. And I hope the Supreme Court, now void of any compassion, it's very walls still crying out for Thurgood Marshall's return, will somehow be affected by what is said here today.

And even over at my alma mater, Howard University—no doubt one of the greatest universities ever to exist, one that my children will tell you that I defend with great vigor when someone tries to take away from its accomplishments by saying too many negative things about it—over there in the "A" Building and on the yard, there are some spots and wrinkles. Like at most institutions, there are some bad attitudes among the staff and students—perhaps in part because of our legacy of slavery—that are also clouded with spots and wrinkles and can benefit from God's word. So, I hope that my message today can somehow make its way over to the main campus on Georgia Avenue and the other campus locations.

This scripture today, coming from Ephesians, theologically speaking is a difficult one for me to fully comprehend. So, I had to first break it down into layman's terms to help me understand about these spots and wrinkles so that I could get a better picture about what God was going to do. I often take my soiled clothes to the dry cleaners, and they sometimes will come back still with some of the spots and a few wrinkles they had when I put them in the cleaners. The cleaning solution didn't quite get all the ink, blood, or grease spots out, and the hot iron didn't quite get out all the wrinkles. And so my clothes sometimes remain in an imperfect condition even after being taken to the cleaners. The best of the dry cleaner's efforts sometimes isn't quite good enough.

When I was a teenager, I had my share of pimples and blackheads, spots all over my face. And even today, occasionally I will look in the mirror and see the wrinkles of age increasing with each year. Many of us, especially our women, try to cover the facial wrinkles with makeup. And that effort to cover up spots and wrinkles has produced a multibillion-dollar business. Maybelline and other such cosmetics companies promise much than they can deliver. And today, on the wealthier side of town, many seek the services of a plastic surgeon to get rid of the spots and wrinkles. I saw on television—*60 Minutes* or one of those type programs—where teenagers were being given graduation gifts of an appointment with a plastic surgeon to have a breast implant or other surgery to improve their appearance or the shape of their body. Thank God I don't have that much money lying around! But even after spending thousands of dollars, many of the beneficiaries of the surgeon's knife come away disappointed and unfulfilled within, still searching for happiness.

We are all full of spots and wrinkles. Many of us have uncontrolled anger, unnecessary fear, deceitfulness, lack of courage, selfishness, nosiness, heads full of gossip and hatred—spots and wrinkles that control our lives. Early in my law practice I heard a lawyer say to the judge as he was representing his client who was about to go away to prison, "But for the grace of God go I." Yes, none of us are perfect; we are all but a few steps away from falling and not getting up. Church, today, I'm happy that God has allowed me to get up when I've fallen.

On Walker Memorial's 114th anniversary, this church and many like it around the country are full of spots and wrinkles. Somehow, as a church body, we have gotten all puffed up and proud and think that we are the elite and the elected and have fooled ourselves into believing that the church is full of the saved and no sinners are to be found among us and that no sinners are welcome. But as we know from the Bible in Romans 3:23, all have sinned and come short of the glory of God, and therefore we need God's grace. Our church of the twenty-first century suffers from yet another malady. We have forgotten what we are supposed to be about. In the words of Dr. William Augustus Jones, pastor of Bethany Baptist Church in Brooklyn, New York, in his sermon "Stewards of the Mysteries," he said, "The big-church syndrome can cause us to mistake numbers for members—to count heads instead of weighing hearts."[17] In other words, it's not the number present on Sunday, but the commitment of those present Monday through Sunday.

17 Rhinold Ponder and Michele Tuck-Ponder, eds., *The Wisdom of the Word Faith: Great African American Sermons* (New York: Crown, 1996), 75

As a body of believers, the Christian church of the twenty-first century has often been in turmoil. Within the last several years in my law office, I received two separate telephone calls from leaders of two separate churches, located only fifty miles apart, soliciting my legal advice. The deacons who called pointed out to me that their churches were in turmoil, one being led by a new pastor who was trying to change everything and demeaning the older church leaders, while the deacon who called me from the other church said we been trying to get rid of our longtime pastor, a man who is tearing up the church and causing members to be angry with one another—pitting one family against another. Amazingly, both leaders asked me the same question: is it legal to put a lock on the church door to lock out the pastor? I have since pondered the dilemma both churches were in.

First, both of those churches were full of spots and wrinkles. But they asked, is it legal to put a lock on the church door? I have concluded that what both church congregations and their pastors were arguing about is, Who owns the church? Who owns Walker Memorial on your 114th anniversary? But my analyses of both telephone conversations lead me to conclude that the congregations and pastors of both churches were attempting to take the deed out of the Lord's name. So even the church, the one institution in our society that is supposed to represent the very best of wisdom, patience, love, and understanding, is full of spots and wrinkles that grown men and women don't know how to get rid of.

Before getting specifically into our scripture today, I must also remind us today that Sunday morning at about this hour, our society is the most segregated hour in the United States. From time to time, I get the opportunity to talk about racial reconciliation in the context of the gospel. Mostly my message on this subject has been at churches of the majority race. But I have begun to ponder how blacks and whites can begin to resolve the oldest and most pressing problem in America today, the spot and wrinkle of the racial divide: how can we reconcile with one another unless we at least occasionally also worship with one another? I read where racism is on the rise among our youth. Jesus gave us a model to follow in his encounter with the Samaritan woman at the well where a Jewish man met a Samaritan woman, and the woman learned about salvation through partaking of that living water.

If the church is full of spots and wrinkles, then that is what can we expect outside of the church. Judge Williams must send our young black men to prison every session of criminal court. He told me one time he often asked them as they stand before him ready to be sent away to prison, "What's wrong with you?" Alex, I want you to know that they are full of spots and wrinkles that only our God can cure. Our communities are full of young women with two or three children from different fathers, and some communities are void of men, real men, who are about something. Too many of our black men are in prison or are stretched out in the streets of Washington, DC, or Durham, North Carolina, dying from gunshot wounds. There is something wrong with this picture. Drugs and AIDS are killing us in record numbers, with the highest rate of new HIV cases being found among black females. The spots and wrinkles of life seem to be taking our joy.

Our text today coming from Ephesians is a difficult one for my little feeble mind to fully comprehend. Even the great writer Paul says in verse 32 that "this is a great mystery," but he goes on to say in that verse, "But I speak concerning Christ and the church." So the remainder of my time today I want to talk about Christ and the church. Many have discussed what this chapter and specifically this verse mean relating to a church without spot or wrinkle. This concept of the church being Christ's bride is illustrative of Jesus's love for the church. We men who have been married know how much we loved our new bride. I remember so well twenty-five years ago this past May 3, how happy I was when I first saw my wife being escorted down the aisle at Duke Gardens on the campus of Duke University. I know many of you remember how you smiled when you saw how beautiful your bride was on your wedding day. And then you took a vow and said, "I will love you and stay with you until death do us part, through sickness and in health." You promised your bride that you would protect her and love her even when her face began to fill up with spots and wrinkles. I heard Dr. Renita J. Weems, the William and Camille Cosby Professor of Humanities at Spelman College, give a memorable sermon at Howard University's Andrew Rankin Chapel Service at Crampton Auditorium. She brought laughter to the audience when she humorously said that when you took your marriage vow,

> You in essence promised that you would love your bride when she was a brick house, but your vow meant that you would continue to love your bride even after she had two or three children, and when there were no more bricks, when she got so big, she just was a house.

Our scripture today is saying as in John 3:16 that "God so loved the world that he gave his only begotten son that whosoever believeth in Him, shall not perish but have ever lasting life." I believe our scripture is saying that no matter who you are, no matter what you have done—you may have killed someone or beat up your boyfriend or girlfriend or been hooked on drugs—but Jesus's death on the cross means that when He returns, He will be coming back for a church without a spot or wrinkle; he won't be coming back for a church that is in turmoil; he won't be coming back for a church with a lock on the door; or where the members are arguing about who owns the church. He will be coming back for a church that has the welcome mat out, a church welcome mat that says, "Come unto me all ye that labor and are heavy laden, and I will give you rest; take my yoke upon you and learn of me, for I am meek and lowly in heart; and ye shall find rest unto your souls. For my yoke is easy and my burden is light" (MATTHEW 11:28–30).

In our scripture today, the church is being described as a bride to demonstrate the extent of God's unconditional love for all of us. His death on the cross means that we all have a second chance and a third chance; that Jesus will wink at our faults. Joe's stubbornness and our hardened hearts, our adultery and our lying, our hatred and deceitfulness—our scripture today is about how God's love is so great that one day He will forgive us of our sins and present us faultless. I heard a sermon by Dr. Gardner C. Taylor speaking from the Book of Jude. He told how another preacher had told the story about how one day, we believers will be standing side by side by our Savior, and the angels who have been with Jesus before the beginning of time would look at one another and ask the question, which one is Jesus? The Bible says in 1 John 3:2 that when God appears, we shall be like him. One day Jesus will present us to himself as a gift, a glorious church without spot or wrinkle, free from any sickness, death, or sin. No one else can do that. As bad as we are, as many mistakes as we have made, Jesus can present us faultless, without spot or wrinkle.

Two years ago, I went on a short-term mission trip with some students from Carolina and Duke to London, England, to learn from and get to know a community of Muslims, Sikhs, and Hindus. As a part of our ministry, we went door-to-door conducting a survey. One of the questions we asked was whether the persons we met ever prayed. One young Hindu man responded, "first of all, Hindus have a million gods." I then asked, "Well which one do you pray to?" He said he "prayed to whichever one happens to be listening at the time."

I'm so glad that I have only one God to pray to—the one that can present me without spot or wrinkle; a God that was before time began, the one who saw there was complete darkness and flung the stars to light up the sky, the one who sat the moon in the right location, the one who humbled himself and sent his Son down to earth in the form of a servant—the one who sacrificed His life for those of us who are not worthy. There is a song that my home church's little children's choir used to sing. It says, "I don't know why Jesus loved me; I don't why he cares; I don't why he sacrificed his life, oh, but I'm glad so glad he did." So, when God calls me home, because I am a believer, my faults won't be held against me. I serve a God who will clean me up and make something out of me and receive me without spot or wrinkle, holy. I look forward to hearing him say, "Well done, well done, good and faithful servant."

God will present himself a church which is holy and righteous; one that I can imagine is full of all races and from all ethnic backgrounds. No, it won't be the most segregated hour on earth like Sunday mornings are today. When Jesus returns, there will be some here at Walker Memorial who don't look like us here today, some will have on miniskirts, and who used to be walking up and down on Fourteenth Street when I first came to Howard University thirty-three years ago; there will be some here at Walker Memorial who don't have any money to put in the collection plate; some who shared a needle for heroin the night before, but who because of God's great love, suddenly cleaned themselves up and replaced the momentary joy of crack cocaine with the unspeakable joy that only God can give. There will be some here at Walker Memorial who once had spots and wrinkles, but who are full of the Holy Ghost. Yes, the Bible says at Matthew 19:30 that the first will be last and the last will be first. I look forward to the day when our brothers will lay down their Uzis and the president and Congress will study war no more. I look forward to the day when there will be no more AIDS. I know two pastors in South Africa who tell me that many homes there are being turned into hospital wards because so many are dying of AIDS in the community, and there have been so many deaths that sometimes survivors don't even cry.

To our youth present here today, I want you to know that the love I'm speaking about today is not the kind of love Usher and Alicia Keys are singing about. That kind of love is short-lived. Those songs expressing sexual love are only temporary, but the love expressed in today's scripture is eternal and unconditional. It is the kind of love that transforms you and allows you to have the courage to tell your friends, no, it's not right to do drugs. It's the kind of love that will allow you to tell your girlfriend that we need to wait to have sex, for sex is special and it is the gift of God. I need for the youth here today to go out and tell somebody about God's love, about how Jesus befriended the homeless and criminals and those hooked on the vices of life. Tell somebody how Jesus is important in your own life. I want you to know He is the strength of my life. If Jesus wasn't a part of my life, I would have given up a long time ago. I need for you to go back to school on Monday and befriend someone who has no friend.

To our senior citizens today, I want you to know that God's love is not the same kind of love that Marvin Gaye and Tammy Terrell sang together in unison about. I know you love some Smokey Robinson, and I do also. Some of you probably think about that song now, "Uh Baby, Baby." But God's love transcends time, age, race, and gender. It is a love that keeps your mind set on Jesus when the pain in your body seems to be getting worse. I need for you seniors to pass on your faith to your children and grandchildren like Elijah passed on a double portion of his spirit to Elisha. I'm asking you to pass on a double portion of your faith to your children and grandchildren (2 KINGS 2:9–11). Let them know that you had some spots and wrinkles in your life, that you have fallen many times, but that Christ's love picked you up and dusted you off and allowed you, as the old folk used to say, to run on to see what the end is going to be. So I want to say today to the members at Walker Memorial, hold on a little while longer. God is coming back for a church without spot or wrinkle.

Walker Memorial, I know today as you think about the many problems of life, you wonder, *How long must we wait, Lord? The spots and wrinkles of life are becoming unbearable. I can't take much more.* In some homes two or three sons have been murdered and some daughters are selling their bodies for crack cocaine. To those grieving mothers, I know you must be saying, *How long must I wait?* Well, one writer has said that the church in general and believers in particular will not be without spot or wrinkle until they come to glory.

But you should not be in despair; today's main lesson is about Christ's love. Even before He returns, He has sent his spirit, a comforter, a healer, and a protector. Last February, my brother and I had a close brush with death on the family farm down in Madison, North Carolina. There on the farm my family had hired tree cutters to cut some of the wood from the farm. My brother and I went down to observe their progress. Upon returning, one of the tree cutters had relocated and began to cut a tree in our path. As we walked and talked, the tree began to fall very close to us. As we began to move quickly out of the tree's path, my brother fell and mysteriously couldn't get up. While he was down, I couldn't move toward him as I was in shock. While we escaped harm only by a few feet, I couldn't sleep that night, thinking about how close death was to my brother and me. I also was feeling guilty about how I couldn't move toward my brother lying in the mud there in the path of the falling tree. It was the next day that I realized the power of God needed to be made manifest in our lives. If I had been able to reach out and help him along, I would have probably said, "I'm so happy that I was able to help him." But I needed to see—as did my brother, who has been preaching the gospel as a pastor for almost thirty years—that God is fully in charge of our lives. No matter who you are and how much you have been blessed to accomplish, God oversees our every move, our every thought.

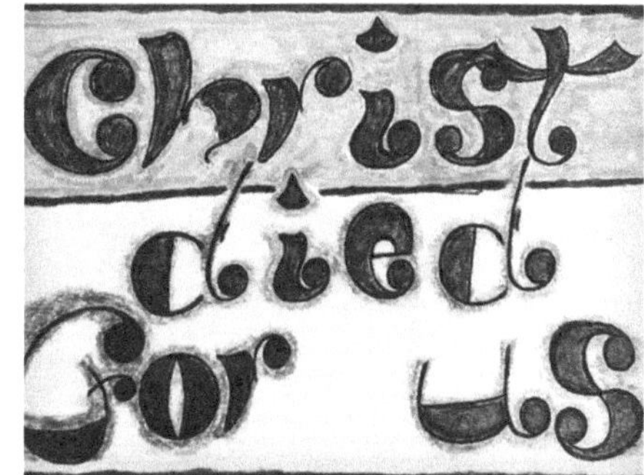

ART BY BILLY D. WEBSTER

I leave you today not knowing whether I will ever be back. Life has many twists and turns. But I am not dismayed. Christ's love for you and me is so great. I know I've likely failed in describing his love for us because his love is indescribable. But I leave you with a prayer that Walker Memorial will be a part of that church Jesus will present to himself without spot or wrinkle. Continue to press toward the mark of the high calling of Jesus Christ.

Weekend Inspiration

November 14, 2009

[I first delivered this sermon, "I'm Running for the Crown: Keep Your Eyes on the Prize," on October 18, 2009, in Durham, North Carolina, at Beacon Light Baptist Church. The sermon, which is excerpted here, is based on scriptures found in 1 Corinthians 9:24–27.]

Today I want to talk to you about staying focused on your spiritual lives. I sense that some Christians have not learned or have forgotten why they need to stay focused on their Christian walk. I can tell you that I have often focused on my academics and other things early in life. In high school, I ran track and played basketball. I spent a lot of time practicing, getting my body in shape, especially in my first love, the game of basketball. I recall running so much in practice that I would sometimes get cramps in my legs. In track, I ran the 100-yard dash and usually the 440 relay. In college, I concentrated on my studies to obtain good grades, keep my scholarship, and get into law school, which was my goal since I was in high school. In law school, I worked hard because I had to; I never knew or met a real lawyer in my life prior to college. I entered law school less prepared than some of my classmates. Until I became a parent, law school was the hardest thing I had ever done in my life. I burned the midnight oil, stayed up late and got up early; kept my eyes on the prize and endured to the end. On October 23, I return to Washington, DC, and Howard University to celebrate my thirtieth law school class reunion. And for that, I can only say to God be the glory!

ILLUSTRATION BY SHAILYN RAMSEY

Praising God Dressed in the Whole Armor of God

ACTS 4:23–30; EPHESIANS 6:11

Men's Day Prayer Breakfast, New Hope Missionary Baptist Church, Greensboro, NC

APRIL 21, 2012

When I was asked to come be your guest preacher today at your prayer breakfast, my first thought was that if there ever was a time for prayer, it is right now, and so I have with great joy joined you here this morning. It is my time of day, maybe because I grew up on the farm right outside of Madison, probably twenty-five miles away as the crow flies. There we had to get up early in the morning before it got too hot in the tobacco fields. But I learned the great lessons of hard work and working together there, and I have my mother and the memory of my father to thank for those lessons. No doubt these lessons that came from hard work and my upbringing of having to be in church on Sunday morning, no matter what time you came in the Saturday night before, played a great role in what and who I am today.

Your theme this year is "United in Praise" from Acts 4:23–30, and in reading this text and from my study of the previous chapter 3 to get the true context of what our lesson is all about, I was led also to go to Ephesians 6:11, which speaks about putting on the whole armor of God. Therefore, I've come today to share some insights on what God has put on my heart about Christian folk being united in praise.

If there has been one thing I have learned in my fourteen years of preaching, and almost thirty-three years of public speaking after graduating from law school at Howard University, it's that unless the Holy Spirit comes, it is all just a speech. So, I ask your prayers today that the Holy Spirit will dwell among us here at New Hope Baptist Church this morning.

Considering the theme of "United in Praise," I suspect some of you present today would like to think that you would be able to return to your homes and tell your neighbors that you were able to get your praise on early this morning. You may be hoping that perhaps you will have an "upper room" experience or even Day of Pentecost experience, where all praised God in one voice. I've come to know that only God can provide an upper-room experience. I've come to realize, though, that if I preach Christ crucified, and that Christ was raised from the dead on the third day, then God can fill in the blanks. God can cover up my insecurity, my uncertainty, and yes, my sometimes lack of faith. Sometimes I need to almost see and feel the prints of the nails in his hands and examine the wound in his side. Before we can get our praise on today, I need to remind you that before we can be united in praise, we need to get to know Jesus for ourselves intimately. We need to sleep with Him, sup or eat with Him, go to Him in prayer in good times and in bad times. Paul said in Colossians 2:6, "So then as you received Christ Jesus as Lord, continue to live in Him, rooted and built up in Him, strengthened in the faith as you were taught, and overflowing with thankfulness." If you do this, Church, then and only then will you be able to become united in praise.

And I personally need—I really need—God to breathe on me this morning so that Jesus can fill me with the Holy Spirit like he did when he appeared to the disciples in the upper room in John 20:19–20. So, pray with me, Church, as we look at what saith the Lord in today's text.

From chapter 3 we find that the early Christians, not long after Christ's death on the cross, were coming together to hear the word of the Lord as espoused by two of Christ's apostles, Peter and John. Among the crowd gathered there in and around the temple in Jerusalem was a man born lame from birth. He lay at the temple gate, which the Bible says was called beautiful. He regularly asked the attendees of the temple to give him alms. Today, we probably would refer to this man as a beggar. You know the well-known story about how when Peter and John approached the temple and saw this man there (we don't even know his name), they looked toward him and said, "Look at us." I find this first encounter by Peter and John with this man instructive. How many times in our goings and comings do we look the other way when we see someone on the corner begging for money? And when the lame man did look upon them, he expected a donation, but got more than he thought was possible. He got a healing. Peter said to him in Acts 3:3–6 (KJV), "'Silver and gold have I none, but such as I have, I give thee. In the name of Jesus Christ of Nazareth rise and walk.' And he took him by the right hand and lifted him up and immediately his feet and ankle bones received strength".

It seems that those who had gathered there in and around the temple were amazed. After all, the scripture says this man was over forty years old and had been lame from birth. Peter and John preached about Jesus to the crowd at the temple and told them that the very one that they had crucified—the God of Abraham, Isaac, and Jacob; the Prince of Peace; the one that you demanded be turned over to the authorities to crucify rather than a murderer—is the one to receive credit for the lame man's healing. A great crowd of about five thousand men heard the preaching of Peter and John, and many believed.

Let me fast-forward to chapter 4 where we find that while Peter and John were boldly proclaiming the word to the crowd, the priests, the captain of the temple, and the Sadducees came upon them. They were mad that Peter and John were preaching through the name of Jesus that he had risen from the dead. This preaching that Christ rose from the dead was not a part of the Jewish Scripture, so the Jewish authorities bound Peter and John and took them to jail since it was in the evening. The next day Annas, the high priest, and many of the priestly order there in Jerusalem, asked Peter, by what power or by what name have you healed the lame man? Thank God for the Holy Spirit, for the Bible says Peter, being filled with the Holy Spirit, answered boldly: it is because Jesus Christ of Nazareth, the one that you crucified, the very one that God raised from the dead, is the one responsible for this man standing before you today. I like Peter's sermon speaking about Jesus. He said boldly and in unmistakable terms, it was Jesus, the one who the builders had rejected but who became the capstone or chief cornerstone, the one and only one through whom salvation can be achieved. Church, do you know Jesus today? I know Him as Emmanuel, God with us, the Alpha and Omega, the beginning and the end. I've found Him to be the bread of life, King of Kings, the light in a dark world. He's the same one, Church, who was living water to the Samaritan woman at the well, the only begotten son of the most high God.

The religious leaders were befuddled by what they heard being preached that day. They could not deny that a miracle had happened regarding the lame man's healing. So the religious leaders, seeing the masses praising God for the miracle they had witnessed, warned Peter and John to quit preaching in the name of Jesus and then released them.

After being released, Peter and John went to their fellow Christians, to those who believed, and told them all about what the religious leaders had said to them. Church, sometimes when we are feeling persecuted and put down by society, we go to everyone except our fellow Christians. Often, we don't want to let others in the church know that we are experiencing difficult times in our lives. We often are ashamed that we have fallen on hard times. But Peter and John went to their fellow believers upon being released. Upon hearing what the rulers and elders had said to Peter and John, the believers lifted their heads and began to pray with one accord. Church, can you imagine what effect it would have if all Christians everywhere or even within the same congregation would begin to praise God in unity?

Church, let me pause to tell you why we need to be praying in one accord today. For one thing, I personally believe in prayer. I have personally seen the power of God working after prayer.

Just a month ago, I was at the UNC Hospitals. I'd just gotten out of my car in the parking deck, and a woman held the elevator for me as I approached. Having served as a chaplain intern there at the hospital in 2001 and considering the scores of times I had been in that parking deck, I didn't recall ever entering the elevator, as I customarily walked up or down one flight of stairs to the bridge that crosses over the street to get to the hospital. But because the woman was kind enough to hold the elevator for me, I decided to get on. We greeted one another and then she said to me, "Sir, I don't know you and you don't know me, but will you please pray for my daughter?" Without hesitation, I said, "Of course I will pray," and as the elevator door opened and we began to walk, I asked about her daughter's condition. She said her daughter was twelve years old, and the doctors thought she had Rocky Mountain spotted fever because her fever had been around 103 since earlier in the week. She told me the doctors were not sure, but she said her fever won't go down. Her child's name was Brandy and they lived down near Clinton, North Carolina. So, by then we were in front of the entrance to the hospital, so I said, "Let's pray right now." And we did.

We departed. I didn't get the mother's name or what room her daughter was in. I thought that would be the last time I would hear Brandy's name mentioned because UNC Hospital is such a huge facility with hundreds of patients. I departed to my destination to see my niece, who had been in the hospital for over six weeks; she had been too sick to get a kidney transplant. While there visiting my niece, I had a conversation with a nurse about my niece and she said, "You know, I am really worried about another one of my patients, and I got the mother's permission to bring in my brother, who is a great warrior, to pray for the little girl. She didn't call any names. And then for some reason, I told the nurse about my experience with the stranger in the elevator and how she had asked me to pray for her daughter, Brandy, who was twelve years old, and her fever wouldn't go down. I told the nurse that she was from down near Clinton. And the nurse began to back up and said to me that is the same patient, and she showed me her name on a piece of paper. Then she said to me that is the way the man upstairs works. We both began to speak about how God answers prayers when the doctors can't figure it out. Just two weeks later I ran into the nurse again, and she told me Brandy got well and went home!

It was not by accident or chance that I had an encounter with someone I had never seen before that day in Chapel Hill. Can you imagine how unlikely it would have been for me to have that experience if it had been based upon chance? Thank God for the mother's faith to even reach out to a stranger like me. I'm glad, Church, I was carrying myself in a way that somehow the woman saw something in me. I'm thankful to God that on that Sunday morning God had dressed me in the whole armor of God. And I'm glad I wasn't ashamed to pray boldly right there in the front of the hospital. I have not always had that amount of courage. At times in my past, I've worried about what others thought. Church, to do the work of the Lord, we can't be ashamed of the gospel. Brandy went home because the Lord I serve brought her fever down, not because of anything

I did, but God has a way of using those who are unlearned ordinary men like Peter and John to get his word out. Church, this experience has increased my faith.

But let me move on and apply these scriptures and the one selected in Ephesians 6:11 to us today. We learn from our text today that it is much needed that we stay together, that we pray together, worship together in one voice. Oh, how many times have I stated that I wished we didn't have denominations? It seems to me to that denominations separate us more than they bring us together. But despite this, we have much work to do together. Acts 4:27–29 teaches us to be servants. Scripture refers to David as a servant and Jesus as a servant. Matthew 20:28 says the Son of Man did not come to be served but to serve. Scripture also refers to the disciples as servants. So, for us to be able to unite in praise we—no matter what profession or walk of life we come from—need to adopt a servanthood philosophy. Servanthood requires us to serve. We will need to get our hands soiled as we put our hands to the plow. We will have to possess the faith of a feet washer. Jesus was a feet washer. I'm impressed with the early Christians. They prayed for boldness to endure the threats and prosecution; they didn't pray that their way would be made easy as many of us do today.

The text also points to other characteristics of the early Christians that we need to learn from today.

We have mentioned the word "boldness" already. As Christians, we are going to have to take chances or risks, to be daring and strong and of good courage, as the Bible teaches (Joshua 1:6; Deuteronomy 32:6). It takes courage to be a Christian, even today. You can't be ashamed of the gospel and be effective in helping to win souls to Christ. But boldness must be tempered with humility. Somebody said you can catch more bees with honey than with vinegar. In other words, especially in today's world where it seems very difficult to get our young black men to stay in church, being bold cannot take on a tone of confrontation. I have learned in dealing with my twenty-two-year-old son that putting my arms around him, encouraging him, and letting him know I love him unconditionally does better than trying to shame him or attack his character. Many of us believers believe that we can draw all men unto Christ. But the Bible says that if Christ be lifted, He would do the drawing. We need to be lifting Christ more today. We are in a battle of survival in many of our churches. Too few men are present; many have lost faith because they see that those who attend are acting as foolish as the young adults are acting. Some preachers are stealing from the offerings and breaking up churches, communities, and families. Who wants to be a part of such an institution?

Before closing my law practice in Pittsboro in 2006, two chairmen of deacons' boards at two different churches located over fifty miles apart called me in the same week asking for legal advice. They explained that their churches were in turmoil; one of them said the preacher had gotten old and was insulting the youth, while the other said that they had a new preacher, and he was insulting the older members. But both deacons asked me the same question: is it legal for the church to lock the preacher out of the church? After much thought, I concluded what both sides at both churches were trying to do was to take the deed out of the Lord's name. I don't know how we ever got to this point in our history—some of us thinking that we as members, deacons, or pastors own the church. I may not ever be asked to come back here, but, New Hope, we got too much foolishness going on in our churches today. I ask New Hope and all churches today a question: How can we be united in praise if we can't be united under the same roof? How can we be unified in praise if the church, the very backbone of society, is engaged in so much foolishness and turmoil, so much so that the ways of the world look more favorable to unbelievers?

Church, to be able to praise God in unity, we need to put on the whole armor of God. I read that we need both offensive and defensive weapons to withstand the wiles of the devil. We need more armor made from love for our fellow man. To be able to praise God in unity, the whole armor of God is needed in order to withstand the devil, who doesn't fight fairly. He doesn't confront you in your face but sneaks up on you and talks behind your back so that you can't defend yourself. Satan engages in spiritual warfare. Satan utilizes a clandestine attack. Some might call it guerilla warfare. Satan is like the Taliban in Afghanistan, the suicide bombers in Iraq; he's an enemy that is hard to defeat. Satan is like the stealth bombers or unmanned drone planes that America has that are undetectable by radar. Often Satan doesn't come during the daylight hours but comes when you are weary; sometimes in the middle of the night when you are drowsy and unprepared. We need more soldiers who are willing to put on and keep on the whole of God 24/7, every day and every night.

We need more armor that is tempered with forgiveness. First Corinthians 13 says that love keeps no record of wrongs. God's armor contains a mandate for reconciliation. It is past time for reconciliation in our churches, in our homes and among our family members. There is much need for reconciliation among straights and gays. It is so very important that as Christians we make every effort to treat every individual with love and respect like they are somebody created by the same God that healed the lame man in our text today. No matter how bad a person is, he or she is one of God's children. I believe if we did this, Church, we would need fewer prisons for our young black males to go off to. We'd have more of our young men in churches, high schools, and colleges and more making livable wages. As I said in one of my previous sermons, we Christians need a new attitude about the way we look at things.

I'm about to conclude this message, but eminent theologian Dr. Gardner C. Taylor wrote the Foreword to the book *The Wisdom of the Word Love: Great African American Sermons,* in part said,

> Love and faith are the spiritual muscles of life. Just as your body is composed of physical muscles—without which it cannot function—without love and faith, the spirit cannot thrive. Faith and love are basic to our existence, the way we look at things, the way we treat people, and the way we conduct our lives.... Today the virtual disappearance of the "love ethic" has had its effect on us all. Our society has become loaded with hate and faithlessness.... We must begin by looking at how we treat other people. In our personal relations, a sense of regard for the value of every other individual will do a great deal to change the way we treat them. *I do not think there is any basis for a "love ethic" that does not largely take into account the preciousness, the importance of the individual. The New Testament gives a sense of one's worth. Christ thought every person was worth dying for; that is the basis of our preciousness.* [18]

But as I leave you here today, I want you to know that one day I decided to follow Jesus, the same one who woke me up this morning and started me on my way. And that is why I can stand before you today hopeful that we will move forward in unity praising a God that is able to keep us from falling. Paul said in his Letter to the Romans, "May the God who gives endurance and encouragement give you the same attitude of mind toward each other that Christ Jesus had. So that with one mind and one voice you may glorify the God and Father of our Lord Jesus Christ" (15:5–6, NIV).

Now that our minds and hearts are ready to praise God, we need to praise Him in the morning, praise Him at the noon time, praise Him when we wake up during the night. Jesus is worthy to be praised. The Psalmist says, "Let everything that has breath praise the LORD" (Psalm 150:6); "Enter into his gates with thanksgiving and his courts with praise" (100:4); "Give thanks to the LORD, for he is good! His faithful love endures forever" (136:1); "Make a joyful noise unto the LORD, all ye lands. Serve the LORD with gladness: come before His presence with singing" (100:20).

Church, we have so much to praise Him about. When we were yet sinners, He died a

18 Rhinold Ponder and Michele Tuck Ponder, eds., The Wisdom of the Word Love: Great African American Sermons (New York: Crown, 1997), Rev. Dr. Gardner C. Taylor, Foreword, in *The Wisdom of the Word Love,* p. 9-10)

cruel death on the cross to set us free; he hung there on the cross between two thieves. They put a crown of thorns on his head, pierced Him in his side.

Jesus, Jesus, we need to praise Him in unity, praise Him all alone, praise Him at work, and praise Him when we go to bed and praise Him when we wake up; praise Him when we can sit down at the dinner table, and praise Him when we get up. Church, we need to praise Him in unity. See where **He** brought us from. Praise Him when the sun comes up and when the sun goes down. We need to praise Him when the winds are calm, and we need to praise Him when the storms of life don't lighten up. We need to praise Him when floods leave you homeless. Praise Him because you got a comforter. Praise Him when you got money and praise Him when you're down to your last dime. Praise Him, Church, when you are all alone and when you come together.

A GIFT FROM AND BY GENE THREATS

His Truth Is Marching On

JOHN 18:38

Shiloh Baptist Church, Greensboro, NC

FEBRUARY 9, 2014

> Pilate saith unto him, "What is truth?" And when he has said this, he went out again unto the Jews, and saith unto them. "I find in him no fault at all."

It is my great honor and blessing to be in the pulpit once again. I was last here to deliver a sermon almost twelve years ago on the fourteenth day of April 2002 on Shiloh Baptist Church's 110th anniversary. I am also blessed to be in this pulpit alongside my friend of almost thirty-five years, Rev. Steve Allen. Some of our children are the same age, and importantly, our careers have paralleled one another. Both of us served in the trenches practicing law in neighboring counties. As you know, Steve practiced here in Guilford and I over in Rockingham County. I say "trenches" because we conducted many battles on cases that were difficult to say the least. I also say we served in the trenches because, while I have never seen Steve's financial records, early in our careers we both often took whatever came through the door. Sometimes what came through the door didn't have any money to pay us, but our parents' upbringing and the love we experienced in our communities and our churches made it very difficult for us to say no, and so we did our best to provide excellent legal services to many people whether they had much money or not.

Preaching at Shiloh Baptist Church, Greensboro, NC, with then-pastor Rev. W. Steve Allen Sr., February 9, 2014

In fact, I represented so many who had little or no money that the North Carolina Bar Association gave me an award, the Pro Bono Services Award, almost thirty years ago in 1985. I think—no, I'm sure—there came a time when my wife got fed up with me not bringing in much money. We were sitting around the dinner table one night and I told my wife that one of my former clients from Sanford had brought some "poke salad," a piece of lean meat and a piece of corn bread, by my office that day. Diane spoke up and immediately said to our three children, "Lord, children, your dad's clients are paying him with 'poke salad.'" But I know that my family and Steve's family never missed a meal. We were kind of like my parents when someone would stop by unannounced as my family sat around the dinner table. They used to say, "We got plenty, such as it is." So my family had plenty, such as it was. And I'm still thankful to God today for supplying our every need.

Regarding similar career paths, lastly Steve and I have been blessed to serve as judges and even to be lifted to a higher calling, that of gospel preachers. My father, now deceased, told me one time even before I went to law school that he didn't think you could be a lawyer and a preacher at the same time. For years, some have asked me, "How could it be possible to be a lawyer/judge and preacher at the same time?" My answer is always the same: "Apparently you don't know the power of God." And my father lived for a quarter of a century to see God bless me to be a lawyer and preacher at the same time. Shiloh, if you don't remember anything else I say to you today, do remember with God all things are possible!

But Shiloh, I know you didn't come here today to hear me talk about myself, so I turn to our text. I want to read from selected verses in the eighteenth chapter of John, highlighting the thirty-eighth verse. I believe there is a word from the Lord found there, possibly relevant and appropriate for this the second Sunday of the Black History Month of February, and so I want to speak on the subject "His Truth Is Marching On."

In today's text we find our Lord and Savior amid a trial, if you can call it that. If there ever was a kangaroo court, the one conducted by the Roman Pontius Pilate, his so-called trial of Jesus was just that. Rather than a trial as we have come to know it, maybe a better word would be "persecution." Christ had been arrested and was first taken to Annas, according to John 18:13.

Annas was father-in-law to the high priest, Caiaphas. The text says that Jesus was bound and taken to Caiaphas (some of the Gospels refer to Annas as the high priest as well as Caiaphas). In any event, in John 18:19–20, Caiaphas and other members of the Jewish Sanhedrin began to ask questions of Jesus about his disciples and his doctrine. Jesus responded I've been speaking openly to the world. I've been teaching in the synagogue and in the temple. I have not done anything in secret. Not believing Jesus had answered the questions directly, one of the officers present struck Jesus with the palm of his hand and demanded that he answer the high priest. Jesus told them, "If I've spoken evil, then bear witness to the evil. Point out to me what it is that I've said that is not the truth. But if I have spoken well, why do you strike me?" This was the beginning of a long night of cruelty to my Lord and yours. How the religious leaders were treating Jesus would be called police brutality today, but rather than coming from the police, it was coming from the religious authorities. Church, the truth is marching on.

While this first mini trial, if you will, among religious leaders was taking place, the text says that one of Christ's own disciples, Peter, was hanging out on the outside in the courtyard, denying that he knew the man called Jesus. Peter was like many of us. Church, in your silence have you denied that you know Jesus? By seeing injustice and wrongfulness committed by others in our presence, many of us remain quiet and, if given a chance, are quick to say, "That ain't my business" or "I don't want to get involved." Our youth are very concerned about being labeled a snitch. I'm concerned today that our sin of silence is aiding and abetting ignorance regarding the truth. But despite our silence, His truth is marching on.

The truth is that Jesus is the one who woke me up this morning, the one who hung the sun and moon in the sky causing the earth to turn on its axis, the one who walked out on the water and calmed the raging sea. Church, despite Peter's denial and our silence for lack of courage, I've stopped by Shiloh today to proclaim that His truth is marching on. I'll get back into our text in a moment, but I need to make my point. Yes, each of us have the right to remain silent under our Constitution so that we don't incriminate ourselves. But the truth needs to be exposed.

A couple of weeks ago I saw a one-man play about the events surrounding the savage murder of Emmett Till, the fourteen-year-old black youth from Chicago who traveled to Mississippi in the summer of 1955. Emmett Till was accused of whistling at a white girl in a store in Money, Mississippi. You may recall the event or reading about it. Some men came to his uncle's house and forcefully picked him up. But these white men took Emmett Till away from the house, took him to a barn, where they beat him about the head and body, gouged one of his eyes out, shot him, and then took him to the edge of the Tallahatchie River, where they shot him in the head and then fastened a seventy-pound metal fan around his neck with some barbed wire and threw him into the river. When found three days later, Emmett Till's body was swollen, disfigured, and unrecognizable. Law enforcement later sent the body to his mother in Chicago with instructions not to open the casket. But at the funeral in the presence of the world, *LIFE* magazine photographers, and others, the mother examined each part of the body that she knew so well and declared to the world, "That is my son." The photo of this unrecognizable corpse was on the front of *LIFE* and on television for the whole world to see. The savagery and wicked deeds done in the dark that we think will never come to light come to light because God is truth and light. John says in John 14:6, in part, "I am the way, the truth, and the life." Church, His truth is marching on.

Shiloh, this being Black History Month, I want you to know that in spite of all that happened to a people because of the color of our skin during over three hundred years of slavery and Jim Crow laws that followed—the rape of our women, castration of some of our men, separation of mothers from their children, brother from brother—in spite of all this, His truth, God's truth is still marching on!

Now let me return to the trial of the century for the truth within it. Caiaphas had seemingly become frustrated because perhaps he didn't get the confession he was seeking. They were trying to get Jesus to confess that he was stating that he was the son of God. Being unsuccessful and realizing that the Jews could not have him executed under Jewish law, Caiaphas had Jesus taken before the Roman judge Pontius Pilate for trial. Jesus was taken to the Hall of Judgment. John 18 says Pilate immediately asked them, "Why you bringing this man to me? What is he being accused of?" They responded, "We wouldn't have brought him here if he was not a benefactor [or criminal as we call it today]. The crowd already condemned him." Pilate said to them, "Why don't y'all judge him according to Jewish law?" They responded, "Because under Jewish law, we can't give him the death penalty." We can only speculate on what was going on in Pilate's mind. But Pilate went back into the Judgment Hall again and called Jesus before him and asked some questions. Pilate asked, "Are you the King of the Jews?" Jesus said, "Are you saying that yourself or did someone tell you that about me?" Pilate pressed Jesus further, "What have you done?" Jesus's answered: "My kingdom is not of this world; if it were, my servants would have fought back to keep me from being delivered to the Jews." Jesus further responded in 18:37, "You say I am a king. To this end I was born, and for this cause came I unto the world that I should bear witness unto the truth. Everyone that is of the truth heareth my voice." Pilate must have been frustrated after Jesus spoke about coming into this world to bear the witness to the truth. At verse 38, Pilate said, "What is truth?" And he immediately went back out to the crowd, and once again told them that he found no fault at all.

Church, today, this would be like the jury coming back with a not guilty verdict. It would be all over, and the judge would excuse the jury and order the bailiff and jailer to free the defendant. But Pilate didn't do that; he knew that during Passover the Jews had a custom that one charged and being held for a crime could be released. So Pilate asked, "Which one shall it be, Jesus or Barabbas, who is charged with robbery?" The crowd cried out, "Don't release Jesus, release Barabbas!"

I imagine Pilate was perhaps troubled in his own spirit. After all, no one had brought him a list of crimes that Jesus was being charged with, such as murder, robbery, or other such serious offenses. The chief priest Caiaphas had not sent Jesus to Pilate with a true bill of indictment specifically setting forth the charges, as we do in American courts. And not only that, but Pilate had seen the crowd out there screaming, "Crucify him, crucify him." Pilate must have been tormented. In the Gospel according to Matthew 27:19, while sitting on the judgment seat, Pilate's wife sent him a message: "Don't have anything to do with this innocent man, for I have suffered a great deal today in a dream because of him." I guess Pilate must have been like some of us husbands today. We don't always follow our wives' advice.

Now being a judge myself, I know that Pilate should not have been influenced by the crowd, but you know, Church, whether you are a judge or involved in any other profession or work, if you don't have Jesus somewhere in your life, you will be influenced not only by the crowd but by all sorts of matters that have nothing to do with fairness, justice, and doing what is right. So today, Church, I'm glad that God has come into my life and created in me a new heart that won't allow me to disregard my oath that I would administer justice to those who don't have any money as well as those who can afford the best lawyer than money can buy. I believe everyone should be able to have a lawyer to represent them. For this reason, I once agreed to represent a man who was a member of the Ku Klux Klan. Reverend Allen, I know that not everyone wants to see me sitting there when they come into my courtroom. Not everyone is seeking justice. I'm glad today that money can't buy me. I'm not controlled by who your lawyer is; I'm glad that God introduced me to Micah 6:8: "God has showed me what is good; and shown me what the Lord requires of me, which is to do justly, and to love mercy and walk humbly with my God."

So, beginning in chapter 19, Pilate took Jesus and had my Lord and your Lord whipped; the old song says they whipped him all night long. The soldiers put a crown of thorns on his head and put him in a purple robe, and said, "Hail, the king of the Jews," and they smote or slapped him with their hands.

And then after this, Pilate brought Jesus before the crowd yet again and told them yet again that he found no fault in Him. But the chief priest and officers, upon seeing Jesus, began to cry out, "Crucify him, crucify him," and so Pilate said, "Take him, for he found no fault in him. In other words, Judge Pilate found him to be innocent of the accusations against him, but because of the crowd, Pilate didn't set Jesus free. And the Jews answered that Jesus ought to die because he made himself the son of God. John 19:9 says that Pilate went back into the Judgment Hall again. He was afraid. After all this, Pilate asked Jesus, "Where are you from?" Jesus didn't say a word. The old gospel song says, "He never said a mumbling word." One might surmise that Pilate was troubled because he didn't know Jesus. Church, do you know Jesus today? If you don't know Jesus, then you don't know the truth! John 17:17 reminds us that Jesus said that he is the truth, and his word is true. I wonder sometimes whether witnesses who come before me and swear to tell the truth, and nothing but the truth so help me God, really know what they are saying. One day one of my newly hired law clerks was visiting our court, and we went into the courtroom to take a picture together. She saw two Bibles near the witness stand and asked me why are there two Bibles? With complete humorous intent, I said some witnesses lie so much that they are required to swear on two Bibles. Of course, we both laughed at my statement.

Young folk, I know some of what you are experiencing. Jobs are not plentiful, but they are more plentiful than when my parents began their family nearly sixty years ago. They didn't have much. I heard my mother say on one occasion that she only had one good dress and had to come home and wash it out every day. But Truth saw that she wanted to make something out of her life, so Truth stepped in. My parents had eight children, and we made do with what we had. Truth stepped in and made a way out of no way. Truth stepped into my family and made a federal judge out of the son of fourth grade and tenth-grade dropouts. Young folk, if you do your best, God will do the rest. You can't make it under your own power. His truth is marching on.

Church, the truth is ever lasting, no beginning and no ending. I lost my mother in the middle of last September and then my sister in November. My mother had studied and knew the Bible so well. I heard her say often that not one jot or tittle would pass away from the law until all is fulfilled (Matthew 5:18). Get in the word today. You can't wait on Sunday for Reverend Allen to teach you. You need to know God for yourself. His truth is marching on. Friday night I heard a pastor say that he used to stay up all night worrying about stuff, but one day he read in Psalms where it said, "He that keepeth me shall not slumber or sleep." So, from that day forward, he said he decided to go to bed and get some sleep, because there was no need for him and the Lord to lose sleep. Church, his truth is marching on.

Let me begin to bring this message to shore. So, Jesus didn't get a fair trial, but we know that he could have had one but for the fact that his fate was in the divine plan. In fact, Christ told Pilate that you only have the power that God gives you. So, Christ went to the cross; he went to Golgotha, to Calvary's cross; he hung there on that old rugged cross; he didn't have to, but he died so that we might have a right to eternal life. He died to cover all our sins; all we got to do is believe. His mother watched them pierce her son in the side. The Bible says blood and water poured out. What manner of love that he would give his life for me and for you?

There he stood between two thieves. One of them, upon expressing his belief, Christ told him, this day, you shall be with me in paradise. The Bible says the soldiers stood all around him casting lots for his garments. One of them said, "Truly this must be the son of God." Like Emmett Till's mother, Jesus's mother, Mary, was able to see her son's corpse after he had died while hanging there on the cross. Mothers and fathers, can you imagine what that would have been like to see your son hanging on the cross? But the truth is marching on.

I'm about to close but I can't leave Truth hanging on the cross and in His grave. For on the third day, Truth got up from the grave, proclaiming to the world that all power was in His hand. So today I thought that I needed to come by and add my voice to Reverend Allen's voice, that truth is all you need. You may not have much money, but know that money can't buy happiness, can't buy contentment, can't buy you a good husband or wife. His truth is marching on. If you want peace, then try the truth; if you want joy, unspeakable joy, then I dare you to try the truth. If you want to be content, then embrace the truth. If you need comfort, the truth will be with you all day and all night. Truth took a little nappy-headed boy off the farm in Rockingham County, North Carolina, where he was born three days shy of sixty years ago. And Truth has been trying to make something out of me ever since. Shiloh, His Truth is marching on. Glory, glory, glory hallelujah, His truth is marching on.

Virtual Sermons and Writings during the Season of COVID, *2020–2003*

Mothers with Sons—Night of Encouragement and Prayer
An Encouraging Word for Mothers with Sons

Zoom Conference—Host: Lori Moss

MAY 26, 2020

I'm grateful to be a part of a discussion dealing with mothers and their sons. In the last three years I have been blessed to become a grandfather to three grandsons and two granddaughters. I must say that my grandsons have been on my mind lately. Each time I have criminal court and see the many young men who come before me who have no relationship with their fathers, and some don't even know who their father is, my spirit is troubled. Each time I see a young unarmed black man shot and killed by a police officer or the hundreds killed during gang warfare in Chicago, Washington, DC, Durham, or Greensboro, North Carolina, I am deeply moved, sometimes even brought to tears in my secret closet. It seems like a black man's life is not valued as much as others in America. I am equally troubled by the seemingly many young men who don't have much drive to get a job, and those who are, educationally speaking, falling far behind their female peers.

Program announcement

COURTESY OF LORI MOSS

I want to give you wonderful mothers a few thoughts, followed by Attorney [Gregory] Moss, who I asked to accompany me tonight. He is closer to some of your children's ages and may have some perspective on how mothers ought to deal with their sons. As in most things in life, there is usually not one size that fits all. What might work for one son won't work for all. My wife's mother, the late Frances Ramsey, who gave birth to seven boys and eight girls, said to me one time, "Joe, all of my children are different."

Teach your children the importance of working.

I want to make five points as quickly as I can and then have Greg say whatever is on his mind:

1. *Give your sons responsibilities from an early age.* As soon as they can walk, begin training them to do some chores. My grandsons started having responsibilities at an early age. My daughter sent us a photo of her sons cleaning their home and raking leaves in their front yard. Their dad and mom have the right idea. Put youth to work as soon as possible!

2. *Encourage your sons.* Today they need encouragement more than ever. Put your arms around them and let them know you have confidence that they can do their schoolwork and achieve greatly. I learned more from raising my son than I did from raising my daughters. They didn't give me any trouble. My son was determined to do what he wanted to do, including not going to church after he'd been out late at night. I had curfew for my daughters, and I saw no reason not to have curfew for their brother. He rebelled because his classmates at Chapel Hill High School didn't have curfews. So I took a hard line and became very angry with him; one time calling him a coward in the church parking lot, one of those times when harmful words come out of your mouth that you will forever regret. God spoke to me and reminded me that love covers a multitude of sins, so I started loving him with all my might. My son became ill his senior year and needed to be hospitalized. My wife and I were hurting. You see, Satan was trying to take our son. As Christians we must make up our minds that our sons don't belong to Satan. It was about that time that I turned to the only thing that I knew to do. All through the day and night, I went into my secret closet and prayed for his healing. I was conducting a trial, and at every recess I went into my chamber and prayed without ceasing. I prayed when I got home, when I went to bed, when I woke up, and when I got into my car. Today my son has brought us so much joy. At thirty he has matured, gotten married and has two lovely daughters. He has become a manager at a Trader Joe's and is much beloved by all his coworkers and management. He has taught himself how to play guitar and writes his own songs and sings often about issues of our times.

Mothers don't give up on your sons. Encourage them every chance you get. I want you to know that all persons, no matter their circumstances—their very souls require validation. If you beat up on them too much—bruise their egos and make them feel worthless—then you can do permanent damage. One day several years ago I said to my son, Evan, "You need to find you a church to attend." He said, "Dad, if God does the drawing of each of us to Him, then why are you trying to do God's job?" But it wasn't until I began to love him with all my might that a change came. He told me just last week that it wasn't until he got to know God for himself that a change came upon him.

3. *Mental illness is rearing its head among many of our youth.* Black parents are still letting the stigma of mental illness keep them from seeking help for their children. A psychologist friend told me that some black teenagers told her that they didn't want to get treatment from a psychologist because they already had two strikes again them: being black and a man, and if they acquire the label of being crazy, then that might take them over the edge. Yes, there is nothing more important than prayer, but God has wonderfully made some psychologists, psychiatrists, and counselors. Sometimes our kids need to talk to someone other than their parents.

4. *Mothers can't be fathers.* No matter whether the father is in the home or nowhere to be found, women and mothers are not fathers. I would encourage you not to put down your son's or daughter's father, as that may affect your son's or daughter's relationship with their own partner. Many children are going to love their parents no matter what you may say about them.

5. Finally: *Pray, pray, pray without ceasing, and when you get tired of praying, pray some more.* The founder and host of this Zoom conference, Lori Moss, told me the other day that it had been on her mind and heart that parents need to take their little ones by the hand and pray for and with them from an early age. What a great thought. I know my faith was formed early in life. So, keep on praying.

The Sin of Silence: Do You Know the Man?

MATTHEW 26:69–75

Providence Missionary Baptist Church, Robersonville, NC

JULY 5, 2020

> The he began to call down curses, and he swore to them, "I don't know the man!" MATTHEW 26:74, NIV

Since fellowshipping with Providence Missionary Baptist Month last month, the perilous times of which I spoke have not eased up. Coronavirus is still raging across America and the world. We continue to see the positive testing numbers go up and observe in wonderment some people who show that they believe they are more powerful than God, refusing to follow the advice of doctors and the science community. When I last spoke to you, I also shared how the world was protesting the cruel death of Mr. George Floyd. Since that time, we've heard about others who have met the same untimely death. Photos on television of officers celebrating the chokehold used on twenty-three-year-old Elijah McClain bring back the images of whites celebrating the lynchings of black men in the 1800s and 1900s. Lord, when will this hatred flowing from hundreds of years of white privilege all end?

If there ever was a time when Christians need to have their voices heard—voices of conviction, voices of faithfulness, voices of truth, voices of courageousness, and voices of love toward men, women, boys, and girls from all walks of life—the time is right now.

In today's text, we see Peter—one of the first of the twelve disciples to be chosen, the one of whom it might be said he was one of Christ's most dependable disciples—denying even knowing our Lord, not once but three times. This is the same Peter who had been up on the Mountain of Transfiguration with Jesus, James, and John, and in a vision saw Moses and Elijah talking with Jesus and heard the voice of God say, "This is my beloved son, in whom I am well pleased" (MATTHEW 17:1–9). This is the same Peter who, on the same evening of his denials, told Jesus that even if he had to die with Him, he would never deny Jesus (MATTHEW 26:35). It was the same Peter who observed Christ walking on the stormy sea and had enough guts to set out to walk with Jesus but lost his nerve when he looked around and saw the fierce winds. But he's also the same Peter who had faith enough to call on the Lord to save him when he began to sink (MATTHEW 14:25–31). Peter's human nature is also shown while Jesus was in the Garden of Gethsemane, preparing for his crucifixion. He had asked his disciples Peter, John, and James to watch for him while he went away to pray. Three separate occasions Jesus returned to see Peter and the others asleep (MATTHEW 26:36–46), and the Gospel of John sets forth that at the moment of Jesus's arrest by the authorities, Peter takes his sword and cuts off the right ear of the high priest's servant (JOHN 18:10). Arguably, this may have demonstrated that Peter had a little mean streak, or as the young folk might say, he, like all of us, might have had a little "thug" in him.

Church, I have no doubt that Peter was capable of great loyalty and love toward Jesus (JOHN 21:15–17). He was indeed a zealot, believing fiercely in what he believed. Perhaps that is why he was given the nickname "The Rock." But these examples of Peter's character shortcomings demonstrate how God uses those among us who are not perfect to do his work. Perhaps it could be said that like all of us, Peter did not have a "stormproof religion," to use the words of the late preeminent theologian Rev. Dr. Gardner C. Taylor. When faced with the storms of life, we are often not up the task. But God uses whosoever he chooses to proclaim His word.

Church, do you know the man from Galilee, the one born in a manger, the one who raised Lazarus from the dead, walked out on the water and calmed the raging sea, the one who said, "Peace be still"? Do you know Him enough to testify publicly, unashamedly about the goodness of God, or will you continue to sin by remaining silent?

Are you one of the silent ones who can't muster enough courage to speak up and tell the world that the Savior has come? When your time comes at the end of your journey, will somebody be able to say that your voice could be heard when speaking up for truth was necessary. Stay with me and pray with me, Church, for a few more minutes.

Dr. Martin Luther King Jr. spoke about the dangers of being silent about things that matter. King urged those that care about the problems in our nation to speak up; we should not be silent. This applies especially to our friends. I have often said that unless those of us who have something to lose don't speak up about injustice and other things that matter, then progress won't take place. In other words, if those of us who are financially secure, own big houses, expensive cars, have savings accounts, money to invest in the stock market, and other wealth don't speak up, then progress won't occur for those who must choose between buying groceries, paying the rent, or buying life-saving medical prescriptions.

Providence and others under the sound of my voice, do you know the man? I challenge you today, for it's time for Christians to speak up loudly and clearly about the injustices that we see all around us. I believe in my heart, that this applies even more so to those of us who have big titles: judges, doctors, engineers, and PhDs. We hide behind these titles sometimes and say that, because I'm this or that, I can't speak the truth. We judges are challenged to remain neutral, but we also must speak out.

Whatever category you find yourself in, I want you to know today that you can't speak up under your own power. It takes the courage that only Jesus Christ can give to speak up. If you walk closer to Christ, He will direct your path and give you directions on the right time and the right place to say what needs to be said. My late mother, Bettie Webster, often told me and my seven brothers and sisters that there is a time and place for all things. Today I proclaim that now is not the time to remain silent.

Church, there is a void, some empty spaces that need filling in our communities. Church, we need some more Christians to make up the hedge and stand in the gap for the land. The silent majority can make a difference in America and around the world. Providence, you have among your congregation Judge Jim Wynn, who has given us a great example of courage in his state and federal legal opinions. He has not been afraid to call a spade a spade. He's called out racial and gender discrimination when he has seen it. He has in his many legal opinions spoken truth to power. And so, when his day comes, I believe it will be said that he left a committed life behind. He, and I, and other judges desperately need the constant prayers of the righteous as we do our jobs. Today I'm standing on the shoulders of my late parents and others who taught me right from wrong in my rural community called Goodwill outside Madison, North Carolina.

So today, I'm not worrying about anything; because I know that I know that I know the one who is able to keep me from falling and keep me from being silent. I can't say like Dr. Martin Luther King Jr. that I have been to the mountaintop and looked over and saw the promised land. But I know that I know that I've been redeemed by the sacrificial shedding of Christ's blood. So, Judge Wynn, I can't stay silent. I know the man who one day took me down to the potter's house and operated on my heart and added some courage and gave me a little more faith. Church, it's past time for all those who know our Savior to speak up, not only to our own race. We do a lot of preaching to the choir. It's also past time to speak to our white brothers and sisters with candor and love about racial and other injustices, and the devastating effect they continue to have on a whole race of people. I've learned that love does cover a multitude of sins. Yes, it will take courage. We need some more Mother Pollards, who I read told Martin King at the time of the Montgomery boycott, "My feets are tired, but my soul is rested." Fredrick Douglass is quoted as saying, "With bravery, there will always be a remedy for oppression."

Church, do you know the man? You might say that your past sinful ways make you unqualified to speak up. But Peter and so many others who God has called demonstrate that God uses the imperfect and the improbable to carry his message around the world. Silence is not acceptable today.

I'm about to conclude. Yes, Peter was imperfect; but his love for Christ allowed God to restore him completely to the body of faith. Christ didn't give up on Him, and He never gives up on us. After Christ's resurrection, He reminded Peter three times before going to his Father to feed His sheep. So, Providence, since you happen to know the man, you need to speak up. Our ancestors reminded us how they got over. So feed His sheep so that they might be encouraged during this pandemic. Feed his sheep, Church, so that our young men won't give up hope despite those who wrongfully abuse them at a traffic stop or some other injustice is done to them.

I have this affinity, this dedication in my heart especially to our young black men.

Occasionally I've returned from the courtroom into the inner solitude of my chambers, my Court office there in downtown Durham, eyes welled up with tears because of the dire circumstances confronting our mostly African American young men that I see in court. It's almost a rarity to find a young black man who has a relationship with his father. In fact, many don't know their father at all. Providence, I'm also asking you today to pray for these young men. Their renewal, new birth, and welcoming back to the house of faith is one of the keys to the future of our communities and our nation. The voice of Jesus keeps ringing in my ear, "If you know me, then feed my sheep."

Providence, I leave you hopeful today. Our youth are demonstrating for a good cause; please support them. Black lives do matter. All of God's children matter. If you want them to come back to our churches to fill the empty pews, then we older ones, while we have an ounce of strength left in our bones, will need to feed His sheep.

I'm encouraged today by God's word. I'm encouraged by some of the old gospel songs: "On Christ the solid rock I stand, all the earth is sinking sand"; "I go to the rock of my salvation; I go to the rock and my redeemer." The sins of silence: do you know the man? A-men.

Knocked Down, but Not Out: The Battle Is the Lord's

2 CHRONICLES 20:15

Oberlin Baptist Church

JUNE 7, 2020

> He said: "Listen, King Jehosphaphat and all who live in Judah and Jerusalem and all who live in Judah and Jerusalem! This is what the LORD says to you: 'Do not be afraid or discouraged because of this vast army. For the battle is not yours, but God's." 2 CHRONICLES 20:15, NIV

I read that the great prizefighter Muhammad Ali won fifty-six of his sixty-one professional fights in his long-storied career and that he was knocked down only four times. Ali was knocked out only once—by George Foreman in 1980, when Ali was thirty-eight years old, had come out of retirement, and some say had already started showing signs of Parkinson's disease. So, for the most part, at least during Ali's prime, he was knocked down, but not knocked out.

ILLUSTRATION BY SHAILYN RAMSEY

As most of Oberlin knows, I was blessed to publish a book on the first African American superior court judge in North Carolina history, the Honorable Sammie Chess Jr. He is most likely the wisest man I have ever met. Many of his kernels of wisdom are quoted in that biography. He speaks of the fact that even trained lawyers are going to experience blows against them no matter how trained or how good they are. In that book, Judge Chess is quoted as follows: "You must have a bearing and an abiding faith in your moral direction." [He said] "You can't be a lawyer if you don't stand up straight." He went on to say, "There will be blows against you, but you will be a man if you take the blows. A man can do remarkable things if you inspire others."

In today's text found in the twentieth chapter of 2 Chronicles, King Jehoshaphat ruled in Judah for about twenty-five years from 873 to 848 before the birth of Christ. I read that he was an able ruler and faithful worshiper of Yahweh. A record of his reign is contained in the final chapter of 1 Kings 22:43 and 2 Chronicles 17:1–21:1. I want to move quickly to the text found at 2 Chronicles chapter 20, and to paraphrase some of what is found there.

There came a time during Jehoshaphat's reign that some outsiders, the Moabites, Ammonites, and Meunites, came to make war against Jehoshaphat and his nation of Judah. Some of his own people came to him and told them a great multitude were approaching from beyond the sea on this side of Syria. Upon hearing this bad news, we learn that Jehoshaphat feared God and set about seeking Him. (I saw a billboard one time along the highway in Eastern North Carolina. It said, "Wise men still seek Jesus.") So, Jehoshaphat, upon hearing the bad news, began to seek God. Church, there is something special about seeking God in humble submission, admitting your many sins, and asking for forgiveness. Forget about correct English: Lord I ain't what I ought to be but thank God I ain't what I used to be. So, King Jehoshaphat brought his nation together to give reference to an almighty God. He declared a public fast. As I understand the text, it seems like the king was having a conversation with God. Church, to have a conversation with God, you need to know Him for yourself. Jehoshaphat reminded God about how He had protected them in times past. Like some of us, he seemed to be saying in his prayer, "Lord God, you know that we are weak, but we know that you are strong." King Jehoshaphat said, "We have no might against the great army that is approaching us."

The king's concern was like ours today during this coronavirus pandemic that has inflicted millions around the world and killed hundreds of thousands with no end in sight, and during this time of the killing of unarmed black men in America by police or white vigilantes for no reason other than the color of their skin. We are experiencing a time in which rioting, and mass destruction are taking place across the nation brought about by the senseless murder of Mr. George Floyd on the streets of Minneapolis by a white police officer. Jehoshaphat was burdened down and praying, "God we don't know what to do." How many of you have said at least to yourself, "Lord, I just don't know what to do"?

Church, have you ever been perplexed, bewildered, and at a complete loss at how to solve a problem facing you? Perhaps you have had an illness. Have you been at a loss of why it is the doctor couldn't diagnose your condition? You went to every doctor that somebody said might be able to help. It might be that you were experiencing a family issue, conflict between husbands and wives. Families with children often have conflict that can be exhausting and make you want to throw up your hands and give up. Our children may lose their minds and forget who carried them for nine months, forget about who nurtured and provided shelter, who supported them in school, and maybe gave a son or daughter their last dollar because of the love we have for our children.

Let me place a pin right here for just a moment. I was asked by a woman of faith in our community, Ms. Lori Moss, to participate in a Zoom program titled *Mothers with Sons* this past week. I heard that many mothers were encouraged by what took place that night. To God be the glory! As I was preparing for today, I saw two quotes about our children that I'll quickly share with you that might also encourage somebody in this service with the relationship with your children.

Eileen Kennedy-Moore, PhD, a clinical psychologist, is writes in her book, *Smart Parenting for Smart Kids: Nurturing Your Child's True Potential,* "The miracle of children is that we just don't know how they will change or who they will become."[19]

Author C. J. Milbrandt, in his book, On your Marks: The Adventure Begins writes, "Have a little faith in your sons. This journey will be the making of them."[20]

Life itself is a difficult journey. There will always be weapons formed against us, but the Bible says those weapons will not prosper. We don't know what God has in store for our children. As parents when we are having our daily prayer, it is okay to remind God that we know that He has made a way in the past and that we are still trusting Him to make a way in the future. Yes, you must fast sometimes and pray all the time, morning, noon, and night. Pray when you get tired of praying; pray when you don't feel like it. The Bible says pray without ceasing. And we must live a life before our children that is pleasing to God.

Let me get back to the text. So, when King Jehoshaphat was pleading with God for protection from the great army that was coming his way, he was completely honest with God. Again, he said, "We don't know what to do but our eyes are upon you." Church, during these perilous times, be sincere and honest with God. Keep your eyes on the prize!

The text says Jehoshaphat's congregation was composed of a cloud of witnesses that included husbands, wives, and little children. Today, families everywhere need to come together, to pray together, humble ourselves, seek his face, and turn from our wicked ways. If we do this, Church, I believe we will hear from heaven and that God will build a fence around our black men in America and heal the nation. He is the one and only one that can change those whose hearts are eaten up with hatred and racism. Rioting and burning down your own community will not get the job done.

I read further on over in 2 Chronicles 20:14–15 that there in the crowd the Spirit was present. Maybe it's me, but it seems to me that when our people only had one good suit and one car, and outdoor toilets, and our drinking water came from wells, the spirit of the Lord showed up more often in our churches than today. But He showed up as

19 Permission granted by Dr. Eileen Kennedy-Moore.

20 Permission granted by C. J. Milbrandt.

Jehoshaphat was seeking God's protection. The Spirit spoke, "Listen Jehoshaphat and all of Judah and all who live in live in Judah and Jerusalem! This is what the LORD says to you: 'Do not be afraid or discouraged of this vast army. For this battle is not yours.'" Oberlin, I want you to know with great clarity today that no matter what you are going through, the battle is not yours. During this season of much stress, thank God we are knocked down but not out. We are still in the race, still in the game. We may be behind in the race, but every now and again, I feel some tailwinds; I feel the wind beneath my wings. So, I feel like going on no matter what the challenge is. I want Oberlin and all those under the sound of my voice to know that in the Lord, the bad police have no power; and they should know that until they rid themselves of those among them who think like and act like the Ku Klux Klan, law enforcement in many communities will not be able to earn the respect of those who they are sworn to protect.

I want Oberlin and those present to know that we will always have battles:

We will likely from time to time get knocked down, but thanks, thanks, thanks be to God, we will not get knocked out—for we are soldiers in the army of the Lord. That old gospel song comes to mind: "I am a soldier in the army of the Lord, I'm a soldier in this army. I don't mind dying in the army of the Lord, I don't mind dying in this army."

Church, I've been challenged many times, rejected, . didn't get accepted in my first three choices for law school forty some years ago; apparently, they didn't know who they were dealing with—didn't know that even then, I was a soldier of the cross. I was knocked down, but I was not knocked out. Never, never, ever give up, young folk. I've never been one to pay much attention to those who tell me I can't do something. Those are fighting words as far as I'm concerned. I already see this Webster stubborn streak in some of my grandchildren. My parents used to call it "hardhead."

When I was rejected at three law schools after graduating with honors from Howard University, I got up and dusted myself off and went to church and I heard the song, "The battle is not yours, it's the Lord's." I heard God would fight my battles, that He is a battle axe, when I am weak, He is strong, and that God has never lost a battle. I heard the old grandchildren of slaves sing, "I've been buked, and I've been scorned, talked about 'sho' as you born." But I'm thanking God today for giving me the strength to get up when I've been knocked down, but not knocked out, I get up stronger and more faithful than ever. Knocked down, but not knocked out. Church, the battle is the Lord's.

I heard somebody say that Jesus beat the devil with both hands tied to the cross. We forget sometimes that God is fighting our battles, getting things ready for us at the right time—"Kairos," His time, not ours. He is busily arranging things in our favor, making a way when we cannot see our way out. As followers of Christ, we should expect to see boulders in our path and deep rivers to cross. The lyrics to "Must Jesus bear the cross alone, written by Thomas Shepherd in the late 17th Century, lets us know that we too will have some hardships, some crosses to bear in this life.

In Romans 8:37 the scripture says no, in all these things we are more than conquerors through Him who loved us. God has a way of making our paths straight and leveling out the jagged places. Isaiah said that the mountains and hills will be made low. But we are good at saying, "Woe is me"; we murmur or complain about so many things that don't matter. Expect to be knocked down, but God will pick you up if you trust Him. He will place your feet on solid ground.

I'm about to close, but I'm sure King Jehoshaphat was feeling anxious about the great army that was approaching. After having fasted and praying, he received instructions from the Lord. God told him not to be afraid or dismayed by reason of the great multitude coming up against them. In verse 16, the spirit said tomorrow to go down against them; come up by the cliff, you'll find them at the end of the brook before you get to the Je-ruel wilderness. God said, "Stand still, Jehoshaphat. You won't even have to fight a battle." The Spirit told Jehoshaphat to stand still and see the salvation of the Lord that will be with you. And before going toward the battlefield, Jehoshaphat and all Judah and Jerusalem bowed down once again and worshiped the Lord. Oberlin, you can't pray enough. So, they got up early in the morning. Young folk, I grew up hearing that "the early bird catches the worm." Laying up in your bed sleeping all day won't get you any place in life. Jehoshaphat and his people followed God's command and went into the wilderness, and when they got to their destination, they saw with their own eyes that the entire opposing army was already knocked down and knocked out. The enemy was already dead; not one weapon had to be drawn—proof of what can happen if you let God fight your battles.

Sometimes we feel like we are already defeated, that mentally we feel like we have been knocked down and have lost the battle even before it begins. But get this, Church, since the battle is not ours to start with, we couldn't lose the battle, because it was not ours to lose.

Knocked down, but not out. The battle is the Lord's.

In conclusion, sometimes I walk around the housing singing a song from my youth, made popular by its author and singer, Walter Hawkins. Part of the lyrics are: "When the battle of life is over, you know I'm gonna wear a crown.

African American Contributions to Religion

On the Occasion of Black History Month,
Oberlin Baptist Church, Raleigh, NC

FEBRUARY 3, 2013

As I began to reflect upon what it is that I would say to Oberlin today about the contributions of African Americans to religion in just a few minutes, I couldn't help but think about the slaves and ex-slaves who endured hardship to be able to worship what was, to most, "a foreign God." Dismembered from their families in Africa and having been brought to these shores chained in the hull of ships—sickened by the rough seas and many treated worse than animals—somehow or another, African Americans accepted a God from those who enslaved them. This fact alone lets me know that there is a God somewhere. I am reminded that God said in Isaiah, "My thoughts are not your thoughts neither are your ways my ways." So today one of the great collective contributions made by African Americans to religion was how we as a people endured the hard aches and mistreatment during slavery while at the same time accepting Christ and spreading the gospel of Jesus Christ. One great contribution by African Americans to religion is the lesson that people of faith must be steadfast and must endure to the end.

Another great contribution of African Americans is the music, the gospel songs joyously proclaimed all over the world. I go back to that "ol' time religion" that was good enough for my grandmother and my mother, and it's good enough for me. We sang in

A GIFT FROM AND BY GENE THREATS

the tobacco and cotton fields, "Ain't gonna let nobody turn me around.... I'm gonna keep on walkin', keep on talkin' marching up to freedom land."

And then I look to the many uplifting songs Mahalia Jackson sang, such as "How I Got Over" and "His Eye Is on the Sparrow," and Thomas Dorsey's "Precious Lord, Take My Hand." I don't have to go that far back as I remember my own mother's rendition of "I love the Lord, down in my heart; I love the Lord, down in my heart. He's good to me, he's good to me, down in my heart. He's all I need. Down in my heart." And Aunt Hazel Moore is still singing, "I've learned how to live holy, I've learned how to live right, I've learned how to suffer, for if I suffer, I'll gain eternal life." And then she ends by singing, "When I see Jesus, no more heartaches, no more disappointment, no more trouble, no more sickness."

The greatest contributions of African Americans may best be found in the millions of sermons that began on the slave plantations by some who could not even read and write, but committed Scripture to memory, and in the northern cities by Richard Allen in Philadelphia and the surrounding states and Isaac Lane who went from slave to preacher among the freed men and women in Tennessee, Texas, and Louisiana. They are just two of the many great preachers of the late 1700s and 1800s. One can never overlook the great contributions of Rev. Dr. Gardner C. Taylor. Time does not allow me to elaborate on his numerous contributions to scholarship and the lives of tens of thousands. Some may forget that while Dr. Martin Luther King Jr.'s legacy is that of a civil rights leader, he was first and foremost a gospel preacher ordained and sent by God. Pauli Murray graduated from Howard University Law School, became a civil rights activist and author, and became the first black female ordained as an Episcopal priest. Many others from all walks of life have preached, unlikely people like Congressman Adam Clayton Powell Jr. of Harlem, New York. On Good Friday night, 1930, he preached his initial sermon. Many of his unsaved friends attended. I read where prostitutes, gamblers, and his drinking friends came to hear him preach. Congressman Powell had a reputation of being able to hold his liquor, and he also had a reputation of being a ladies' man. There were those among the crowd who were simply curious, wondering how it could be possible for Adam Clayton Powell Jr. to be called to preach. God's magnificent, unmatched, and transformative power was revealed that Good Friday night: Thirty-seven people joined the church.[21] There are too many others to mention, but I can't ever forget about the many who rode the dusty roads of the South, whose names have not been recorded in the history books—those who

21 From Ponder and Tuck-Ponder, eds., *The Wisdom of the Word: Faith*, p. 46.

were compensated only by a good meal on Sunday and, if they were lucky, something to take back home from the gardens of the old farmers in their congregations. All these preachers, notwithstanding their level of education, had sense enough, like the Apostle Paul, to preach Christ crucified, and that's why I say that God-sent preachers may be our race's greatest contribution to Religion in American and the world.

Can Anything Good Come out of Nazareth? And what about Bertie and Martin?

JOHN 1:43–46

Providence Baptist Church, Robersonville, NC

APRIL 18, 2021

> The next day Jesus decided to leave for Galilee. Finding Phillip, he said to him, "Follow me." Philip, like Andrew and Peter, was from the town of Bethsaida. Philip found Nathanael and told him, "We have found the one Moses wrote about in the Law, and about whom he prophets also wrote—Jesus of Nazareth, the son of Joseph." "Nazareth! Can anything good come from there?" Nathanael asked. "Come and see," said Philip. JOHN 1:43–46, NIV

My sermon today comes straight out of Nazareth and out of Eastern North Carolina but could very well come out of every nook and cranny in America today. I have a great love for history, and in recent years I have been doing some ancestry research on my own family tree. Recently I had a brief conversation with my career law clerk, attorney Pedra Lee, about her family tree, and she has consented for me to relate a relevant part of a conversation she had with me about family. At the outset I will tell you that Ms. Lee is one of the hardest-working students of the law and best legal writers that I have ever met. Her understanding of the sometimes very difficult factual and legal issues of our cases is off the charts. And she has an attitude and heart of servanthood. In short, Ms. Lee is a great law clerk and a person who everyone in the Middle District of North Carolina loves to encounter. She was born in Martin County over in Williamston, and her family trees of the Lee and Wynn family roots go far back in time over there in Bertie, specifically, the town of Windsor.

In my conversation with Ms. Lee about ancestry, she told me that she had asked kinfolk a question relating to her family. I got the impression that one family member responded in a manner that informed her more than she expected. The phrase "getting an earful" might adequately describe the conversation. I sensed that my law clerk might have heard some things that one might not be talked about ordinarily. So often in our communications about family ancestry, we get responses that often don't paint a perfect picture. That's because the human experience has never been and never will be perfect. In discussing family history, in prior generations we would often get a response from relatives along the lines of a conversation that I overheard during my youth about where one of my own late great-grandfathers was from. The relative said her mother told her, "Child, y'all better leave that alone." I've always wondered what that meant. One might assume with little if any evidence that there may have been something scandalous about my great-grandfather's conception and birth or perhaps about how he had lived his life. I surmise that because of the racially divided American experience and the horrendous suffering brought about by slavery, the question of mixed racial heritage often was taboo, and our ancestors of generations past didn't want to talk about it because it was too painful.

But I've stopped by Providence Baptist Church this morning to tell you that despite how sometimes our minds lead us to only think of negative information when considering family heritage, that something good has come out of Nazareth, Bertie and Martin Counties. Well, for one thing, while my law clerk lived and went to school in Newport News, Virginia, her life was molded and shaped by a strong family bond of loving parents, aunts and uncles, cousins, and the unconditional love of her grandmother Pearl there in Bertie. She spent many a weekend and summers there and can still feel the sandy soil of Bertie County. The love of family was and continues to be so great that she will never forget where she came from.

And, Providence members and others who are a part of this service, please don't spend even one second trying to figure out who said what, how and why. If you do so you will miss the message that I'm trying to convey to you today. More important, powerful, and insightful than anything my law clerk told me, in response to what her relative had said, was that she told another family member, "I will never judge, because I need to be afforded some grace myself."

My, my, what began as a brief conversation on ancestors ended with a reminder to me of what Jesus would say or do. Church, there is much good that has come out of Bertie and Martin and all places big and small.

Church, as a people we have continued to get things all twisted as to what is important in our Christian walk. We tend to value gossip and specialize in repeating information that is not necessarily factual and often degrading or demeaning of others. As Matthew 7:3 reminds us, we are good at noticing the speck of sawdust in our brother's eye, yet we don't pay any attention to the plank in our own eye. As a result, we end up doing what young folk call "throwing shade."

Some of us even today have the unbridled gumption to tell our daughters that they can only be good on their backs—or that his or her very birth was a mistake. Providence, the Bible makes it so clear that all have sinned and fallen short of the glory of God. But

I want to leave you with an encouraging word today. Something good has come out of Bertie and Martin and all places large and small, urban and rural. But more importantly, something good has come out of Nazareth.

I once met the late attorney John Harmon, who grew up in Windsor there in Bertie and practiced law for many years over there in New Bern. I attended the memorial service of another great Bertie County native, the Honorable Frank Balance Jr. I read that at his "Going Home" funeral service, Congressman G. K. Butterfield remarked that "Frank Balance was a servant leader. He was one that cared about the least of these in our communities. And Congressman Butterfield said that Eastern North Carolina is better because Frank Balance came our way." And God is still raising up lawyers and other noteworthy persons in Bertie. During a recent court session not many weeks ago, I met a young attorney whose name is RaShawnda Murphy. She had been salutatorian at Bertie High School, graduate of the University of North at Chapel Hill, and an honors graduate of North Carolina Central's law school. She law clerked for the former chief justice Cheri Beasley. Attorney Murphy has gained an associate's position in a reputable law firm in Greensboro. I understand she is the only person of color in that firm. And finally, from Bertie, NBA basketball player Kent Bazemore went to high school in Bertie, and Google says he makes $15 million and change a year for the Golden State Warriors.

And what about Martin County? I've been blessed to get to know my friend the Honorable James Wynn Jr., a very proud son of Martin County and Providence Baptist Church. He grew up over there in Robersonville and has, for over thirty years as member of the state and federal judiciary, exemplified many times over that something good can come out of Martin. As a member of the highest appellate court in North Carolina and the federal Fourth Circuit Court of Appeals in our nation, Judge Wynn has courageously breathed new life into the Constitution and made it applicable to all people through his judicial decisions, not just to the rich and powerful but also to those who can't speak for themselves.

And I recently read the obituary of Judge Wynn's late father, James Wynn Sr. No wonder his son is standing so tall. Evidently his dad had broad shoulders. What would that community be like without the likes of James Wynn Sr., who did so much to help build up your community? I read that he was a farmer, a self-taught carpenter, and a friend, teacher, and mentor to many, and I see that he was faithful to the end. Nothing better could ever be said about anyone when one gets to the end of one's journey. Never give up, Church, no matter what happens to you, and like James Wynn Sr. endure to the end.

So, there is much good that has come out of Bertie and Martin. I implore you today that rather than searching for the mistakes in life that some may have made, we need to encourage each other. We need not and should not spend one second thinking and talking about stuff that God forgave many years ago with his death on the cross.

For one thing, as my career law clerk said, all of us need some grace. None of us are so bad that grace can't turn us around. Over there in 2 Corinthians 12:7, I read where the Apostle Paul had a thorn in the flesh, but he concluded in 2 Corinthians 12:9 that God's grace was sufficient for him. Therefore, I proclaim today that His grace is sufficient for me and you. And over there in 1 Timothy 1:15, I read where Paul considered himself chief among sinners. Thank God Christ came to save sinners.

Providence, no matter who you are, no matter how much or how little we think we have accomplished, we all need a little grace that only Christ can give. We need to be careful about judging others too quickly. Something good has come out of Bertie and Martin and places large and small.

And then when you get through testifying on the highest hill and molehill in Eastern North Carolina that you can find about the goodness of the people there in Bertie and Martin; when you get through building up the self-esteem and dignity of your neighbors and your children, some of whom have lost hope; when you get through putting your arms around that man or woman who may have a drinking or drug problem, telling them that you love them; go tell somebody what and how Phillip responded to Nathaniel's question in today's text, about whether anything good could come out of Nazareth. Phillip responded, "Come and see." Church, I invite you to just come and see a country boy whose ancestry was from Nazareth. Come and see one who can change your heart, transform your life; come and see the one who has all power in his hands; come and see the one who can heal the minds of those sitting in judgment, who can heal the brokenhearted and disappointed.

I've run out of time, Church, and must conclude, but I heard the late Dr. Gardner C. Taylor say that no matter where a preacher starts his or her sermon from the pulpit, you must end up at Golgotha. In other words, the pastor-preacher can start at Genesis and end up in John or whatever Bible verse one pleases. But no matter where you start, Dr. Taylor said you must end up your sermon at Calvary's Cross, where I first found the Lord. It was there by faith, at the old wooden cross, two pieces of wood nailed upon the other where my wounded and imperfect sinful heart was mended and put back together, and my life was changed.

Philip said, "Come and see," Nathanael; come and see, Providence, the one who was born of a virgin named Mary; the one who suffered and died on Calvary's Cross. The soldiers placed a crown of thorns on his head and pierced him in his side; the Bible says that blood and water came streaming down. Can't you see it, Church? Come and see the giver of redeeming grace that my law clerk reminded me about, the giver of eternal life. Come and see the one that gives us a second chance and a third chance. Go tell somebody how one day you were lost and now you are found, was blind but now you can see. Come and see, Church, the good that has come out of Nazareth. Come and see with your own eyes. There is something good that has come out of Nazareth, Bertie, and Martin, and throughout the land.

"Whosoever Will"

REVELATION 22:17

On the Occasion of the Graduation of Ms. Brianna Collins and Ms. Tanaya Gay, Oberlin Baptist Church

JUNE 11, 2017

> The Spirit and the bride say, "Come!" And let the one who hears say, "Come!" Let the one who is thirsty come; and let the one who wishes take the free gift of the water of life. REVELATION 22:17, NIV

Today is a special occasion that we here at Oberlin Baptist Church have designated as a time to honor two outstanding high school graduates who are daughters of Oberlin: Brianna Collins and Tanaya Gay. It is a time of reflection and a time of looking forward to what God has in store for them and for others who love the Lord. Congratulations, Brianna and Tanaya. Well done! You have overcome just one of the many obstacles and tests that no doubt you will encounter in your lives, and all of which you will have to decide about. We here at Oberlin have been blessed by your willingness to share your youthful vigor and vitality and unashamedly your talent of singing and spiritual dance with us. We pray for your continued walk with the Lord.

God has led me today to share a few moments, not only with these graduates, but with all those who have gathered here today at Oberlin. My text is found in the Book of Revelation, chapter 22, verse 17. IT reads as follows: "And the spirit and the bride say, Come, and let him that heareth say, Come. And him that is athirst come. And whosoever will, let him take the water of life freely." From this text, I want to talk to you for a few minutes on the subject "Whosoever Will."

Today I'm standing partially with my judge's hat on but mostly with my preacher's hat, recognizing that I cannot do anything without the power of God. I want to issue a summons to you all, not just Brianna and Tanaya. But I want to issue a summons—a court order if you will. But it is unlike any other order I sign from time to time when someone does not show up for court as they are required to do. This summons is more akin to an invitation, and it is titled "Whosoever Will." It is one that, if you study it carefully, read what the commentaries say about it, pray over it, and seek divine guidance, you will find that some will understand it, and some will heed the call of the invitation to choose eternal life over eternal damnation. The Invitation is in big bold letters, **Whosoever Will.**

Other scriptural verses also set forth the invitation. To our youth, the Bible says at Luke 18:16 and Matthew 19:14, "Suffer the little children to come unto me and forbid them not, for such is the Kingdom of God. In Matthew 11:28–30, the Bible makes the meaning of the summons even clearer. That text say, "Come unto me all ye that labor and are heavy laden and I will give you rest. Take my yoke upon you and learn of me, for I am meek and lowly in heart; and ye shall find rest unto your souls. For my yoke is easy and my burden is light." Whosoever will.

Oberlin, if you are burdened down with sickness, not getting any relief, whosoever will.

If you or someone you know is hooked on drugs and alcohol, legal or illegal, whosoever will.

If you have any other addictions, perhaps a sex addiction, whosoever will.

If you lack understanding of where you are in your relationship with God, your wife, your husband, or your children, whosoever will.

If you are confused about who you are, whose you are, where you came from, or where you are going, whosoever will.

If you are wondering about your DNA genetic makeup, whether you are straight, gay, or neither of the above, whosoever will. I heard a summary of a quote several years ago given by a preacher citing one of the greatest preachers and religious scholars who ever lived, Rev. Dr. Gardner C. Taylor, who passed in recent years. Dr. Taylor had been asked to be a guest lecturer or be a part of the program which, if my recollection serves me well, was held at the Hampton Ministers' Conference held annually in June of each year. At the conference, at that time, many of the participants could ask the guest lecturer any question that may have been burning on their hearts. So, one guest asked, and I paraphrase, How could it be proper, lawful, and godly for some churches to have a gay pastor? I suspect being in an auditorium full of learned preachers that perhaps the guest asking the question may have been like the learned lawyer who stood up to test Jesus over there in Luke 10:25; he asked, "What must I do to inherit eternal life?" You know the story. Jesus said, "What is written in the law?" He answered, "You shall love the Lord your God with all your heart, and with all your soul, and with all your strength and all your mind, and your neighbor as yourself." Jesus told him he'd answered correctly: do this and you will live. The story continues because the lawyer sought to justify himself. . . . Like Jesus, Dr. Gardner was learned in the Bible and was ready to answer the preacher who asked how it could be that a gay preacher could pastor a church. I can still hear Dr. Taylor's voice as he answered that my Bible says, whosoever will.

I had the opportunity to speak at my home church within the last year or so and one of the things I told them about themselves is that when I was a child, I grew up thinking that the worst sin that one could ever perform was that of being an alcohol abuser, or a "drunk," as such persons in the community were called. I told Goodwill Baptist Church that we did a great disservice to those mostly men, but some women too, who walked the roads and throughout the community. They were talked about without anyone trying to encourage them. No wonder our churches are half to three-fourths empty today. Whosoever will. If we had just told them, "Whosoever shall call on the name of the Lord, shall be saved" (ROMANS 10:13).

We are guilty of judging, putting ourselves in God's shoes; how could God choose so-and-so to teach Sunday school, or become a deacon or trustee, or let alone be called to preach? Whosoever will. Oberlin and friends gathered here today; Jesus met a Samaritan woman over there at Jacob's Well in Samaria. Jesus treated her with respect and offered her a dipper full of that living water that only He could give. Jesus told her, "Whosoever"—there's that word again—"Whosoever drinks of the water that comes from the natural well shall thirst again, but if you drink from that living water that I give, you will never thirst again" (JOHN 4:13). Whosoever will.

If you are feeling lonely today, wondering why and how God could take away your husband at early age or an only child; wondering how your father could abandon you to take up with another woman, leaving the family destitute and living in poverty: whosoever will. If you have been blessed to get up in age, your eyesight is growing dim, may need a walker to keep from falling, your children live far away, and you feel neglected and all alone, Revelation says, whosoever will.

Young folk, if you don't have any money to go to college but have determination, a hard work ethic, and God on your side, the summons says whosoever will. In August 1972, I was preparing to leave the tobacco farm for Howard University. I had never been to Washington, DC hardly knew what a city block was, only had a little money, but had a praying mother. But as I was getting ready to leave home, she told me to put God first in my life and work hard. Essentially, she was telling me, whosoever will.

Church, if you are having one crisis after another, whosoever will. I have a brother who hasn't talked with me or any of my brothers and sisters in several years; apparently his mind is messed up, angry about the family selling the farm after my mother's death. He won't answer his phone, even blames us for Mama's and my sister's death, even though my mother died of Alzheimer's disease one month shy of eighty-four. Messed up in his thinking—I wish, I wish that I could get word to him, that whosoever will.

To Tanaya and Brianna, you are two beautiful young ladies. I'm afraid that unless you continue to carry yourselves in a dignified manner that is pleasing to God, that many young men and even some old ones will see in you only the outward appearance and not see your brilliant minds and the goodness of your hearts. Proverbs 31:30 says that charm is deceptive, and beauty is fleeting, but a woman who fears the Lord is to be praised. The Apostle Paul teaches in 1 Corinthians 6:19–20 that your bodies are the temple of the holy spirit, who is in you, whom you have received from God. You are not your own, you are bought with a price. Therefore, honor God with your bodies. Let me make it even plainer to you by using street language. Somebody was correct when they said, "If you lie down with dogs, you will get up with fleas." Young folk, if you put all kinds of alcohol and drugs into your bodies; if you drink excessively, then you are not honoring God with your bodies. I am guilty of having done that sometimes when I was in my late teens and early twenties. I could have died in the process. I did some bad things while growing up and at Howard University. I was not always faithful to my girlfriends while away in college and law school. I am still a work in progress. Thank God I am a long way from where I used to be. You see, one day God took me down to the potter's house and started working me over, molding something better out of me. I found as I have drawn closer to God that He has drawn closer to me. It's been decades since I abused alcohol or anything else that affected my judgment. It is very important to keep a clear head. For some reason, God has spared my life, and that's why I'm standing before you today. Three of my law school classmates died of HIV-AIDS, one was murdered in Richmond over thirty years ago; it remains an unsolved murder. I know God has poured out his favor and grace upon me. I know that I cannot repay Him for all He has done for me. All I can do is to have a grateful heart and try to give back a portion of what God has blessed me with. Whosoever will.

I'm about to close out, but Tanaya, Briana, and others gathered here at Oberlin today, there is nothing more important than staying prayed up. Pray in the morning, pray when you get through praying, pray when you eat lunch, and pray when you get finished. Pray when you wake up and pray when you put your feet on the floor. Pray in the shower and pray when you are putting your clothes on and when you are taking them off. Pray without ceasing, as the word tells us in Thessalonians. Pray, Church, for the sick, and pray for those who are well, pray for friends and even for your enemies. Pray, Church, for Oberlin and all other churches. Pray for the Taliban and ISIS that they might come to their senses. Pray in your secret closets; pray in the classroom and on the job. Prayer changes things. Whosoever will, let him pray. I wish I could tell you more to encourage you. But fear God and keep his commandments. Commit yourself to Him and stay connected to the vine. Be honest with yourself and be honest with others. Place others above self. Bread cast upon the water will return fourfold, and a thousandfold. Whosoever will.

Young people, Jeremiah said over there in 29:11, "'For I know the plans I have for you,' declares the LORD, 'plans to prosper you and not to harm you, plans to give you hope and a future.'" You are going to have to keep a clear head to get ahead in the future. There are some in our society who would like to take us back to the 1940s, 1950s, and 1960s. You can expect trials and tribulations in your life. Jesus said over there in John 16:33, "I have told you these things so that in me you may have peace. In the world you will experience tribulation." Paul said on another occasion that he was troubled on every side. But Jesus said, "Be of good cheer, I have overcome the world." Whosoever will.

A GIFT FROM AND BY GENE THREATS

A Call to Witness

The McIntyre-Whichard Legal Fellows Program, Raleigh, NC

NOVEMBER 15, 2022

> But you will receive power when the Holy Spirit comes on you; and you will be my witnesses in Jerusalem, and in all Judea and Samaria, and to the ends of the earth. ACTS 1:8, NIV
>
> You are witnesses of these things. LUKE 24:48, NIV

I was elated to learn that one of my mentees and former interns, Trey Ellis, is a member of an organization to which one of my longtime legal colleague's and friend's name is attached, the Honorable Willis Whichard. Before being invited to speak here tonight, I had not ever heard of the McIntyre-Whichard Legal Fellows Program, so I am glad to be with you here tonight. I see on your website that this organization is about "Community, Counsel and Calling." It is about building community through personal relationships between Christian law student "fellows" and attorneys, connecting all members of the mentorship program with one another to foster strong, lasting relationships. Counsel is about matching fellows with forward-thinking lawyers of integrity who can offer counsel, wisdom, and insight into the professional realities of being a Christian attorney. And calling is about pairing aspiring lawyers with practitioner role models who can walk alongside and encourage them as they seek out God's calling in their life.

What does it mean to be witness for Christ?

As lawyers, judges, and Christian soldiers we are called to be witnesses of our faith. We are to show who we are as demonstrated by our words and actions. For forty-three years now I have sought to represent Christ in all aspects of my life. It takes courage to do the work we are called to do.

My mind goes back to my days of practicing law in my hometown of Madison, up in Rockingham County, North Carolina, from 1980 to 1986. I was frequently in the news headlines. I stood on the side of right and not wrong. I committed to speaking up for those who could not speak for themselves. A client of mine who had been discriminated against and cheated out of wages killed his boss. As my client holed up in a warehouse, law enforcement threw in a smoke bomb, and the warehouse caught on fire and burned. However, my client died because of a self-inflicted gunshot wound. The community assumed that law enforcement had purposely burned him alive. The US Department of

Justice and state officials came to town, and the matter received a lot of publicity. During this time, one of my cousins went into a convenience store there in town. He heard a young fellow make a threat toward me. After having read the headlines in the newsstand, the young man said that "Joe Webster ought to be killed." My cousin called to tell me what he had heard. One night when I was in my office all alone, I must admit to you that I thought about my wife and my three young children—about how they were depending on me for food and shelter. So, I abruptly went home to check on my family.

Some of you may know that I wrote and published a biography of the late Honorable Sammie Chess Jr., the first African American superior court judge in North Carolina. He had an awakening himself where in the midst of a dream, he saw that he was in danger as a civil rights attorney in the 1960s—during the civil rights struggle. Many came to hate him and his good friend Julius Chambers, whose car, home, and office had been firebombed. Chess had received some threatening calls to his home. But in the dream, the then-attorney Chess died. Let me read a paragraph on pages 88–89 from his biography:

> I had a vision that I could be killed. I was shown all of the ramifications of continued support for civil rights through the work I was doing as a lawyer. The vision took place in the early 1960s shortly after my friend Julius Chambers's house had been bombed and later his office was firebombed. It was also at about the same time Julius's car blew up just prior to him getting into it. He had attended a meeting in New Bern, North Carolina. My dream was that my life was in jeopardy. I believe I had that vision so that I could make an informed decision. I decided to do it my way. I immediately conquered the fear of death. I was liberated. My fear was conquered because of my acceptance of death.

So, attorney Chess decided to be a Christian witness and continue doing his work as a civil rights attorney. For the most part, he lived a peaceful and forgiving life. He learned through experience that if you keep on doing what you are doing, eventually your enemy will become your friend. Chess said he wouldn't stop talking to those who disagreed with him. One man said he thought Chess was the devil incarnate. Chess never stopped talking to him. And by the time the man died, he'd asked Chess to do his eulogy—the only person who spoke that day. In the early 1960s Chess traveled to the western part of North Carolina to try a case. It was the only trial his father ever witnessed. He won the trial. On he and his dad's way out of the courtroom, the opposing attorney was walking in front of them. A white man approached the opposing lawyer and said, "You look like you got beat up by a bobcat." The opposing lawyer responded, "I just got the s— beat out of me by a nigger lawyer." He didn't know that Chess and his father were behind him. Chess and his father kept on walking toward the exit of the courthouse. Sometimes in life, as attorneys or in our personal lives, we have to show who we are by walking away from a fight.

As a member of this great organization, you have a duty to speak up, boldly and kindly and respectfully. If this deeply divided nation is to heal, it will be you, those present in this room, who have a faith the size of a grain of mustard seed, to bring the nation back together. Healing won't come from the far right or the far left, but from those among us who have been called to witness. Trey Ellis, I heard your message at your law school graduation. God didn't give you all that talent to be silent. I may not live to see all that God has in store for you, but I want you to know that a change is going to come, and that you will be a catalyst for change in a positive direction. Never forget whose shoulders you are standing on and in whom you have placed your faith.

If Chess were here tonight as our guest speaker, he would tell you that you need a moral compass. Your compass can never deviate from the direction God has called upon you to follow. Your values as lawyers and judges and as human beings must be evident by all who observe your walk. You must walk the talk. It's now enough to be able to tell somebody that you belong to this organization. That is not enough. I try to use my position of authority to bring lawyers and others to a place of making a difference in this world. The last several years I have been telling lawyers seeking admission to the federal court that they need to be doing something to improve America. As part of their oath, they swear or affirm "to support and defend the constitution of the United States against all enemies, foreign and domestic." After administering the oath to them, I talk a few minutes about what that means. I know that will mean different things to different people. But to me it means at least we need to open our mouths and speak truth to power. It means that private lawyers must take on pro bono cases.

I stand before you today having taken on many court-appointed cases and civil cases involving indigent litigants. Twenty years ago, I agreed to represent a member of the Ku Klux Klan because I believed then and I believe now that everyone is entitled to be represented by a lawyer. That is the only way that they can receive justice. It is the only way for the playing field to be made level. This case was one of the most difficult ones I have ever been involved in as a practicing attorney. I was appointed because he had fired his first attorney because he didn't want his first court-appointed attorney, a black female state public defender. And I knew he didn't want me to represent him, but I did the best that I could do.

In my forty-three years of being in the legal profession, I've never forgotten or forsaken my calling to make a difference in my community, my church, and my profession. Tonight, I call upon each of you to get to know those who are not like you. I sense that is part of the vision of this organization's founders. I try to stay close to those who are poor and discouraged. I'm so deficient in this, though. However, in my judicial capacity, I let those who come before me, most of whom are poor and minorities, know that I see them. I understand their plight. Many years ago, my wife and I were inviting some friends to our home for dinner. I recalled the scripture that tells us to invite the poor. I couldn't think of one person in that category that I knew there in Chapel Hill. We have so many problems in our country. I began a program called CourtCares in my present position, in which we reach out to middle schoolers in the Durham County Schools. We invite them to our court. As a result of this program, I learned that some Durham students live in hotels. I met a counselor who told me that he had two or three middle schoolers who were shot in drive-by shootings. This is our call to witness. Thank you for inviting me to share with you tonight.

Eulogies/Eulogistic Expressions

Fighting the Good Fight: He Chose the Road that Leads to Calvary— A Service of Memory for the Life of the Honorable Sammie Chess Jr.

2 TIMOTHY 4:6–8

St. Stephen Metropolitan A.M.E. Zion Church, High Point, NC

JULY 30, 2022

> For I am now ready to be offered, and the time of my departure is at hand. I have fought a good fight, I have finished my course, I have kept the faith. Henceforth there is laid up for me a crown of righteousness which the Lord, the righteous judge shall give me at that day: and not for me only, but unto all of them also that love his appearing. (1 TIMOTHY 4:6–8)

Sammie Chess Jr. is an excellent example of a man who in his professional and personal life fought the good fight. He is an example for all of us to follow. He lived a long, fruitful, and purpose-filled life. Like Judge Chess, no doubt, in this battle we face daily called life, we are going to come up against many obstacles. To use the words of poet Langston Hughes, life for Chess was no crystal stair. It had tacks in it and some splinters. As Chess confronted the situations that he found himself in as a lawyer and trial and administrative law judge, he fought the good fight. In life we find some who fight with weapons of war such as guns and bullets, some fight with sharp objects such as knives and swords, and some will use their tongues to try to take advantage of your weak moments. This is not the kind of fighter Chess was.

Our text comes at the end of a long life of the Apostle Paul. No doubt he was weary and probably felt he had given all he had to the cause of Christ. Just one example of what he experienced on his Christian journey, we find him in 2 Corinthians 7:5 saying, "When we were come into Macedonia, our flesh had no rest; we were troubled on every side; without were fightings, within were fears." Like the Apostle Paul, sometimes, throughout his life, Judge Chess found himself surrounded by trouble.

If Sammie Chess Jr. were able to speak today, he would say that when he was born in the middle of the Depression on the dirt floor in a poor man's house without running water or electricity at the edge of a cotton field in the Bull Pond community outside Allendale, South Carolina, there was trouble on every side. He'd say my grandmother spoke of night riders (the Ku Klux Klan). The year of Chess's birth in 1934 witnessed thirteen recorded lynchings in the United States, and only the Lord knows how many unrecorded ones were lynched. The Great Depression took its toll on ordinary Americans, no less so for those of African descent.

But as Chess grew in stature, he grew in wisdom and grace. He was the wisest man I ever met and got to know—thanks in part to the farm life he saw for the first nine years of his life and because he had wise, hardworking, and industrious parents and grandparents. He was among the five million African Americans who migrated from the South to the northern and midwestern urban and industrial regions of our country. For three years he experienced a glimmer of hope in Harlem, New York, before moving to High Point, North Carolina, where he saw once again trouble on every side; that same year, 1946, saw the North Carolina legislature pass a law prohibiting the burial of black and white human beings in the same graveyard. Chess saw trouble on every side.

Like the Apostle Paul who saw the discrimination in the first-century Christian church, Chess saw with his own eyes the "colored only" and "white only" signs and the stairways leading up to the balconies of movie theaters in High Point, where blacks were relegated to sit. He heard with his own ears the calls for justice and equal treatment, which must have had a profound effect on him. And just like the Apostle Paul, Sammie Chess Jr. chose the road that leads to Calvary. Calvary is where that old, rugged cross was found—two wooden logs crisscrossing the other. But it is also symbolic of the hardship that one will experience if you devote your life to Christian principles. It was where Chess found his deliverance from fear that gave him the courage to continue his work as a civil rights lawyer that he had committed himself to.

Calvary was where he found the courage to fight the good fight. Going back to his law school years, Chess knew what his purpose was. After two years in the army, he returned to open his law office in High Point in 1960. Whatever his classmates may have had in their minds to

A Service of Memory
for the Life of
The Honorable Sammie Chess, Jr.

Sunrise
March 28, 1934

Sunset
July 23, 2022

Service
Saturday, July 30, 2022—11:00 a.m.

St. Stephen Metropolitan A.M.E. Zion Church
1012 Leonard Avenue
High Point, North Carolina

The Reverend Dr. Reginald M. Keitt, Officiant
The Honorable Joe L. Webster, Eulogist

COURTESY OF SANDRA CHAVIS CHESS

do with their legal education, Chess just wanted to uplift and make a better life for his people. He didn't have a desire to make a lot of money, although I heard him say many times that "bread cast in the water" will return fourfold. He said he made a commitment to the Lord if He would help him make fifty dollars a week so he could support his family, he promised the Lord that he would use his training to help elevate the quality and standard of life of his people. However, Chess cast much bread in the water, and it returned to him fourfold, including most importantly a long life and good health. He took on many clients and cases that most lawyers wouldn't undertake because of little or no pay, or because they'd think it would hurt their business or just simply because they didn't have the courage. Chess fought the good fight.

Yes, Chess chose the road the road that leads to Calvary. The road to Calvary is often filled with disappointment and pain. To use the words of the old hymn, "Time is filled with swift transition." You are healthy one day, and the next you might be diagnosed with stage 4 cancer. We are caught up in the maddening race, to paraphrase the words of the late Rev. Dr. Gardner C. Taylor, to obtain things that perish—things like big cars, big houses, and expensive jewelry and such. If we avoid this, then the road to Calvary will be manageable and even rewarding. Sometimes you will have to climb seemingly insurmountably high mountains: I like that old spiritual, "We are climbing high mountains trying to get home." Often, we must trudge our way through thickets and high waters, and there will be many boulders in our way. Like Chess experienced, someone will use some derogatory phrase to describe you because of the color of your skin. Chess would have me to tell you today that if you hold to God's unchanging hand, everything will be all right. It won't matter what they call you. You just keep on fighting the good fight.

Chess would have me to tell you that more than ever, America needs fighters who fight the good fight today, post–January 6, 2021. It has been said that this nation is in a battle for its soul, for democracy, the rule of law, and its Constitution, and for the other principles for which our country was founded. If you choose the road that leads to Calvary, you will find, like Judge Chess, that you won't ever be in the boxing ring alone. The same one that was walking around in the burning fiery furnace with the three Hebrew boys Shadrach, Meshach, and Abednego who refused to bow down to the king over there in the third chapter of Daniel will be there with you. Sandra, Eva, and Janet, there will be some lonely and dark moments ahead, but if you follow the principles Sammie Chess Jr. lived by, you will never be alone. As Martin Luther King Jr. said in one of his sermons, Jesus promised never to leave him alone, "No never alone."

Chess wasn't always as courageous as he would become. There came a time early in Chess's life in the mid-1960s, about when one of his best friends, the late Julius

Chambers, had his car bombed in New Bern, North Carolina, and his home and office bombed in Charlotte—that Chess began to have the same fears that the Apostle Paul must have felt in the early years of Christianity when he arrived in Macedonia, He was weary because he had no rest. He encountered trouble on every side and reported in 2 Corinthians 7:5 NIV "conflicts on the outside, fears within." Chess must have felt the same way during the civil rights struggle. He could see and hear the demonstrations in downtown High Point, not far from his office. It was in the 1960s when he was faced with the most pivotal point in his life. He had to make a decision about whether he would continue to pursue a career path that subjected himself and his family to harm and even death. Chess had a vision that his life was in jeopardy. He felt strongly that he had the vision so that he could make an informed decision. So Chess decided to do it his way; he would continue his important work. He immediately conquered the fear of death; he was liberated; his fear was gone because of his acceptance of death.

Yes, Church, Chess fought the good fight. I have a question for all those under the sound of my voice, and that is, will you fight the good fight in this crazy world of gun violence against one another, against little children while in school, those worshiping in church, and disparate treatment of persons of color by some bad police officers, and those who are standing honorably and righteously in the gap and fighting the good fight for democracy and the Constitution as Chess did for all of his professional career and beyond? He considered himself a soldier of the Constitution. Chess felt that for us to fight the good fight, "one must have an abiding faith in one's moral direction"—that, as lawyers, you can't be a lawyer if you don't stand up straight. Chess said there will be blows against you; you will be a man if you take the blows. He went on to say that a man can do remarkable things if you inspire others. You can even disarm your opponent if you stand up straight and practice these principles. He concluded by saying you can't think about consequences, but you must think about what the Constitution requires.

Chess was always thinking about others, especially those who were getting their faces smashed on the picket lines, or thrust onto the sides of buildings by high-powered water hoses, or those like the four little innocent black girls—Addie Mae Collins, Cynthia Wesley, Carole Robertson, and Carol Denise McNair—who were attending Sunday school at the Sixteenth Street Baptist Church in Birmingham when bombs exploded on the Sabbath Day planted by four Ku Klux Klan members. (A fifth little girl, Sarah Collins, lost her right eye in the bombing that day.)

Chess grieved about the many others who died for the cause of equality. I will never forget the one day of the many days I sat with him in his dining room or on his back screened porch. He got choked up almost to tears talking to me about the great sacrifice of others wounded or killed in the civil rights struggle. Seeing the expression on his face, it was as if he was feeling the pain himself. As he talked, it was clear to me that he could still see the bloated, mutilated, and unrecognizable face of Emmett Till down in Mississippi; the television images of the late Congressman John Lewis being beaten on the Edmund Pettus Bridge in Selma, Alabama; and Viola Greg Liuzzo, a white lady who was killed by Ku Klux Klan members as she transported a black male volunteer from Montgomery to Selma in the aftermath of the Selma civil rights march. Compared to them and so many others whose names we will never know, in Chess's opinion, his own sacrifice was miniscule and unimportant in comparison to these heroes. Chess was not about getting praise for anything he did to make this world a better place. He never wanted that; he told me that he did things because it was the right thing to do.

As a trial lawyer, Chess sometimes had to fight for his dignity and respect. I'll tell you about two incidents, one demonstrating his physical strength and fallibility, the other demonstrates his moral strength, his true character. Early in his law practice, he and other local lawyers from High Point and the area were gathered around with the assistant district attorney waiting to negotiate dispositions for their clients. Al of them had in their hands one or more court files; we called them "shucks" back in the day. Chess had one, and suddenly without notice, the prosecutor reached up and jerked the shuck out his hand. Chess's dignity as a human being was at stake. And I'm sure the suddenness of the moment played a role in how Chess handled what had just occurred. Chess reached down, grabbed the prosecutor by the collar and lifted him, and told him what he would do if ever did that again. Church, I pondered whether to tell this as a part of Chess's eulogy as a eulogist usually tells only the best parts of one's life. However, I decided to do so because, first, Chess approved of it in his biography, and like the Apostle Paul, Chess had a thorn in the flesh like all of us do. And sometimes human beings can be pushed to the limits. Not one of us is perfect in our actions every second of our lives.

The second incident demonstrates the essence of how Chess handled conflict in most instances. It occurred in Gastonia, North Carolina. It occurred in the aftermath of a civil jury trial on the homecourt of the opposing attorney. It was the only case his father, Sammie Chess Sr., ever saw his son participate in as a trial lawyer. He won the case, and he and his father were walking down the hallway heading toward the exit a little distance behind the opposing attorney in the case. A white fellow was coming in their direction and as he approached the opposing counsel, the man asked him. "What in the world happened to you? You look like you been in a fight with a bobcat." And the opposing attorney, not knowing Chess and his father were close behind him, responded, "A "n"-word lawyer just beat the 'you know what' [the lawyer used a four-letter word beginning with "s" and ending with a "t"] out of me." Chess and his father continued toward the exit without saying a word. Church, Chess fought the good fight. Church, as believers sometimes, the good fight requires you not to even say a word. You can win a fight without casting one blow. But it's obvious who won that fight. Indeed, victory prevailed both in the courtroom and outside of it.

Chess left us so many universal truths that will endure forever—many that he learned from his parents and grandparents. Maybe one day some young person will hear or read about Judge Chess and might be encouraged by his life. I've never met a judge other than Judge Chess who was once a high school dropout. His grandmother told him, "You are better than nobody and nobody is better than you." Chess said one of the greatest lessons in life is that "With perseverance we can achieve." Chess reminded me that it's not where we start, but where we end up that counts. And the race goes not to the swift, but those who endure to the end. "Do any task that you undertake with all your might. There is no meager task or great task. They are all tasks, and they require the same attention and dedication. If one wants to succeed, one must do that, and they will be able to do things that usually spell success for people who practice perseverance and dedication to a task undertaken."

"One of Chess's favorite scriptures was, "What shall it profit a man to gain the whole world and lose his soul?" Mark 8:36. Chess didn't lose his soul. I think that I observed that the closer he got to this past Saturday, July 23, the closer he grew to his Savior. I heard that recently while listening to a recorded sermon he was moved by the Spirit. Over the last few years, he would often preach a sermonette to me. I told him that since I was an ordained preacher, I believed that I would have to give him a license to preach. Based on his life's work alone, he was qualified in every respect. He was not perfect; none of us are. All of us fall short of the glory of God. He had long ago accepted Christ in his life and knew for certain where his help came from. You may be asking, Webster, how do you know he had accepted his redeemer? Some preacher said many years ago, "Well, I'm glad you asked." Over there in the seventh chapter of Matthew, the scriptures make it clear. You shall know a tree by the fruit that it bears. Chess bore a lot of good fruit because long ago he chose the road that leads to Calvary. He chose the road of love for his fellowman; no matter the person's race or national origin, no matter what denomination or creed, he chose to love those who despitefully used him. He forgave his enemies. Chess told me that if you disagreed with his perspective on things, he would not stop speaking to you, but he would keep on speaking to you and one day you might change your mind.

Many people didn't understand Chess's work as a civil rights lawyer. Some despised him, especially those who did not know him. An example of this was that a white man who lived near his office told Chess that for years he thought he was the devil incarnate. But later, after getting to know him he found him to be a good man. Later the man came to Chess and told him he wanted him to do his eulogy, and that he was the only one who would be speaking at his funeral. After hearing this, I concluded that therein lies the remedy to racial and other divisions in our country. We must get to know one another.

I'm about to close this eulogy, but earlier this week I got a call from a reporter from the *High Point Enterprise*, the local newspaper in this town. He asked me something to the effect of what was the one thing I thought stood out most in Chess's contributions to this nation. You know how it is when someone asks you a question when you have other things on your mind, and you have not had a chance to give thought to the question presented to you? Well, I went around the world in my thoughts and comments to the reporter about the many contributions of Judge Chess. But it finally came to me that as civil rights lawyer, trial judge, and community leader, perhaps his greatest contribution was his perhaps unintended contribution to the reconciliation of black and white people in a, then and now, still deeply divided nation.

Two other giants of Chess's generation here in this Guilford County, North Carolina, community have spoken of his contributions to society.

On the occasion of Chess being selected for the North Carolina Bar Association's Liberty Bell Award, retired North Carolina Supreme Court Chief Justice Henry Frye wrote a letter and said to Chess, "You have had a marvelous and exciting career, improving the administration of justice in North Carolina while also improving the lives of its citizens." And retired North Carolina Senior Resident Superior Court judge W. Douglas Albright once said about Chess, "Confronted and strapped by a legal and social system

The Honorable Sammie Chess Jr., the Honorable Julian Mann, and me at the Office of Administrative Hearings, Raleigh, NC

flawed by invidious discrimination and unequal treatment under color of law that fed racial injustice, Judge Chess, with malice toward none and charity for all, faced daily insults with quiet dignity and recurring slurs with amazing grace."

Improving the administration of justice in North Carolina and improving the lives of its citizens with quiet dignity and amazing grace does describe the Judge Chess who I came to know well. Now more than ever, we can say with certainty that because of the life that Judge Chess lived, eagles and doves fly together. There is an African proverb that says, "He ain't dead so long as you keep calling his name." Family and friends, I promise you that for the rest of my life I will keep calling his name. As I bring this message to shore, I hope that I have said something that will bring some comfort to his wife and children and those who have been grieving his passing as I have been the last week. But we should be rejoicing today for there is a crown of righteousness awaiting Judge Chess because he fought the good fight. He finished his course. He kept the faith. He chose the road that leads to Calvary. To God be the glory for a life well lived. Amen.

God's Grace Is Sufficient: Eulogistic Expressions at My Father's Funeral

APRIL 2, 2003

> In 2 Corinthians 12:9, a portion of the scripture found there is as follows: "And he said unto me, my grace is sufficient for thee: for my strength is made perfect in weakness."

Over the last couple of months, and especially the last few days, my family and friends have had the opportunity to reminisce about my daddy and some of the good times we had and what he meant to us. We also have been praising God for sustaining Daddy over all these years and thanking him for the mercy shown to him and our family during Dad's illness.

Our daddy was imperfect. He had a thorn in the flesh. He was sometimes stubborn, hardheaded, and had a temper: traits that many of his children inherited. He was outspoken about things he believed in. It bothered him when people didn't do what was right. I heard him say many times, "That just ain't right." Some have said he was a fighter, and he was. Even though slender in build, he was a strong man. Back when Hurricane Fran came through Chapel Hill in 1996 and caused great destruction to my family's home and automobiles, he came down with his chain saw and sawed a huge tree in two even though he had emphysema and perhaps even cancer then.

A CELEBRATION OF THE LIFE
and
HOMEGOING
of

Deacon James Edward "Tom" Webster
Sunrise July 3, 1925 — Sunset March 29, 2003

Wednesday, April 2, 2003
2:00 O'clock p.m.
Goodwill Baptist Church
Madison, North Carolina

Dr. John A. Jackson, Pastor

Funeral program for my father, James E. Webster

My dad was a hard worker and a highly principled man; therefore, he went to work every morning early and came home late. But we are grateful that he came home to our mama and eight children. I never heard of him running around on my mother. He was devoted and faithful. I never heard of him hurting anyone except the time a man stole a ham from the family. God's grace is sufficient.

My dad was an honest man; I never heard about him beating anybody out of what wasn't his. Some have said he was from the old school, and he was. On the inside of this man, who many misunderstood, there was a good heart that grieved, sometimes about his own imperfections, about his thorn in the flesh. But God's grace is sufficient.

As most of you know, he tried to farm and public work too. There came a time when I believe he gave up on making farmers out of his boys. Perhaps he had reason to because we recall the times when:

1. The time the pigs got out and as they ran through the woods after the pigs, Daddy asked my brother James to call the pigs, and my brother said, "Here pig, here pig."

2. The time my daddy asked my brothers J.T. and Billy to go put the harness on the mule as we were priming tobacco that morning. They went ahead of Daddy and me and when we got to the stable, they had put the harness on upside down. My dad said, "I believe y'all are the biggest fools I've ever seen in my life."

3. The time my daddy asked Billy to get behind the mule and plow the tobacco. The problem was my brother Billy didn't know gee from haw, and consequently the mule plowed all over the field with my daddy watching in disgust, and my mama was in the front yard hollering, "Lord, have mercy."

4. And finally, the many occasions when I got sick in the tobacco fields and Daddy would shake his head and say as he sent me to the house, "Boy, you better go on to college." And I decided to take him up on that advice—I went as long and as far away as I could.

But God's grace was sufficient even on the farm.

So yes, our daddy was stubborn and outspoken when he thought that what was being done was wrong.

During my dad's last months, he shed a lot of tears as God took him down to the potter's house and reworked him and continued to mold him and shape him. So early last Saturday morning, as a light rain fell outside of his hospice room in Winston Salem, as his eyes looked steadfastly toward heaven, as the death angels began to sing, "Holy, holy, God's grace is sufficient," God came suddenly in the middle of the night to take him home because He is faithful to His promises. God grace is sufficient. It was sufficient for my father with all his imperfections—his stubbornness, his temper, his sometimes-untimely outspokenness. And God's grace is sufficient for those of us who remain.

So, we've been thanking God for not letting him suffer and linger too long. He lingered just long enough for the family to be able to tell him how much we loved him and how proud we were of his accomplishments. And he just lingered long enough for God to take away the thorns in the flesh and present him faultless. So, we are happy today, for God's grace is sufficient.

Eulogistic Expressions on Occasion of the Funeral of Kenya Javon Webster: Love One Another

JOHN 13:34

Goodwill First Baptist Church, Madison, NC

MAY 8, 2012

> A new commandment I give you: Love one another. As I have loved you, so you must love one another.

I give honor to God, my fellow members of the cloth in the pulpit, others who may be in the audience, and those who have traveled from near and far. I've been honored by my sister Kathy to say a few words on this Homegoing service for my niece Kenya Javon Webster. There is a word from the Lord over there in John 13:34. After Jesus had foretold his disciples about the fact that he would be betrayed by one of his own, He said to the disciples, "A new commandment I give unto you, that you love one another, as I have loved you, you also love one another." Kenya Webster, in her short thirty-two years, demonstrated to all who knew her what Jesus was talking about. She made no difference in people regarding race, gender, or whether those she met were rich, poor, or didn't fit society's description of what it means to be beautiful. Somehow or another, Kenya knew that it was important to value every human being. To use the words of eminent theologian and preacher Dr. Gardner C. Taylor, who wrote in pertinent part, "There is no basis for a love ethic that does not take into account the preciousness, the importance of the individual." Dr. Taylor went on to say that the "New Testament gives a sense of one's worth. Christ thought every person was worth dying for, that is the basis of our preciousness."[22]

You see, society has a way of disfavoring or looking down on those who might be misshapen, disfigured, or overweight or anyway different from the norm. Kenya was a beautiful, talented, courageous young lady who lived a full life while she struggled over half of her life with liver disease brought on through no fault of her own. She shared her musical and other talents with others, and so she too thought everyone was worth her time and the sharing of her talents.

In conclusion, my sister Kathy gave me the privilege of sharing Kenya's last months on earth as she fought to live. Kathy, my sister Patsy, my wife Diane, and I held on to

22 Rhinold Ponder and Michele Tuck Ponder, eds., The Wisdom of the Word Love: Great African American Sermons (New York: Crown, 1997), Rev. Dr. Gardner C. Taylor, Foreword, in *The Wisdom of the Word Love*, p. 9–10.

Kenya's hands after the breathing machine and medicines had been discontinued, as she took her last breaths Thursday of last week at the University of North Carolina at Chapel Hill Hospital. That was a powerful experience that I will never forget. To Kenya's first cousins, aunts and uncles, and friends gathered here, Kenya would have me say to you, love one another as Christ and I have loved each of you. Uplift and embrace one another; reach out to those who don't have anybody. God needs some more burden bearers. Love one another. Kenya was a drum major for love. Love will take you a long way in life. Love one other! To God be the glory!

ART BY BILLY D. WEBSTER

Graveside Service of Charles Truby Watkins Sr.: "God Is Love"

LAMENTATIONS 3:21–25

Carolina Biblical Gardens, Raleigh, NC
Joe L. Webster, officiating

JULY 21, 2001

> Yet this I call to mind and therefore I have hope: Because of the Lord's great love we are not consumed for his compassions never fail. They are new every morning; great is your faithfulness. (LAMENTATIONS 3:21–23)

> Blessed are they that mourn for they shall be comforted. (MATTHEW 5:4, KJV)

I know that it is difficult to see God's love during suffering, amid just having lost a loved one to death. It is hard to see God's love when you think of the fact that you just lost to death that beloved son Truby, who only lived to be fifty-four years, short years. It's hard to see God's love when you reminisce about how Truby suffered over the years, how in recent years he had been to the hospital on numerous occasions. It's hard to imagine that God could be love when you consider the fact that sometimes Truby could be contrary and stubborn and sometimes a free spirit to his own detriment. I know it is difficult for you to see God's love when you consider that Truby, while possessing on the one hand a good heart that caused him to want to bring joy and laughter to all around him, at the same time had a defective heart, perhaps from birth. But during the pain that the family endures today, God's mercies are new every morning. Great is thy faithfulness. I am here today to let Truby's family and friends know that God's love is present even during our tears over this great loss. After all, God allowed Truby to be the first born to two parents who must have felt great joy as the flowers bloomed on April 16, 1947. Great is thy faithfulness. After all, Truby wasn't stillborn, and his mother didn't die giving birth. Truby was born with two good legs and two arms and could see. He was even blessed to faithfully serve his country in the military. As the spring of 1947 brought forth new life, as you held him tightly in loving arms, as you spoiled him, all knew that a child born of a woman was born to die. But I want the Watkins family to know that even during death, Jesus is love. To this great Watkins family, who has been pulling together all these years, Jesus is love; his compassions are new every morning. Great is thy faithfulness. After all, he woke us up this morning. As you looked up, you didn't see Truby, but you could see, you could remember the good times, those times when Truby told a joke and had you in stitches, you were laughing so hard. Jesus is love. After all, each of us who wanted to eat this morning had access to plenty. After all, while in today's era of modern medicine, while Truby only lived for fifty-four years, God shared him with you for almost twenty-thousand days. God's compassions are new every morning, not just every now and again, or every once in a while, but as our scripture makes clear, every morning. Great is thy faithfulness. To the Watkins family, God's love is everlasting. It never fails. It allows us to go on amid trouble, amid sickness, and yes, amid death. I know Truby's youngest child and others must be wondering why Daddy had to go; why, God, if You are love, if You are a compassionate God, why didn't You let him live a little longer, that you wanted to tell him something or go to a ball game with him one more time, but we still must give thanks for his mercy. God's compassions are new every morning. Great is thy faithfulness. Amid your tears and sorrow, I want you to know that you can count on mercy and compassion tomorrow morning just like this morning. The Bible, in Saint Matthew, chapter 5, verse 4, "Blessed are they that mourn, for they shall be comforted." The word "shall" means that comfort will come to those who mourn. It is not conditional on something else happening. You can count on it. I personally find comfort in the scripture today, because when you go to bed tonight, you can look forward to waking up to new mercy and new compassion. It is not new just every now and again, or every once in a while. It is new every morning; great is thy faithfulness.

So, we must conclude by saying that the greatest demonstration of God's compassion is that he gave his only begotten son, not after fifty-four years, but Jesus died in his early thirties not to a comfortable death in the hospital, but to a painful death on the cross, so that we would have a right to eternal life. So, to those who remain, the least you can do is to accept God's invitation by believing on Him that grants life, believing on the One who has been merciful to us every day, the One whose compassions are new every morning. The least you can do is to devote your life to the One who was gracious to share Truby with you for just a little while. Great is thy faithfulness. Praise be to the Lord. His compassions are new every morning. Great is thy faithfulness.

Eulogy of James "Jimmy" Sharpe
"Lord Search Me"

PSALM 139:1

Union Baptist Church, Winston Salem, NC,

APRIL 1, 2017, 1 P.M.

You have searched me, LORD, and you know me.

I am honored and blessed to have been asked by my sister-in-law Viola Sharpe to participate in this service today as the Eulogist. She called on Wednesday night and said, "Would you do the eulogy?" She went on to say, "You know him." I quickly responded that I would do so. For some reason or another, Tink had faith in me to come up with the right words during this time of bereavement and contemplation about the future. Perhaps she knew that I know beyond a shadow of a doubt that I can't do anything on my own, let alone know what to say in times like these. So today I look to God for guidance and direction. Perhaps my wife, Diane, also knew that I would look to God for guidance in carrying out this task of putting together a eulogy. She came home late Thursday after visiting her sister and niece in the family home. She found me in my bedroom with my Bible and books all around me trying to acquire a message, one not for Jimmy, for his works have already spoken for him. I saw in his obituary what I already knew to be case: that he was a very caring family man, always concerned for others. He loved hosting family and friends' events, passionately watched sporting events in person and on television, loved tailgating and sharing with others. But upon my wife returning home, she asked how I was doing—I responded with a sigh—and said I don't have a sermon yet. She responded, "Well, you just got the assignment." And I said something like, "Well, the funeral is Saturday." So hopefully that was yet another family member expressing confidence in me because she knew that I would look to the hills from whence cometh my help; that I would lean on the one who woke me up this morning, the one who said come and follow me.

But let me move on and take my text before you accuse me of preaching a sermon before the sermon.

I go back to Tink's call to me when she said that I knew Jimmy. Yes, I did, but more importantly God knew him. He knew his heart. The psalmist says in chapter 139, verse 1, "You have searched me, LORD, and you know me."

During times of struggle—times of bereavement such as sickness and the death of a loved one—we often forget there is a higher power—one that knows us. Yes, we often forget that He knows us because He made us—each of us; the scripture says that He knows every hair on our head.

Down around the thirteenth verse of today's text, it says, "For you created my inmost being, you knit me together in our mother's womb. David goes on to say, "I praise you because I am fearfully and wonderfully made; your works are wonderful, I know that full well." Viola and Jamese, Marcellus and other family members, the Bible says that Jimmy was fearfully and wonderfully made! Rejoice knowing who made him. God made him when He used His hands to mold and carve out a handsome black man from Wilson, North Carolina. God's eyes saw Jimmy's unformed body even before he was in his mother's womb. God searched him so He knew him when Jimmy sat down, and God knew Jimmy when he rose. God knew long before he would make a step, say a word, think a thought, take in a breath of fresh air. God knew his every thought, his every wish, his every desire. God knew his transgressions and He knew his good traits and bad traits. He knew his strengths and his weaknesses. And He knows everyone of us here today. The text says God is familiar with everything about us. Before we utter a word from our mouths, God knows about it. The God that gave life for seventy-two years to Jimmy Sharpe is an omnipresent God. One of the old preachers in my youth said, "He's so high you can't go over him; so low you can't get under Him; so wide, that you can't get around Him." He's ubiquitous; He's everywhere. As we go about our daily lives, we forget about who He is and whose we are. In today's text, David was a man after God's own heart who had done some bad things in his life, yet he recognized the preeminence of an almighty God. Lord, search me.

In our text today, David asked some rhetorical questions that he already knew the answer to. He said, "Where can I go from your spirit? Where can I flee from your presence?" He answered his own question when he said, "If I go up to the heavens, you are there. If I make my bed in the depths, you are there. If I rise on the wings of the dawn, if I settle on the far side of the sea, even there your hand will guide me, your right hand will hold me fast."

God knows all about what about the family is experiencing today. Tink, God knows. When family and the visitors go back to their homes, you won't be alone. God said He would never leave us nor forsake us. You will remember the annual beach trips, and how Jimmy didn't like the sun so he'd stay behind to cook while you and Jamese would go to the ocean. In your quiet moments you will think you hear Jimmy's voice calling you Baby Doll, Honey, Tinkerbell, Sweetheart, or Sweetie Pie. You will recall the tailgating at A&T

and the long weekend Diane, myself, and others got snowed in at your home during the MEAC basketball tournament weekend. You will miss the laughter, the good times, and the bad times. But God said He wouldn't leave you alone. Jamese, God knows your inner thoughts. He knows the desires of your heart and promises you that if you delight yourself in Him, He will give you the desires of your heart. He knows your present sadness, your disappointment; He feels your loss. God knows you will long for the days when he bought you animal crackers from work each day when you were eight years old; about the first college apartment for you and your roommate—that your dad wouldn't allow you to live in substandard housing. No doubt you will recall again and again how your dad looked after you when you got sick and traveled long distance to see about you when you were suffering from a common cold. You will remember how your dad taught you by example to look after your mother as he took care of his own mother. Jimmy brought her groceries and bought her favorite ice cream sandwiches and even while sick bought you groceries during your recent layoff from work. What I want you to know through today's lesson is that God is a way maker; that God is father to the fatherless. I stopped by Union Baptist to tell you that I know a little bit about what you are experiencing. I lost my parents and a brother and a sister. So I know the pain of losing a loved one. Most of us here do. But more importantly God knows about your pain. For He has searched us and knows our every need. He knows that you will need an extra portion of His grace. I know that I know that I know, and I am a witness that God's grace is sufficient.

God knows our good and our bad. All have sinned and fall short. Over there in Romans 7:21 (NIV) even the Apostle Paul said when I would do good, evil is present with me. So, Paul makes it clear that like all human beings, he also struggles with sin.

Even if you're thinking in your mind, *Why couldn't it have been someone else? Why didn't God strengthen my father so that he could have gotten up from his dying bed?* I want you to know, Jamese, that God has not forgotten about you. He will wrap His arms around you; He will be a father to you. He will be sunshine on a rainy day. He will allow you to remember what your daddy taught you through his sharing and giving to others—even those who he didn't know. It is normal to be upset sometimes, even to be upset with God. God made that quality as well. You see, God loves you, Jamese; God loves you, Tink. God is close by. Even death can't separate His love from us. Romans 8:38–39 says, "For I am persuaded that neither death nor life nor angels, nor principalities, nor powers, nor things present, nor things to come, nor height, nor death, nor any other creature, shall be able to separate us from the love of God, which is in Christ Jesus our Lord."

David concludes this great psalm by being honest with God about how he felt about those who are rebellious against the Lord. He asked God to slay them and says that he has nothing but hatred for them. I never heard Jimmy say that he hated anyone. Jimmy wasn't a hater. David recognized that his own heart needed fixing. In the last four lines of this song of David, he says, "Search me, God, and know my heart; test me and know my anxious thoughts. See if there is any offensive way in me and lead me in the way everlasting."

I believe that early Wednesday morning, Jimmy Sharpe said, "Search me, Lord; search my heart; and if you find anything that shouldn't be, remove it." As for me, I'd rather see a testimony than hear one any day. In Jimmy I saw a testimony. I didn't need to search him, but all of us need to ask God to search our hearts and remove anything that shouldn't be there.

CHAPTER THREE

The Importance of Prayer

Two men went up into the temple to pray; the one a Pharisee, and the other a publican. The Pharisee stood and prayed thus with himself, God I thank thee, that I am not as other men are; extortioners, unjust, adulterers, or even as this publican. I fast twice in the week, I give tithes of all that I possess. And the publican, standing afar off, would not lift up so much as his eyes unto heaven, but smote upon his breast, saying, God be merciful to me a sinner. I tell you, this man went down to his house justified rather than the other: for every one that exalteth himself shall be abased; and he that humbled himself shall be exalted." (LUKE 18:10–14 KJV)

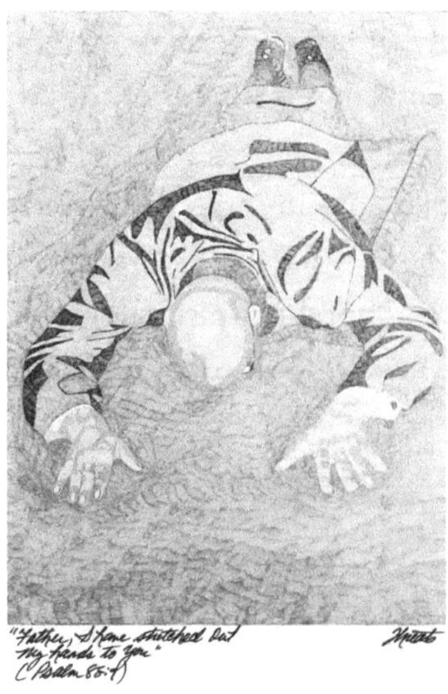

A GIFT FROM AND BY GENE THREATS

Our Prayers Are Not in Vain

LUKE 18:1–8 NIV

Oberlin Baptist Church, Raleigh, NC

DECEMBER 10, 2017

> Then Jesus told his disciples a parable to show that they should always pray and not give up. He said: "in a certain town there was a judge who neither feared God not cared what people thought. And there was a widow in that town who kept coming to him with the plea, Grant me justice against my adversary. (vs. 1–3)

We are living in uncertain times. There are divisions among people in the United States and around the world. My late father, James E. Webster, a longtime deacon at Goodwill Baptist Church, would be shaking his head right now with all that is going on even just here in the United States. He was a big proponent of doing what is right rather than doing what was wrong. He used to go to church and came away disappointed with some things he was seeing and hearing from the pastor, and, looking to me for answers, he'd say, "Boy, is there book on that?" He died in 2003, but bewildered by what he was observing in the church, he used to say, "I don't know what to believe anymore." Nevertheless, he continued to attend church whenever the doors were opened and kept his faith to the end.

ILLUSTRATION BY SHAILYN RAMSEY

Jesus often spoke in parables, and in today's text we find him speaking to God's people in a parable. A parable is a simple story used to illustrate a moral or spiritual lesson or truth. If there is one thing we need to hear today, that s the truth. We've heard enough mentioned in Washington over the last year of the words "fake news." So today I just want to talk not about the "fake news," but the good news coming from the mouth of our Lord and Savior Jesus Christ.

In today's text of Luke, chapter 18, the first verse tells us the purpose of this moral or spiritual lesson, this truth from the mouth of Jesus, and what he sets forth as the purpose of this parable is that men ought to always *pray and not faint*. The NIV says basically the same thing, except it says we should always pray and not give up.

In this parable, he uses an unlikely character, an "unjust judge." We usually don't think in terms of the terms "unjust" and "judge" in the same sentence. The words "judge" and "unjust" side by side seem to be what we call an oxymoron. They just don't seem to go together. But as long as we use humankind as judges, there will be in the mix some who are unjust and unfair and those who practice partiality or show favoritism. This judge who Jesus uses to get his point across to the disciples must have been one of the worst in history. Can you imagine a judge who does not fear God nor care about what people think about him or how he ruled in cases before him or her? But the text says that "there was in that city, a judge, which feared not God neither regarded man." Such a judge would be a dangerous person to be wearing a black robe with the power to judge right from wrong and truth from untruth. This judge, Christ uses to make his point, would not have cared one bit about the words of Micah 6:8, "He hath showed thee, O man, what is good, and what doth the Lord require of thee, to do justly, and to love mercy, and to walk humbly with thy God?" Unjust judges can do a lot of damage to the system we have established to administer justice, just like unrighteous or selfish preachers and pastors can do a lot of damage to the Christian church.

In the very next verse, verse 3, Jesus uses a widow to set the stage for what he is teaching his disciples. We don't know much about her; like the judge, we don't know her name or lineage. We don't know how long her husband had been dead, whether they had children or any other family. Widows back in Jesus's day couldn't rely on a monthly Social Security check or fall back on some other retirement account, but upon her husband's death was thrust into poverty and may have had to rely on other family or neighbors. Widows even today are vulnerable, often the victims of fraud or otherwise being taken advantage of. But Jesus said this widow came before this unjust judge seeking justice. We know she had an adversary, an opponent, possibly someone who had taken from her, owed her money, or did her wrong. But we learn in the text that she had the wherewithal, the courage, to go before the judge and beg for justice.

I have the great privilege to have served eleven of my thirty-eight years as an attorney as a judge, first for the State of North Carolina and the last six as a federal judge. In my present capacity, I have the opportunity to hire what we call law clerks and to extend opportunities for externs for course credit from the nearby law schools. I usually end my interviews with: Would you recognize injustice if you saw it? My thinking is that if you have never seen injustice or thought about it, how would you know how to dispense justice? A few of them, believe it or not, have trouble answering the question. They have not at any time in their lives, because of race or skin color, had to walk to the upstairs in the movie theater as I did as a child in my hometown. They have not yet grasped why the Black Lives Matter movement was started or been in the face of a police dog, like Rev. John Leaston as a young man experienced while chained to a post down there in Alabama in the late 1960s.

But let me get back to the text so I can move on with a word from the Lord.

We learn in the text that the widow was persistent, she knew something about persevering, something about not giving up. She knew about pushing forward, not taking "no" for an answer. No doubt she had some difficult days both before and after she lost her husband. How many of you have had some difficult times in your life, when you were too sick to get out of bed, or were down to your last dime, when perhaps you wanted to give up, but you couldn't give up, because, for one, you know that if you give up, then your children wouldn't have a chance.

But this widow woman in Luke chapter 18—perhaps I'm speculating also she may have known the Lord for herself. So, the widow kept coming back to the unjust judge, please grant me justice against my adversary. And the judge apparently kept saying no. But the widow kept coming to the city to see the judge. So, finally the judge said to himself that even if I don't respect God nor have any respect for people, this woman is causing me trouble. In fairness to the judge, at least he recognized that he wasn't what he ought to be. And since I am a judge, I will say that sometimes lawyers and those coming before you do kind of get on your nerves. Sometimes your patience runs thin, and you must get a hold of yourself before you say something you shouldn't say. So, the judge, rather than allowing the woman to wear him down and perhaps embarrass him, says in the fifth verse, I'm going to grant her justice, so she doesn't keep coming here and bothering me. I can hear him say, "That widow 'bout to get on my last nerve." What do I care, it ain't going to cost me a penny to grant her what she's asking? So, the unjust judge granted justice to the widow, not because it was the just thing to do, but because he didn't want to get worn down, and he got tired of her coming before him.

And then in verses 6 and 7, Jesus says to his disciples, listen to what the unjust judge is saying. If this unjust judge grants the desire of a widow, then surely the God of Abraham, Isaac, and Jacob, the I am, the lily of the valley, the one who listens to his chosen ones, surely God's people who are saved through the grace of Jesus Christ, who cry out day and night, will He not do justice swiftly. Church, I have no doubt that Jesus will do just like he said.

The question that Oberlin needs to ponder and pray about today is contained within the eighth verse: "When the son of man comes, will he find men and women, boys and girls, those who say they are believers; will he find us faithful?" Or will we be like three of Jesus's disciples, Peter, James, and John in the Garden of Gethsemane, on the evening before Jesus was crucified, who Jesus told to watch and pray so they would not fall into temptation? The spirit indeed is willing, but the flesh is weak, and they fell asleep (MATTHEW 26:41–43). And when he returned, he found them asleep again. Church, once you put your hands to the plow, there's no turning back. Church don't get weary. When the Lord returns, will He find us preachers and pastors preaching the gospel in season and out of season?

Oberlin, do you also believe that our prayers are not in vain? Some of us have been given the gift of prayer. I believe my mother could get a prayer through. When you have eight children as my parents had or fifteen like my wife's parents, you better know or at least seek to get a prayer through. Do you believe that prayer changes things? Do you believe the word in Thessalonians that says we must pray without ceasing? Do you believe the scripture in 1 John 5:14 which states this is the confidence we have in approaching God: that if we ask anything according to his will, he hears us. Do you believe as it says in 2 Chronicles 7:14, that "If my people, who are called by name, will humble themselves and pray and seek my face, and turn from their wicked ways, then I will hear from heaven and I will forgive their sin and will heal the land." Jeremiah says, in 29:12, "Then you will call on me and come and pray to me, and I will listen to you." Even Job, who had lost all he had, including all his children, says in Job 22:27 that "you will pray to him, and he will hear you, and you will fulfill your vows." Church, our prayers are not in vain. James says in 5:13, "Is anyone among you in trouble? Let them pray. Is anyone happy, let them sing songs of prayer." Mark says in 11:24, "Therefor I tell you, whatever you ask for in prayer, believe that you have received it." We are even taught in Matthew 5:44 to pray for our enemies and pray for those who persecute us." Paul in Romans 12:12 says, "Be joyful in hope, patient in affliction, faithful in prayer." The Psalmist in 145:18 says, "The LORD is near to all who call on him, to all who call on him in truth." Proverbs 15:29 says, "The LORD is far from wicked, but he hears the prayers of the righteous."

Church, when we are too sick to pray; Romans says in 8:26 that "in the same way, the Spirit will help us in our weakness. We do not know what we ought to pray, but the Spirit himself intercedes for us through wordless groans." Timothy 2:8 says, "Therefore I want the men everywhere to pray, lifting up holy hands without anger or disputing." And James in 5:16 says, "Therefore confess your sins to each other and pray for each other so that you may be healed. The effectual fervent prayers of the righteous availeth much."

Church, rather than telling a suffering person you come across that you will be praying for them, don't delay. Do it right then. I'm personally getting forgetful and may forget all about it if I wait until later.

So Church, I ask you again, when Christ returns, will he find some faithful among us who have persisted and persevered like the widow woman who wouldn't give up seeking earthly justice? I want you to know that God's court of justice is open 24/7, not just during the week. He hears our cries during the sunrise, during the noon day, while we are sleeping, and all times in between. He hears the cries of those who have lost a loved one.

I sent a note to one of my pastor cousins. I said, "What do you say to one who tells you that the police came to their door at 2 a.m. and the officer said, 'Sir, your son had been killed in a car accident?'" Or what do you say to that family whose home had been destroyed by the floodwaters caused by the hurricane? Or what do you say to a grieving mother who says someone had just killed her only child? I was hoping for more direction, but his text message said, "There is not much you can say, but to pray and hopefully they have a relationship with God." So often it comes down to prayer. Prayer is the most important gift you can give.

Church, do you have a close relationship with God? Are you being faithful? Have you made up your mind that you are going to run on and see what the end is going to be? Jesus says in the eighth verse, that God will avenge those that cry unto him, but he also asked when he returns, will he find faith on the earth? Church, when the trumpet sounds and Jesus comes in a cloud and returns, will you be looking to the hills from whence cometh our help? How many will there be who have been constant in prayer, enduring in love, faithful in worship, dedicated, and devoted? How many will have persevered and not gotten weary? Church don't get weary. Galatians 6:9 teaches us not to be weary in well doing: for in due season, we shall reap if we faint not.

Therefore, as I'm about to bring this message to a conclusion, I want Oberlin and others gathered here to know, as I see it, that these two words—the primary objectives of this parable, prayer and faith—go hand in hand. You cannot have enduring, lasting faith without prayer, and you cannot have effective, sincere, and heartfelt prayer without faith! Our prayers are not in vain.

I sense some at Oberlin would just as soon give up. God sent me here to tell you, Don't give up, Oberlin. Hold on a little while longer! We shall reap what we sow! But we must be faithful. Hebrews 11:6 says that without faith, the Christian life cannot be what God intends it to be. We must have belief so strong that we can indeed walk by faith and not by sight. "For faith is the substance of things hoped for the evidence of things not seen" (2 CORINTHIANS 5:7). "Faith is trusting something that you cannot explicitly prove" (HEBREWS 11:1). Don't give up, Church. Don't give up, pastors, ushers, deacons, and choir.

After opening the doors to the church, we want to conclude the service with prayer, prayer for our church, prayer for this community and the world, prayer for our president and Congress, our governor and state legislature that all who have power will see the need to have regard for God and respect for his or her fellowman. We need to pray for those who are hurt by the laws that they pass. I seldom hear anyone mentioning that word "poor" or "widow" or "destitute" in Congress or in the legislature halls anymore. So let us pray that those who are enriched by greed will somehow have a change of heart and share more of the bounty of this country with others who cannot lobby for themselves as the widow in today's text.

Don't give up, Church. Endure to the end. Yes, I sense that many here at Oberlin have gotten weary but learn from the widow in today's text. Keep on praying, keep on seeking God. Keep on loving your enemies. Keep on being faithful.

Lord, Revive Us: Don't Let Us Sleep Too Long

MATTHEW 26:36–46

First Night of Revival, White Rock United Holy Church, Chapel Hill, NC

MARCH 24, 1999

> Then Jesus went with his disciples to a place called Gethsemane, and he said to them, "Sit here while I go over there and pray. He took Peter and the two sons of Zebedee along with him, and he began to be sorrowful and troubled." Then he said to them, "My soul is overwhelmed with sorrow to the point of death. Stay here and keep watch with me." Then he returned to his disciples and found them sleeping. "Couldn't you men keep watch with me for one hour?" he asked Peter. He went away a second time and prayed.... When he came back, he again found them sleeping, because their eyes were heavy. So he left them again and went away once more and prayed the third time, saying the same thing. Then he returned to the disciples and said to them, "Are you still sleeping and resting? Look, the hour has come, and the Son of Man is delivered into the hands of sinners. Rise! Let us go! Here comes my betrayer!" MATTHEW 26:36–46 (NIV)

In our text tonight, we find Jesus in the Garden of Gethsemane. Jesus knew His time had come to fulfill His Father's will that He be sacrificed for the sins of man. Jesus, as He was both human and divine, was like any one of us facing certain death: sad and sorrowful. I imagine there were many reasons he was sorrowful in addition to the fact that he was soon to be crucified. But first, let me paint a brief picture of a major event leading up to Jesus's walk in the Garden of Gethsemane.

Jesus and the disciples had just completed the Passover meal. As you know the Passover meal was in celebration of the Israelites' deliverance from bondage in Egypt. We refer to this Passover meal that Jesus shared with all twelve of his disciples as the Last Supper (MATTHEW 26:17). As a part of that meal Jesus and his disciples celebrated what we have referred to for many years as Communion.

During this somber occasion, Jesus reminded the twelve disciples that one of them would betray him. Have either of you ever had a friend betray you? If so, then you may have just a little idea why Jesus may have been so sorrowful when he thought about how Judas would sell him out for thirty pieces of silver (MATTHEW 27:3). And He knew He would have to experience the cruelest of deaths: crucifixion, death on the cross.

White Rock United Holy Church

Revival

March 24 – 26, 1999

Elder Robert A. Siler, Pastor
Rev. Joe L. Webster, Guest Evangelist

932 White Rock Church Road
Chapel Hill, North Carolina 27514
(919) 933-0593

First night of three-day revival

So, with unimaginable burdens on his mind, Jesus came to the Garden of Gethsemane with all of his disciples except Judas. Jesus asked a small favor of his disciples—the same close friends who had seen him heal the sick, give sight to the blind, and even raise Lazarus from the dead (JOHN 11:43–44).

In Matthew 26:36, Jesus asked his disciples to "sit ye here, while I go and pray." And it was Peter, and the sons of Zebedee, James and John, who Christ asked to walk with him to one corner of the Garden away from the others so he could pray. Luke's version says that Jesus went about a stone's throw away from the others and kneeled to pray (Luke 22:41). Sometimes we need to get away from the crowd to enter our secret closet so that we can communicate with the Father. Sometimes we need to tell our family and friends to wait for me while I go and pray.

In verse 38, Jesus said, "My soul is exceeding sorrowful, even unto death, tarry ye here, and watch with me." Luke 22:44 says when Jesus was praying, he was sweating, and his sweat was like great drops of blood falling to the ground. And Jesus went a little further and fell on his face, and prayed, "My father, if it be possible, let this cup pass from me, nevertheless not as I will but as thou wilt" (MATTHEW 26:39). Can you imagine what must have been going through the minds of Peter, James, and John as they observed Christ in so much agony? After all, they had seen him work many miracles.

I am a strong believer in prayer. I'm finding that God always answers my prayers. It may not always be the answer I think I'm seeking, but God answers prayers. One day not long ago at my office, I locked the doors and prayed because nothing seemed to be going right that day. Fees weren't coming in like I needed for them to come in. I felt so stressed out. So, I locked the door and had a little talk with God. And to my surprise, the answer came back in the form of a question. God said to me:

> Haven't I always taken care of you and supplied your needs? Didn't I heal you when you went to the hospital not long ago? What about that night when I healed your son when you woke up and found him having a severe seizure? What about that evening when you and your three children were around your wife's bedside in the hospital when her fever wouldn't go down after surgery, and I answered your prayers and Diane's fever went down that very moment for the first time?

That day in my office, prayer changed things. It opened my mind to my situation. God let me know that He had never neglected me in the past, and He would continue to be my side if I just trusted in Him. The Bible says if we abide in Him and His words abide in us, then we ask what we will, and it shall be done unto us (JOHN 15:7). God is faithful to answer our prayers. But Lord, revive us. Don't let us sleep too long.

So, Jesus asked his disciples to watch while he went to pray. And after Jesus had prayed, verse 40 says he came onto the disciples and found them asleep. Jesus said unto Peter, What, could you not watch with me one hour? In other words, Can't you stay awake at least one hour? I imagine in his great suffering Jesus may have said, "Don't you know my time is near? I'm getting ready to be crucified and go home to be with my father." Church, today we're sleeping when we ought to be praying. Lord, revive us. Don't let us sleep too long.

In verse 41, Jesus said yet again to his disciples, "Watch and pray, that ye enter not into temptation, the spirit is willing, but the flesh is weak." Church, no matter what we do, we can't change the fact that everyone of us is born in sin, and we don't have the power to change ourselves. There is a song I was listening to which is part of the Alvin Ailey *Revelations* collection. The song says, "Fix me, Jesus, fix me." "Fix me for my long white robe. Fix me for my starry crown. Fix me for my dying bed. Fix me for my journey home. Fix me, Jesus, fix me." Church, if we are not fixed, this old flesh will sin. Church, we often sin today because we're falling asleep when we ought to be praying. Lord, revive us. Don't let us sleep too long.

In verse 42, Jesus went again, the second time, and prayed, saying, "O my Father if this cup may not pass away from me, except I drink it, thy will be done." In other words, Jesus, being both human and divine, was yet again praying to his Father, that he'd rather not have to carry this burden that had been given him. He was saying to His Father, but if it is Your will, He would die on the cross. If it was His Father's will, he would allow them to spit on him and pierce him in the side. Church, we too have a cross to bear. Matthew chapter 16, verse 24, says that if any man will come after me, let him deny himself, take up his cross, and follow me. One songwriter wrote, "Must Jesus bear the cross alone and all the world go free? Yes, there's a cross for everyone, and there's a cross for me." I believe Jesus was teaching us how to pray, yet today our prayers are selfish. He was also teaching us how to live as well as how to die. I don't know about you, but I'm trying to spend as much time preparing to die as I am preparing to live. I believe God would have me say tonight that if you are not spending any time preparing to die, then you are asleep and need reviving. Lord, revive us. Don't let us sleep too long.

And in verse 43, Jesus came and found them asleep again, for their eyes were heavy. Church, Jesus just keeps giving us a second chance and a third chance to stay awake and serve him. I imagine Jesus, in his human nature, by this time probably was saying to his closest friends, his disciples, and I believe Jesus is saying to us tonight: After all I have done for you; I've even taught you to pray as John taught his disciples (LUKE 11:1–4). I've made you fishers of men (LUKE 5:1–11). I've even promised you eternal life if you will just keep my commandments and take up the cross and follow me (MATTHEW 19:16–17 AND MARK 10:17–21), and yet you can't even stay awake to watch and pray during my darkest hour. Peter, James, and John, I even took the three of you with me up into the mountains where you saw me changed before your very eyes, and you saw Moses and Elijah, and you heard a voice out of the clouds proclaim that I was His beloved Son, yet you can't even stay awake for a little while (MATTHEW 17:1–5). Lord, revive us. Don't let us sleep too long.

And in verse 44, Jesus left them, went away again, and prayed the third time, saying the same words. You would think that by this time, Jesus would have said to his disciples as the ninth verse in Proverbs 6 says: "How long wilt thou sleep, O sluggard?" But verse 45 says, "Then cometh He to his disciples and saith unto them, sleep on now and take your rest, behold the hour is at hand." Church, I'm comforted to know that even in this time of great sadness for my Lord, and yours, God sent him comfort. Luke's version of this Gethsemane event says in 23:43, "and there appeared an angel unto him from heaven strengthening Him." Church, even in our darkest hours, even when we're on our death-bed, God sends the angels to be with us. So we ought to stay awake and see the salvation of the Lord. Church, we don't have to go it alone if you will just love Him and trust Him. He will send us a comforter (JOHN 14:15–16). God, revive us. Don't let us sleep too long.

How is this Bible lesson relevant to us today? Church, our children are hooked on crack cocaine and being born with the AIDS virus. Yet we are sleeping when we ought to be awake and in constant prayer. Tonight, I can't emphasize enough the importance of prayer. First Thessalonians 5:17 says that we must begin to pray without ceasing. Our children are going to prison in record numbers. Across this state, from the coast to the mountains, I have visited state prisons. They are mostly filled with young African

American and Hispanic men, yet we are still sleeping. Our youth are committing suicide in greater numbers, something African American children didn't do in great numbers in years past, yet we are sleeping. We ought to be wide awake and praying that God would come into their lives and deliver them from evil. As a lawyer, I see young black men, even many who have not yet gone to jail, suffering and struggling to be men. It's especially sad because they don't have the Lord in their lives, and they seemingly have lost all hope. Can you imagine what it would be like not to have the Lord in your life in times like these? We need to wake up and be an encouragement to others. For our young people to put away alcohol and drugs and get fornication off their minds, they need all of us who are believers to stay awake just for a little while. Our young men and women need for us to be awake and to keep them in our daily prayers. Lord, revive us. Don't let us sleep too long.

Just like I believe Jesus was calling out to the disciples in the Garden of Gethsemane, I believe Jesus is calling out to White Rock and Barbee Chapel and Alston Chapel and Holy Trinity and First Baptist, and the Methodist, and the Catholic Churches and all those who are called by His name to humble ourselves and pray, and seek his face and turn away from our wicked ways, and stay awake just for a little while. Then Jesus will hear from heaven, and will forgive our sins, and will heal our land (2 CHRONICLES 7:14). Lord, revive us. Don't let us sleep too long.

Church, I need somebody to stay awake tonight and pray with me just for a little while. Jesus needs somebody to wake up and remember where He brought us from. Jesus needs somebody here at White Rock to wake up and remember that you haven't always had this fine church here. We need to wake up and remember that unless those within these walls go forth into the hedges and highways and take by the hand some bruised and beaten brother or some sister who has been abused and misused, then these walls and beautiful windows will all be in vain. I need somebody to remind our youth that our great-grandfathers and -mothers were slaves and had nothing, yet Jesus supplied their needs. Jesus is calling for us to wake up tonight and remember that He is a way maker and a mind regulator and that He died for us on Calvary's cross. Jesus is calling on us tonight to watch as well as pray. Lord, revive us. Don't let us sleep too long.

Some of us need to wake up and truly be born again, like Jesus told Nicodemus, that you need to be born of the spirit and the water (JOHN 3:1–21) Jesus needs somebody to stand up with a sober mind and a clear head unaffected by alcohol and drugs and say, "For God I'll live and for God I'll die."

Christian folk need a revival of the spirit, a revival of our minds, and a revival of our hearts. Some of our hearts are so messed up that you wouldn't help somebody if your very life depended on it. We are filled with jealously for one another. As soon as one of us gets near the top, the others will try to pull him back down. I read where a well-known superior court judge up in Washington, DC, William Thompson, who recently died, used to say that we should "work hard to achieve. Take somebody with you on the way up."

We have too many cars, too many fine houses, too much money in the bank that is just drawing interest and not being used for the purpose of the upbuilding of His Kingdom. I know too many seventy-five and eighty-year-old men and women who are still holding on to the first dollar they earned and still trying to get more just for the sake of having it. We are too selfish. God would have me say tonight that He is not pleased with us and that we need to wake up. We've been sleeping too long and need to be revived. Lord, don't let us sleep too long.

We need to wake up before it's too late. The sun is going down on many of us. We need to remember that the same Jesus who prayed in the Garden of Gethsemane is coming back for a church without a spot or wrinkle. St. Matthew chapter 26, verse 64, says Jesus is coming in the clouds of heaven, and in John 14:1–3, Jesus says in my Father's House are many mansions and that he has gone to prepare a place for you, and that He will come again. According to Revelation 1:7, the Bible says, "Behold, he cometh with clouds and every eye shall see him." As the song says, "I want to go back with him when he comes. Church, don't let Him catch you with your work undone, He's coming again so soon." We need to be ready when He comes again.

Church, Jesus is coming back for those who have been awake in Him; for those who have placed their whole heart and belief in Him, those who have kept his commandments; for those who have watched and prayed during the good times and the bad times, for those who have a clean heart.

Lord, revive us. Don't let us sleep too long.

Prayer of Comfort
Deacon Swade Sanders Funeral

Deacon Swade Sanders, Member, Oberlin Baptist Church, Raleigh, NC; Homegoing Service, Poplar Springs Christian Church, Garner, NC

MAY 14, 2022

Heavenly Father, I come before you and this great cloud of witnesses that have gathered for this Homegoing service for your servant Deacon Swade Sanders. I have been asked to say a prayer of comfort for his family. God, I first ask you to anoint me for this purpose. For I acknowledge that only you, and not my words, can provide the comfort and peace that Deaconess Sanders and her family need right now during this season of sadness, sorrow, and anxiousness about the future.

Heavenly Father, at the outset we acknowledge that in the Book of Job 14:1 we learn that man born of a woman is of few days and full of trouble. We thank you, God, for giving Deacon Sanders more than a few days. You gave him more than thirty thousand days, most of them healthy ones. So, we rejoice in his long life and contributions to his community and state.

Lord, your holy word in John 14, seemingly speaking to the saddened, disappointed, and bereaved, says, "Let not your heart be troubled, you believe in God, believe also in me." And David says over there in Psalm 23, "The Lord is my shepherd, I shall not want; the Lord will lead us beside still waters and restore our souls; and that even when we walk through the shadow of death, we don't have to fear evil. His rod and his staff will comfort us." And the Psalmist says over there in Psalm 46 that God is our refuge and strength, a very present help in trouble.

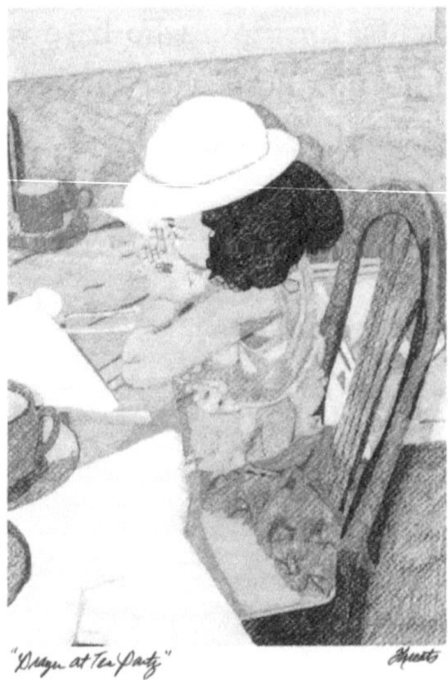

A GIFT FROM AND BY GENE THREATS

So Heavenly Father, no other help I know today, as I try to offer just a little bit of comfort to the family, I pray that the family will remember to look to the hills from which cometh our help. Our help cometh from the Lord and no other. God knows your heartache; God knows your pain; God knows your disappointment that Deacon Sanders was called home. Heavenly Father, I pray the Sanders family will keep pressing toward the mark of the high calling of Jesus Christ, and I proclaim today that if you do this, everything will be all right.

And Deaconess Sanders, after seventy-one years of marriage, even late at night when you feel like you are all alone, after the children have returned to their respective homes, I pray that God will give you strength, lift you up in your weakest and most lonely moments. To the Sanders family I pray that during the storms of life that will surely come, God will fill you with His Holy Spirit and shine upon you so that you will have peace; that the lily of the valley, that bright and morning star, that chief cornerstone will provide comfort and unconditional love to you that only God can give, and that you will feel the Savior's spirit present more than ever. And lastly, I pray that the ties that bind your family together will be mended, if torn, and as David said, that even your very souls will be restored. This is my prayer, this is my hope, and this is my assurance, my proclamation based upon an abiding faith. Family, God is faithful and true, to his word. Amen.

Invocation for Downtown Rotary Club

Durham, NC

MARCH 7, 2022

> Heavenly father, we know the scriptures say that in all our ways we should acknowledge you, and you will direct our paths. –PROVERBS 3:6

This afternoon we thank you for all that you have given us—life, health, comfort, food, raiment, for the sunshine and the rain, and even the cloudy days in our lives. We thank you for the leaders of our nation, state, and this Downtown Rotary Club.

We pray for forgiveness, for we all have committed transgressions inconsistent with your Holy will for this Rotary Club, and inconsistent with the mission of the Rotary Foundation to advance world understanding, goodwill, and peace by improving health, providing quality education, improving the environment, and alleviating poverty. We need an extra portion of your guidance, for our understanding of your will is so lacking.

I know that I personally need to be taken down to the Potter's House to be remolded and reshaped, and yes, given a new heart, a new birth, so that I might be all you would have me to be. I pray for courage, patience, grace, and for more humility as we interact with our fellow humankind. We pray for reconciliation of the races, ethnicities, different cultures, gender groups, and many faiths around this state, nation, and world, so that we might have peace on earth. I think of and pray for those who are senselessly being slaughtered and suffering in Ukraine and in other parts of the world today.

I cannot neglect to pray for those who are conspicuously absent from this room today—the poor, the unwelcomed, those that don't meet the criteria of this organization—for many more would be here and would contribute much if they could afford to be present. I pray for access to justice for all, and that we will eventually get to the time in history that someone would be able to say as the Prophet Amos said over there in Amos 5:24, "that justice roll[ed] down as waters and righteousness as a mighty stream." Amen.

Invocation: Fortieth Anniversary Ubiquity Reunion Prayer Breakfast

Howard University, Washington, DC—May 13, 2013

God of Abraham, Isaac, and Jacob, and God of Harriett, Rosa, Martin, and Malcolm, and borrowing from the words of James Weldon Johnson's lyrics to "Lift Every Voice and Sing," "God of our weary years, God of our silent tears," who has lead Ubiquity over these 40 years; we honor, praise, and say thank you almighty God for all you have given us: life, health, and strength, and so much more. Thank you for giving some Howard University students the vision to sow some seeds that grew into Ubiquity, an organization of fun-loving students and believers in community and public service to humankind. We thank you, God, for Howard University, the capstone that has educated tens of thousands from around the world. Your mercy and unconditional love allowed us to travel back to celebrate this Fortieth Ubiquity Reunion, and so we say thank you this morning.

We say thank you even for those brothers and sisters whose lives seem to have been cut short: Eric King, Ron Croxton, and others. We say thank you for those who could not return this weekend for whatever reason. You have lifted us to a higher place over the last forty years, and we will never be able to thank you enough.

Ubiquity Prayer Breakfast, Howard University

Now, God, we pray for deliverance and forgiveness of our sins, our shortcomings, for at times we have forgotten who made us, shaped us, and allowed us to persevere on this journey called life. You have propped us up and were so merciful to allow us to lean on your shoulders when we did not have anyone else to lean on.

We pray that you will increase our faith, our love for you and for each other. Bless our families. Because we can look back and see that you brought a whole race out of slavery, Jim Crow, and abject poverty, we know that you can sustain Ubiquity another forty years, and another four hundred years.

To God be the glory. Amen.

Invocation at Dedication and Open House, Office of Administrative Hearings

Raleigh, NC

DECEMBER 5, 2008

Heavenly Father, we know the Scripture says that in all our ways we should acknowledge you and that you will direct our paths (PROVERBS 3:6). And so, on this special occasion of the dedication of this new home of the Office of Administrative Hearings of the State of North Carolina, we first give honor to You, King of Kings and Lord of Lords.

God, we thank You for all that you have given us—life, health, comfort, food, raiment, for the sunshine and the rain, and even the cloudy days in our lives. We thank you for the leaders of this State and of the Office of Administrative Hearings whose vision helped make today's occasion possible.

As we dedicate this brick and mortar, we pray that it is symbolic of more than the evidence of the completion of a larger barn to store up our goods—our law books and court files and other things that we already have too much of—or a place to make us look good, feel comfortable, and boast about. But we recognize that we cannot begin anew in this building without also being transformed ourselves. And so, we pray for forgiveness for the leaders of this state, the governor, legislators, the judges, the advocates, and those who are visitors. We ask for forgiveness because all have committed reversible error and fall short of the ideal of perfection in all that we do and say and fall short of the glory of God. And so today as we dedicate this building, we also pray for guidance, for wisdom, for understanding, for reconciliation among the races, different cultures, religions, and genders. We pray for patience, for courage, for humility, stamina, and more grace as we begin anew in this place.

We pray for those who are conspicuously absent from this ceremony—the less fortunate, the homeless, the severely disabled, the mentally ill, the blind, the little children, the ones who are unemployed in these uncertain and difficult times, the ones who couldn't afford to be here even if they wanted to be here. We pray for those who will come into this building who have been traditionally denied equal access to justice, the ones who cannot afford a lawyer, those for whom this building was constructed and without whom there would be no need for a new building. We pray that you will pour out your abundant blessings upon them.

God, and so as we begin anew during this historic moment, we pray for a double portion of teaching. Teach us, God, what it means to be fair to all sides of a dispute, evenhanded, unbiased, and unashamedly committed to the cause of justice. And so, when our time at this place has passed, we pray that all will be able to say that within these walls and throughout the state of North Carolina wherever administrative law judges and other Judges preside, that in the words of the Prophet Amos (5:24) that justice rolled down as waters and righteousness as a mighty stream. A-men.

Funeral Committal—Celebration of Life for Travis Durant Ramsey Jr.

Durham, NC

FEBRUARY 25, 2024

With little advance notice during the funeral service of Travis Durant Ramsey Jr., I was asked by the funeral director to say a prayer and perform the Committal. Before praying and citing the words of Committal, I took liberty to say the following words to the audience:

> I believe God took Travis home early in life so that those of us who remain will, finally, finally, finally, learn not to judge, and to love one another, not just people who are like us.

And afterwards: "If even one among us who remains will commit to these words, then Travis's life and God's purpose for him will have achieved a great victory! I am fully committed!"

CHAPTER FOUR

Rev. Dr. Martin Luther King Jr. Birthday Celebration Oratories

Wake Forest Rev. Dr. Martin Luther King Jr. Holiday Celebration

Friendship Chapel Baptist Church, Wake Forest, NC

JANUARY 21, 2021

It is a great honor for me to be the keynote speaker on this 2021 Wake Forest Martin Luther King Jr. Holiday Celebration program. I am especially pleased to be a part of a program that recognizes the achievement of the up-and-coming youth of Wake Forest and surrounding communities. Your presence means that you have competed well and been selected by the committee that judged the competition. Congratulations to each of you.

Before I speak the words to the youth that I have prepared for them and others under the sound of my voice, I find it entirely appropriate to pause to say that my heart is heavy, my cup is running over with sorrow and sadness about what COVID–19, the coronavirus has wrought around the world. Nearly four hundred thousand have died in the United States alone; four thousand people a day are now succumbing to this illness. Millions of others have been infected, and the number of grieving the losses is far into the tens of millions. So my heart and prayers go out to everyone affected by this pandemic. No one has been spared. Personally, I have lost two second cousins and one first cousin to COVID. May God cover us with his magnificent and unmatched love.

This evening, I want to give my best efforts to encourage those who have been a part of this competition to always seek to aspire to the ideals and lessons we learn from the life of Dr. Martin Luther King Jr., including his leadership in the struggle of African Americans for equality, justice, and civil rights. Let me first describe just a few of the characteristics of Dr. King that our youth and all people all should strive to emulate.

Preparation

The first is that King was a learned man. He prepared himself for the tremendous task at hand. He graduated from Morehouse College (now University) and then later got his PhD, became an ordained minister, and in the process studied and learned about peaceful, nonviolent protest. He therefore became a great leader who caused many to join in the struggle that would not have had he advocated violence. So, he had followers, black, white, and from every walk of life. So, prepare yourselves, gain all the knowledge you can; you will need it as you become a leader in whatever career aspiration you may have. Somebody said, if you want to be a preacher, be prepared. If you want to become a lawyer, teacher, engineer, doctor, writer, mechanic, plumber, be prepared. Be the best in whatever you choose to do in life to support yourselves and your family, and as you go out into the world, help make it a better place. That will require hard work. Burn the midnight oil—an old phrase no doubt coined when we didn't have electricity in this country—which means you may have to stay up late at night studying. When your friends are at the party, sometimes you won't be able to attend.

In the process of getting prepared for the continuing struggle for dignity as a black man or woman, you likely will be rejected by some universities. I was rejected from some law schools, but I didn't give up. Like King, you must persevere. Never, ever give up, young folk. The law schools didn't know where I came from; they didn't know I came from hard-working, God-fearing stock, that I had a "How come I can't?" attitude. They didn't know that I came out of the hot tobacco fields and textile mills in the Goodwill community. They didn't know the stuff that I was made of. Some of my ancestors were landowners going back to the 1800s. They won't know that those of you who have won in this competition have been through peaks and valleys; they won't know the obstacles that you have overcome—they won't know the high mountains that you climbed to get where you are. So don't let no one—not your parents, other relatives, school counselor, or anyone else—tell you that you cannot be successful in college or in whatever other endeavor you put your mind and heart to.

I've been blessed to reach the height of a federal judge. In my court there in Durham, about eight years ago my staff and I started a program called CourtCares. It is geared to middle schoolers, sixth-, seventh-, and eighth graders who are brought to our court. We teach them about the federal courts, the Constitution, and we just try to get them to become good, law-abiding citizens by staying on the right side of the law. We have a little mock criminal trial where they act as the jury. In each session we have a guest speaker from different walks of life. One of our guest speakers, a retired

African American general, encouraged the students to believe that they could achieve. He told them that they can be great. One of the students, a little girl, spoke up. She said, "I can't be great because I am a mistake." My heart sunk down low that day. For one thing, I thought to myself, *What mother, father, grandparent, uncle, or aunt would be so heartless and so stupid to tell a little girl that?* I could tell she had been seriously damaged, internally wounded and discouraged! But the general tried to assure her that despite what anyone says, you still can be great if you put mind and heart and a hard work ethic to whatever you want to achieve. This week, a young black student-athlete football player at the University of Alabama, Devonta Smith, became the eighty-second Heisman Trophy winner. Because of his size, many doubted whether he could excel at such a high level. But I understand that in his acceptance speech he said, "If everyone else doubts you, have confidence in yourself." In the words of the Apostle Paul there in the 1 Corinthians 15:58 (KJV), you need to be "steadfast, unmovable, abounding in the work of the Lord as you pursue your goals.

Love Your Neighbor!

And then after you have been to finishing school, after you are prepared, you must, like Dr. King, learn how to love your enemies. That's a very difficult thing to do, but we are commanded to do so. And it will get you far in life if you could just learn to love your enemies and those who despitefully use you. I need for you leaders of today and tomorrow to take this love that I speak about to a new level. Our future is depending on you. We need leaders who know that there is no race of people that is superior; that all lives matter, including especially black lives that have been trampled on for over four hundred years in America. Several years ago, I published a book on the life of Judge Sammie Chess Jr., the first African American superior court judge in North Carolina. I quote him in the book, as he spoke of those who were mentors in his life. One of those people was his grandmother. She told him, "You are better than nobody, but nobody is better than you." I'm asking you to reach out and touch the hands of those who are different from you, those who not only look different, but those of a different faith or those who have no faith at all, and those who are less fortunate than you. I heard a preacher from Africa say that unless we get close enough to hear the poor chew their food and hear their cries, we cannot feel their pain. In this part of North Carolina, and this country, most of us don't go to bed hungry. But some do, and I need for those who are here tonight to care about those who are in need. We need to get close enough to people to hear them chew their food and hear their cries. Dr. King is crying out from the grave that we need to share more of what we have with others. If you want to know what love looks like, study Dr. King's life. The Bible teaches that there is no greater love than one who is willing to lay down his life for his friend.

You Cannot Achieve Anything without God

And then each of you need to know that without God you cannot achieve anything. Dr. King was a man faith. He was not perfect; he like all of us have our flaws, our weak moments, and our bad days when our faith is tested. But without God, you cannot become successful. None of us can do our jobs successfully. I would not be a federal judge if I sought to judge fairly under my own power. When I was 18 years old, preparing to go off to Howard University and Washington, DC, my late mother said to me, "Joe if you put God first in your life and work hard, someone will see you trying, and someone will help." Nearly 50 years later, people are still trying to help me. People love to help those who are trying to help themselves. Most importantly, without faith, your life will end upon your earthly death, but for those who put their trust in God, will be granted eternal life.

Dr. King was a Peacemaker

The last point I want to make to you about Dr. King that all of us should seek to emulate is that King was a peacemaker. The Bible over there in Matthew 5:9 says, "Blessed are the peacemakers for they will be called the children of God."

You may have seen the television coverage on January 6, the anarchy, the insurrection of mostly white men and women who took over the Capitol of the United States; looting and trashing the Capitol building; some proclaiming that this country was going back to 1776; some with Confederate flags, putting many in fear for their lives spurred on by President Trump. I understand five people died because of the domestic violence that Trump and his mob followers wrought that day. They are the opposite of peacemakers. The singing group, the Chi-lites, in 1974 had a hit song, "There will never be any peace until God is the conference table." Young people, middle-aged people, and senior citizens under the sound of my voice, we need to seek peace, using Martin Luther King as our example of peace. I have frequently said over the last decade that if those among us who have something to lose—meaning those who have a good-paying job, those of us who have big houses, money in the bank—don't stand up for peace, don't stand up for justice, don't stand up for right and stand up against wrong, then our system of justice will never be fair. The world we live in will never believe that black lives matter. Our young black men will continue to be feared by the police officers who carry the guns, and so their first instinct will continue to be to shoot them down often without cause.

As a judge, I'm called upon to be fair and just in all my decisions. I try to do that every day. Some say that I should not signal in advance what I stand for, that maybe I should demonstrate my impartiality only through my court rulings, that I should not speak truth to power. But I can't ask of others what I am not willing to do myself. Plus, I have a higher calling on my life. I believe that the truth will set me free. Not only that, but I took an oath almost forty-one years ago to support and defend the Constitution of the United States against all enemies, foreign and domestic. So for whatever time I have left I will continue to use my energy to do just that, speaking more forcefully, with even more conviction about equal justice under law and the rule of law that requires all persons to be treated the same.

If encouraging America to live up to its promise of equality to all men and women, and somehow insisting on it, somehow violates my oath to support and defend the Constitution of the United States, foreign and domestic, then so be it. I take my oath seriously and my calling seriously. They are not in conflict. Unarmed young black men and women deserve not to be gunned down like wild animals by untrained, overzealous, and often prejudiced police officers. Parents and other loved ones of these men and women of color ought not to have to be worried every time their teenager goes out the door. On this occasion of celebrating the life and legacy of Dr. Martin Luther King Jr., this injustice must end.

Young people, I'm about to close, but I hope that God will reveal to you that which He has revealed to me: that my life is not my own. Therefore, when you have been as blessed as I have been, you won't be able to be quiet when you see an injustice, when you see another person bullying a classmate or anyone else. And when my and others' voices grow silent, I hope that you too will take up the Martin Luther King mantle of love, peace, and a fully committed faith in God.

I hope that you will keep nudging America to live up to its Declaration of Independence, which states that "All men are created equal; that they are endowed with unalienable rights, among them are life, liberty and pursuit of happiness." I ask you to constantly remind those in power to live up to this. You will have the blessings of many, and most important, the assurance of God. You will be comforted and assured by the scripture that says, "If God be for you, then who can be against you?"

Conclusion

Finally, in conclusion, to those who have participated in the contest to recognize our youth of this community, I want to leave you with two scriptures. The divine word of God is far more important than anything I've said to you tonight. I encourage you to start right now: memorize them, study them, keep them in your heart and live your life by them. My late mother taught me the first one early in my life, and I recently sent that one to my three adult children by text. The first one is found at Matthew 6:33:

> But seek ye first the kingdom of God and His righteousness and all these things will be added unto you.

And in Mark 8:36 it says,

> For what shall it profit a man to gain the whole world and lose his soul?

To those under the sound of my voice, I ask for your prayers. If I can be of assistance to any of you here, get in touch with me. I will freely give you my advice about whatever you want to talk about. Those who invited me here have my permission to give my telephone number and email address to you. May God continue to bless you and keep you.

Sanford–Lee County Branch NAACP, Eighth Annual Martin Luther King Jr. Birthday Observance

Sanford, North Carolina

JANUARY 16, 1994

I am extremely happy and honored to be here today and to have been asked to play a role in this annual observance of the life and contributions of one of the most outstanding Americans who has ever lived, Dr. Martin Luther King Jr.

The Sanford–Lee County Branch of the NAACP should be commended for helping keep Dr. Martin Luther King Jr.'s dream alive. To begin my comments, I want to talk about the number-one problem facing North Carolina and the nation today. I want to summarize a brief article from the December 1993 edition of *Essence* magazine, titled "Violence, a Life Changed Forever."

As with too many black mothers across the length and breadth of America, the life of an African American mother, her son, and family were drastically changed forever by a firearm and a teenage assailant who pulled the trigger. The toll this tragedy has taken on all affected is indicative of the suffering and grief experienced by many families in the neighborhood called Homewood, a community in Pittsburgh, Pennsylvania where gunfire and other violence are a frequent occurrence. During the last thirteen years, this family's mother, her husband, brother-in-law, nephew, and three stepsons have been shot. And last February her twelve-year-old son was shot—maliciously gunned down because the teenage victim made the innocent mistake of calling another teenager by the wrong name.

The victim of this one violent occurrence was sitting on the front porch with his girlfriend when some young persons from the neighborhood passed by when he called out one of them by the wrong name. His mistaken identity of a teenager by the wrong name resulted in the victim being shot in the neck, which cut through his sixth and seventh vertebrae, leaving him paralyzed from the chest down, with only the partial use of his hands and arms. At the time this young teenager was told he may never walk again.

This life-changing event could not have been foreseen in earlier times when one's life was valued differently and there was respect for the well-being of others. The mistake of greeting someone by the wrong name caused great harm to an entire family. Today, a mistaken identity, or accidently bumping up against another person in a crowd, can cause one to be shot. "The young assailant approached the victim and said to him,

'That's not my name.'" The assailant then pulled out a gun and hit Dion in the head with it. In defense of himself, the victim punched his assailant. The teenage assailant pistol-whipped him. The aggressor then aimed his gun and fired. The victim's girlfriend ran inside her house and locked the door, leaving her friend slumped on the porch.

When the police arrived a short time later to investigate, another tragedy occurred that is an example of man's inhumanity to man—an indication that in the minds of some, a black man's life in America has less value than of the majority race. Apparently to the police officers, it was just another example of the many instances of violence in the black and brown communities that they encounter daily. The *Essence* magazine article stated that because the police officers had not seen the shooting, and did not see any blood, they concluded the victim of the assault had not been shot, and instead of calling for an ambulance, they searched him for drugs. He was left lying on the porch for an hour before an ambulance was summoned to the scene.

The delay in receiving treatment may have contributed to the victim's paralysis. The boy's mother stated "that her son could still move his body shortly after he was shot. He was barely hanging on by the time he reached the hospital. His mother commented further, "If I could take his place, I would." She looked toward her son sitting in his wheelchair watching television. "It hurts so much just to walk in front of him."[23]

Today as I reflect on the life and great works of Dr. Martin Luther King Jr., I cannot help but think that if he were living today, he would still be fighting to bring down the walls of racism and bigotry that still pervade our nation. But I believe that more than anything else, his crusade today would be to take his message of nonviolence into the neighborhoods, and into every city and town across this nation. He would be working around the clock to end the useless bloodshed taking place today, especially among the African American youth. So today in my brief comments, I want to encourage the NAACP here in Sanford and Lee County to take up the torch that Dr. King passed on to us and encourage you to begin the dialogue that will allow us to concentrate on saving our youth before another generation is lost.

As the article which I just summarized illustrates, our youth are killing and maiming each other in record numbers. In 1990 homicide was the leading cause of death of young black men. African American children are killing each other with guns and by taking cocaine and other drugs. Our children are committing violent crimes and going

23 Over the last thirty-one years since the publication of this article, violence, especially black-on-black crimes of violence in all communities of the United States has increased. On average, more than 12,400 black people die from gun violence each year, 15,548 such deaths in 2021 alone. Black Americans die from gun violence at nearly 2.4 times the rate of white Americans. Giffords Law Center to Prevent Gun Violence, giffords.org.

to prison in record numbers. While blacks only represent 12 percent of the nation's population, they represent 44 percent of the inmates in our state prisons and local jails in 1991. Nationwide, more black males are incarcerated in federal prison than are enrolled in colleges and universities at a cost of twenty-five thousand dollars per year in North Carolina.

If Dr. King were still alive today, he would also find that our youth are living in poverty now, just like they were twenty-five years ago. Two of every five black children live in poverty. African American children are also doing poorly in our public schools. Not only have we not made a great deal of progress academically—two of every five over age sixteen have no high school diploma—but black children are suspended at a rate far greater than white students. In Wake County, for example, black students are suspended at twice the rate of white students.

As I survey the condition of our youth, I cannot overlook the fact that, today, our fourteen- and fifteen-year-old youth are giving birth to children. A black child has only a one in five chance of growing up with two parents. Don't misunderstand me. There are many children who have grown up to be very successful from single-parent homes. Contrary to what Dan Quayle implied during the presidential campaign, a mother or a father and a child can constitute a family. However, this phenomenon today is causing many children to grow up never knowing what it means to see a man get up and go off to work and be responsible and to help the young children to be nurtured so that they grow up to have self-esteem and to know the hard work ethic which is so important. I can tell you today that I can still see my own father get up before daybreak and come home after sunset from work, and that has a lot to do with my own success today.

So today, as I reflect on the life and legacy of Dr. Martin Luther King Jr., I cannot help but having a message that cries out for our youth. All of us should take heed to the African proverb: "A community that does not take care of its youth and elderly is doomed to failure from within." Attributed to Mahatma Gandhi is an equivalent truth: "The true measure of any society can be found in how it treats its most vulnerable members."

So, what must we do here in Sanford and Lee County and across the nation to end the killing and to restore responsible conduct in our youth?

First, we must begin to restore hope in our youth. I strongly believe that where there is hope, there is pride. Unfortunately, many of our youth still aren't very proud of even their own heritage. I once read a story about a little black boy that emphasized this lack of pride or self-esteem in oneself brought about by the color of his skin.

> A little black boy went to a county fair and observed a balloon vendor blowing up balloons—all different colors. Some were red, some blue, some black, some yellow, and some white. He watched as a red balloon went up into the air, and then a blue one and then a white one. And he watched them go out of sight. As he stood there watching, the young boy asked the vendor, if you let a black balloon go up, will it go up as high as the others? The vendor responded to the young man, "It's not the color of the balloon, but the stuff inside that makes it fly."

So Dr. King would tell the NAACP today, that we must begin to instill in our youth that it's what's inside that counts. It is how much courage you have, how much desire, how much willpower, and how hard you want to achieve: that's what really counts. It's not what color you are or tall you are. It's not whether you are rich or whether you are poor. But we must tell our youth repeatedly that it's what's inside that matters. And so pride, which our youth lack so much of today, will be restored if there is hope.

I also believe that where there is pride, there will be respect for self. Respect for self means drug and alcohol abuse will decrease. Fewer young girls will become pregnant, and fewer young boys will disrespect young girls by insisting on sex as the number-one condition of friendship. If there is respect for self, there will be respect for others. If there is respect for others, clearly there will be fewer crimes, fewer robberies, fewer funerals with weeping mothers. If there are fewer crimes, there will be a need for fewer prisons—and so more of our youth will become contributing members of society.

So the NAACP, to use a basketball term, must begin to do a full-court press to offer hope to our children and thereby give them a credible alternative to crime and violence. President Bill Clinton, during the presidential campaign, said we don't have one person to waste, and we don't! We must draw upon all the citizens of this and other communities, those with education and those without, those who are doctors and those who are not, those who are janitors and those who are not. We don't have one person to waste. For those we give up on will be those who rob, kill, and rape and become wards of the state prison. I read a quote attributed to a great singer, Lionel Ritchie, who quoted his father as saying,

> That a three-piece suit and a briefcase didn't impress him all that much. That a person with a mop and a broom might have the answer that you need. But if you carry your head too high, you might miss the answer.

So for the NAACP and other organizations and individuals to play a role in restoring hope and pride and respect in our youth, you can't carry your heads too high. Our youth are down here. If you carry your heads too high, you will miss what they are saying. You might have to get into the hedges and highways and come down to the level where the youth are to be found.

Almost one hundred years ago, at a time when African Americans were not long out of slavery, when W. E. B. DuBois and others were saying blacks needed to obtain a liberal arts education—while others advocated trade schools, such as those which taught brick masonry and carpentry, as the best means to overcoming poverty—Booker T. Washington said, "We must cast our buckets down where we are."

You see, today, where our youth are—are in the streets with guns, and in the drug houses, and in a state of hopelessness. So we must cast our buckets down where we are. This organization must go quickly to reach our youth before they get hooked on crack cocaine and before they are arrested, and before they drop out of school, and before the young girls get pregnant and before the young men develop disrespect for young women and the elderly.

There are examples of work being done to help the youth. There are Big Brother, Big Sister programs, and programs to teach our youth how to read. There are many programs to show them we do care. The NAACP and other organizations and individuals in the community, no matter what race, should seek out our children who are at risk and spend time with them. The real answer to the crisis in our communities can only be reached one child at a time. We can't wait for government programs and handouts. We must put our hands out to touch someone.

Sure, there is still racism in this country. But my parents didn't let it stop them. They didn't have much book sense, but they had sense enough to work hard and to know God and the power of prayer.

I personally am inspired by my own parents who had eight children and parents like my wife's parents who had fifteen children and reared fourteen of them to adulthood in rural Orange County. Before my mother-in-law, Frances Ramsey, passed, I asked her how they made it during the 1940s, '50s, and '60s with all those children. I remember vividly her response: "Sometimes I would go to the cupboard and the cupboard would be bare, but there was always food on the table." So their tremendous faith and sacrifice brought them through the hard times.

And yes, there was racism all around my wife's parents. They had no indoor bathroom or plumbing, but there was laughter in the house, and sharing with each other and with their neighbors, and giving and respect, and hard work and honesty, love and forgiveness being taught and practiced by example in the confines of that old wooden house. Some of you may be saying, *What does your family and your wife's family have to do with anything?* Dr. King would have all of us to know today that we must go back to the values that brought us out of slavery and segregation to get a handle on the violence and hatred that are separating the haves from the have-nots, blacks and whites, Jews and Arabs, Protestant and Catholic.

Dr. Martin Luther King Jr. said that "all meaningful and lasting change begins on the inside." If this NAACP chapter and if this community devote your hearts and souls to changing the direction of your young people here in Lee County, then you will be successful. You will see a reduction in violent crime, and you will see more young people graduating and assuming responsible roles of leadership in this community. Lee County can be a role model for others to follow. You can't do it, though, if some of you are squabbling about who is in charge or who the leaders will be. You must agree or agree to disagree and move on. No one has the answer solely within himself. The silent majority must solve the crisis facing us today. Go over to your schools and talk with the teachers and determine who needs help. Go other places where our youth can be found. It is not going to be easy, but Dr. King would have us to know that you can do it if you try. He would say, just look how far we have come. He said, "The ultimate measure of a man is not where he stands in moments of comfort and convenience, but where he stands at times of challenge and controversy."

In conclusion, I am reminded of the aftermath of the death of one of my and my wife's best friends, Margaret Porter, who died four years ago leaving behind a husband and four young daughters, ages one to eight. I went to Virginia with her husband to select a casket and make other arrangements for her burial. As we sat there in her parents' living room looking through a high school yearbook, we saw just underneath Margaret's picture the words, "It's not the triumph, but the struggle. The essential thing is to have fought well."

A GIFT FROM AND BY GENE THREATS

So when the battle to save our youth is over, we will be judged not by where we came from, but what we have done to help somebody. All that will matter is whether we have fought a good fight. Our youth are crying out for attention. Only individuals can give them what they need, one child at a time. So Dr. Martin Luther King Jr.'s dream today would be that the NAACP, the church, and individuals throughout the community should take charge of their own destiny and work with our youth one child at a time.

Thank you so much for inviting me here today to play a part in this annual observance to honor the memory and contributions of one who gave his life so that we could have freedom and equal rights. We can best honor him by going to work this very day to help solve the problem of crime and violence among our youth.

Excerpts from Keeping the Dream Alive through Unity by Understanding and Working Together

Zion Baptist Church, Reidsville, North Carolina

JANUARY 17, 2011

I accepted the call to be here this morning to help you celebrate the life and legacy of a great man, Dr. Martin Luther King Jr., to whom who we are all so truly indebted. But also, I accepted the invitation, to use the words of our president, Barack Obama, because of the "urgency of the moment."

"Keeping the Dream Alive through Unity" is like the word "love," in that it is an action verb or phrase. It is easy to say but hard to carry out. I stopped by here this morning to remind you of the work you have committed to undertake. It requires putting aside self and putting your fellow man and the community and nation first. Oh, how I'd love to come here today and say that all is well, that King's dreams have all been fulfilled, that we don't have any more work to do. But it seems that the work ahead may require even more hard work and dedication than in the past. It will require even more understanding than in the past. Yes, we must be unified and try harder to understand and work with each other to keep King's dream alive.

Reverend Martin Luther King Jr. Banquet, Reidsville, NC, January 17,2011
PHOTO COURTESY OF JAMES ANDERSON

In January 2008, in a frozen field overlooking the Capitol in Washington, DC, I was present to hear President Obama say in his inaugural speech that the time has come to put away childish things. Our nation, at the crossroads of a critical time in history, needs to put away childish things and come together and work together for the good of the whole nation. We can't be role models for our young people if we are bickering and fighting with one another. It is no wonder that many of our youth are out of control.

In order for me to know where I was going with this theme today, I had to remind myself—and I knew I needed to remind you—of what Dr. King's dream was about before you put your hands to the plow. Today not only are we experiencing difficult economic times, but the family structure we had as a nation in the 1950s and 1960s has disintegrated right before our eyes. Rather than going off to work, Daddy is going off to prison, leaving many communities with only women, children, and senior citizens left. And sometimes, increasingly even the single mother is so messed up on cocaine that grandmothers and extended families have to intervene. You can see the results of a disintegrating family in our communities, in the churches, our workplaces, and universities. I'm confident King would say we must rededicate ourselves to our families.

Dr. King's dream of equal justice under the law and equal employment opportunity is still unfilled. Economic justice is still lacking in America. Dr. King's dream of educational opportunity for all has mixed results. It's going to take a lot of effort to keep Dr. King's dream alive to work on this and other problems in America today.

Dr. King's dream of equality in health care for all Americans remains unfulfilled. King spoke of the huge racial and ethnic disparities in health care coverage which is so great that it shocks the conscience. There remains—and it seems to be increasing—huge racial and ethnic disparities in health coverage. Our nation's economic health will be severely threatened unless the health of the poorest and hardest workers who have the most labor-intensive jobs, is not addressed by those with the ability to do so. After all, the poor built this country and remain the pistons that keep the nations engines running smoothly.

I'm sure Dr. King would say that his dream didn't include our young folk killing one another; it doesn't include gang membership and gang warfare. I encourage you to utilize mediation in the county's schools and communities to solve problems before they escalate into violence.

If he were alive today, I believe Dr. King would say maybe we've been dreaming for too long; maybe it's time to wake up and go to work. I believe King would say that if you want to keep his dream alive, you must put your hands to the plow. There can't be any turning back. You will lose your credibility if you do that. He would say that it is a moral imperative for those of you who are retired and have some time on your hands to go into your local elementary, middle, and high schools to let some young brother or sister who is struggling know that you care about them. We need some more lawyers, judges, teachers, nurses, ministers, and doctors who are socially conscious, who care more about helping their communities and less about making a lot of money. The desire to help somebody has been the motivating factor in my own life's work, and I ask for your prayers as I continue to try to make a difference.

As we think about the message of Dr. King's dream, and the huge commitment you have undertaken to keep Dr. King's dream alive, I must take a moment to tell you that it is past time for blacks and whites to enter into a spirit of reconciliation. Jesus stopped by Jacob's well to fellowship with a Samaritan woman and to teach us that blacks and whites, Jews and Gentiles, Protestants and Catholics, Christians and Muslims must begin to drink from the same well. We've been distrusting one another too long. We must also reconcile with sister and brother, mother and father, straights, and gays.

As we reflect on how we can keep Dr. King's dream alive through unity by understanding and working together, our president needs each of you here today to help him do his job. Whether you like our governor, congressmen, or senators, they need you to help them do their job. They need your support and encouragement. They need some foot soldiers to help them.

I encourage you to keep coming together; come together more often in a spirit of cooperation, unity, togetherness, and love. You will never be able to work together in unity if you don't understand one another. Only then will you be able to keep Dr. King's dream alive by understanding and working together. Be encouraged. Keep striving for peace.

Redefining the Dream: For This Cause

Excerpts from an April 11, 2009, speech presented to the Eighth District Black Leadership Caucus, Raeford, NC

MAY 7, 2009

When Brother Rogers gave me the theme for this evening, "Redefining the Dream," the first thought that occurred to me was that we must first step back in time and determine what Dr. King's dream was about and whether his dream has been completely fulfilled. I look out into the audience tonight and see that there are some of you who remember when it seemed that it was unlawful or illegal for black men and women to do anything: to vote, to eat at the lunch counter in restaurants, and even to dream or aspire to be somebody. During those times, the masses of our people were still feeling so shackled in the shadows of slavery that had ended one hundred years earlier that we dared to dream. Today, some say we should forget about slavery, forget about Jim Crow, forget about being spit on, being insulted, being abused, being raped, being forced to use hand-me-down books in separate but unequal school buildings, and being told as a people we had no right to vote, to hold office, no right to equal rights under the law.

There was Medgar Evers, who was willing to give his life; Fannie Lou Hamer, who had the courage to go to Chicago to the Democratic Convention and stand up and say I've come too far to turn around. And there was Rosa Parks, whose feet got tired of standing up on the bus in Montgomery. And there was Martin Luther King Jr., who first publicly articulated the dream of the silent in front of hundreds of thousands and millions on television. There were thousands of others whose names we will never know, who gave their lives so that we could have three black judges here tonight. I give honor to those bold soldiers who had the courage to stand up and say I dare to dream about a better future for my people! So tonight, I draw courage from reading and knowing my history.

I want to pause for a moment and tell you that I'm thankful that I got to know, as a friend, Dr. John Hope Franklin who passed away a couple of weeks ago. Dr. Franklin, the eminent historian and civil rights advocate, would say we need to be teaching our children our history now, so they too can dream. Someone once said that you cannot get to where you want to go unless you know from where you came.

So, in many ways, as noted in King's I Have a Dream speech, America has not made good on the promises it made years ago. King compared these unfulfilled promises to what happens when one issues you a check that bounces because of insufficient funds. When I consider whether King's dreams have been fulfilled, I can't help but see the floodwaters in New Orleans after Hurricane Katrina in 2005. For some reason I can't get that picture out of my mind: poor folk on top of rooftops begging and pleading for help; even some of the disabled in hospitals couldn't get out in time for their lives to be spared. I remember King's campaign on poverty. When I saw people on rooftops and wading through filthy waters in New Orleans and those who lived among filth in the Superdome for many days, somehow King's dream and his plea for a safety net for poor people, the right to receive adequate food, shelter, medical care, and protection had been forgotten. Our own government could not figure out that poor people often can't afford cars, buses, or trains for safe passage out of New Orleans—and so many perished. I heard that one hundred hours after the storm hit, thousands upon thousands had not received any food or and water. I kept thinking that if those were not poor people, the government's response would have been much different. And so, we have to demand better for those who can't take care of themselves. We must demand that America live up to the true meaning of the Declaration of Independence that proclaimed that all men are endowed with certain inalienable rights: the right to life, liberty, and the pursuit of happiness.

Yes, we must continue to review Dr. King's dream and seek to apply it to our times. Our times today are just as difficult. While we can sit at the lunch counter, many are unemployed and don't have money to pay for a meal. If King were alive today, I believe he would say that just as we preached the need for a peaceful struggle without violence in the 1960s, our young people must put away their guns and stop killing one another. They must put away their guns and love one another. We, as a people, must stay in school. Our young people must not give up. I see too many young black men standing on the corner and on the front porches of their parents and grandparents' homes—having given up on finding a job. We must rededicate ourselves to our families. Yes, I believe Dr. King would find it necessary to say to our young black men that anyone can become "a baby daddy," but it takes effort to become a father. As I have found with my own three children, you have to work at being a parent. There is no one book or one formula that fits all.

I believe Dr. King would say that he was first and foremost a man of faith—that he found it necessary to go down on his knees in the midnight hour as he was threatened with bodily harm and even death, locked up and spied on by the FBI. After arriving home to be with his family from a long meeting one night, Dr. King received a telephone call from a man using the n-word and threatening Dr. King's life. In times like those, King got down on his knees and prayed. How many of you here have found it necessary to get down on your knees in the midnight hour? I stopped by here tonight to tell you that these problems we are experiencing today are too great for us to handle on our own.

We must remember that America, as great as is, does not have the answer to all of the world's problems, and our blessings don't make us better than others in the world. My friend, John Hope Franklin, wrote that,

> . . . when this country and the Western world understand that there's no monopoly on goodness and truth, nor on skills and scholarship, we can begin to appreciate the ingredients that are indispensable to making a better world. That is perhaps the greatest lesson of all.[24]

A Hindu man I met in London who believes he has a million gods still belongs to the one God that I serve. We must love him just as much as we love our own children. Somehow, it is through the true love that only God can give that we can reconcile or make peace with those who are not like us. This is my dream tonight.

Tough times are not new here in the Eighth District. In the days when cotton was king, God brought you out. He made a way out of no way for your great-grandparents; some of your great-grandparents were slaves, and then sharecroppers. So, as we rethink, redefine, and relive Dr. King's dream and try to apply it to today's difficult times, I encourage you not to get weary. I need for you to become dreamers and say: for this cause, I will dedicate my life; for this cause, I will forever be faithful; for this cause, I will do what I can to help those less fortunate than myself; for this cause, I will tell my children and grandchildren about my hopes and dreams for them; for this cause, I will keep on keeping on; for this cause, I'm going to stay on the battlefield; for this cause, I'm going to look to the hills for which cometh my help; for this cause, I'm going to be a role model for young people; and for this cause, I'm going to do what I can to make King's dream a reality.

24 John Hope Franklin, *A Life of Learning,: in Race and History: Selected Essays, 1938–1988* (Baton Rouge: Louisiana State University Press, 1991).

CHAPTER FIVE

Other Selected Writings

Chaplain Internship at University of North Carolina–Chapel Hill Hospital

AUGUST 2001–DECEMBER 2001

By the spring of 2001, I had been accepted as a chaplain intern at the hospital on the campus of University of North Carolina at Chapel Hill. In July 1998, I had preached my initial sermon at Goodwill Baptist Church in Madison, North Carolina. I had not considered my calling to be one of a traditional pastoral ministry. I was engaged in the full-time practice of law at the time, and I knew that I wanted to continue my work as an attorney-at-law, which I considered to be a calling also. My call was to make a difference in my community and state. I had hung my shingle once again, in January 1995, this time in the small, mostly rural town of Pittsboro, North Carolina, fifteen miles south of my home in Chapel Hill. This is how I made a living for my wife and three children, at the time the ages of nineteen, fifteen, and twelve. Therefore, I entered the Chaplain's Internship Program with no goal of becoming a full-time chaplain at the University of North Carolina Hospital or any other hospital. It was one of the many opportunities I considered in life that might help me carry out my commitment of making a difference, especially in my dual callings of law and recent ordination as a Baptist minister in 2001.

My first recollection of my internship program was that early in the program, the entire hospital was placed on alert in the days following the terrorists' bombing of the World Trade Center in New York, the Pentagon in Washington, DC, and the plane crash in Pennsylvania on September 11, 2001. I recall a large gathering of persons in the hospital chapel to discuss the fact that many of the seriously injured might be transferred to UNC–Chapel Hill Hospital for treatment, and that we might be called upon to offer pastoral services to those patients. It was a critical time in the life of the hospital and for those of us who were called upon to minister as chaplains. I also recall that different faiths were represented among those gathered in the chapel to draw strength from one another, and the many prayers for the injured and the loved ones of the nearly three thousand innocent victims who perished on 9/11, as this time has been forever etched in history.

The Chaplain's Internship Program was composed of several parts. There was the seminar part, the part that required each student to visit a certain number of patients each week, the part that required the students to write a summary of the visits with the patients, and the part that required each student to meet with the director of the Program to discuss our summaries. One of the first patients I visited was sitting on the side of her bed rejoicing that she felt better than she had in many years. She was recovering from a kidney transplant. She had been on dialysis for years. So, I sat down beside her on the bed and had prayer and talked about her long journey to recovery. I wrote a summary of this visit, and in my first visit with the director of the program to discuss my visits, he said I was wrong to sit beside the patient on the side of her bed. Until this day, I still believe I was right, and the director was wrong. I could tell the patient truly enjoyed my company, and we both rejoiced in tears as I prayed for her continued recovery. As I recall, the program director stated that I was invading the patient's space, although there was never any indication that I made the patient feel uncomfortable in any manner by sitting on the bed beside her. It also seems that somewhere in the back of my mind there was some discussion about there being a difference between sympathy and empathy and being shown an illustration of a man trapped in a ditch and a man reaching down to help him out of the ditch rather than the man getting down in the ditch with the man to help him out. It is possible that I was taught this distinction at some other time in my life. Finally, many years later someone reminded me that the director's objection to my sitting on the bed beside the patient probably had more to do with the possibility of my spreading germs to this patient, although I have no recollection of the director discussing this factor with me.

Other patients I recall visiting included a man brought in by ambulance who had been in an accident causing one hand to be almost totally severed from his arm. His hand was barely attached. Whenever the hospital's code blue rang out, the chaplain intern had to report to the emergency room and then report to the attending physician to let him or her know of the chaplain intern's presence. I would take notes, make entries in the patient's medical record, and listen to what the physicians were saying. I heard this patient say to the attending physician, "Will you be able to save my hand?" The doctor did not respond. I observed him call the Duke University Hospital to consult. The next day I went by to visit this patient, and I saw that the hospital was not able to save his hand. I found the patient asleep and elected not to disturb him. I wondered to myself what I would have said to him if he had been awake.

I have another vivid memory of an elderly African American woman of great faith. In my visit with her, she told me that she had been diagnosed with cancer, but that she didn't believe she had cancer. She also said she had been told she had been in a coma. While in the coma, she said she had "seen the feet of Jesus and heard his mighty voice." She told me that Jesus had asked her whether she wanted to go back to where she was. She replied yes, and when she woke up, she saw a nurse standing beside her bed looking very frightened. The patient asked the nurse, "Why are you looking so frightened?" The nurse replied, "Because we just disconnected your life support." This patient spoke of this experience with certainty and confidence that it had happened.

Another memorable experience with a patient occurred when I checked in with the reporting nurse one day. She said to me that a young woman on a certain floor had a stillborn child and I needed to go see her. She also told me that she had several previous miscarriages. I proceeded to her room. Upon arrival I observed the young patient was looking very stoic and all alone. She didn't say a word as she lay in bed. I immediately saw her stillborn child in a container sitting on a table beside the patient's bed. What could I say? Should I tell her not to give up on having a healthy child? Being the father of three healthy children, I did not have the words to express my heartfelt thoughts. I tried to offer words of comfort. My training provided direction for offering a short funeral service for the stillborn child. I carried out the program, and I'm certain ended with prayer as I always did. And then I departed.

Another experience involved an elderly man dying of cancer. No family was present. I could see agony all over his face. Above his bed was the sign "NPO." I came to learn that this meant "nothing by mouth." He could have nothing to eat or drink. I stood beside him and held his hand. I prayed for him, and a short time later wrote a poem titled "Death Bed,"[25] that described what I observed and felt that day as I sought to minister to this patient.

And last, I ministered to two families who were toiling over when to disconnect life support for their loved ones. One was a pastor of a church in Moore County, North Carolina, whose wife was dying. He later invited me to preach at his church's Homecoming Day service. To God be the glory for these experiences as a chaplain Intern, and I will always be appreciative of those within the internship program for affording me this opportunity.

25 37 See "Death Bed" poem in Chapter 10 Joe's Book of Poetry

When Man Says No, God Says Yes at His Time: Never Give Up

Chapel Hill, North Carolina

DECEMBER 14, 2022

I want my children and children's children to know that I applied for many jobs and positions over my long career for which I was not hired. These included three vacancies on the North Carolina Court of Appeals; an election to the State District Court for Orange and Chatham Counties, North Carolina; and faculty positions at the University of North Carolina at Chapel Hill and North Carolina Central University School of Law. I was not selected for either of these positions. Those in position to appoint me to the Court of Appeals or to the law school faculty said, "No," but God said at his time (Kairos). God said yes to my appointment as a state administrative law judge (ALJ) in 2006 and to my present position as US magistrate judge for the Middle District of North Carolina in 2012. After being denied a faculty position by University of North Carolina–Chapel Hill and North Carolina Central Law Schools, I was later appointed as an adjunct professor of law at the Norman Adrian Wiggins School of Law at Campbell University, which I held until my appointment as a federal magistrate judge.

Also, on two occasions I sought election to the alumni trustee position on the Howard University Board of Trustees. Often, I have reflected on the fact that I would have been under additional stress to fundraise for the university as a board member if I had been successful. This task would have been more difficult because of the restrictions set forth in the Code of Judicial Conduct. I lost in the alumni trustee position by less than two hundred votes on each occasion. Also, on two occasions I was nominated by fellow Howard University alumni for the prestigious Distinguished Alumni Achievement Award given at the annual black-tie Fundraising Banquet. I was not selected for this recognition.

I am glad that my Redeemer knows me better than I know myself. I'm convinced that the judicial positions I did get appointed to were much better suited for my talents, judicial temperament, and my desire to make more of a difference in our judiciary, my profession, and my community. I also know that our time is not God's time and so we must be patient and wait on the Lord. Moreover, in due time three alumni achievement awards came my way, including being recognized at the Mid-Eastern Athletic Conference Basketball tournament in Raleigh, North Carolina, and being selected to the Hall of Fame by the Howard University Alumni Association of the Research Triangle Park.

That organization commissioned a video titled *Judge Joe Webster—A Life of Calm Purpose,* which has been produced and viewed hundreds of times in North Carolina and around the country. The video also won in a competition for short films. The video covers my childhood in my hometown of Madison, North Carolina, and my small community of Goodwill where I grew up and began to flourish; my matriculation at Howard University; and my career accomplishments as an attorney, judge, family man, and ordained minister.

I implore my children, my children's children, and all who may read these words not to ever give up, no matter how many times you are turned down for a job or other position you are seeking. Put God first and work hard, and someone will help you, no matter how many times you are turned down for a job or other position you seek. Soon to approach my sixty-ninth birthday, there are those who are still helping me over fifty years later after receiving this advice—most importantly, including God, who makes everything possible.

My Mission Trip to London, England

Chapel Hill, North Carolina

SEPTEMBER 20, 2022

In early March 2003, I was offered the opportunity along with some students from the University of North Carolina–Chapel Hill, Duke University, and North Carolina Central University to travel to London, England, as a part of a short-term mission program sponsored by Chapel Hill Bible Church in Chapel Hill, North Carolina. At the time I was a Stephen Minister at the Bible Church. Our purpose was to minister to and learn from the large Muslim, Sikh, and Hindu communities located in the area located near the Heathrow Airport. We stayed in a church and could hear the flights departing and approaching Heathrow.

Spending time with women of the Muslim faith on mission trip in London, England, March 2003

We spent our days visiting the local Muslim mosque and Sikh and Hindu temples and praying with and visiting residents of the area. While some of our group was in the field knocking on doors to interface with residents, the others in our group stayed behind to pray constantly. The highlight of my trip to London occurred when my group knocked on the door of a residence. A young Hindu man came to the door. One of the questions we were asking those we met was whether they prayed? The man responded, "First of all, Hindus have a million gods." Being short on knowledge or tact concerning the Hindu faith, I asked him, "Well, which one do you pray to?" His response was unexpected. He said, "Whichever one happens to be listening at the time." I chose not to ask any more questions.

Another recollection from my journey to London was that it took place toward the end of my father's battle with cancer. I struggled whether I should travel that far from home since I did not want to be there if his condition worsened or even worse if he passed while I was four thousand miles from home. I discussed this matter with my family and my father's doctor. The doctor felt it would be safe for me to be away for one week. I am certain that I prayed that my father would not pass before I returned home. My father did survive, although he was in a hospice in Winston Salem, North Carolina, not far from Baptist Hospital where he had been hospitalized. He survived until late

March. However, while I was in London, one of my mission partners brought me the telephone one day, handed it to me, and said, "It is your wife, Diane, and she said it's not about your father." I took the telephone, and she said it was about one of my best friends, Reverend Robert Siler. He had died suddenly the night before. She didn't have many details, but I later learned he had a congenital heart condition. Indeed, this was an unexpected occurrence that put a real damper on my trip to London.

I am a better person for having spent time in a foreign land, for having spent more time than I ever had in constant prayer, and for spending time with those who are of different faiths. Much of who we are is based on who our parents are. I am appreciative of Mark Acuff, the then-pastor of Chapel Hill Bible Church, and others who made it possible for me to travel to London and for my family who encouraged me to travel there despite my father's illness. Their faith and prayers allowed me to travel and return so that I could spend some quality time with my father before he died March on 29, 2003.

Sixty Years—Applying My Heart unto Wisdom

FEBRUARY 2014

The 60 years, 21,915 days, 525,960 hours, 31,557,600 minutes, and 1,893,456,000 seconds have passed so quickly since my birth on February 12, 1954. The Psalmist in 90:12 instructs, "So teach us to number our days, that we may apply our hearts unto wisdom." What a powerful lesson to live by! Paraphrasing James 4:14, the Scriptures further remind us, "We don't know what tomorrow will bring. For what is life? It is like a vapor. It appears for just a little while and then it vanishes away." The older I get, the more I reflect on these two Bible verses. One of my colleagues on the federal court sent me an email the other day that said, "Every year I age, I am amazed at how much more quickly it seems to go. There are days I think the planet is spinning faster and faster!" One of my great lawyer mentors, now in his early eighties, told me the other day that he "was seeing a lot of people die at age seventy-eight or seventy-nine." The tone of his voice implied that he was wondering how much longer he had to live. For thirty-five years I have observed this great public servant apply his heart unto wisdom, and I suspect that is why he is still with us, still vibrant and making a difference in his community, state, and nation.

Lately there has been quite a bit of discussion in my household and from two of my adult children living in the nation's capital about what I wanted to do for my sixtieth birthday. The other day I asked my wife, Diane, why is so much made of one's sixtieth birthday? She replied, "Because when you turn sixty you are over the hill." Recently I recalled someone making a comment to me, "Sixty years old, that's a big one." My, my, I had not thought that I was going over the hill, as if I would not ever again have enough energy to climb back up the hill. Presently my mind and body say I can still climb the hill with God's help if I continue to apply my heart unto wisdom. I saw basketball greats Kareem Abdul-Jabbar and Michael Jordan—after they had lost a step or two, and after even some had said they were "washed up"—apply wisdom as they continued to rise above more youthful athletes. More recently, I've seen Ray Allen shoot three-pointers with great accuracy as he inches closer to age forty.

Even with applying my heart unto wisdom, I know that Father Time has no respect of persons. As we grow older, it takes a little longer to recover from minor surgery, and even a cold or a muscle strain. More rest is needed to recover from a long road trip or a vigorous workout. Mental fatigue sets in a little earlier than when I was thirty-five. Where I laid my car keys becomes a mystery on some days. My son told me the other day that he solves that problem by putting his keys the same place every day. Perhaps too at age twenty-four, he has also learned to apply his heart unto wisdom. Aging seems to affect how much sleep one can get on any given night. On a recent Sunday I heard a pastor say that a night's sleep for him is limited to four hours each night. I must say on most nights I can better that by a couple of hours and can take a nap on weekends or other days that helps replenish lost sleep.

I have been so very blessed to learn from some great people in my life who applied their hearts unto wisdom. My father and mother, James E. and Bettie E. Webster, lived to be seventy-seven and eighty-three, respectively and shared their wisdom with their eight children. I have learned from some great lawyers, judges, and theologians, who were twenty or thirty years my senior. I have talked to them as often as I could. Long walks and talks with esteemed retired lawyer Walter F. Brinkley, formerly of Lexington, NC, talks with Henry E. Frye, former chief justice of the North Carolina Supreme Court, and the late former pastor, Rev. Dr. Elliott James Mason Sr. of Los Angeles, to name a few, helped give me great perspective on how to apply one's heart unto wisdom. But I have also learned from many who are thirty and forty years younger than I am. I have learned much from my own children. I have learned from them through trial and error that loving them unconditionally is the greatest tool within my parental arsenal. I have also learned so much from my wife. Her perspective comes from her giving heart, the heart of a mother. Once, an elderly woman whose name I have long since forgotten told me that we should love our children so much that they will want to obey our commandments. In our brief talk I sensed that she had been applying her heart unto wisdom.

Life is so short! As I number my days, I hope to be able to continue to apply my heart unto wisdom. I do not know what tomorrow will bring. Nevertheless, it is my heart's desire that I might be able to continue to try to make a difference in the years, months, days, and seconds that lay ahead, whatever number that might be.

A Service to Honor God

Goodwill Baptist Church, Madison, NC

JULY 14, 2018

I am overjoyed this afternoon. My heart is full. Most importantly, my mind is made up to endure to the end. So, I first give honor to the one who woke me up this morning, to the author and finisher of my faith. I hope that God is pleased with what has taken place today.

I give thanks for the abundant grace and mercy that God has bestowed upon me; for his favor in my life, favor that I do not deserve; for the doors that have been opened for me, doors that were closed to my ancestors and the doors that have been opened for me that I didn't know existed over the last twenty years—no, I should say for the entire sixty-four years of my life. I am grateful for this great crowd of witnesses that surrounds us this afternoon (HEBREWS 12:1). I am glad to be home again; to a church that my paternal great-great-great grandpa John H. Gibson donated two and a half acres of land upon which Goodwill Baptist Church was built in the first few years of the 1900s. He and others of our relatives who lie in the graves outside of this church would be so proud that we are still honoring God, demonstrating that John H. Gibson and the labor of his neighbors has or has not been in vain. My first memory of this place was hearing the testimony of people like Deacon Welbert Carter's mother, born in the early years after slavery ended, who stood over there in that corner by her sister, Belle, testifying to the glory of God. When she sat down, another elderly brother or sister would stand up and sing a song; they had a way of singing that told the world just how far God had brought them; usually just a few words: "If I couldn't say a word, If I couldn't say a word, I would just wave my hand." So, I'm grateful today that I grew up in this village called Goodwill.

A SERVICE TO HONOR GOD
on the occasion of the
20th Anniversary of the Call to Ministry of
Reverend Joe L. Webster

Saturday, July 14, 2018
2:00 PM
Goodwill First Baptist Church
1036 K Fork Road, Madison, NC 27025
Rev. James S. Moore, Pastor

20th Anniversary Service of Joe's call to ministry at Goodwill First Baptist Church

Thank you, Goodwill Church and Goodwill community. Thank you for praying for me—the Bible says that the effectual fervent prayer of righteous man availeth much. Keep on praying. It is a praying time in our country right now. Thank you,

Pastor James Moore, for saying yes when I called to say that it had been on my heart to honor God today. Some might have said that you have to be a pastor to have an anniversary service. Thank you for "roasting me kindly." The word says whosoever will. Thank you, deacons, trustees, officers, ushers, Goodwill choir, you have done a beautiful job today as you do always. I see and feel your love and pride for me every time I come home. I mention you in my sermons often because in this village called Goodwill you have been, to use the words of our ancestors, "sending up timber," praying and preserving through the storms of life. My parents and relatives out there who have gone on, thank you for not giving up, for persevering.

Thank you, master of ceremonies: my friend of forty years, Rev. Steve Allen from Greensboro, who God first called to be an outstanding lawyer in Greensboro and then told him some years ago that I have some greater work for you. Close your law office; I need you to pastor your home church, the historic Shiloh Baptist Church. Thank you, Steve, for answering God's call.

Thank you, Oberlin Baptist Church, for adopting me into your family and for coming over one hundred miles to be a part of this celebration today. UMOJAH, the gospel choir, sang from their hearts. Pastor Young, thank you for coming today. You have been preaching your heart out—sometimes to just a few—But God hears your cries, and He will answer at His own time. Thank you, Reverend Leaston: God hears your prayers. Keep on praying.

Thank you to all who participated here today; no less so to those behind the scenes, not just those out front.

I thank my children and grandchildren who are present. God has answered my prayers. My daughters, Briana and Camille, and my son, Evan, who as a manager of his place of employment couldn't be here in person, but thanks to technology, appeared and expressed how he felt about me as his father. I've seen with my eyes the gift that God has bestowed upon my three children. I am so proud of the work you have undertaken. I see the respect your friends have for my daughters when I visit DC. To my wife, Diane, you have given me and our children and the community so much of yourself. When you are married to someone who is also married to their calling—and in my case, two callings—that is a difficult situation. Thank you and I am so proud of you.

Thank you to my career law clerk, Ms. Pedra Lee. You are the best of the best in all that you do. Thank you for making me look good as a judge—but thank you most for giving God the praise. These choirs were powerful today. Thank you. I am so grateful to both choirs.

Thank you, Sister Chalmers, for your dance of praise this afternoon. Your commitment to your faith is evident; your courage is commendable and encouraging.

To my brother Rev. Dr. James A. Webster, the word you brought from the Lord was right on time. Your sermon coming from St. Luke, chapter 17, verses 11 to 19, today on the ten leopards who were healed but only one came back to thank Jesus was so appropriate, for I did come back today to say thank you to Goodwill for all you have contributed to my life's work. Thank you, James, for saying yes to the spirit in 1975 when you answered the call to preach the gospel. I will always remember that hot summer day when you did your initial sermon here at Goodwill.

Aunt Hazel, you sang at my initial sermon on July 18, 1998, and you are still allowing God to use you twenty years later. Thank you, Minister Lillie Moore, for saying yes to participating today.

Thank you, Food Committee. When asked about what I wanted on the menu, my only request was that you include some pinto beans. Thank you, law clerks, for coming today. John Brogdon came all the way from Atlanta, Georgia. Thank you for allowing me to mentor you and others. Too many names to call out; those who have come from far and near. I read a scripture, John 15:15 that says in part, "Without me you can do nothing." So, Church I'm going to keep leaning on Jesus for the rest of my life.

I will forever be grateful, for all that each of you have meant so much to me in my life's work.

CHAPTER SIX

My Ancestry and the Importance of Family

My Ancestry

The families that I descend from are very large. I have many cousins, known and unknown. While I am not aware of any formal or scientific count that has taken place, suffice it to say that I have multiple hundreds of first, second, and other cousins considering my Webster, Moore, Hairston, Ziglar, Gibson, Brown, Strickland, and Taylor family relatives. Perhaps because of my being brought up in the church, and attending annual family reunions, the longevity of many of my relatives who lived into their eighties and nineties has allowed me to learn much about my ancestry. My paternal great-grandmother, Lucy Gibson Ziglar, lived to be 103, having been born in 1885 and died in 1989. Her daughter and my paternal grandmother, Annie Ziglar Webster, lived to be 97. My maternal grandmother, Ressie Moore Hairston, lived to be over 90 years old. Many other relatives of their generation and the following generation lived to into their 80s and 90s. With the help of family members and modern technology, in particularly access to Ancestry.com and other research engines, much of my family tree has been pieced together going back two hundred years to the 1820s.

My paternal great-great-great grandfather, John H. Gibson, and his wife, Lucy Johnson Gibson, are listed in the 1870 Census, the first census after the Civil War, and in the 1880 Census. They were listed along with their children, including my paternal great-great-grandfather, Samuel H. Gibson. In the 1880 census record, the household of my paternal great-great-great grandparents included two persons with "Goin" surnames (Lottie and Nat H. Goin). The Gibson family is listed as mulatto. My limited readings on the Goins (Goin), Gibson, and Moore families revealed that these

Joe L. Webster

Family Tree 2024

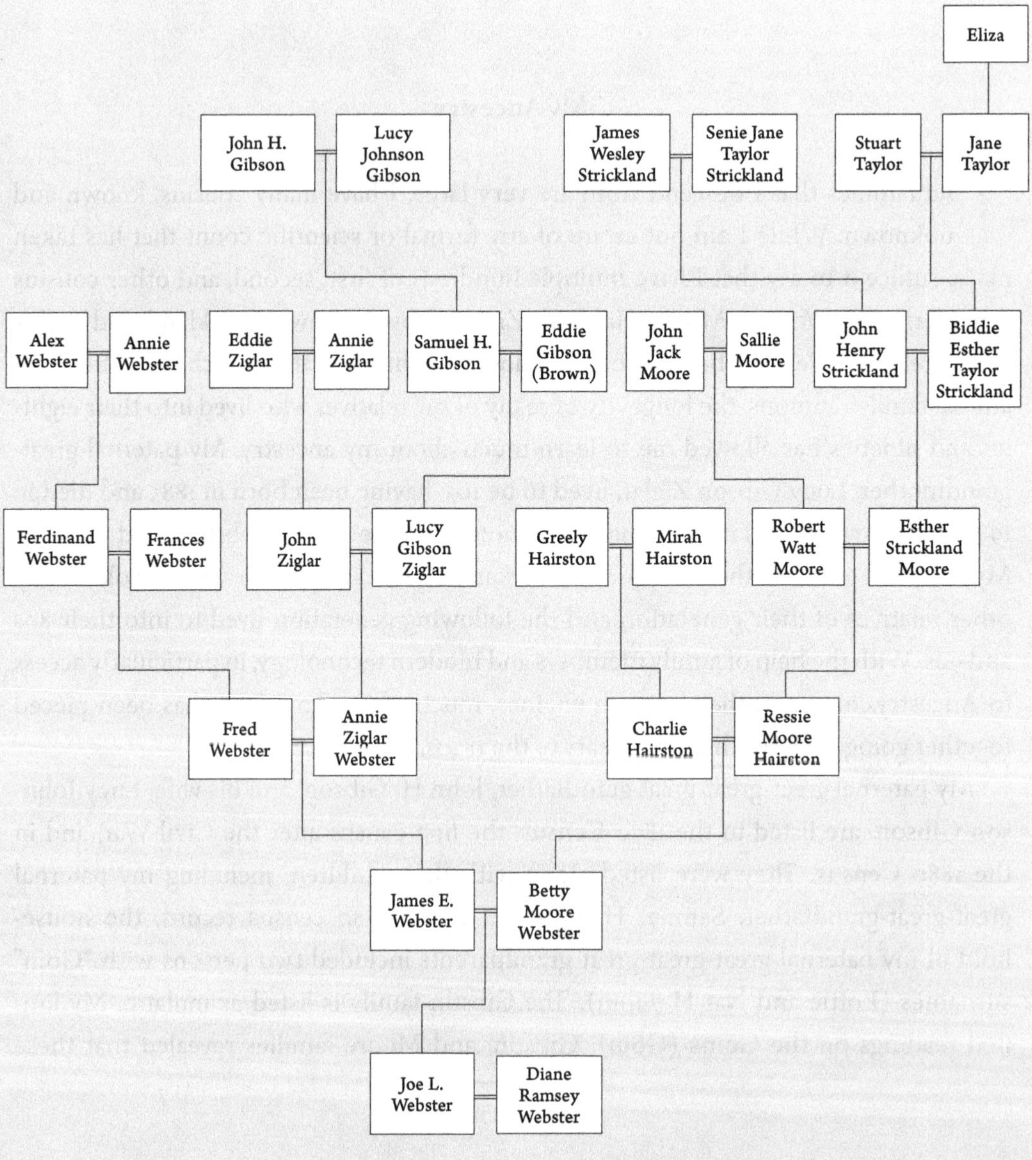

Eliza

John H. Gibson — Lucy Johnson Gibson
James Wesley Strickland — Senie Jane Taylor Strickland
Stuart Taylor — Jane Taylor

Alex Webster — Annie Webster
Eddie Ziglar — Annie Ziglar
Samuel H. Gibson — Eddie Gibson (Brown)
John Jack Moore — Sallie Moore
John Henry Strickland — Biddie Esther Taylor Strickland

Ferdinand Webster — Frances Webster
John Ziglar — Lucy Gibson Ziglar
Greely Hairston — Mirah Hairston
Robert Watt Moore — Esther Strickland Moore

Fred Webster — Annie Ziglar Webster
Charlie Hairston — Ressie Moore Hairston

James E. Webster — Betty Moore Webster

Joe L. Webster — Diane Ramsey Webster

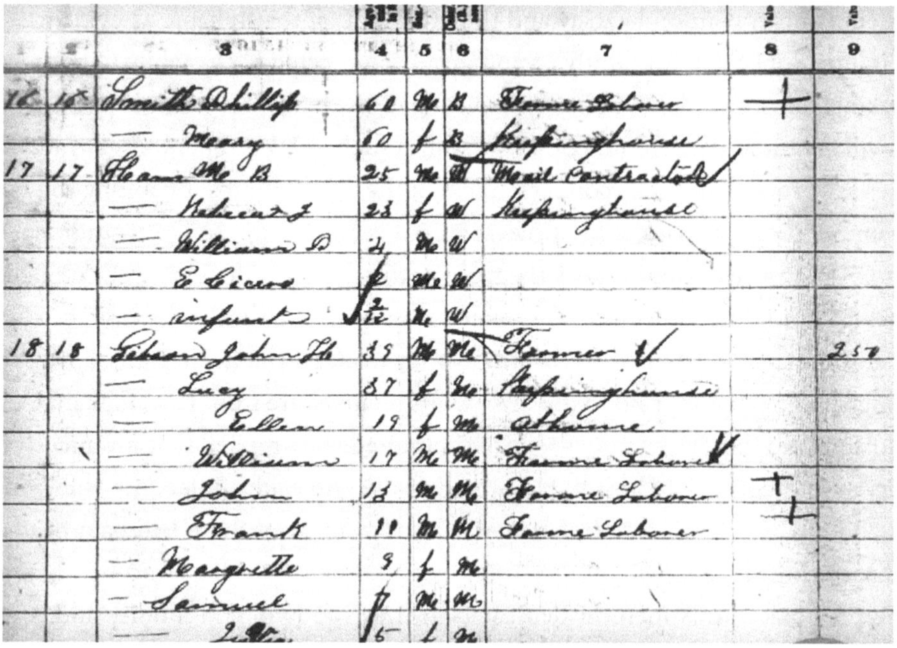

1870 Census record of Joe's paternal great-great-great grandparents, John H. Gibson and Lucy Johnson Gibson

surnames belonged to a group of people known as Melungeon. Some of the literature suggest that the Melungeon group of people were triracial, a mixture of whites, Indian, and some small part black. Other literature suggests that this group of people were part Portuguese or came from the Lost Colony. None of this has been scientifically proven. My brief research did not uncover whether the two Goin's listed in the 1880 Census were related to my ancestors.

It is for these reasons that my memoir includes brief mention of the "Goins" ("Goin") family and "Goinstown" area of Rockingham and Stokes Counties.[26] Regarding the Gibson black and white family connection, I cannot recall the exact source, but I distinctly recall a relative mentioning to me that many years ago, someone told him that he overhead a white Gibson man who lived in the eastern portion of the Goodwill community, say to a black family member, "Tell cousin Lucy I said hello," referring to my great-grandma Lucy Gibson Ziglar. And, as I leaned in law school at Howard University, this

26 My research reveals that Rockingham County was the heart of Melungeon county in North Carolina. My research indicates there exists no formal designation for the Goinstown area. Historically, other than in Rockingham and Stokes Counties in North Carolina, many Melungeons lived in East Tennessee. The 1834 Tennessee Constitutional Convention referred to the Melungeons as "free persons of color" (Bonnie Bell, The Melungeons: Notes on the Origin of a Race 1992. 66. In 1877, Tennessee gave the Melungeons a separate legal existence and recognized them under the title "Croatian Indians" (Bell, vi) The Gibson, Goins, Moore, Harris and a few others have been mentioned as some of the surnames of those non-white families that moved into the Goinstown area of Rockingham and Stokes Counties pre-civil war.

statement is hearsay upon hearsay and therefore not all that reliable as evidence. Still, there is little doubt that my family is biologically connected to the white Gibson family of Rockingham and Stokes County. And of course, the many fair-skinned persons of the Goodwill community, including other surnames such as Webster and Ziglar, and other families are proof of this interconnectedness of the racial groups inhabiting the Goodwill community going back at least two hundred years. No doubt DNA studies, if they were to be performed, would speak the truth of this connectedness as well. While I was practicing law in Pittsboro, North Carolina, I was in court awaiting my case to be called for disposition, and I sat next to a white attorney from Durham. He learned I was from Rockingham County. He said to me, "My wife's relatives are from Rockingham County in Madison, and their last name is Gibson." I immediately replied that my ancestry, my great-grandmother was a Gibson. He turned to me and said, "In fact my wife's uncles' heads all look just like yours" (referring to fact that most of them had bald heads like me). I could only laugh.

The portions of this memoir dedicated to the Goodwill community and particularly to my own ancestry and whether any portion of my ancestry were slaves, and what portion were free cannot be completely answered, for my research was very limited in this regard. My limited research does not include any evidence that the white Gibson, Moore, Ziglar, Brown, Hairston, Strickland, and Taylor families were slave owners in Rockingham or Stokes County, North Carolina. However, the 1850 Slave Schedule of Daniel Taylor in Pittsylvania County, Virginia includes my maternal great-great-great-grandmother, Senie Jane Taylor, as a slave born about 1828. She later married my maternal great-great-great grandfather, James Wesley Strickland. The 1850 Slave Schedule of Daniel Taylor also lists my great-great grandfather Stewart Taylor as a slave, and that he was born about 1820. He later married my great-great grandmother Jane Taylor. [27]

My ancestry research leaves an unanswered question that will likely go answered throughout time. I wondered whether the late 1800 and early 1900 Census records listing the race of the Gibson, Webster and Strickland lines of my family tree as mulatto were the results of my African ancestry engaging in a consensual relationship with one of my European ancestors, or was it—as often was the case during the sad and despicable period of slavery and later years—the product of forceable rapes of my female relatives' bodies, spirits, and their human dignity? The historical records are replete with proof that especially slave owners and others exercising white privilege and taking

27 The Taylor family reunion historical report is consistent with the Slave Schedule of Daniel Taylor.

liberties with their slaves at will, produced many children, who they later sold off to other slave owners, often depriving the birth mothers of their children for the rest of their lives. This must have been extremely agonizing, to say the least. I have often thought about how inhumane all aspects of this cruel process must have been, including the sale of the slave owner's own offspring. Throughout the long period of slavery in America, the slaves were treated as livestock and were listed in most instances in the Census records only by age.

But even after slavery was abolished, the treatment of former slaves, persons of mixed race, and even free persons of color frequently involved indignity, disrespect, and physical abuse as horrific as for those who had been enslaved. Warren Eugene Milteer Jr.'s book, *North Carolina's Free People of Color, 1785–1885*, gives many examples of this maltreatment.[28] As I have done research, and matured in age and wisdom, I cannot say with any degree of certainty whether my African ancestry during the years of slavery and Jim Crow was subjected to savage violence by those who had the power to do so. It is also uncertain whether some of my ancestors were the product of natural human attraction, affection, and consent. The evidence is overwhelming and sufficient to conclude that enslavement of a human being by another human being, in and of itself—with all the indignities that go along with the condition of involuntary servitude, including degradation of the human spirit, even without assaultive conduct by the slave owner against the slave—was a "crime against humanity."[29] The very thought of slavery sickens me, but personally, I know that I came into being by the grace of God, and as set forth in Psalm 13:14: "I choose to praise Him because I am fearfully and wonderfully made"; and I can proclaim like David did in this text about the Lord of Lords, "Your works are wonderful, [and] I know them full well." Also, I know that I know that I know with unquestionable certainty who I am and even more importantly, whose I am. And that is sufficient for me, no matter what others may think of me.

28 In the fall 1849 term of the Rockingham County North Carolina Superior Court, two men were indicted for the assault of a free man of color, having cut off his ears. The two men pled guilty and served prison terms (Milteer, *Free People of Color* (Baton Rouge: Louisiana State University Press, 2020), 185–86. And one August criminal complaint was filed against a man for assaulting a free woman of color in her own home in Stokes County, NC (Milteer, *Free People of Color*, 186.

29 Crimes against humanity consist of various acts such as murder, extermination, enslavement, torture, forcible transfers of populations, imprisonment, rape, persecution, enforced disappearance, and apartheid, among others according to the International Criminal Court (ICC)

Joe and Diane's wedding, May 3, 1980, Duke Gardens, Durham, NC

Joe and Diane's wedding vows

Joe and children at home, Chapel Hill, NC

1994 judicial campaign photo

Joe and family on vacation, Sea Island, GA

Joe and family on his 70th birthday

Joe and Diane celebrate thirty-fifth wedding anniversary at Eiffel Tower, Paris, France, May 3, 2015

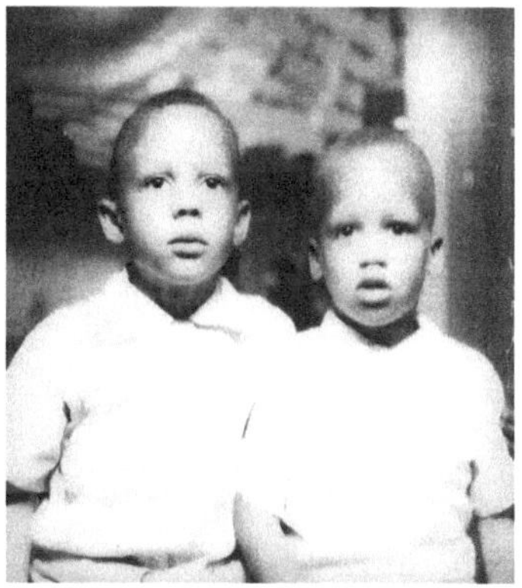

Joe's parents and siblings

Joe's parents' first home on 98-acre farm, March 1966

Joe's parent's home on farm, circa 1970

Joe's parents

Joe's parents' 50th wedding anniversary

Joe's siblings and mother

Family gathering on birthday of late brother,
Rev. Dr. James A. Webster, April 28, 2023

Grave marker for my parents— James E. Webster, 1925–2003 and Bettie E. Webster, 1929–2013—buried in the Goodwill First Baptist Church Cemetery

TOP Joe's paternal great-grandparents Ferdinand and Frances Webster and their children. BOTTOM Children of Frances Scales and Luther Scales

Webster family reunion, c. 1990–2000

My paternal grandfather Fred Webster and paternal grandmother Annie Ziglar Webster

Joe's great aunt and uncle, Mable and Sonnie Brown

Moore Family Reunion, Charlotte, NC, August 2019

My maternal great-great-grandfather, John Henry Strickland, and his daughter, my maternal great-grandmother, Ester Strickland Moore

Maternal grandmother
Ressie Moore Hairston

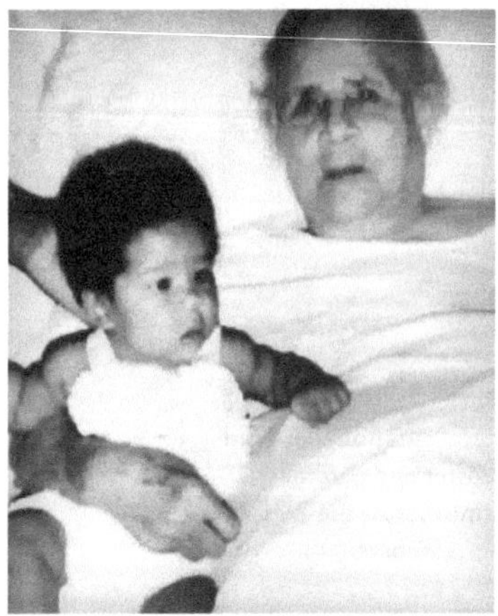

My paternal great grandmother, Lucy Gibson Ziglar and my daughter, Briana

Eight of my paternal great-great-grandmother Addie Gibson Brown's eleven children (children of Samuel H. Gibson and Addie Mitchell Gibson, and Johnny Brown and Addie Mitchell Brown)

Joe's extended family by marriage to Diane Ramsey Webster: her parents and all fourteen children on their farm in Rougemont, Orange County, NC, circa 1984

The Importance of Family On the Occasion of the Seventy-Fifth Annie and Roman Martin Family Reunion

Bonner Field House on the campus of Oak Ridge Military Academy, Oak Ridge, NC

AUGUST 5, 2012

> God setteth the solitary in families: he bringeth out those which are bound with chains; but the rebellious dwell in a dry land. —PSALMS 68:6 KJV

It gives me great pleasure to be standing before you today. The Martin Family and the Annie and Roman Martin Memorial Scholarship Inc. will always be dear to my heart. It was forty years ago this month that I went off to Howard University with a piece of paper which stated that the Annie and Roman Martin Scholarship Inc. had awarded me a scholarship for five hundred dollars. It meant to me then and still means to me today that somebody among the family saw that God had highly favored me and they saw promise in me. That one act of giving highly encouraged me. Your act forty years ago validated what my mother told me as I got ready to get my brother, Rev. Dr. James A. Webster's, car, who would be driving to Howard University and Washington, DC. My mother, now suffering with Alzheimer's disease, said to me (hear me, young people, because this might be the most important advice, I could give you today for your future success), she said, "Joe, if you put God first in your life and work hard, somebody will see you trying, and somebody will help you." I continue to bear fruit from my mother's advice forty years later. For it was just a couple of days ago when I received a telephone call from the chief judge of the US District Court for the Middle District of North Carolina that I had been selected from many excellent applicants to serve an eight-year term as a United States magistrate judge for the Middle District of North Carolina. So, if you see me in tears today, know that they are the result of the joy of the Lord that is in my heart. So, to God be the glory for the five-hundred-dollar Martin Family Scholarship and Mama's advice forty years ago.

Today I want to issue a challenge to the Martin Family Reunion. Being the first recipient, I have firsthand knowledge of your forty years history of awarding the Martin Scholarship annually to one or more recipients. I have occasionally contributed to the fund, and fifteen years ago I accepted your invitation to come to McMichael High School to present some number of scholarships to worthy students. I can only imagine the thousands who have benefited from the life's work of the honorees. From Ann Dalton I have learned in the last few days via email that your family has also undertaken an initiative of working with Rockingham County Schools to bring literacy training to the students and develop a RAMMS Scholar. And as important as anything else your family is doing, Ann said in her email to me that by coming together annually, you "celebrate family." The importance of family and celebrating family is so important today in a time of division, strife, and the disintegration of family throughout our communities, throughout the nation and world.

In today's text in Psalms, the Psalmist speaks about one of the benefits of family. The King James Version says God sets the solitary in families. The New American Standard Version says God makes a home for the lonely. You like me have heard of violent prisoners being placed in solitary confinement—all alone, separated from all other inmates. I think a lot about our young men today—too many going off to prison if their childish mistakes are bad enough. They find themselves separated from their families. But the word of God says, He setteth the solitary in families and bringeth out those which are bound in chains. The New American Standard says He leads out the prisoners into prosperity and the New Living Translation says He sets the prisoners free and gives them joy.

To this great family gathered here today, not to minimize all you are doing, but I must charge you with doing even more than you are already doing in order to strengthen the family. Every family ought to have a prison ministry component, but just as importantly, all families this size ought to have a requirement that the able-bodied members heed the call of the Big Brother and Big Sister programs so we can help our youth before they stray into criminal activity and help steer them in the right direction. If we don't offer our youth the benefits of family at an early age, then they will find refuge in a family called a gang. As families, we must do what the government is unable and powerless to do. Throughout history the family represents love; it represents strength, it represents structure, instruction and a firm foundation. Family offers second chances and third chances and tenth chances. When all others have given up, family represents the last resort for our youth and young adults. Families represent forgiveness.

Mothers and fathers here today, I know you want to give up on that disobedient son who is hanging out all night, drinking and doing drugs, or that daughter who is not taking care of her own body. But Martin Family, if you ever take your hands completely off them, they will become, as today's text says of the rebellious—they will dwell on dry land.

I want to pause to read a script from Tyler Perry's movie, *Madea's Family Reunion*. I know many have seen the movie at the theater or on television. I'm no Cicely Tyson who I'm about to paraphrase, but her words ring true today even more than when the movie was first shown seven years ago.

In Tyler Perry's movie, there is a segment about the family gathering for a family reunion, the first one that the family has had in many years. They gathered at the family home that their ancestors had toiled to purchase from the widow of the slave owner. The renowned actress Cicely Tyson's character reminded especially the youth and young adults gathered there that they had a greater obligation to their families and community than they had been exhibiting, She reminded them that they came from ancestors who had a hard work ethic running through their veins. She wondered out loud to them, What had happened to them? She asked, What happened to the pride, dignity, love, and respect that their ancestors once had? She reminded and challenged the young men first—that they were much needed and encouraged them to take their leadership role among the family and society. And then she challenged the women to do better. She reminded the women that they were more than physical bodily attributes—that they were beautiful and strong. And then she concluded by telling those gathered to turn to the person next to them and grab them, hug them, and offer that person a shoulder to lean on. She told them to let their family member know that they are available to talk to and to feed them if needed.

So, young men and women, I need for you to contribute more to the family. I know that you are becoming discouraged about the high unemployment figures you are witnessing firsthand. I ask you, though, What if your grandfather and great-grandfather Roman Martin had given up? What if Roman Martin had said, I'm going to abandon my wife and children if Madison Throwing Company won't hire me or if the Washington Mills in Mayodan won't even take my applications because of the color of my skin. Where would your family be today? So, I need for you today to get up off the sofa, cut the television off; put down your iPads and iPods. Go tell the nearest McDonald's or Hardee's that you're not too proud to flip burgers. In honor of Roman and Annie Martin and your parents who sacrificed so much, I need for you to get down to the community college or university of your choice as quickly as you can and tell them you come from a proud heritage of schoolteachers and other professionals. Tell them that your family's first scholarship recipient of forty years ago told you that you could make it if you put your mind and heart to whatever you chose to do with your life. If you don't know where to start, see me after I sit down, and I'll give you my telephone number and I will offer you whatever I can in advice and direction. If you need an advocate, I'll personally go with you or find someone to go with you and offer encouragement.

Young men and women, I want you to know today that I didn't always have courage. As a child, I was so very quiet and shy. Somehow another, God answered my mother's prayers. If you have a criminal record and can't get a job for that reason, I want you to know that God has been issuing pardons for all of us here in this room. Many of us just didn't get caught driving drunk or stealing in our youth. God can grant you an unconditional pardon and reveal to you someone who is willing to give you another chance. Whatever you need, God has it. I am begging you today to take that first step to recovery. As the text says today, God will loose you from your chains.

Young men, I need for you to pull up your pants. I don't want to see your underwear. Most mature men and women aren't going to hire you with your pants hanging down below your bottom. Young women, tell the young men walking around like penguins that you come from a proud heritage of black men who worked hard and respected black women. Don't go out with them, or heaven forbid, sleep with them. Tell them they must change. Marriage is still important. Encourage your brothers, cousins, and male friends. Tell them Judge Webster said to never, ever give up. I'm here today to encourage each of you to never, ever give up. As our text says, God will even bring you out of bondage. Even in these seemingly desperate times for many, God is still sitting on the throne. I still must call on him daily to keep my focus; I must call on him to help me do justice in my legal work. I call on him to keep my family safe and keep my spiritual mindset where it ought to be.

Men and women, whatever age you are, don't let others define who you are. If God be for you, then who can be against you?

Today I want to end by sending out a shout-out to my former teacher Eudoxia Dalton, who refined my reading skills. I didn't want her to tell me that I was "reading like a square-wheeled bicycle," as she told some of my classmates. I want to send a shout-out to my earthly father, who is gone on now, but who only went to school up to the fourth grade, and my mother who now lives in an assisted living facility and suffers from Alzheimer's disease. They raised eight children and bought a ninety-eight-acre farm with hard work, dedications and faith. They moved us from the outdoor toilet and well water to indoor plumbing. So I send a shout-out to them for leaving a legacy that I could emulate and become successful.

In conclusion, never underestimate family and how important it is. Celebrate family each day. Tell your parents, "Thank you." Tell them that you love them. Cherish your family. That's the best thing you have. As the Fifth Commandment found in Exodus 20:12 states, "Honor your father and your mother, so that you may live long in the land that the LORD your God is giving you" (NIV).

> Children are a heritage from the LORD, offspring a reward from him. Like arrows in the hands of a warrior are children born in one's youth. Blessed is the man whose quiver is full of them. PSALM 127:3–5

Joe and Diane's three children

Granddaughters

Grandsons

Papa's Early Observations of My Grandchildren

FEBRUARY 26, 2022

L.J., ever since I saw you and A.C. huddled up with Camille on the bed so many years ago, I knew then that you and your sister were special. I remember that time we were visiting DC and you and A.C. were in the car with me and others. I kept saying, "My my," and you said, "Mr. Joe, are you saying 'Mama'? I know you must have thought something was deeply wrong if I, a grown man, was crying out, "Ma-ma." I think I recall you got a big laugh out of it. I have never met more well-mannered and respectful young persons than you and your sister. I watched you grow up right before my eyes. If some guy is trying to date you at University of Maryland, tell him you must get Mr. Joe's permission first!

A.C., I could just say, "Ditto to what I just wrote about L.J." However, I have also been so impressed with your maturity, IQ, and respectful manner. I always love when you call to say happy birthday or to greet me for some other milestone or holiday. You have such a sweet-sounding voice that makes me so happy to hear from you. I have observed you read more books since I have known you than I have in my sixty-eight years of life. I'm impressed! I hope I live a long life so that I can see how successful you and your sister and other siblings are in life. And oh, I will never forget the summers you and your sister traveled to Chapel Hill to stay with Papa and Lolli!

R.L., I will forever remember how mature you were when you were born. Eyes wide open, it was like you wanted to talk then. If you had been able to speak, you would have said, "What's going on? I've been trying to be born for weeks. I'm ready to start making my mark on life." You started talking and acting grown earlier than most. "Rambunctious" could be your middle name. You favor me when I was a little boy, but you talk ten times more than I did when I was a little boy. You have that trait exactly like your mom.

N.E., as soon as you learned how to talk, you started acting "silly." You are a fun-loving child and like to help your mom cook cakes. You often squint one eye when you are looking at people as you are acting silly. If I can borrow a term from your mom that suits you very well, that is, you are "animated." Sounds like I'm describing your Grandma Lolli. Destined for Hollywood!

H.J., the thing I remember most about you is just how extremely physically strong you are. I guess you had to be because you had to let your big brother know you were not going to let him beat up on you simply because he is older and taller. I observe how you seem to end up on top if you and Ramsey get into a wrestling match. Ironically you are a "mama's boy." Like your uncle Ed, you will be an excellent cook because you are around your mother helping her cook so much. You have been quiet for so long, but you have found your voice—learned to ask for what you want and if you don't get it, you take it. You are rambunctious like your big brother, and you look up to him.

E.C., it seems like since the day you were born you looked like you could be a model in a fashion magazine or that you are dressed to go to a prep school, even though you are just going to be around the house playing. Oshkosh brand should hire you to model for that company. You frequently call for Papa, and as I see you on FaceTime or in person, you won't speak to me, or you look the other way. You favor your late great uncle Billy Jack. I can already tell you will enjoy telling jokes.

A.S., your smile is contagious. Your smile speaks a thousand words. I can't help but smile when you smile. It is not a fake smile but real. I will never forget how you started crying when I visited you recently. I had to come back and let you know I would come back later to see you. I hear you occasionally fall on the floor, as the terrible twos sometimes do when upset. I have not yet seen that, so I'm believing someone has done something to upset you if that happens.

To all my grandchildren, I love you all so much, and you bring so much joy into our lives.

Sincerely, Papa

A Tribute to My Grand dog, Polo

JANUARY 25, 2024

Polo, a teacup Yorkie, was the only dog that I ever called a family member. I had never gotten close enough to a dog to understand that a dog had the ability to love and to be loved. I could tell Polo knew he was loved by Briana and her family. In his youth, he was very happy. Polo was given free range to run around any room he desired in his adoptive home. He often laid in Briana's lap as she watched television. I was never comfortable holding him. I realized that was my problem, and nothing that Polo did, caused me to fear him. He was always kind and gentle.

In Polo's later years, as his health began to decline, I felt so sorry for him. Each time I saw him, he seemed to have lost weight and laid around for long periods of time. Finally, the second weekend in October 2020, the year COVID swept throughout the world, Polo said goodbye. Briana grieved his death at least for the long weekend our family gathered in Virginia Beach. As I observed Briana's tears, I shed tears myself.

Granddog Polo

Prior to Polo's death, I felt like God had begun to prepare Briana for Polo's homegoing and for what God had in store for her a few years prior to Polo's death. God did so by giving Briana one son, and then another son. During Polo's long decline, my thought had been that God was giving Briana someone else to love—that through Polo, God was preparing Briana to become a mother. I am happy God gave us Polo. I told my friends I had a grand dog. They often laughed because they knew I was afraid of dogs in general. Like any other family member, I will forever remember Polo. He was such a wonderful little dog, and I miss seeing him when I visit my family in the nation's capital.

A Mother's and Father's Love for a Son

OCTOBER 26, 2023

After my parents' deaths, after much deliberation, my brothers, sisters, and I decided to sell the family farm. One day my brother James called to say that there was a trunk on our parents' back porch. He said the items within it seemed to belong to me. I traveled to Madison to examine the contents of the trunk. To my surprise, it contained a treasure trove of handwritten letters from my mother and others beginning with my sophomore year at Howard University in 1973 and continuing through my junior year in 1975. I have chosen to make them part of my historical record because of their importance. I'm not sure that I would have been as successful in undergraduate school without her frequent and consistent encouragement to me as shown in these letters. I looked forward to receiving the letters in part because many of them would have a money order or cash for twenty-five dollars, forty dollars, or some other amount that may seem small today. However, Mama's contributions to me were as meaningful as two hundred dollars or more today. The letters also demonstrate how Mama painstakingly took the time to communicate with me—an act of love that I'm not sure I truly appreciated at the time. More important than the amount of money that Mama would often enclose in the letters, as a parent and grandparent myself now, I know now that it was her way of encouraging me to hang in there and not give up. Mama had a big heart, and her steps were ordered by the Lord.

Having four younger brothers and sisters, I tried not to worry my parents during my college years. I knew they needed to support my younger siblings. While in college, most often I did not disclose to my parents any sickness I might have. I knew how much my mother worried about her children. However, one day I told my older brother James that I had had a terrible cold, and he shared that fact with Mama. He later told me Mama started crying when she heard that news. To my surprise, on a Saturday afternoon, my father knocked on the door of the residence where I was living—at the time located at 40 Buchanan Street NE, Washington, DC. I answered the door. My dad had in his hand a new overcoat my mother had purchased for me and ten dollars.

Mama later told me in one of her letters that she had sent twenty dollars to me, but "Tom had used ten dollars of it on his trip up to DC." Now that's a mother's and father's love for a son. Mama just couldn't bear to think that the cold of winter in DC had given me a bad cold, and so buying me an overcoat and insisting that my dad drive it three hundred miles from home to DC was the answer. She wanted me to have that coat immediately. I have never forgotten my parents' contributions to me as a student and even after my graduation.

I recall that my dad bought me my first car, a 1963 Chevy II Nova, in the summer of 1975 just prior to me returning for my senior year at Howard. I drove it to and from home to DC many times. It had some issues, but it survived my entire senior year.

My dad also bought me a Ford Maverick, and I drove it until I totaled it in an accident my first year in law school. And finally, while I don't recall the details, I am sure that it was my dad who helped me get my 1970 Volkswagen to finish out my education at Howard University Law School. I still drove the Volkswagen when I met Diane. She will recall that the trunk, located in the front of the car, had to be tied down with a rope to keep it from opening while being driven.

I have so many memories that demonstrate how important it is to have the support of family. Even after I had graduated from law school and passed the bar, my parents always demonstrated their willingness to help me. They borrowed money to assist my wife and me in purchasing our first home in Chapel Hill, which I repaid monthly until paid in full. Having been in private practice in my hometown during six of my first seven years after law school graduation, it was often feast or famine. My income varied from month to month. A considerable number of people stepped forward to help me, even years later, as I became a sole practitioner for the second time in 1995 in Pittsboro. Pastors in Chatham County welcomed me and stepped forward with some financial assistance as I began my law practice. At the time, I was the only African American attorney with an office in that county.

But this short recollection is about a mother's and father's love for an undeserving son, who found out that I could never repay them in money. But rather I sought to do all I could to make them proud of me by trying to do good toward my fellow man. I think they were proud of me. On more than one occasion I heard my dad say to others, "Joe is a lawyer and preacher too." He had passed on three years before I became an administrative law judge in November 2006. Dad would have loved to see me presiding in a trial. Having a limited education himself, I'm sure he would have recognized how far God has brought the Webster family. Today, I am still rejoicing myself about how good and merciful God has been to my family. If I could pass on a few things to my children and my children's children, it would be for them to give God thanks daily for God's love and favor for our family. I would also pass on to them the importance of reaching back and helping others up the ladder, or as some would put it, paying it forward. I would also remind them that it is futile to get caught up in pursuing material things; for as the Bible says, "For what does it profit a man, if he shall gain the whole world, but lose his soul?" (MARK 8:36). Finally, I would also like for my children and their children to remember that no matter how difficult the road ahead appears, God promised not to forsake us or leave us. I'm a witness to His promise!

Confessions from Papa

JANUARY 6, 2024

Over the years as I have sought to live out my callings as husband, father, lawyer, judge, and preacher, I have often grappled with my failings, my imperfections, my past and present sins. I grapple with how much of my sinful nature I should reveal, especially to my wife, children, friends, and others. And I have wondered how specific I should be, how far back I should go to tell of who I am and what God has created in me. I am confident that those who know me well already know much of what I say here.

As I undertook the task of putting together this voluminous publication that I have named *Dual Callings of Law and Ministry: Grounded in Faith, Family and Service.* I reviewed hundreds of pages of sermons, published news articles, photos of family and friends, and evidence of honors bestowed upon me for some of the work I have been blessed to do over the last forty some years. I have given much thought to the notion that I am not worthy of such praise, that I am not deserving of some of the praise that has been hyped upon me by mortal human beings like me. Being truthful with myself, I want my children's memory of me to be not only of the sermons or speeches I have given or a snapshot of the accomplishments that are highlighted within this memoir. Rather I would prefer for my children, grandchildren, and anyone else desirous of reading it that they know that my life was about more than a lifelong journey and quest for achievement. It is also an example of one seeking to leave the legacy of a committed life. I fear that my achievement might give them the impression that I am not "human." I want them to know that I know that my flaws and imperfections are just like anyone else's. I also don't want my grandchildren to one day read the contents of this memoir of their grandfather and say to him- or herself, "I can never accomplish all that my papa did, and so there is no need to try."

What I would say to my children and children's children is that whatever I might have accomplished was not under my own power but was through and by my Lord and Savior Jesus Christ and because of the example of hardworking and Christian parents and others in the community where I grew up—the little community called Goodwill. I have told my children and others about how my mother told me when I was leaving for Howard University as a freshman student, "that if I put God first in my life and worked hard, somebody would see me trying and somebody would help me." I can't begin to call the names of those who have helped me along the way. I suspect many who helped me saw my needs, my insecurity, and how shy I was early in my childhood. They most certainly saw many who were smarter than me academically. I have never viewed myself as a scholar of the first order but overcame with hard work and favor from on high. In fact, in mid-August of 1972, I arrived at Howard University and was required to take a semester of remedial reading. But many helped me nevertheless because of what my mother said to me; many saw the promise in me. Many have witnessed that it is not where you start but where you end up at the end of the journey.

Getting back to my reason for drafting this confession, I have always known that while I have personally helped some people along the way, deep down I have known that I have a selfish streak. Spending time with my grandchildren over the last five years, I have noticed that all of them seem to have been born with a selfish streak also—often not desiring to share their toys with their brother, sister, or cousin, let alone a stranger. As God has prospered me, I have sought to share what I have with others less fortunate than me. What I have been blessed with to share with others fulfills my oft-stated assertion that to whom much is given, much is required.

Apparently, I was born with the Webster temper. I didn't realize to what extent that affected my marriage or relationship with others, especially those closest to me. I didn't really realize how bad this flaw is, especially when I am under stress. I regret that I didn't realize what affect it has had on my wife especially. If I had known just how bad it was, much earlier I would have had an introspective examination of myself and gotten help for myself. When you have some good character traits such as caring about others, sharing with others, and being respective of others in general, sometimes it's hard to see the bad parts about yourself. And those who love you—your wife, your children, your best friends—often will not tell you face-to-face about the bad parts of yourself until much damage has been done.

Also, I was not born with as much patience as I wish I had. It has taken a lifetime for me to grow in this regard. Over the years, especially those who are closest to me have observed my lack of patience in dealing with them. My wife, Diane particularly has observed that my temper plus lack of patience is not good for a relationship. I have often cut her off in the middle of her expressing her thoughts to me about a particular matter, rather than hearing her through.

If I had given careful thought to how I made Diane feel, specifically, how I abruptly cut her off when she expressed herself to me, then likely I would have understood why she viewed my reaction as being disrespectful or uninterested in her opinion and changed my ways earlier in our marriage. I've had to apologize to her for this character flaw and ask God for forgiveness. Perhaps, like the Apostle Paul, I have a thorn in the flesh. Mine may be even worse than Paul's, as having a thorn in the heart and mind is even worse than whatever thorn Paul suffered from. I find comments from my law clerks and externs about my patience with attorneys, litigants and others who come before me in Court to be contrary to my thorns. Hopefully I will continue to grow in patience and temperament with those who I love most and who are closest to me. I need even more grace as I battle these flaws.

At times, I find myself not being as congenial as I should be. I'm not always up to being in large crowds. I tend to like smaller, more intimate groups of people that I might engage in conversation—perhaps one-on-one. While I enjoy meeting others I've never met before, I also love the solitude that comes with being in the quiet of my own home.

I don't always say what's on my mind, especially to those who one would think it would be easy—like my wife of forty-four years. I guess I'm afraid that I might hurt Diane's feelings or that I might be rejected myself. There is no doubt that loved ones should forthrightly discuss whatever is on one's mind. Bearing one another's burdens is a Bible verse that applies to married couples as it does to all others. An example of this phenomenon is years ago when my wife and found it impossible to have a balanced budget because of my private law practice—the days of "feast or famine" as I called it back then. Some months were bountiful while others produced much less income than was needed to cover my law practice expenses and personal bills and living expenses. I didn't want Diane to have to worry about our financial woes. One day I finally had the courage to discuss this matter with her. She responded that I should not worry about hurting her feelings; that she was a grown woman, and she could take it. She concluded her thoughts with, "That's what companions are for." Yes, I knew that, but because of my love for her I just didn't want to her to carry the heavy load that I was carrying.

Next, I must say something about faith, or my inadequate faith. Yes, I have quoted the scripture that says one should have faith as small as a grain of mustard seed, and that faith is the substance of things hoped for and the evidence of things not seen. I know that the Scripture says that one should trust in the Lord with all one's heart and do not lean unto your own understanding. I know that Christians live by faith and not by sight; and without faith, it is impossible to please God. I believe in these scriptural mandates and others; however, my human, educated part of me wants to create doubt. I need, as my relative George Brown used to sing, "Just a little more faith, that's all I need." I know that to have more faith, I need to study the Scriptures much more than I do and grow closer to God.

There is much more that I could say but I will conclude by saying that there are some sinful acts that I have committed that I have not fully forgiven myself for, although I know that God has long ago forgiven me. Just one example is when I look back at how immature, dishonest, and selfish I treated several female friends during my late teen and early adult years when I was in college, I wish I had done things differently. I hope that I will find the courage to talk with my grandchildren, especially my grandsons, to be frank with them and seek to convince them they should always respect and be honest with their female friends—and one girlfriend at a time is best. I will tell them that "no" really does mean "no." I will tell my granddaughters that men will only treat you as good or bad as you allow them to do so. It is my opinion that if a man is faithful in his relationship while dating, then he is more likely to be faithful with his wife. While I have not been a perfect husband to my wife as described herein, I have been completely faithful to her from the time I met her on June 26, 1979, and throughout the forty-four years of our marriage. I've heard it said by many Christians that there are no large or small sins, that a sin is a sin. Nevertheless, in my opinion, infidelity is one of the greatest of sins of all and will often destroy the bonds of marriage. If that happens, what else is left in the marriage? Therefore, I have taken the vows I stated during my wedding on May 3, 1980, seriously, and still do forty-four years later.

Yes, I know and preach with confidence that Jesus died for our transgressions, our faults, our sins. Long ago I accepted Jesus as my Lord and Savior. Consequently, He blotted out my transgressions and made me whole. First John 1:9 tells us if we confess our sins, He is faithful and just to forgive us of our sins and cleanse us of all unrighteousness. I am also comforted by Christ's admonition to those who would stone the adulterous woman to death as found in John 8:7–11; "He that is without sin among you, let him first cast a stone at her." All have sinned and fall short, as I heard preachers of my youth proclaim a thousand times. Christ says to just go and sin no more. In John 3:16 we are given a prescription for salvation: "For God so loved the world that whosoever believes in Him shall not perish but have everlasting life." And finally, Romans 10:9–10 says, "That if thou shalt confess with thy mouth the Lord Jesus, and shalt believe in thine heart that God hath raised Him from the dead, thou shalt be saved." I have been completely pardoned from my sins.

> I heard a great sermon by Dr. Howard John Wesley on January 7, 2024, pastor of Alfred Street Baptist Church in Alexandria, Virginia. I paraphrase my understanding of what I recall he said about what it means to be pardoned by those who have the authority to pardon as in the case of the president of the United States. Dr. Wesley said the president of the United States has the power to pardon any federal

> crime. He said his research showed that one must accept the pardon for it to be effective. Similarly, he believers one must accept Christ's pardon for it to be completely forgiven.

I have accepted and confessed my sins, and therefore when my appointed time comes, I will be confident that I will have an eternal home not made by man's hands. My earthly vessel with be no longer, and as Job said at 19:26, "Even after my skin worms destroy this body yet in my flesh shall I see God." I believe with all my heart, soul, and mind that all believers will have an eternal home, as found in Job 3:17, "where the wicked shall cease from troubling and the weary shall be at rest." This is my confession to my family, my wife, my children, and children's children and all those who read these words. To God be the glory!

Reflections on Thirty Years of Marriage

APRIL 17, 2010

By the grace of God, and the prayers of family and many others, Diane and I have remained together for thirty years through the good times and bad times, in sickness and good health. We took seriously our solemn vows to remain dedicated and faithful to one another.

Together we have sought to make a difference for our children, extended family, community, church, and our alma maters. In our imperfection, we have fallen short many times. However, our high and low moments have been leveled out by our great love and respect for one another. Over time, we have learned that "being in love" and "loving and respecting one's life partner" are two different things. The latter is much more important as a foundation for a lasting relationship. As a married couple, our individual and collective flaws have been overshadowed by our willingness to forgive one another for sometimes being selfish, impatient, hot-tempered, and even worse. Love does cover a multitude of sins, as the Holy Scriptures make clear.

We invite you to be with us
as we begin our new life together
on Saturday, May third
nineteen hundred and eighty
at two-thirty in the afternoon
Sarah P. Duke Gardens
Duke University
Durham, North Carolina

If you are unable to attend, we ask
your presence in thought and prayer

Diane Ramsey
and
Joe L. Webster

Invitation to wedding of Joe and Diane, May 3, 1980

As I consider the last thirty years and look forward to whatever time together Diane and I have left, as it was with our parents, the importance of keeping the family together has and will continue to be a great motivating factor in our marriage. We owe so much to our parents, children, and extended family. Both of our parents were married to the same spouse for over fifty years and between them produced twenty-three children, sacrificed much, and laid the foundation upon which Diane and I stand today. Our three children have given us the great blessing, privilege, and struggle of parenthood. Our shared hopes and dreams for them have helped us to grow closer together and helped us make a difference in all that we have sought to achieve.

To God be the glory!

Alzheimer's Disease: My Mother's Long Ride Home

AUGUST 12, 2012

For most of the last decade, my mother has suffered with Alzheimer's disease. The disease is one that destroys your thinking skills, memory and the personhood that you had before becoming afflicted. One's ability to engage in activities of daily living such as feeding oneself, bathing, dressing, grooming and toileting are very often complete lost to the disease. Frequently it causes its victims to lose the memory of their children and other loved ones. I short it is a very terrible disease!

While much is known about Alzheimer's, there is so much more to learn about the disease. We know that it affects millions of Americans, and like many other diseases, affects the African American community disproportionately compared to the rest of the U.S. population. Alzheimer's, like cancer, has no respect for persons as to race or socioeconomic status. We don't know what starts the disease process, although damage to the brain can begin 10 to 20 years before any symptoms appear. The wife of my late friend, esteemed historian and author Dr. John Hope Franklin, died of Alzheimer's disease as did Ronald Reagan.

My mother, Bettie Ester Moore Webster, who will be eighty-three on October 10, 2012, was born just weeks before the stock market crashed in 1929. Mama was born into poverty, but worked hard and prayed out of it, as did hundreds of thousands of her generation. Her maternal grandparents raised her in North Carolina's rural counties of Rockingham and Stokes. I am quite certain that her maternal grandfather, Robert "Watt" Moore, born in 1863, may have lived part of his life as a slave, although my brief study has not revealed proof of this fact. Great-Grandfather Watt's second wife and my mother's namesake, Ester Strickland Moore, was born in 1888. She was Watt's second wife, as his first wife, Maggie, had died.

Somewhere in the Moore or Strickland gene pool, perhaps in my great-grandfathers or great-grandmother's, or the next generation, this terrible disease called Alzheimer's struck with vengeance. My mother's mother, Ressie Moore Hairston, died of severe Alzheimer's at the age of ninety. My mother is the spitting image of her mother. Several of my mother's aunts and uncles have suffered from the disease as well. Occasionally when I momentarily lose track of my car keys, cell phone, or something else of importance, I ask myself whether my ancestors' disease will become my plight or that of my three children or their children's children.

Alzheimer's is not usually an illness that you wake up with one morning like a sore back or a headache. To the contrary, it seems to sneak up on you over a period of time. The signs of the disease in Mama became more noticeable after my father's death in 2003. On one occasion, a couple of years after his death, I remember visiting my mother. When I arrived at her home in Madison, North Carolina, I was not surprised to find her in the kitchen cooking. Mama was a prolific cook; she had to be, having been married for fifty-seven years and raising six boys and two girls. But that day I saw her sitting at the kitchen table with the stove on, boiling eggs. I sat there for twenty minutes or so talking with her as the eggs continued to boil. Mama had a couple of ingredients on the table, but she didn't seem to know what to do with them. It was as if she had forgotten how to make the deviled eggs that she had made many times during my youth and adulthood. Mama just sat there. I could tell she was struggling to know what to do next. I finally reached over and cut off the gas flame under the boiling eggs.

Later I began to get reports that Mama had misplaced her keys to her car and home on numerous occasions and they couldn't be found anywhere. Still later, the family received reports that Mama was observed sitting in her car in the parking lot at the church where she had attended for over half a century, located just up the road from her home. The only problem was that there was no church service going on and none planned for the times Mama was seen there. And then Mama was diagnosed with Alzheimer's disease. It was no surprise. What followed were frequent accidents due to incontinence and hallucinations of unimaginable events involving persons she had known all of her life. On top of this, the family had a great fear of Mama "walking off"—all part of the decline and what I choose to call Mama's long ride home.

Science has made much progress in the diagnosis of Alzheimer's disease and the availability of medications designed to slow its progression. Prior to Mama's diagnosis, as a Statewide Visitor for many years, I learned much about the disease from my involvement with the African American Community Outreach Program (AACOP) at Duke University's Bryan Alzheimer's Disease Research Center since its inception in October 1995. But nothing I learned prepared me for dealing with the illness so close to home. To date there is no cure.

The medications prescribed seem to have little or no effect on Mama. Mama's once congenial, talkative personality seems to be gone now. Oh, how we miss her biblical teaching and words of encouragement! An occasional responsive smile reminds us of days gone by. I don't remember the last time Mama started a conversation. She responds to questions, but only briefly, often in a defensive manner. I ask, "Do you know who I am?" Her response, "You know I know who you are." I choose not to follow up with, "Well, who am I?" I don't want to embarrass or frustrate her.

Sitting there in her room at the assisted living facility not many miles from where she has spent all her life, she is still my mother and I love her just as much as I ever have. I honor all that she has done for her family, church, and her community, far too much for me to write about here, except to say that Mama sacrificed her all as long as her mind and body were working in unison. There has never been one selfish bone in her body. The last few months we've noticed more sullenness and sleepiness. The old adage of "once an adult and twice a child" comes to my mind when I think of her. It hurts so much to see her in this state, in her long ride home.

Mama's long ride home is over.

Mama's Long Ride Home Is Over: Bettie Ester Moore Webster

OCTOBER 13, 2013

On August 12, 2012, I blogged, "Alzheimer's Disease: Mama's Long Ride Home." On September 16, 2013, at 5:25 a.m., Mama finally arrived home, dying peacefully at the Morehead Hospital in Eden, North Carolina. I suspect her death certificate will record that she died of pneumonia. At the end her frail body of eighty-some pounds was too weak to fight off the complications of severe pneumonia that had taken hold of her less than a month from her eighty-fourth birthday. We wept during the three days leading up to her passing to the other side of Jordan. But we had wept numerous times before on our visits to see Mama in the assisted living and then nursing home as we watched her slow but steady decline. So, our grief was nothing new. In the end, my sister Patsy, who was there with Mama when she took her last breath, remarked to my nephew Derrick, "Mama doesn't have Alzheimer's anymore." In some ways it seemed that Mama's arrival home had snatched up death. I am reminded of the scripture found in 1 Corinthians 15:55: "Oh death, where is thy sting, oh grave, where is thy victory?"

We find some solace in the rich legacy that Mama left behind. Like Dr. Martin Luther King Jr., she left a committed life behind. Bettie Ester Moore Webster did that and more. She left a legacy of love for others and self-sacrifice. She loved her God, her Goodwill church community, and her family. In short, Mama loved everyone. As my niece Jasmine Scott orated to the congregation at Mama's Homegoing service on September 19, 2013, Bettie E. Webster's life can be summed up in a few words: "She walked the talk." My own brief eulogistic remarks that day spoke of Mama's advice to me as I left for Howard University forty-one years ago last month. She said, "Joe, if you put God first in your life and work hard, someone will see you trying, and someone will help." My brother James remembered one of Mama's favorite songs and led the congregation in singing, "I'll Overcome Some Day." "If I live right, I'll overcome some day. If I walk right, I'll overcome some day." Mama, you have overcome the dreaded Alzheimer's disease—no more sickness, no more pain, no more worry, and no more disappointment! During the funeral service, my aunt Hazel Moore sang a powerful song of praise, "When I see Jesus, Amen." It was about God's power and promise of everlasting life.

Mama, your long ride home is finally over. Hallelujah! To God be the glory for the glorious life you lived!

Hurricane Fran

SEPTEMBER 1996

The winds roared as we sought a safe place to ride out the storm.
The rains had not ceased all the day long, and we sought to protect ourselves from harm.
We gathered as a family downstairs, all five of us snuggly fitting in our bathroom.
There was hardly enough space to move yet we were not full of gloom.
We could hear the trees fall upon our house, not knowing what damages had been done.
With only our flashlights in hand
Being the man of the house, for some reason, I thought it my duty to go upstairs and see whether
damage could be seen but I quickly returned to my wife and precious children
A squeal or moan occasionally came from the mouths of the little ones we love.
But my faith was in the one from above.
The sound of the wind and rain was frightening, only God could determine our plight.
Dawn finally came and we saw trees down all around us with a huge pine tree that flattened
two of our cars parked in our front yard.
We walked around happy to be alive, but to see all the damage was hard.
The winds had hardly ceased to rumble when neighbors passed our way.
Glaring at the mass destruction in contrast to the beauty of that sunny day.
This must be the worst day in your life, one visitor said.
Not really, I replied, my family and I could be dead.
Material things can be replaced, I told him.
We had no reason to be saddened or grim.
So, we are not in despair about Hurricane Fran.

Recognizing that this was God's own plan.
Despite the physical damage, we still had our wealth.
For we survived that night in good health.
We thanked God for sparing our lives, and we will never forget that long, long night.
Our family was spared from injury or death only by God's own might!

316 Carlton Drive, Chapel Hill, NC—The power of Hurricane Fran, September 1996

Our home after renovations. "The greatest and unmatched power of God to resurrect all things."

How Come I Can't?

JUNE 17, 2010

If my father had lived until July 3 of this year, he would have celebrated his eighty-fifth birthday. Unfortunately, James Edward "Tom" Webster succumbed to cancer seven years ago this past March. It was not until I was older and had children of my own that I fully appreciated what a great father Tom Webster was to his eight children. My father, or "Daddy" as we referred to him, only completed the fourth grade, but accomplished more than many people with more formal education. He was from the old school and did things the hard way. He and my mother bought land and a house early in their marriage and later made it part of the deal to acquire a ninety-eight-acre farm in 1966. All my father's jobs involved arduous labor. He began driving a brick truck at a time when drivers had to load the trucks by hand. He began farming tobacco when plowing was done by mule. I remember how exasperated he was when two of my older brothers put the harness on the mule upside down and when one of my brothers didn't know "gee" from "haw," the mule plowed up a lot of Dad's tobacco. I remember my father leaving home early before we arose from bed and returning often after nightfall. Nevertheless, he always came home daily. "I love you" was not a part of my father's vocabulary in my childhood. He would "thump" the heads of his boys when he arrived home from work. It hurt, but that was Dad's way of demonstrating his love for us.

My father was a man of faith mixed with stubbornness and perseverance. He was a deacon in our church in the same community where he grew up. He did not always have the right understanding of Scripture and often did not agree with the pastor's way of doing things, but he never quit the church. I would often see him beside my mother, both on their knees, bedside reciting their nightly prayers. It took a lot of praying to provide for eight children in rural North Carolina beginning just after World War II ended. We were never hungry. Often someone from the community would stop by unannounced at dinnertime as we were gathered around the kitchen table. My parents would greet them by saying, "Come on in and join us. We have plenty, such as is." Indeed, we did. During the summer months, we had fresh corn, green beans, squash, potatoes, tomatoes, and "fatback" meat. My father seemed to be satisfied even if he had just a glass of buttermilk mixed with corn bread. Fried chicken was often the treat for the Sunday meal. I loved Mama's pinto beans, a southern staple year-round. During the winter, Daddy killed hogs and we often had sausage or ham for breakfast and liver or tenderloin for dinner.

My parents were married for almost fifty-seven years when my father died. Since both of them were strong willed, their way of communication included lively discussions about trivial matters. On one occasion, late in my father's life, he and my mother were "fussing" about something when my mother said, "Now, Tom, you can't be that ignorant." Probably without thinking, my father instantly responded, "How come I can't?" I break into laughter every time I think about that comment. But that was James Edward "Tom" Webster. His legacy to his family is a hard work ethic and a "How come I can't" spirit that didn't allow him to quit or succumb to obstacles. One of my uncles told me that even in the early years when money was very scarce, "If you bought a Coke [Coca-Cola], Tom could buy one." Daddy was no beggar. On his deathbed, as tears flowed down my cheeks, Daddy talked with me about how he had always worked hard for a living. My father's "How come I can't" spirit served him well and will continue to serve his children and his children's children for many years to come. Well done, Daddy. You too made a difference for your family and community. "Happy Father's Day," Daddy!

CHAPTER SEVEN

Contributions to the Legal Profession and Community

Be Inspired: Printed Remarks in the North Carolina Bar Association Foundation's 2008 *Champions of Justice* program book

COURTESY OF NC BAR ASSOCIATION

JULY 13, 2008

How time flies! This past June marked the twenty-third anniversary (1985) of my being awarded the second Pro Bono Service Award given by the North Carolina Bar Association. The award came in the sixth year of my legal career. It was at a time in my career when I was still taking almost everything that came through the door, whether the clients could afford to pay me or not. In the Charles Hamilton Houston and Howard University traditions, I knew that it was imperative for me to be a social engineer in my hometown, which had never had an African American attorney in its 161-year history. So, seeking to zealously represent limited-resource clients was what I knew and loved most. In addition to my own clients, I took on as many referrals as the Legal Services office in Greensboro could refer to me. Many of the clients had cases and causes that no one else would undertake. I must say that at the time, I did not know what reward was at the end for me. I just knew then what I know now: that to whom much is given, much is required. I had too many bills and too few assets to join the [North Carolina Bar Association] prior to being awarded the Pro Bono Service Award. However, I became wealthy from the satisfaction I received from helping others who were less fortunate than me. It takes courage to represent the poor. At that time, I didn't know that I had courage. Since receiving the Pro Bono Service Award, many doors that I didn't know existed have been opened, and many opportunities have been presented to me. I'd like to think that I made a difference serving as chair of the Minorities in the Profession Committee, the NC Board of Law Examiners, or as an administrative law judge in the NC Office of Administrative Hearings. I continue to heed the call of that old professor at Howard University to "go down there and make a difference."

Madison lawyer's position helps him reach poor

By MARK EDELEN
Leader Staff Writer

Courts aren't kind to the poor, Madison attorney Joe Webster believes. The poor can't afford a lawyer. They can't defend themselves. And, more often than not, they lose.

That, Webster says, is injustice. Injustice the controversial Eden resident has experienced firsthand and seen around him in his 31 years. And now Webster has been honored for his work to see that that injustice doesn't happen.

At the North Carolina Bar Association's annual meeting in Asheville in June, Webster was awarded the 1985 Pro Bono Service Award for representing about 60 poor people at no charge since November 1982. He has also handled 30 more cases for a reduced fee.

"It just seems a flaw in the system if those people don't have the right to representation because they can't afford it," he said. "Everyone should have the right to justice.

"I see so many that will try to be their own attorney and represent themselves," Webster said. "They aren't educated in the law or cross-examining. And the trial results show it."

Webster knows what it is to have to get by without much.

The family of eight children grew up on a small farm three miles outside of Madison, where his parents still live. His father, James, works as a driver for Pine Hall Brick & Pipe Co. in Madison; his mother, Bettie, took a job at Macfield Texturing to help support the family.

"It certainly helps if you can understand where these people are coming from," Webster said. "I wouldn't say we were poor. But growing up on the farm, we definitely learned what it was to work hard."

While Webster worked hard on the farm, he did the same at Madison-Mayodan High School. Hard enough to gain his 1972 admission intoHoward University in Washington. He got his law degree from Howard in 1979.

There Webster learned to speak his mind.

He remembers joining the lines at the White House and the U.S. Supreme Court Building protesting cases such as the 1978 Bakke decision, which ruled minority-admission quotas at colleges illegal.

But Webster also remembers the advice a professor gave him before he came back to North Carolina: "If you're not going to go down there and make a difference, then you might as well stay up here."

After graduation, Webster made a difference.

He became a staff attorney for Legal Services of the Southern Piedmont in Charlotte, which provides free legal service for the poor. After a year and marriage to his wife, Diane, he moved back to Madison to become the town's first black attorney and only the third in Rockingham County.

Now home, Webster still speaks his mind. In November 1984, he sued the city so he could use a blue two-story colonial house on Decatur Street as his office. In October, Webster accused the Madison Board of Adjustment of racism for turning down his request.

Webster made news again in ear-

(See Webster, L2)

Attorney Joe Webster

Joe being sworn in as a newly licensed attorney, Superior Court of Rockingham County, Wentworth, NC, late August 1979 (introduced to the court and bar by well-known Madison attorney, A. D. "Lon" Folger

L2 Rockingham Leader
Greensboro News & Record, Thursday, Aug. 1, 1985

Webster

From L1

ly June when he went to the Western Rockingham School Board to ask that more black teachers be hired and retained.

"Every time a black teacher leaves, they're replaced by someone white," he said. "Those kids are missing out on good role models."

Webster put himself in the spotlight most recently after Dolphus (Bud) Ziglar, who was black, fatally shot his white boss and himself before his body burned in a warehouse fire.

After the deaths, Webster asked the Madison Board of Aldermen to consider filling city appointments with more blacks.

"There are so many people so discouraged with the way the system works that they take matters into their own hands," he told the aldermen.

Webster said he has never tried to make himself a leader in Rockingham County's black community.

"I'd rather stand behind people and offer support," he said. "But, unfortunately, my profession thrusts me to the front more and more."

That's not the case with the for-free cases Webster handles. They are referred to him by Central Carolina Legal Services in Greensboro. The cases can't be criminal and most often involve real estate disputes or domestic troubles such as divorce and child custody, Webster said.

"Some people might say that's not very important," he said. "But what's more important than the future of a child? After all, the children are our future."

The reason behind the for-free work is simply what Thurman Hampton, the county's first black lawyer, calls Webster's belief that "his law degree and profession are of little help unless he can do some good with them."

And Webster does do good, District Court Judge Peter McHugh said. McHugh said he's never been able to tell which cases before him Webster is handling for free.

"That may say as much as anything," he said. "He's a strong advocate for his clients. He puts as much time and expertise in the cases that he's handling for free as the ones he's charging for."

Asked why he does the work, Webster simply quotes from the Bible, John 12:48: "For unto whomsoever much is given, of him shall be much required."

"I've certainly been blessed," he said. "I'm just giving some of that back."

Greensboro News & Record Thursday, October 30, 1986

Voice for Rockingham blacks leaves for position in Raleigh

By ROBIN ADAMS
Staff Writer

MADISON — Rockingham County's black community will be losing one of its most vocal spokesman soon when attorney Joe L. Webster moves to Raleigh to take a job with the state.

Webster, 32, will be working in the human resources section representing state medical and social service agencies. He will begin his new job Dec. 1.

Webster has taken on controversial cases and often represented people who have little or no money.

When black school secretary Barbara Fretwell was suspended, an action that drew accusations of racial discrimination, it was Webster who negotiated with Western Rockingham school officials and got a settlement that both sides could agree upon.

Webster

That suspension lead to Madison's first and only protest demonstration in February. It was Webster who organized and led the demonstration.

When the family of Dolphus (Bud) Zigler, a 58-year-old mechanic who shot and killed his employer and himself, needed representation, they called on Webster.

It was Webster who wrote to City Manager Steve Routh requesting the formation of a city human relations commission as a result of the Zigler shootings. A commission was formed.

Webster has argued before the city Board of Aldermen that blacks be considered for board and commission appointments. He has argued to the Western Rockingham

(See Webster, D5)

Webster From D1

chool Board that they should hire more black teachers.

Webster, one of only three black ttorneys in the county, says his ight for "what's right and just" has nade him the subject of lots of criticism, but he has no regrets.

"Everything I have done has been n an effort to make a difference," Vebster said. "I've always tried to dvocate and demonstrate what was ight."

He said he hopes to have been a nodel for others. His own models vere Thurgood Marshall and the Rev. Martin Luther King Jr.

Webster, one of eight children of ames Webster, a driver for Pine Hall Brick & Pipe Co., and Bettie Vebster, a textile mill employee, rew up on a farm about three miles rom Madison.

He graduated from Madison-Mayodan High School where he played n the basketball team and ran rack. He entered Howard University in 1972 and graduated from the w school in 1979. While in school e was a member of Phi Beta Kappa.

From 1979-80, he served as a staff ttorney for Legal Services of the outhern Piedmont in Charlotte, hen moved home.

He credits a former Howard law rofessor for encouraging him to ke an active role in the community.

"This professor said, 'If you're not ing to go down there and make a fference,' then don't go at all.

"No doubt if I had not come back Madison, there would have always been that feeling that I did not do all that God wanted me to do," Webster said.

He hates to leave Madison.

"Of course I have mixed emotions, but I feel that I have been offered a good opportunity," he said. "This position will be in the best interest of my family and me."

Others hate to see him leave. "I've enjoyed working with Joe," City Manager Routh said. "I'm sorry to see him go."

But his new employers are happy.

"We are pleased that Mr. Webster is joining our staff and not just because of his academic background and experience but because of his record in community service," said John Simmons, administrative deputy attorney general. "This is exactly the kind of people we want to join our office."

Webster will be honored Saturday when he receives the Community Service Award from the N.C. Association of Black Lawyers. Last year, he received the 1985 Pro Bono Service Award from the N.C. Bar Association for representing many clients for no charge or at reduced rates.

He is married to Diane and has two children, Brian, 4, and Camilla, 6 months. He serves on the board of directors of the N.C. Association of Black Lawyers Landloss Prevention Project and the Best Friends of Rockingham County. He is also a member of the NAACP, Madison Masonic Lodge No. 568 and trustee and member of Goodwill Baptist Church.

WITH PERMISSION OF *GREENSBORO NEWS AND RECORD*

BARNOTES

Joe L. Webster of Madison (left) was presented the 1985 Pro Bono Award by 1984-85 President E. Osborne Ayscue, Jr. during the Annual Meeting. To learn why Webster was selected, turn to page 5.

Receiving Pro Bono Service Award, NC Bar Association Convention, June 1985—Of all the commendations I have received in my career, this one recognition in 1985 did more for my career advancement than any other. It came at a time when I was laboring in the trenches of law practice in my hometown of Madison, NC, and I was not widely known in the legal profession. Shortly afterward, I became a member of the NC Bar Association and chair of the Minorities in the Profession Committee. In 1989, I was selected as a member of the NC Board of Law Examiners and later chair of the board. COURTESY OF NORTH CAROLINA BAR ASSOCIATION

'ick Thigpen, Sue Perry, Len Elmore and Joe Webster speak at press conference.

Elmore Sends Message To Youth

The N.C. Bar Association is pro- ιoting academics among athletes by roducing a public service announce- ιent featuring former Atlantic Coast 'onference basketball star-turned- ιwyer Len Elmore.

The NCBA hopes the video will en- ›urage youth—especially minority :udents—to further their education nd consider legal careers in North arolina.

During the 30-second spot to be dis- 'ibuted to television stations across ιe state, Elmore encourages young ɜople to plan for a career off the court γ studying hard, staying away from rugs and by putting academics before :hletics.

"A small percentage of youngsters :ay in college and only 1 in 500 of those will go on to play pro ball," Elmore said. "Even then, the average NBA career is just about four years. It's imperative that student athletes look ahead and plan for a career."

Elmore, who played for the Maryland Terrapins in the '70s, played in the National Basketball Association for eight years. A Harvard Law School graduate, Elmore is now an attorney in New York City and is a TV analyst for college basketball games.

The video production evolved from an idea of the N.C. Bar Association's Minorities in the Profession Committee which was looking for ways to get more blacks interested in a law career.

"In the broadest sense we are simply trying to urge all students to stay in school and prepare for life after sport: said Joe Webster, chairman of the coı mittee. "But we hope that youı blacks will see what Len Elmore h: done and will want to follow in h footsteps and become lawyers."

North Carolina has the fewest nuı ber of lawyers per capita in the Unit‹ States. In addition, the committ‹ found that while blacks make up : percent of the state's population, on 4 percent of lawyers are black.

N.C. Bar Association Presideı Richard E. Thigpen Jr. said, "This pr duction is an example of the NCB/ significant and long-range commi ment to promoting opportunities in tl legal profession for future minorit practitioners in the state." □

Former president of NC Bar Association, 1988–1989, Richard "Dick" Thigpen; chair of Minorities in the Profession Committee Joe L. Webster; and committee member Sue Perry with former NBA player and Harvard Law graduate Len Elmore COURTESY OF NORTH CAROLINA BAR ASSOCIATION *BAR NOTES* (JUNE/JULY 1985).

Thirty-five years later, Dick Thigpen and present vice president of the Bar Association board, Joe L. Webster, in attendance at the 2024 Bar Association meeting in Blowing Rock, NC. COURTESY OF MARK HOLT

Board of Law Examiners and Executive Director in the 1990s

WITH PERMISSION OF THE NC BOARD OF LAW EXAMINERS TO THE EXTENT THE BOARD HAS AUTHORITY TO GRANT PERMISSION

(L-R) Board of Law Examiners Members and Spouses, The Honorable Leon and Michelle Stanback, Jerry and Sheri Collins, Joe and Diane Webster

Joe with two of his fellow NC Board of Law Examiner members, (L-R) Eric Michaux and Karl Adkins, at bar grading session

Board of Law Examiners
of
The State of North Carolina

RESOLUTION OF APPRECIATION
TO
JOE L. WEBSTER

The Board of Law Examiners of the State of North Carolina, in meeting duly assembled on this the 10th day of January 2003, in Raleigh, North Carolina, does hereby adopt the following Resolution of Appreciation:

WHEREAS, JOE L. WEBSTER of Chapel Hill, North Carolina, was elected by the North Carolina Bar as a member of the Board of Law Examiners of the State of North Carolina in August 1989, and he served as a member of this Board from August 1989 until October 2002.

JOE L. WEBSTER contributed immensely to this Board by bringing to it his high ethical standards and his broad knowledge of the law. He represented the Board of Law Examiners well in his dealings with the members of the Bar in this State. He freely shared with the members of the Board his numerous talents and strong legal abilities. He unselfishly gave a great deal of his time to the operations of this Board, having served on numerous committees, including the Finance and Audit Committee, Chair of the Drafting Committee, and the Executive Committee. He further served as Chairman of the Board from August 1998 through October 2000. His dedication to and firm leadership of this Board has earned him zealous respect from the Board and the Bar.

JOE L. WEBSTER has worked diligently, faithfully, and with dignity to uphold the high calling of the legal profession in North Carolina by helping to assure the proper qualification of applicants to practice law in our State. He treated all those dealing with the Board and appearing before the Board thoroughly and with courtesy.

NOW, THEREFORE, BE IT RESOLVED that the Board of Law Examiners of the State of North Carolina does hereby express to *JOE L. WEBSTER* its sincere appreciation and gratitude for this outstanding, devoted, and dedicated service to this Board and we gratefully acknowledge the exemplary service he gave to this Board, which has brought distinction to him, the Board, and to the legal profession of North Carolina.

BE IT FURTHER RESOLVED that this Resolution of Appreciation be made a part of the permanent record of the Board of Law Examiners of the State of North Carolina and that a copy be delivered to *JOE L. WEBSTER* in recognition and appreciation of his dedicated service.

SEAL

Thomas W. Steed, Jr., Chairman

Resolution of Appreciation, Board of Law Examiners of the State of North Carolina

VOLUME 101 NUMBER 1 SPRING 2017
JUDICATURE

64

Saving Our Profession

It's up to us

By Joe L. Webster

Judicature 101, no. 1 (Spring 2017). Duke University School of Law, published by the Duke Law Center for Judicial Studies, and reprinted with permission

Saving Our Profession: It's Up to Us

SPRING 2017

A number of years ago, a man told me he had been charged with a crime. I asked him how his case was going. With all sincerity and with an honest demeanor, he said, "Well, I've had to spend a lot of money to help me get out of trouble. I had to pay my lawyer a large attorney fee, and then I had to give him some money for the district attorney and the judge also."

I was not completely stunned by his response, because earlier in my career I had heard similar comments by those charged with crimes. Well, as sincere as he came across, I suspect that the man was repeating to me what his attorney told him to justify a large and perhaps excessive attorney fee, not that any money was ever paid to the district attorney or the judge. But if that is what happened, it was inappropriate and unethical for whatever reason it was said.

There may be some in the legal profession who believe the profession is just fine as it is. There may be some who haven't heard or have just been out of touch with some disturbing realities that affect our profession and criminal and civil justice system negatively. But I believe our profession needs saving, and we must be the ones to save it.

What must we save our profession from? Here I will address a few of the biggest challenges: increasing public distrust of the legal system, lack of excellent legal representation available for indigent defendants in serious felony cases, lack of excellent legal representation available to lower- and middle-class citizens in civil cases, and real and damaging racial disparities in the way our system delivers justice.

These are big challenges, but as you'll see, I think there are meaningful things each of us can do to make a difference.

Honesty and Trustworthiness. I read online about a poll that rated twenty-two professions regarding honesty and ethical standards. The polling showed lawyers to be rated thirteenth out of the twenty-two professions, listed just above members of Congress, advertising practitioners, and car salespeople. Even journalists were rated higher than judges.[30] So you see the problem we face with respect to our reputations for honesty and trustworthiness: two of the most important character traits members of our profession can possess.

30 Gallup Poll, Honesty/Ethics in Professions, www.gallup.com/poll/1654/honesty-ethics-professions.aspx).

There are lawyers who violate the rules of professional conduct by using various tactics to obtain business from people who had gotten speeding tickets or other traffic violations. One of the attorneys sanctioned in my district had a website named "tixfixer.com." One would think that this lawyer would have known that the use of the word "tixfixer," which gives the impression that he could fix tickets, would only cast a negative light on lawyers and the legal profession in general.

The number of our fellow lawyers stealing from their clients' trust account funds does not seem to be decreasing, if you look at state reports of attorney disbarments or other disciplines.

In the area of criminal law, I believe that part of the problem is that, as a profession, we have not even figured out a way to clearly explain to laypersons how it is that attorneys can and indeed should represent those charged with the most heinous crimes, even when the defendants have told the attorney that he or she did the crime. Nor have we adequately explained to laypersons the distinction between being found "not guilty" and being "innocent" of the crimes for which a person is charged.

These are just a few examples of reasons that our profession has fallen into serious disrepute. What is required of us as lawyers and judges in these few examples I have just given and in general? I doubt that many of us take advantage of the teachable moments we often have with our fellow members of the bar. I also know that we need to do a better job of explaining the role of an attorney and, most importantly, in policing our fellow members of the legal profession in complying with the rules of professional conduct. If we don't adequately police ourselves, then others outside our profession may be called upon to do so.

Zealous Representation for All. The very first words of the preamble to the American Bar Association's rules of professional conduct state, "A lawyer, as a member of the legal profession, is a representative of clients, an officer of the legal system, and a public citizen having special responsibility of the quality of justice." Paragraph 6 of those rules, in part, states that, as a public citizen, a lawyer should seek improvement of the law, access to the legal system, the administration of justice, and the quality of service rendered by the legal profession. "A lawyer should be mindful of deficiencies in the administration of justice and of the fact that the poor, and sometimes persons who are not poor, cannot afford adequate legal counsel." And finally, in the thirteenth paragraph of the preamble to the American Bar Association's model rules, it states that "lawyers play a vital role in the preservation of society."

If we as a profession could do just a couple of things that would change the perception of the legal profession and our system of justice, it would be to provide access to justice for all who had business before our courts and to allow our voices to be heard in the many injustices we see manifested in our society. All of us, including we judges, must do a better job of providing access to justice as relating to our courts.

I was on the indigent appointment list for most of my career. One of the most difficult cases I ever had was one in which I had been appointed to represent the defendant.

While I was practicing law down in Pittsboro, North Carolina, I was in court one day, and here was an assistant public defender who stood before the judge making a motion to withdraw from one of her client's cases. I was busy making final preparations to argue my case, and so I wasn't paying much attention to what was going on. I did see a tall, ponytailed, tattooed man standing beside her. I heard the judge say, "Yes, I'll allow you to withdraw." And then the judge, Hon. Leon Stanback, started looking in the direction of the lawyers seated beyond the bar. And then I heard him say, "I think I'll appoint attorney Webster. Are you still on the appointment list?" At that point in my career, I had my hands full with the many cases, both criminal and civil, I was handling, so I hesitated and then said, "Yes, your honor, I'm still on the appointment list." But immediately the assistant public defender addressed Judge Stanback and said, "I don't think it would do any good to appoint Mr. Webster." Judge Stanback said, "Why not?" and asked the public defender and me to approach the bench. The judge leaned forward and said, "Why not?" and the public defender responded, "My client is a member of the Ku Klux Klan." The judge then turned to me and asked, "Will that give you any problems?" I won't go into the entire sidebar conversation, but I agreed to be appointed to represent the defendant.

I did so because I believe each person charged with a serious crime ought to have a lawyer—not only any lawyer, but one who will fight zealously for their client and a lawyer who cares about him or her and their plight. It turns out that one case may have been the most difficult criminal case I have ever had in all of my years of practice. For one thing, the defendant made threats to me about what he would do to whoever came forward to testify. There came a time when all my meetings with him took place in the courthouse rather than my office, because frankly I had some fear, and I owed it to my wife and my children to be cautious.

It was the only time in my career when I had to consult with the state bar on what I was allowed or required to do. I pondered whether I should attempt to withdraw or report the threats to do bodily harm to law enforcement or the court. However, I know that I made the right decision to remain in the case because this man needed compassionate, zealous representation. My personal abhorrence to what my client and the KKK has stood for over the years took a backseat to my belief that one is innocent until proven guilty and that even individuals charged with the most heinous crimes imaginable deserve competent representation. And I strongly believe there is no doubt that our system of justice works best when there is zealous advocacy on both sides of the aisle. And so I said yes when asked to take on this case.

While practicing as a solo practitioner for most of my career, sometimes I struggled to make ends meet, and my family had necessities unmet. While I was in private practice, one day a client, Ms. Beasley, brought me some poke salad and a piece of pork and a piece of cornbread. And that night at dinner, sitting around the table with my wife and three children, I told my wife about Ms. Beasley's kind gesture. My wife instantly said to our children, "Lord, children, your daddy's client's paying him with poke salad."

I tell you about these personal memories of my days as a practicing lawyer because of the need today for our profession to be even more generous with our time and treasure than ever in the past. We have even more financially poor among us than thirty-seven years ago when I began to practice law. Of the 1,173 civil filings in the Middle District of North Carolina during the 2013 calendar year, 680, or approximately 58 percent, were pro se.

Our federal Middle District judges recently implemented a pilot program involving the appointments of attorneys to represent pro se litigants in appropriate civil cases. My research shows that there is no shortage of lawyers in the Middle District. Just in Durham, Guilford, and Forsyth Counties alone there are approximately four thousand active lawyers. What is required of us? Many of those four thousand active lawyers who practice before the federal court or who have experience in the federal court ought to take up my challenge to volunteer for the pro bono panel of attorneys who can help breathe life into the words "equal justice under law." The success of our system of justice in part depends on our response to this call.

As you know, in contrast to most serious criminal cases, there is no civil Gideon.[31] in most cases that entitles a civil litigant to a lawyer. While I sat as an administrative law judge for six years, just prior to taking on the responsibilities as a US magistrate judge four years ago, I used to look out from the bench and sometimes see two assistant attorneys general on one side of the aisle and a desperate-looking elderly lady or man on the other side who didn't know even one rule of civil procedure or rule of evidence. In my mind, I often said to myself, *There is something wrong with this picture. How can this be anything close to equal justice under law?* Often,1963 I felt helpless sitting there as the judge and jury!

Over and over again, those of us who sit in civil cases involving pro se litigants find ourselves compelled to follow the rules of civil procedure and rules of evidence, but, at

31 Giden v. Wainwright 372 U.S.335 (1963) The United States Supreme Court ruled unanimously in favor of Gideon, guaranteeing the right to legal counsel for criminal defendants in federal and state courts. No such right is guaranteed in civil cases.

the same time struggling to provide a venue that looks just a little bit like a venue where justice might be found. The words "equal justice under law" must be more than the four words that appear on the western facade of the US Supreme Court building there in Washington, DC. Yes, we as practicing lawyers and judges must give meaning to those four words. This means that more attorneys may have to be paid with poke salad or paid nothing at all to provide access to justice.

The need is urgent: In recent years, DNA has proven in numerous cases that our system of determining guilt is not perfect, and many innocent people serve lengthy prison sentences before being exonerated by DNA or other evidence. North Carolina has seen several such exonerations in recent years, thanks to the work of dedicated attorneys, law students, and other volunteers. More excellent experienced advocates must make themselves available in capital and other serious felony cases where justice might slip away if a good lawyer is not present.

So having a competent lawyer is an important element of gaining access to justice. However, even those in the middle class are finding it very difficult to hire a lawyer. For someone who makes $15 or $20 an hour, an attorney informing them that his or her services are billed at $250 or $300 per hour is not even comprehensible, let alone affordable. If our profession puts such a high dollar value on its services, then who will be able to afford our help? Even without a lawyer, in the simplest of speeding tickets in state court, the cost of court is at least $185. The cost of filing a civil lawsuit in federal court is $400. Some families don't have that much income per month. Fortunately, we have in America laws that allow indigent parties to at least file a lawsuit without paying the filing fee, if he or she qualifies.

Addressing the Racial Inequities. Access to justice is much broader than a person's ability to get into court with a lawyer. It begins long before a lawsuit is filed, and in many instances, it involves no lawsuit at all. The news has been filled with headlines about police shootings of black men. According to a ProPublica analysis of federally collected data on fatal police shootings, young black men are twenty-one times at a greater risk than their white counterparts to be shot dead by police officers.[32]

I have a six-foot, two-inch, twenty-seven-year-old, brown-skinned son who is one of the most respectful, hard-working, talented young persons I have ever met. My family, my wife, and two daughters worry about what could happen to him, especially if he happens to be in the wrong place at the wrong time. The wrong place at the wrong time could be lawfully driving on his way to work or in a store shopping or any other place in America where he has a lawful right to be. In the midst of rejoicing about the birth of my

32 ProPublica, *Deadly Force in Black and White,* www.propublica.org/article/deadly-force-in-black-and-white.

first grandchild in early 2017, my wife and I and other family members discussed what the future holds for him and other black and brown males, and what we as parents and grandparents will need to instill in our sons and grandsons in order for them to survive, flourish, and achieve the success unquestionably expected of others. These same concerns are on the mind of many persons of color around the nation.

What does this have to do with you, and what is required of us in the legal profession? First, we must recognize that racial profiling is real, and that lawyers and others of goodwill should speak out against it. As the number of shootings have increased, it is more difficult to defend some among law enforcement who seem to shoot first and ask questions later. I have concluded that unless fair-minded and forward-thinking people of goodwill of all colors and professions—and especially people who have something to lose—don't open our mouths and speak the truth, then our system of justice and all that we've been hearing about on the news won't get any better.

Our legal profession has long been considered a beacon of hope, a bastion of protecting our constitutional rights and freedoms that we hold dear. But we also have been the first to stand up for what is just and right. Here is what is at stake: Unless we as a profession speak up, then those who have less to lose will lose confidence in us as a profession. Not only are these young, mostly men of color entitled to equal justice under law, but they are also entitled to equal dignity under law. Law enforcement officers have a very difficult job. Guns and violence seem to be everywhere around the world, especially here in America. But even those who are in the wrong have a right to be brought to justice to have their day in court. They can't be brought to justice if they are gunned down in the street. This is what is on the minds of persons of color around the nation, and all of us should be equally concerned and seek to remedy it.

You may not know how difficult it is for every African American judge in the nation to see the disproportionate number of minority defendants standing before us in criminal court. I have read that one-third of the black men in America are involved in the criminal justice system, whether in prison or on probation or parole. In recent years, more and more people have recognized that our sentencing guidelines are too tough in some cases, and Congress and the Supreme Court have softened the guidelines.

What is required of us? Let me first say that, compared to how I grew up in rural North Carolina here in the Middle District, I hardly recognize the world of some of those who come before me. Recently one young man before me had seven children by seven different women, none of whom he'd been married to. He was accused of selling drugs and somehow had not worked in over twenty years. Most of those we see in criminal court don't have a father at home, and increasingly, some don't even know who their father is. Many of them are angry. No one will offer them a job. Many believe that society doesn't value their lives, and many standing before the court don't value their own lives. Over the years I've learned that the human spirit needs to be validated in order for a person to have self-worth. And so many of our youth have all but given up on living; some say they don't believe they will live long anyway.

What is required of us? First, every one of us should become a mentor to some young girl or boy outside of our own families. We must fight to keep them in school and give them hope. We must go into the public schools and put our arms around some young boy or girl whose father is in prison, whose mother is strung out on drugs, and who often cannot read well and is struggling with a lack of self-esteem.

We should become ambassadors of the legal system to young people. My clerks and I invite Durham middle school students to our court and chambers once per month during the school year. We encourage them to stay on the right side of the law, to be respectful of each other and their teachers and other school officials. We make every effort to show them that we, the court system, cares about them. We introduce them to the federal court by conducting a mock criminal trial and allow them to act as jurors and to decide the guilt of the defendant. We then discuss with them fundamental principles of our system of justice, such as that one charged with a crime is presumed innocent until proven guilty beyond a reasonable doubt and that a defendant has the right to remain silent. And, last, we invite a guest speaker from the community each month. Among our guest speakers have been an airline pilot, a scientist, retired college head football coach, actress, police chief, drug-sniffing dog and his handler, head manager of a grocery store, retired head basketball coach, former Ringling Brothers Circus clown, physician, assistant US Attorney, and convicted drug dealer who is now a successful businessman. All have given compelling stories of how they have overcome the challenges of life to become successful.

Those of us who can afford to do so must contribute our money to colleges and universities for scholarships for those of our young men and women who cannot afford some college or training beyond high school. Only then will they be able to compete for a job that at least pays a living wage. As judges, when these young men and women come before us, we must treat them with as much dignity and respect as we would the most respected person in society. And as judges, we must also seek to offer them hope as they go off to prison. I have found that to be respected, you must give respect, no matter what a person's station is in life. This is what I meant when I said that all are entitled to equal dignity under law. Even though in my court most are not successful in being released pending trial or further proceedings in their cases, nevertheless I try to give them hope. I encourage them not to give up. I sense that for many of them, I may be the first grown man who has ever tried to encourage and give them hope, even if I have ruled that I cannot release them pending trial because I find they are a danger to the community or a flight risk.

What else is required of us? Our profession must recognize that there is strength in numbers, and so we must seek to partner with other groups, especially those that are already in the trenches working to right this ship of despair in their communities. I have written and stated before that, in my opinion, lawyers have not been good stewards of our profession. We must begin to mend our profession by increasing our efforts to do "good" toward our fellow man, whether it is with our lawyer or judge hat on or in our individual capacities.

I have been blessed to get to the federal bench because I went back to my hometown thirty-six years ago. In 1985 I was awarded the North Carolina Bar Association's Pro Bono Service Award for doing good in my hometown and Rockingham County. Before that time, I suspect that hardly anyone knew who I was, just six years into my legal career. Three years later I was asked to serve on the North Carolina Board of Law Examiners and later became chair of that board. And after six years as an administrative law judge, I was sworn in as a federal magistrate judge. Before my appointment as a federal magistrate judge, there was a lot of hard work and disappointment along the way. I tell you how I got here not because I'm being boastful, but so that I might convince at least some of you there is a reward for doing good in our profession. But the real reward is not in being recognized but the joy that comes from knowing you have tried to help someone along the way.

I am of the opinion that the legal profession has a role to play in promoting racial and ethnic reconciliation. One of the great privileges I've had as a magistrate judge is presiding at a number of naturalization ceremonies, where usually twenty-five or thirty countries are represented by newly made citizens. Looking out among the audience, I tell them that there is a great need for Americans of all nationalities and creeds to come together and get to know one another. Notwithstanding the painting of America as red and blue states by politicians and others, we are, as indicated in our Pledge of Allegiance, one nation under God, indivisible, with liberty and justice for all. I also tell them of the African proverb that says, If you want to walk fast, go alone, but if you want to walk far, go together.

If we as a profession walk together with others, this will undoubtedly help mend the fractured communities we have in America today and will also help save our profession. I am confident that we, all of us—both lawyers and judges—will rise to the occasion and continue to play a vital role in the preservation of society and also in making this a better world.

The Honorable Sammie Chess Jr., A Giant among Judges and Men

Published in Judicature *102, no. 2 (Summer 2018)*
by the Bolch Judicial Institute of Duke Law, c. 2018,
Duke University School of Law, and reprinted with permission.

PERMISSION GRANTED BY LAURA GREEN AND HIGH POINT ENTERPRISE TO USE PHOTO OF JUDGE CHESS

> There can be but few men in the society who will have sufficient skill in the laws to qualify them for the stations of judges. And making the proper deductions for the ordinary depravity of human nature, the number must be still smaller of those who unite the requisite integrity with the requisite knowledge.
>
> —FEDERALIST NO. 78 (ALEXANDER HAMILTON)

On a dirt floor of a tenant house located at the edge of a cotton field in the rural Bull Pond Community outside Allendale, South Carolina, a giant was born in the midst of America's greatest depression. Named after his father, Sammie Chess the junior was refined by a close-knit family, faith, and the deeply segregated South. The Hon. Sammie Chess Jr. ("Chess") rose to become the first African American superior court judge in North Carolina and one of the first in the United States south of Washington, DC. Governor Robert "Bob" Scott had the courage to appoint Chess as a special superior court judge in November 1971, at a time when previous governors had not had the courage or desire to do so.

After graduating from North Carolina Central Law School, passing the North Carolina bar exam in 1958, and serving his country in the army from 1958 to 1960, Chess, like other African American pioneer lawyers of his generation, hung his shingle; he practiced law in High Point, North Carolina, and, like many of his race, accepted his calling as a "social engineer" (P. 28)[33] to take on a deeply fractured society, full of racial prejudice and invidious discrimination, which badly needed to be challenged and corrected. It was as a civil rights lawyer that Chess first made his mark on society. Chess was serious about the oath he took to defend and protect the Constitution and viewed himself as a soldier of that Constitution (P. 67). His imprint was felt in numerous legal cases affecting the lives of thousands of people in High Point and beyond. As one of the cooperating attorneys of the NAACP Legal Defense Fund, Chess was an attorney of record in *North*

33 All page references relate to Joe L. Webster, *The Making and Measure of a Judge: Biography of the Honorable Sammie Chess Jr.* (Chapel Hill, NC: Chapel Hill Press, 2017)

VOLUME 102 NUMBER 2 SUMMER 2018
JUDICATURE
Published by the Bolch Judicial Institute of Duke Law. Reprinted with permission. © 2018 Duke University School of Law. All rights reserved. judicialstudies.duke.edu/judicature

SAMMIE CHESS, JR.
SUPERIOR COURT JUDGE, NORTH CAROLINA

SAMMIE CHESS JR. VIEWS HIS PORTRAIT, WHICH IS ON DISPLAY IN THE NORTH CAROLINA SUPERIOR COURT, HIGH POINT, N.C., AND IN THE COUNTY COURTHOUSE IN ALLENDALE, S.C. PHOTO BY LAURA GREENE, *HIGH POINT ENTERPRISE*, 2015.

A giant among judges and *men*

by Joe L. Webster

THIS TRIBUTE IS BASED ON JUDGE WEBSTER'S BOOK, ***THE MAKING AND MEASURE OF A JUDGE: BIOGRAPHY OF THE HONORABLE SAMMIE CHESS, JR.*** (CHAPEL HILL PRESS, 2017.) ALL PAGE NUMBERS REFERENCE THE PRINTED BOOK, AND ITALICIZED SECTIONS ARE EXCERPTED FROM THE BOOK.

PRINTED WITH PERMISSION OF *JUDICATURE* DUKE UNIVERSITY SCHOOL OF LAW, PUBLISHED BY THE DUKE LAW CENTER FOR JUDICIAL STUDIES. PHOTO COURTESY OF LAURA GREEN AND HIGH POINT *ENTERPRISE* NEWSPAPER.

Carolina Teachers Association v. the Asheboro City Board of Education, Robinson v. Lorillard Co., and *Addison v. High Point Memorial Hospital.* He also was an attorney for the plaintiffs and the public face of the lawsuit initiated against the High Point Board of Education to desegregate the public schools. During the pretrial and trial stages, Chess, along with the lead attorney (renowned civil rights attorney and friend Julius Chambers) and others, represented the plaintiff in an employment racial discrimination case, *Griggs v. Duke Power Co.* On March 8, 1971, the US Supreme Court decided for the plaintiff and held that employment tests must be job related. *Griggs* was the first racial discrimination case brought under Title VII of the Civil Rights Act of 1964 to come before the US Supreme Court on its merits and quickly became a landmark decision. *Griggs'* author, the late Supreme Court justice Warren Burger, identified *Griggs* as the most important case handed down by the Court in his first two full terms (P. 69).

What distinguishes Judge Chess from so many other lawyers and judges who have served our state and nation well? He is a man of unsurpassed courage, grace, determination, and strength of character that allowed him to overcome obstacles not experienced by most other lawyers and judges of his generation. Chess is guided by a moral compass. He said,

> You must have a bearing and abiding faith in your moral direction; that you can't be a lawyer if you don't stand up straight. There will be blows against you, but you will be a man if you take the blows. A man can do remarkable things if you inspire others. You can even disarm your opponent if you stand up straight and practice these principles. You can't think about consequences, but you have to think about what the constitution requires. (PP. 66–67)

In the early 1960s, Chess traveled to Gastonia, NC, to his opposing attorney's home turf to present a civil case, the only case his father ever witnessed. The jury ruled in his client's favor. After rendering their verdict, many of the jurors, who were highly impressed by the manner in which Chess had argued his client's case, came down out of the jury box asking for Chess's business card, desiring him to be their family attorney. However, whatever joy of victory Chess experienced was tempered by what he and his father experienced when they were leaving the courtroom. As Chess and his father walked some distance behind his opposing attorney out of the courtroom into the hallway leading toward the exit, a man came toward the opposing counsel. The man spoke to opposing counsel and asked him,

> "What in the world happened to you? You look like you have been in a fight with a bobcat." The opposing counsel responded, "A nigger lawyer just beat the shit out of me." Without saying a word, Chess and his father continued to walk toward the exit. (PP. 87–88)

Later as a trial judge, in many of the courts where Chess presided, the various court officials such as clerks, bailiffs, and other law enforcement had never seen a black lawyer, let alone a black judge. During one assignment, Chess traveled to a distant court and

> [Chess] remembers pulling into a parking space which was marked with a sign indicating that the space was for judges only. "This deputy came rushing up to me saying, 'Are you crazy, what do you think you're doing?' 'I didn't say anything.' He said, 'Can't you read?' I said, 'Deputy, I am the judge.' All of a sudden, it came to him that he heard there was a black judge. I told the deputy, 'It's OK. This is something you have not been accustomed to.'" (P. 106)

These are but a couple of examples that prove Chess was the right person to become the first African American superior court judge in North Carolina. While many others would have been offended and ready to take measures in their own hand, Chess was not willing to bring himself to the level of a Klansman. He was well grounded and rooted in love and forgiveness, which was embedded in him by his parents and extended family. His grandmother gave him advice that served him well. She said, "You are better than nobody, but nobody is better than you." Chess also said, "My way isn't to get angry. If you disagree with me, I'm not going to stop talking to you. I'm going to keep talking and try to persuade you, and eventually you may come to see things the way I do."

Chess distinguished himself by carrying himself in a professional, nonconfrontational manner that undoubtedly did much to combat ignorance and prejudice. Perhaps unbeknownst to him, Chess's manner garnered respect and promoted reconciliation among persons of different racial backgrounds and from all walks of life. To use the words contained within President Abraham Lincoln's second inaugural address, Chess's life's work and the manner in which he carried it out did much to help "bind up our nation's wounds."

Notwithstanding Chess's manner of dealing with racial prejudice, he learned early in his career that not everyone would understand his work as a civil rights lawyer. He learned that some would despise him. During this period a white man near Chess's office approached Chess to tell him that he saw him as being the "devil incarnate." Later on, however, after getting to know Chess, he learned that Chess was a good man. Several years later Chess was asked to do the man's eulogy (P. 153).

Lest anyone conclude that Chess was a "yes man" or somehow too weak to stand up to the arduous work involved in representing clients as a civil rights lawyer during the height of the civil rights struggle, his strength of character was unquestionable. No one ever accused Chess of being weak. Strength of character includes the ability to walk away from a fight if necessary. However, Chess proved he was only human on one occasion as exemplified by the following incident that occurred at the High Point, NC, courthouse in the early 1960s, a rare occasion in Chess's professional life where his always calm-and-collected demeanor was challenged. Chess described the incident:

> A number of attorneys, including myself, had "shucks" (court files) in our hands waiting in line to discuss dispositions with the prosecutor. All of a sudden, the prosecutor reached up from his seat and snatched the shuck from my hand. I immediately reached over and pulled him up from his seat, cocked my fist and looked him in the eye and told him, "If you ever snatch anything from me again, I'll crack your jaw." (P. 61)

Judicial Wisdom

Chess says, "My agenda is to be open and do justice in every case that comes before me as God and conscience show me what justice is in that matter. That's all I take with me on every case." As a private lawyer and then judge, he advocated for "justice for all people, regardless of race, societal background, or education. I think of myself as just a man and now a judge. I'm going to try to do justice in every case that comes before me." Chess saw the absolute need to treat all who came before him with respect. He said, "The court must always stand high in the opinion of the populace. The governmental system must show respect for every citizen. If it can do that, it can survive" (PP. 105, 115).

Judge Chess understood the great responsibility of being a trial judge—that the role of judge is, in some respects, like that of being an umpire. However, Chess's judicial philosophy was much more than one that called upon him to call balls and strikes. He said,

> Judges have a greater responsibility than to just sit there and rule; judges have a responsibility to make sure that defendants make an informed decision; to make sure that it is not the time constraints

> of counsel that are the basis of the defendant's decision. Defendants are at a disadvantage of expressing themselves. They have had conferences with their counsel; they don't want to anger their counsel. The defendants know they are at the hands of their counsel and that after the judge is gone, they are in the hands of their counsel. As judge, I had a responsibility to take that weight off of the defendant. He says, "I'm not there to protect lawyers. I have a duty to see to it that the atmosphere is proper, that the conditions are appropriate for a defendant getting a fair and impartial trial; if the judge fails in this regard, then he or she has engaged in a major failing. My concern was to pierce the veil and see that the conditions exist to best ensure those concerns." (P. 111)

In December 1971, shortly after taking the oath of office, Judge Chess was interviewed by a newspaper reporter. In response to the reporter's questions, Chess acknowledged that many across our nation were questioning the legitimacy and fairness of our justice system, and whether it could be saved. His solution, that of placing competent people in all levels of our courts who have the requisite integrity and knowledge, no doubt would go a long way toward mending our justice system today. Chess said,

> "There is nothing wrong with the system.... What the courts need," says Judge Chess, is a better implementation, more dedicated people who will inspire confidence and "devotion to try to effect a good system." Judge Chess said, "It seems we are not meeting the great needs of the people." He points to what he describes as "dissatisfaction among various age and racial groups." Young people are asking questions like, "Can it endure?" "Does it meet the needs?" The judge says young people are accusing the establishment of hypocrisy and notes that "we do not live up to the principles of our government." "They're asking questions about whether or not government is meeting its responsibilities.... My feeling is that we have got to have people in the system who can inspire confidence in the system from the magistrate's level to the Supreme Court." (P. 104)

Chess has commented on another huge problem facing the courts today: the very large number of pro se litigants who seek redress in the state and federal courts.

> The United States system of justice, whether involving criminal or civil cases, is an adversary system. There is no exception to this rule. Therefore, many cases are won or lost because of the skill or lack of skill of the lawyer representing the parties. Even worse are situations where one side is represented by one or more skilled lawyers, and the other side has to rely solely upon laymen's knowledge in representing themselves in the pursuit of justice. Chess saw many such cases as a Superior Court judge and as an Administrative Law judge. (P. 123)

Related to the pro se litigant problem facing our courts, Chess also pondered a question that has vexed many judges that care about fairness throughout time. To what extent should a judge seek to level the playing field, and thereby promote justice, which is the ultimate end of all civil disputes or criminal prosecutions? Chess resolved the issue by stepping into the fray when necessary to promote justice.

> "How does the judge try to see that a fair and just trial takes place without tipping the scale to one side or the other?" Chess believes strongly that indeed it is the job of the trial judge to see that the game is played fairly without having the tremendous power of "undue influence" affect the outcome of the case. While a judge is an independent arbiter, Chess also believes strongly that the judge's role includes a duty of making sure that there is not a miscarriage of justice. The judge plays a unique role. He or she is in a tenuous position. There is no need for a judge to enter the fray when the adversaries are equal. Equal adversaries can take care of themselves. If the judge sees that an injustice is taking place, then the judge should step in and make sure that injustice doesn't continue. As soon as the problem is corrected, then the judge should step back and allow the litigants to continue. (PP. 123–24)

Judge Chess was not the kind of judge that would never admit error. Neither was he ever offended or opposed if the losing party gave notice of appeal in open court as some other judges seemed to disdain.

> He agrees that he and all judges have failures and, like the most respected judges in American history, commit error from time to time. Judge Chess, like most judges who have tried many cases over

> their career, has had the court of higher authority reverse his decision. However, Chess is confident that, with regards to all the failures or mistakes he made as judge, he tried to admit them and go about correcting any error in judgment immediately. Chess says, "I tried to proceed honestly and honorably in all of my doings. Whatever I've done did not vary far from who I am. My idea was that I wanted to be accurate and if I was in error in some way, I wanted to be corrected. I welcomed being corrected because in my error I might do injustice in some way. I believe that is why the system is tiered so you will have many eyes. I never made a lawyer think I would be offended by any appeal. Any injustice done would not be intended. I tried to get for an individual the fairest trial possible. I wanted any error in the facts or law to be brought up and corrected so that the individual would get the fair trial to which he is entitled. I have no ego that transcends that responsibility. My responsibility is to ensure an individual a fair and impartial trial. I have no personal interest in the case. I'd rejoice if someone points out something that was contrary to a fair and impartial trial. To do otherwise would be subverting rather than upholding those principles." (PP. 111–12)

Chess also has offered advice to the highest courts in the land. He spoke to the division and lack of camaraderie that affects not only our society in general, but our court system as well. The division and lack of respect for those even on the same court is evident in the dissenting opinions of various courts.

> There is a great need for the court's decisions to become final, not in the sense that a ruling has been handed down by the court, but that it has been handed down in a manner that most observers believe that the court's decision is a fair and just result. If there is no finality, then friction continues. This continued friction will be like a scab on the skin of our system of justice. It will continue to fester. (P. 122)

In our still deeply divided America and world today, we can learn so much from Judge Chess. In a time of many voices who are the purveyors of hate and further division in our society, we need to hear more from voices of reason and moderation. For over a half-century, Chess was and remains such a voice. Lawyers and others can learn from his example that you can be an advocate and agent for change designed to make this world a better place. Chess proved, like others among his contemporaries, that you can be an agitator and go against the system in an attempt to seek fairness and justice, and still gain the respect of others, including your adversaries. A man of integrity, Chess has carried himself in a dignified manner in and out of the courtroom, which allowed him to stand out among lawyers and judges of not only his time but also the generations before him and after his retirement. His rise to prominence gives hope to those among us who have lost hope and been denied respect because of poverty, race, or other circumstances beyond our control.

Chess is a shining example to others of how, with hard work and perseverance, one can rise above his or her circumstances in life. Indeed, Chess is "among those few men in society" who possessed an abundance of the "requisite skill in the law, integrity and knowledge" that Alexander Hamilton wrote about centuries ago as being integral to qualifying for the station of a judge. Because of this, Chess commanded the respect of all who appeared before or got to know him. Perhaps retired judge W. Douglas Albright of North Carolina's 18th Judicial District Superior Court said it best: "We are all better off as a result of Sammie Chess Jr., being among us.... When his time comes, he will have left this world a better place" (P. 158).

Comments on *The Making and Measure of a Judge: Biography of The Honorable Sammie Chess Jr.*

Joe: A good author takes the reader on a journey. Sometimes the journey is smooth and safe for the reader, sometimes the journey allows the reader to peer into an abyss. Joe has written a book which, for me, fulfills both. The book celebrates the safety of law and order; however, it does not shy away from the chaos of the abyss called prejudice. This book, *The Making and Measure of a Judge: Biography of the Honorable Sammie Chess Jr.*, allowed me to go on a great journey. In the farms and fields of South Carolina in the 1930s, to Harlem in the early 1940s and then to North Carolina later in the 1940s, young Sammie Chess came of age. Encouraged by educators not to give up on education, the future judge studied and worked in High Point and Durham, NC. During the turmoil of the 1960s Sammie Chess was an African American lawyer in High Point, NC, who made a commitment to "work within the system to make life better for all Americans." About the time we were all thinking about our last Christmas in high school, Sammie Chess Jr. became a superior court judge, the first African American superior court judge in North Carolina. Joe has given the reader the opportunity to understand how Sammie Chess Jr. gave him (and many others) an example of a life lived to the fullest. With the strength of strong, proud parents running through his veins, Judge Chess overcame prejudice with faith and courage. I recommend, to all my friends in the MM Class of 1972, that you take this journey with Joe ... the journey of getting to know Joe's mentor. As I read this book I wondered, *How long did it take Joe to write this?* Then I realized a lifetime. —Gloria Horne

---

Joe, I have finished reading your book, *The Making and Measure of a Judge,* and I wanted to let you know how much I appreciated the fine work you did on this book. Biography has long since been one of my favorite literary genres, and I was very pleased with this particular example of such.

One of the great needs that I have as a prayer minister is to gain understanding in the areas of human brokenness and suffering. I am especially interested in gaining insight into the qualities and conditions that best allow those subjected to gross, systematic injustice to cope with and even flourish in such circumstances.

While reading the story of Judge Sammie Chess Jr. I had two pressing questions in mind:

1. What did this man possess and utilize that allowed him to make such a drastic transition from a position of abject poverty to one of highly significant social power?

2. What effect did such a dramatic change in life circumstances have on his personal outlook on life?

As to the first question, I was pleased to see that along with the usual touted methods of education, hard work, and perseverance, Judge Chess gives a great deal of credit to the role that faith played in his life. I got the impression that, through all of the adversity he had to endure in pursuit of his goals, his true ambition was to respond in humility and service to a calling from something he deemed far greater than himself.

This brings me to my second question. I did not get the slightest hint from the book that Judge Chess ever allowed his success to sway him to use his acquired power for bitter or vengeful purposes. It appeared to me that Judge Chess's outlook on life remained one of deep personal conviction to use his life in service to others.

As I was progressing through the book, I began to marvel at the notion that one who had to struggle so fiercely against a prejudiced and unjust system could then, after acquiring a position of power and influence in that system, turn around and commit himself so ardently to being fair and impartial in dispensing his duty.

Being personally convinced that such an achievement does not happen by accident, I wondered if you had come to a similar conclusion and would offer some insight as to what motivated the Hon. Sammie Chess Jr. to consciously pursue such a noble course.

Thus, I was greatly pleased to find on page 152 that you had done exactly that. "You treat people the way you want to be treated." Sounds like the Golden Rule to me.

Frankly, I find it truly inspirational to see that one man's remarkable submission to a simple assertion of fundamental truth could produce such abundant blessing to those whose lives he touched.

Well done, my friend, Michael Lilly

Joe, It is Sunday afternoon and Wrightsville Beach is full of people, some still looking to park, some looking to swim and others just wandering around, happy to be here. And I have just finished the Chess biography. What a magnificent person, jurist and lawyer. With this biography, you have touched many emotions: extreme sadness, profound respect and admiration, happiness and love. I have felt each. Strongly. And also felt regret, not only for the indignities and deprivations imposed upon a large segment of our society, but—on a personal note—because I have spent years not being acquainted with Judge Chess and not having shared in his friendship and wisdom. I do hope, even at this late date, you will help me share some of that friendship and wisdom by arranging our taking Judge Chess to lunch when you come to Greensboro. As complete as your history was, you have made me want to know him even better. Thanks for giving me the opportunity to read this splendid biography. I've enjoyed it so much, I'm sorry I've finished. Have a good week. I plan on being back July 5th. —Woody Tilley

---

Date: January 11, 2021 at 5:42:52 AM EST
Subject: your dad's book
Hi Briana, Hope you've had a restful weekend. My recovery strategy from the horrors of last week was to dive into your dad's book, which I had skimmed but until this weekend had not read all the way through. The back cover said Judge Chess was one of the wisest men, so that seemed like just what the doctor ordered for me. There were many passages I liked and found eerily relevant to this very moment, and even provocative in their own way: "So I had been wondering to myself how Judge Chess could become a fair and impartial judge toward the majority race as he carried all of that history and baggage of resentment and perhaps anger for what had been done to his people in America for centuries." "You treat people the way you want to be treated, not the way you are treated. I didn't let them set my standards. If a Klan member can bring you to his level, then you are not well rooted"—Judge Chess responding to your dad. "Therein lies the remedy to much of the racial and other divisions that dominate American society today: the failure of people of different racial or ethnic backgrounds to get to know one another." Please thank your dad for me and tell him that I found his insights timely and timeless. How are you doing? —Billy Shore

The Making and Measure of a Judge: Biography of the Honorable Sammie Chess Jr.

Dispensing Justice While Offering Hope: United States Magistrate Judge Joe L. Webster

Pedra D. Lee, Law Clerk to the Honorable Joe L. Webster

THE MIDDLE GROUND VOLUME 4, ISSUE 2, OCTOBER 2014
(COURTESY OF MIDDLE DISTRICT OF NORTH CAROLINA FEDERAL BAR ASSOCIATION)

"Do you know what *injustice* is when you see it?" That was the final question presented to me while interviewing for a law clerk position with the Honorable Joe L. Webster, United States Magistrate Judge for the Middle District of North Carolina. I had no problems answering the question because I had experienced and witnessed injustice in my short life. What puzzled my mind, however, was Judge Webster's purpose and intent for asking the question. Nearly two years later, I now understand that the thought of injustice was not just a question, but also a teaching point. On that day Judge Webster wanted to convey a simple message that I and others in the legal profession have a responsibility and obligation to promote justice while offering hope to those in need.

Judge Webster's compassion for people and justice originated in the Goodwill community near the small town of Madison, North Carolina, where he was raised by his parents, the late James and Bettie Webster. He was the fourth of eight children and lived in a community where most people lacked education and opportunities beyond their reality. Like many others, Judge Webster's family did not have an indoor bathroom or running water for most his childhood. Although such necessities were absent, Judge Webster was always surrounded by positive role models, people who worked, persevered, and exercised their faith in God to get through the challenges of life. His parents and others constantly encouraged him to work hard and give his best in everything he set his mind to do.

It's no surprise that Judge Webster desired to return to his hometown one year after graduating from Howard University School of Law in 1979. It was there where he saw a need to help people in a community that he cherished, and the only place he ever called "home." Sadly, it was also the place where he once saw injustice while trying to hang his own shingle in Rockingham County. In 1984, four years after becoming the first African American attorney in the history of Madison, Judge Webster had to file a lawsuit against the town of Madison. The town's Board of Adjustment voted to block him from opening his law office on a street where other businesses had already been established, including another law office, dental office, and real estate agent's office. This uphill battle did not deter him from his dream of helping those who needed his services. Instead, he leaned on the morals and values embedded in him by his parents and overcame the obstacles before him. In 1985, his efforts to serve others in his hometown were recognized by the North Carolina Bar Association when he received the Pro Bono Service Award, one of his greatest honors in life thus far.

Judge Webster has embraced many roles on his journey to the federal bench, serving as General Counsel for the Mid-Eastern Athletic Conference, Associate Attorney General for the North Carolina Department of Justice, Deputy Director for Legal Services of North Carolina, Town Attorney, Adjunct Professor of Law at Campbell University School of Law, and Administrative Law Judge with the Office of Administrative Hearings for the State of North Carolina. He has also worked hard to be the best husband to Diane Ramsey Webster for nearly thirty-five years. Together they have three successful children. Despite his opportunities for advancement in his legal career, Judge Webster never lost sight of his reasons for choosing the legal profession: serving the poor and doing everything possible to promote a fair justice system.

Although he now sits on the federal bench and is no longer engaged in the practice of law, Judge Webster still knows what injustice is, and remains compassionate about his obligation to dispense justice while offering hope to the community. In one of his most recent projects, Judge Webster opened the doors of his courtroom to youth in Durham County Schools through a program he started called CourtCares. Students are introduced to the federal court system, encouraged to stay on the right side of the law and be productive citizens, and challenged to maintain respect for adults as well as their peers.

Whether it's inspiring youth through CourtCares or addressing defendants in criminal proceedings, Judge Webster continues to make an impact on the lives of people by simply being who God called him to be. As a result of my time with Judge Webster, I have a better understanding of injustice, and more importantly, I accept my responsibility to promote justice while offering hope to those in need.

COURTESY OF EFREN RENTERIA

CourtCares Program in Judge Webster's court was launched in April 2013 for Durham, NC, middle school students to introduce them to the federal courts; to encourage them to stay on the right side of the law; to abstain from alcohol and drug abuse, gun violence, and bullying; and to be good citizens in general. COURTESY OF EFREN RENTERIA

FRIDAY, SEPTEMBER 18, 2015
PAGE A4 THE HERALD-SUN | DURHAM, NORTH CAROI

Students get close look at court, cell

BY KEITH UPCHURCH
KUPCHURCH@HERALDSUN.COM;
919-419-6612

The Herald-Sun | Keith Upchurch

Mayor Bill Bell talks to Carrington Middle School students Thursday at the federal courtroom in the U.S. Post Office.

DURHAM — Students from Carrington Middle School got a front-row seat in a federal courtroom Thursday and sage advice from Durham's mayor about how to stay on the right side of the law.

The program, called CourtCares, began in April 2013 to reach out to students in Durham Public Schools. It was launched by Judge Joe L. Webster and staff of the U.S. District Court for the Middle District of North Carolina in Durham.

"We want you to know that you're special and that your lives matter," Webster told the students. "Whatever happens to you in life, we want you to never give up. Keep striving to be the best that you can."

Mayor Bill Bell said people's choices determine their futures.

"Who you choose as your friends is very important," Bell said. "How you spend your time is very important and who you spend it with."

Bell, 74, said his life as a child in Winston-Salem was much different than youngsters experience today. He said he had no car or social media and his choices were limited.

The mayor emphasized the importance of respecting oneself and others, including teachers.

Bell also said knowledge is one thing nobody can steal from you.

"They can take away your clothes and money, but they can't take what you know once it's up here (in your head)."

Courtesy was another topic Bell discussed.

"Saying 'yes sir', 'yes ma'am', 'please' and 'thank you' are simple words, right? But you will be amazed what it can do for you," he said. "Think about your manners when trying to get something; it makes a big difference."

Bell alluded to violent crime in Durham and said many offenses are committed by those between the ages of 16 and 30. He said that when he first became mayor 14 years ago, students who are 16 today were only 2.

"If someone had wrapped their arm around that person and helped them make the right choices, they might not be in the situation they're now in," Bell said. "You need to ask yourself: 'Am I going to be in a courtroom when I'm 16?'"

During a question-and-answer session, a student asked Bell if he favored the death penalty.

Bell paused for a few seconds, then said "No."

"It's easy for me to say that, but I know if somebody close to me had committed a crime that warranted the death penalty, I'd have to think over and over about that. But no, I don't believe in the death penalty. I don't think it serves as a deterrent."

"We want you to know that you're special and that your lives matter. Whatever happens to you in life, we want you to never give up. Keep striving to be the best that you can."

— Joe L. Webster
Durham Judge

After Bell's comments, students participated in a mock trial of a man accused of stealing a tax refund check from a woman's mailbox.

The jury deadlocked, with the vote split about 50-50.

Students voting to convict said the prosecution had proved its case, while others said the case was full of holes.

Perhaps the most eye-opening experience was when students got a look at the tiny holding cell for defendants. No one wanted to stay inside more than a few seconds, and some refused to go in at all.

"Man!" said a student. "That place is small!"

The Stigma of Mental Illness

COURTESY OF NORTH CAROLINA LAWYER, NC BAR ASSOCIATION

NOVEMBER 2013

Mental illness, especially anxiety and depression, is on the rise among adolescents and young adults in America. Like many other illnesses affecting the physical body, mental illness's effect on poor and minority communities is huge, and its cost to society in general is incalculable. Many families, irrespective of race, ethnicity, or nationality, are affected by the painful and debilitating illness of depression and other forms of mental illness. These illnesses often go untreated because of the age-old stigma that accompanies the diagnosis.

Several years ago, I met a young man who told me of his struggle with depression. He told me he had enrolled in college and, without warning, became very depressed. He did not know what was happening to him. He stopped associating with his classmates and stopped going to class. There were days when he could not even get out of bed. His mother took him to the doctor, but when the doctor diagnosed him as suffering from severe depression requiring immediate in-patient treatment, the mother refused to admit him. Being a person of faith, she thought she could help him get well.

The stresses of the legal profession most likely affect its members disproportionately. In recent years around the state there have been several suicides among members of our profession. Each member of the legal bar should do his or her part to get rid of the mental health stigma. On December 20 and 27, 2008, I accompanied several others, including psychologist Dr. Alfiee M. Breland-Noble, to the Shaw University campus to appear on the radio talk show *Traces of Faces & Places*. We discussed adolescent mental health, depression awareness, and suicide prevention. I had the opportunity to describe the many ways in which I see the manifestation of poor, unmanaged mental health in the juvenile justice and adult court systems as well as the stigma associated with mental health within diverse communities. Another guest, whose teenage son had committed suicide, emphasized the significance of parents having the ability to distinguish between "typical teenage behavior" and clinically significant depression. Dr. Breland-Noble mentioned on the program that some of her own patients had discussed that their reluctance to seek treatment was because they felt that as a black male in America, they already had enough strikes against them. "Being black and crazy" would make life even more difficult for them, they remarked.

Indeed, young black males, who disproportionately make up those appearing in state and federal criminal courts, are particularly affected by undiagnosed mental illness.

Often, they end up being the victim of our court system, which most often is ill equipped to address the emotional and behavioral problems that lead many juvenile offenders into the judicial system.

As contributing author of the article titled "Juvenile Mental Health Courts for Adjudicated Youth: Role Implications for Child and Adolescent Psychiatric Mental Health Nurses," in a 2011 publication of the *Journal of Child and Adolescent Psychiatric Nursing,* I wrote, "The court system, like society in general, continues to ignore the fact that many of our juveniles come from broken homes, broken dreams, and broken minds brought on by mental illnesses that they cannot control. Society, including the judicial system, has done far too little to rid society of the stigma that goes along with mental illness.

A recent *Washington Post* article (July 9, 2013) reported that therapists from some major metropolitan areas have seen an increase in the number of African Americans seeking help for mental illness. The North Carolina Bar Association's BarCARES program, a confidential short-term intervention program that provides cost-free services to members of participating bar groups and their families, has also seen increasing numbers of those seeking professional care.

We need more members of the bar and others to publicly tell of their struggles with mental illness and how they have overcome and been successful in spite of their mental illness. It is not difficult to find well-known examples. Thank you, television reporter Mike Wallace, for telling your story. Thank you, Mary J. Blige, Janet Jackson, Drew Carey, Halle Berry, Ellen DeGeneres, and others who have publicly talked about their own experiences with depression or other mental illness. Perhaps unknowingly, you have contributed to the commendable goal of ridding society of the stigma related to mental illness. To those who suffer on a daily or periodic basis with depression or other mental illnesses, be encouraged and know that you are not alone, and just as importantly, there is treatment that will help you.

"Joe L. Webster's return home to make a difference."

BY DAN HURLEY

YOUNG LAWYERS DIVISION PRO BONO, FALL 1985, P. 26

PERMISSION GRANTED BY AMERICAN BAR ASSOCIATION

Shortly before Joe L. Webster graduated from Howard University Law School in May of 1979, a professor at the Howard University School of Religion asked him what he wanted to do with his degree. Webster said he would go back to his poor, rural hometown of Madison, North Carolina, to become the first black lawyer the county of Rockingham had ever had. The professor said to him, "If you're not going to go down there and make a difference, you might as well stay up here."

"I've always remembered that," says Webster, who has since won the North Carolina Bar Association 1985 Pro Bono Service Award for his work in Rockingham County. "Certainly, there would have been far fewer obstacles working for the government or a large firm in Washington. But I knew I would have to come down here and speak up for those who were unable to speak up for themselves."

Pro Bono Profile
Young Lawyers Division
American Bar Association
Barrister, fall 1985

COURTESY OF THE AMERICAN BAR ASSOCIATION

In making the award to Webster, the NCBA noted that "Mr. Webster has devoted hundreds of hours to advising and representing poor persons in Rockingham County who cannot afford to pay for his services. As the only attorney in Rockingham County who participates in the organized pro bono program, Mr. Webster's assistance is particularly important since the closest legal services office is 40 miles away. "Since he signed up at the program's inception in November 1982," the award citation said, "Webster has done an outstanding job of handling more than 60 pro bono cases [and] 30 reduced fee compensated cases through the private bar involvement program at Central Carolina Legal Services. Whenever necessary, he has willingly continued to represent these clients, at no further fee, even after the CCLS funds to compensate him have been exhausted."

Webster is just part of the success story that the NCBA has had since starting its Pro Bono Project. When the program began three years ago, only two counties in North Carolina were served by bar association–supported pro bono programs. Today, such programs serve poor persons in 16 counties. Webster began his work in legal services immediately upon graduating from Howard, when he received the Reginald Heber Smith Fellowship to spend one year at the Legal Services Center of Southern Piedmont, in North Carolina. "A number of my classmates chose to work with large firms and corporations," he recalls. "But I never lost the desire and dream to go back home. To be honest with you, I felt that this was what God wanted me to do."

After his year with Southern Piedmont, Webster returned to his hometown and set up a private practice. Fortunately, he found a number of clients who were willing and able to pay his fees, "I'm not saying I don't like to make money," says Webster, "I'm in this to make a living. But I live in a county that is primarily made up of textile workers. For the last few years, the industry has really been suffering. So, if I turned down everyone who couldn't afford to pay attorney's fees, I would have very few clients."

Webster is the first to admit that working with poor people can often involve unique problems. He has represented many clients who did not have a car and lived 17 miles away. He says, "I've even made house calls."

Why does he do it? "My parents raised me, my five brothers and my two sisters, to help each other," he says. "You shared what you raised in the garden, and you shared other things. My parents helped our neighbors, and they helped us. So, it's just part of my makeup to help people."

At times his policy of never turning down a request for pro bono services can be tiring. "No matter how many times you help one person," he says, "there are that many more out there who still need help. Sometimes I get discouraged. But I take a long weekend off and that allows me to come back and keep going on. I'm not burned out. I feel you need to give it one hundred percent while you're at it."

Webster also finds time for his wife, Diane Ramsey Webster, who works as his assistant, and their three-year-old daughter, Brianne Monet. In addition, Webster is a member and trustee of the Goodwill Baptist Church and serves on the board of three local civic groups. "Once you get involved with one organization," he says, "everyone wants you to work for their group, too."

But after making his house calls, sitting at meetings, spending time with his family and working late into the night, Webster still wakes up each morning eager to start it all over again. "This is the first job I have ever liked going in to work every day," he says.

And maybe that is payment enough for his pro bono service.

Interview of Joe L. Webster

John Gehring, 2014 North Carolina State Bar Journal

COURTESY OF THE NC STATE BAR

> *He hath* shewed *thee,* O *man,* what is good; and what *doth the* Lord require of *thee,* but *to do* justly, and to love mercy *and* to walk humbly with *thy* God? (MICAH 6:8, KJV)

Joe L. Webster and I have been friends for most of our adult lives, having met early in our careers as "country lawyers"—one from Madison and one from Walnut Cove. I started my practice in Walnut Cove as a "not from around here" young lawyer carrying a strange last name, wearing wire-rimmed glasses and a bow tie–something then unheard of in Stokes County. Joe grew up in Madison, was graduated Phi Beta Kappa from Howard University, and was one of the first African American lawyers in Rockingham County, and the very first in his hometown of Madison—something also unheard of in our area. Needless to say, we were not welcomed by some of the unenlightened segments of our communities.

Joe left Madison pursuing an uncertain horizon, and I remained in Walnut Cove as a country lawyer. The certainty of his horizon soon became crystal clear as milestone after milestone was reached. A few of these milestones were: as a sole practitioner, receiving the Pro Bono Lawyer of the Year award by the North Carolina Bar Association; serving as chairman of the North Carolina Board of Law Examiners; being appointed as a North Carolina administrative law judge; and now serving as a federal magistrate judge for the Middle District of North Carolina. All of these milestones were reached by his calm purpose to help change things from the inside, fully realizing that his goal was service to mankind!

I cannot help but think that the above-quoted verse from the Book of Micah epitomizes the life of Joe L. Webster. And thus, my interview with him:

John Gehring (JG): Your journey from country lawyer to magistrate judge has been long and successful. Please tell me about your childhood in Rockingham County and the influences which guided you.

Judge Webster: While I did not know it at the time, growing up in rural Rockingham County, North Carolina, was the perfect place for me. There were plenty of role models there, models of hard work and persevering spirits, and while my father only went to the fourth grade and my mother, the tenth, like so many of their peers, they overcame the lack of education and other obstacles with hard work and faith in God. These two lessons alone have carried me farther than I ever dreamed was possible. Other than my parents, many uncles, aunts, and teachers in my formative years lived exemplary lives and encouraged me to become all that I could become.

Looking back on my life as a youth brings back mostly fond memories. I have fond memories of my five brothers and two sisters and many cousins growing up in the same community. I was the fourth-born child to my parents. My parents had five boys before having their first girl. There were many happy times around the kitchen table. Early in my youth I recall having to stand up at the table to eat because there were not enough chairs. During the first eleven years of my life, my family didn't have an indoor bathroom or running water. We never complained about that because we didn't know anyone else that had such luxuries. Shortly after I turned twelve, my parents bought a farm, and we had our first indoor bathroom. With indoor plumbing came hard work in the scorching-hot sun of rural Rockingham County. Occasionally I had allergic reactions to the chemical contents on or in the tobacco. As I left the field too sick to continue, over forty years later I can still hear my father's voice, "Boy, you better go on to school." He saw that I was not cut out to be a farmer.

Also, when I was twelve years old, I remember my sixth-grade teacher, Mrs. Searcy, at the all-black Charles R. Drew High School (grades 1–12) passing out to each student papers that I now know to have been consent documents which, if signed, would allow the students to attend "the white school" as we called it then, under "freedom of choice." To this day I still do not know why I was one of the students who chose to help integrate the Madison-Mayodan Schools. Other than me telling my parents that is what I was going to do, I don't remember any advice my parents gave me. Looking back, I believe that they trusted my judgment even as a twelve-year-old child. The first day of school in my first integrated environment was uneventful, although I remember well waiting anxiously at the bus stop and taking my first steps onto the bus. It seems I recall that all eyes were on me and every step I made until I found an empty seat. Only once under freedom of choice did I experience any intimidation or violence, and I could not know then whether a few remarks made toward me as I was alone in the school's bathroom were because of my race. Two years after my freedom-of-choice experience, mandatory integration took place in my school district. My greatest highlights of my high school years involved my being a starting guard on a basketball team that went 27-0 before losing our first game in the semifinals of the 3A State Tournament. I recall quitting the team once or twice during my junior year. I was not mature enough to handle being relegated to being a bench player, so I quit the team, but later rejoined. I have never been a quitter since then. This too helped me understand the importance of team play and perseverance especially during adversity.

JG: Judge Frank Freeman of the old Seventeenth Judicial Bar always let us know when we argued cases before him that there was both the letter of the law and the spirit of the law to be considered. We have had countless discussions about these concepts. Have your thoughts about these ideals changed as you have worked as a defense attorney and then pro bono advocate to law examiner and then to your judicial positions? Can both of these visions of the law work side by side in the federal district court?

Judge Webster: It has been written that the letter of the law versus the spirit of the law is an idiomatic antithesis, which suggests that in interpreting a law, there are two choices; one of interpreting the law literally, or the other, focusing on the intent of the law. I do not believe that the letter and spirit of the law have to be viewed only as the antithesis or polar opposites of one another, although these concepts have been viewed as opposites for two thousand years. Even some of Shakespeare's plays incorporated these two concepts. I believe both of these views of the law not only can but must work side by side in the federal district court and other courts. During my career as advocate and judge my ideas about the concepts of letter and spirit of the law have not changed, even though my role as advocate and impartial judge are different. Late last year I took an oath that I would "administer justice without respect to persons and do equal right to the poor and to the rich, and that I will faithfully and impartially discharge and perform all the duties incumbent upon me as a United States magistrate judge under the Constitution and laws of the United States." My oath requires me to administer justice in a manner that all will understand and consider as being fair and just.

JG: At what point in your life were you called to the ministry and when were you ordained? How has being a minister impacted your life? Your commitment to helping young people is an example of your faith in action. The humming of gospel hymns while at work may be another example! Will you be able to continue your work with young people while also serving as a magistrate judge?

Judge Webster: I was called into the ministry in the summer of 1998 and ordained in 2001. My ministry's impact on me is incalculable at this time, yet I know that my life and that of my family have been impacted. Long before I accepted my ministry call, I sought very hard to avoid even the appearance of impropriety, an imperative thrust upon not only ministers but lawyers as well. So, in many ways, my life has not changed considerably. I have also subscribed to the view that "to whom much is given, much is required." I do know that there is a constant pull on my life to do good and that my life is not my own. I know that I must do all I can to help others. Yes, our youth and what they are experiencing right now stays on my mind. It seems that our youth today, especially our African American males, are having more difficulty than perhaps my ancestors did when, in comparison, they had so little in material things. For example, on April 3, 2013, I presided over initial appearances and detention hearings in Greensboro. I conducted fourteen hearings. All were African American men except one. Most were in their twenties or thirties, and many of the cases involved possession of firearms by felons and illegal drug offenses. Most were not employed or were underemployed. All were single and many had fathered children yet had little or no means to support them. Most had not graduated from high school. As I sat there listening attentively, I could not help but wondering, *How did we get here and what can be done about it?* This is the one of the most critical problems facing America today!

I find it ironic that you ask about whether I can continue to reach out to our youth. If anything, I believe the blessing of becoming a United States magistrate judge means that I must do even more to help our youth. On April 11, 2013, my chambers in Durham will begin a monthly dialogue with students coming to our court and chambers from the middle schools of Durham. I have named it "CourtCares." I sense that in society—and especially the populations that the courts serve—most do not believe that the courts or anyone else cares about them, which is far from the case. Maybe by telling them my story and the story of other guest speakers who have fallen and found the strength to rise up again and become successful, the students might be able to overcome the obstacles facing them. We also plan to conduct a brief mock criminal trial with myself and my law clerks and staff as judge, prosecutor, and defense counsel. So, yes, I plan to continue my outreach to our youth and pray that at least some will be affected by what we say and do.

JG: Congratulations on your becoming a United States magistrate judge! What are your duties and what type cases do you hear? Is your court the place where Blue Ridge Parkway speeding tickets are heard? Have you enjoyed your new work thus far?

Judge Webster: Thank you for your congratulations and well wishes. I have many duties as a United States magistrate judge. In criminal cases, I preside at initial appearances and detention hearings. Those arrested for a federal crime must be brought before a magistrate without unnecessary delay. The federal "detention hearing" is analogous to the state court bond hearing. Risk of flight and danger to the community are the two main issues in each detention hearing. Magistrate judges also issue search and arrest warrants pursuant to motions filed by US officials, including members of the US Attorney's office. And yes, getting a speeding ticket or committing other "petty offenses" in national parks, in the VA hospital, or on other federally owned land could land you in front of a magistrate judge. However, the greatest majority of my time is spent on civil court filings. The Article III Judges refer civil cases to magistrate judges to research and write memorandum opinions and recommendations. Also, if all parties consent, magistrate judges can handle all aspects of the civil case assigned to them, including presiding in trial of the case. And recently I fulfilled the duty of presiding at a naturalization service and administered the oath to sixty-one of my fellow Americans from thirty-six foreign countries. It was a joyous occasion, and I must say that tears welled up in my eyes as the preliminary video was being shown. All my fellow citizens came up to take their picture with me, and one elderly lady from the Congo on the continent of Africa told me it took her fourteen years to become a citizen. I'm entering my fifth month of work as a magistrate judge, and I absolutely love it! I know that I still have much to learn and hopefully much to give.

JG: Do you have any further comments for the lawyers of the State of North Carolina?

Judge Webster: It is my opinion that members of our honored profession have not been good stewards of our profession. Unless we figure out a way to make our services more accessible to the poor, we will lose the battle to save our profession. This burden is on our backs, and it is ours alone to bear. Clearly many have done their part, but most have not. We will either continue to look the other way and accept the unleveled playing field presented by pro se litigants, or as a profession make some critical decisions about doing all we can to promote the fairest system of justice possible and to do equal right to the poor and to the rich as my own judicial oath dictates. This dilemma is the number-one problem facing America's system of justice today. I am confident that our profession has among its ranks scores of thousands of men and women of goodwill and knowledge who will undertake to solve this critical problem.

A Campaign for a Judgeship, 1994

While employed as the deputy director of Legal Services of North Carolina in Raleigh, I learned of a vacancy as a state district court judge for the district composed of Orange and Chatham Counties. I made up my mind that I would seek that position even after learning I would have to resign my position with Legal Services. There was in place at the time a federal statute mandating that no lawyer working with a Legal Services program could seek "partisan political office." I fit in that category as I would be running in the Democratic primary set for May 3, 1994. My wife could not believe that I would take such a chance and so she kept asking me was I sure that I had to resign to run for the judgeship? I had investigated this matter and decided to move forward with my decision. I had no idea how this would affect my family's financial position should I lose. I did not know just how badly this affected my wife. My thinking was that if I Jost the race, I could practice law as this was what I knew more about than anything else, having previously engaged in a solo practice in my hometown for over six years. I lost! Badly! I promised my wife that I would never run again, although years later I would ask the governor to appoint me to the North Carolina Court of Appeals, which would have required me to run a statewide race to retain the position a short while later. Thank God neither of the governors I asked to appoint me did so.

Joe's campaign for state District Court Judge
Orange and Chatham Counties, NC

There was nothing about running for elective office that I enjoyed. For one thing, at the time, I could not be involved with fundraising; I had to appoint a committee for those duties. On the other hand, I had all the responsibility if the committee violated any of the election laws. *How could this be?* I thought. Second, I didn't like campaigning. Every day I felt like I needed to be somewhere in the district, speaking to some group of individuals. Sometimes I'd ask my wife and three children to accompany me. One Saturday, after campaigning all day in Orange County attending "teas" (I recall such small group gatherings at churches and homes where tea and other soft drinks and appetizers were served), we attended our last event. Upon entering the basement of a home in Hillsborough, my four-year-old son vomited in the middle of the floor. This was a sign to me that he had enough of campaigning. I don't think my family ever accompanied me again to a campaign event.

On election night, I gathered with a few supporters where we listened to the radio and heard the precinct voting results come in. Shortly after the voting results began to come in, it was clear that I could not win. I was too far behind to make a comeback. I recall that I won only one precinct among the scores of precincts in Orange and Chatham Counties. It was one of the smallest precincts in Chatham County.

While losing was hurtful, I'm glad I took that chance. I felt that I had experienced something that I could pass on to other candidates in future campaigns. I imagine that making myself known throughout the district must have helped me when I hung my shingle to practice law in Chatham County some eight months after the election. Someone once said something to the effect that what doesn't break you makes you stronger. The most important thing I've learned with all my attempts to gain certain positions over four decades (most of them I did not obtain) is that I need to trust in God and be confident in the outcome. For my time is not God's time. His time (Kairos) is what I need to be praying for. So long as my steps are ordered by the Lord, everything will be all right. Eighteen years after the election in which I lost badly. God elevated me to the position of United States magistrate judge for the Middle District of North Carolina. I became the first African American to hold this position in the Middle District of North Carolina. I enjoy coming to work every day! To God be the glory!

Naturalization Ceremony

Durham, NC

JANUARY 26, 2018

Good morning. This is the beginning of the sixth year that I have had the privilege of presiding at these ceremonies to administer the oath of allegiance and to make some remarks to those gathered eager to become citizens of the United States.

To be given the opportunity to administer the oath to you is a great honor for me. With all of America's imperfections—including the great divisions that separate us by race, gender, economic status, political affiliation, even the death and destruction of gun violence and other problems of great magnitude—America is still a great country. Where else in the world might I, the son of a man who only went to the fourth grade in school, become a federal judge? This is still the land of opportunity, and those of you who have taken the oath today are truly blessed! I hope that you will always remember what a privilege it is to be a citizen in this land we call the United States of America. All Americans should examine the question of what this privilege of citizenship means. Some of us have taken the privilege for granted, but I hope that not one of you here will ever take it for granted. For if you do take this privilege for granted, you will lose your determination to keep on working hard to overcome the many obstacles that lie ahead—many of the same ones that brought you to this room today.

It also brings me great joy to stand before you and observe the beauty of what each of you individually and collectively bring to this room, this state, and this nation. You are all so beautiful to me!

Looking out over the audience is like looking out over a meadow on a warm, sunny spring day in North Carolina. It's like I'm looking at a meadow that contains many shades of many colors of flowers, all beautiful and full of life. There is strength in diversity and therefore there is strength in this room. Don't ever let anyone tell you differently; your presence makes America a better place. Why do I say that? That is so because each of you brings to the table your own cultures, traditions, faiths, gourmet foods, music, dress attire, accents, work ethics, and much, much more. I see the strength of diversity in my own family. All three of my adult children are married to those who were born or lived for much of their lives in countries outside of America. My children are married to spouses who were born in or lived much of their lives in Haiti, Trinidad, and Turkey.

This audience reminds me of my days as a student at Howard University in Washington, DC, way back in the 1970s. There were dozens of foreign countries represented on that campus, and I am a better person for having learned from many of them.

As a federal judge, and in my individual capacity, I hope that each of you will often reflect upon this day and what it means to you. I hope that you will not forget who you are and what you have to offer this country. I encourage you—no, I implore you—as you climb the ladder of success to reach back and help someone else up the ladder. I am a member of the Downtown Durham Rotary Club. Rotary, which has chapters all over the world, has a motto. "Service above Self." Placing others above ourselves should be the goal of all of us present here today.

Now, having been granted this great privilege of citizenship, there is one thing that I ask of you. I ask you to try to get to know one another and those who live in your communities. You here don't know one another, and I am not asking you to exchange telephone numbers, email addresses, or Facebook information. I guess what I'm saying to you is that longtime citizens of America need to learn from what you have brought to this country. It is so important for the American people to try to come together. As I said moments ago, divisions are evident. The media and politicians have characterized the individual states as red states and blue states. And in spite of those who are determined to divide the races, nationalities, and many wonderful cultures of this country, we are one nation under God, indivisible, with liberty and justice for all.

Speaking about the great division in our country at the present time, the president of the North Carolina Bar Association, Kearns Davis, in the February 2017 edition of the *North Carolina Lawyer* magazine, clearly and concisely sets forth one remedy that will help heal our nation.

> The ties that bind our society are strong, but they need mending. We need to listen to each other. We must listen critically, to be sure—bad ideas should be rejected, and abhorrent ideas exposed—but we must listen respectfully.[34]

Let me say a little more about placing others above self as being an attribute of good citizenship. Today I need for you to know and be clear in your minds that with citizenship comes responsibility. Citizenship and the freedom and opportunity that come with it are not a free lunch ticket; it is not a free ride. I heard someone say one time, "Don't you know that freedom is not free?" We have so many people who need your help: the poor, homeless, the disabled, and senior citizens who have only the nursing home attendants who care for them daily. Those of you who have lived in places where nursing homes are unheard of, where the elders are cared for in your homes, you can bring a

34 Quoted with permission of Kearns Davis.

Naturalization ceremony with visiting friend Rev. John Leason

Naturalization ceremony accompanied by career law clerk Pedra Lee, 2024

different perspective to the concept of what it means to love one another. Love is a universal language that all of us understand. I've found over the years that love even heals the wounds from the death of a loved one. Some of our longtime citizens by birthright who have been here in America for many generations—those who have forgotten that their ancestors also came from some other place, those who are able-bodied and supposedly of sound mind, some who have more money than they could ever spend—have somehow lost their way.

There is an African proverb that says, "If you want to go fast, go alone, but if you want to go far, go together."

I believe that there are many among you here today who know what it's still like to go together. I ask you to teach us, those who have lost our way, to teach us by example, how to go together. We can accomplish so much more as a nation if we go together.

I know that many of you have had to go through much difficulty and hardship to get here today.

The very first time I presided at one of these ceremonies, an elderly woman from the Congo on the continent of Africa told me it took her thirteen years to get to this ceremony. She is a great example of perseverance! So, I know that there has been much sacrifice along the way to citizenship. And you will now and in the future run into those who place obstacles in your way. Some will seem insurmountable. But don't give up, fellow Americans, no matter what happens to you. Never, ever give up! You might think you are all alone and no one else cares. But never give up! The courage, willpower, sense of purpose, and faith that got you here will keep you from failing. My mother used to tell me that where there is a will there is a way. I want to encourage each of you to continue to work hard and strive to do your best. If you do this, America will be so appreciative that today you all became fellow citizens of these United States of America. Congratulations, my fellow Americans, and I wish for each of you the very best in the days to come.

Remarks upon Taking the Oath of Office as US Magistrate Judge for the Middle District of North Carolina

DECEMBER 14, 2012

This afternoon I stand before you with a grateful and humble heart. I am grateful to God and all those whose shoulders I stand upon. It's great being here in the heart of Greensboro and the Middle District. Being here reminds me of the great trailblazers such as attorney J. Kenneth Lee, Judge Elreta Alexander, and Judge Sammie Chess in High Point and Judge Richard Erwin and attorney Annie Brown Kennedy in Winston Salem. Greensboro and the Middle District have been home to some of my greatest role models. You don't get any better than attorney Walter Brinkley over there in Lexington and Justice Henry Frye and attorney J. Donald Cowan here in Greensboro. They have been extraordinary examples of citizen lawyers and I'm very happy that they have been a part of my journey to the federal court.

In the United States District Court
For the Middle District of North Carolina
Greensboro, North Carolina

Special Session

Investiture of

Joe L. Webster

as

United States Magistrate Judge
For the Middle District of North Carolina

Friday, December 14, 2012
3:00 pm

The Honorable William L. Osteen, Jr.
Chief Judge, Presiding

The oath of office as US Magistrate Judge for the Middle District of North Carolina, December 14, 2012

There are a multitude of people to thank for lifting me up to a higher place. Many are here in the audience and many who are not here today. I am grateful to those who agreed to be a part of this special occasion, including my brother Reverend James A. Webster, who did the invocation and reminded us of what is important. I'm especially thankful to my friends Justice Patricia Timmons-Goodson and Judge Julian Mann, two persons who I deeply admire and respect for their devotion and contributions to the legal profession and state of North Carolina.

Today I am indebted to the distinguished judges of the Middle District who are sitting on the bench. They like many others in my profession over my thirty-three-year legal career took a chance on me. I am especially grateful to immediate past Chief Judge James A. Beatty Jr., who was chief judge for all the hiring process that resulted in me being chosen for this great honor. I value his leadership and that of Judge William L. Osteen Jr. as well as the other judges on this court. I recognize that they could have chosen many others, but they chose me and for that I am truly grateful. I can say without reservation that all the court, including the clerk's staff, have reached out to me and helped make my transition from the state administrative court to federal court much easier than it would have been.

I stand before you with great admiration and thankfulness to my parents, James and Bettie Webster, for their unwavering sacrifice and unconditional love shown toward my five brothers, two sisters, and me. Growing up twenty-some miles from here out on the farm in the Goodwill community of Madison, from as far as I can remember, my parents taught us the importance and value of love and respect for everyone. They taught us right from wrong, something sorely missing in many of our families today. My father passed almost ten years ago. He only went to the fourth grade, but he was a hardworking and courageous man. He, along with my mother, were married for almost fifty-seven years, and they exemplified a hard work ethic, "how-come-I-can't" stubbornness that has stayed with their children. As a result, my siblings and I have tried to raise our own children to believe that they can accomplish whatever they set their minds to. My dear mother, who suffers with Alzheimer's, is such a great woman of faith. We planned for her to be here today, but she came down with a virus and could not attend. I'm also thankful that my brothers and sisters are here to bear witness to this service today.

I must also recognize Diane, my wife of thirty-two years, who has had the patience of Job through her dedication to me and our children. She stood by me when I committed to community and public service, and the great financial sacrifice involved from the outset of my career. I'm also grateful to my three children; Briana, Camille, and Evan. I see myself in each of them and I am pleased with their career paths, but most importantly Diane and I am pleased with how they treat everyone they meet. Today I'm also grateful to have my son-in-law, Ed, and Lys and Ariana to join us as a part of our family.

I must say that on my journey to the federal court, my home community of Goodwill and the church by the same name consisted of many relatives and neighbors who worked very hard in the tobacco fields and textile mills of Rockingham County. Many of them have lived admirable and exemplary lives and encouraged me along the way. I see that a number of them are present here today. I want to say thank you for all you have done to help me.

I see some youth here today from my adopted church of historic Oberlin Baptist Church in Raleigh. They are our future; the ones who will wear the black robes and care for us when we can no longer care for ourselves. Young people, I just want you to know today that I believe in you, and you should never give up on pursuing your hopes and dreams in life. This court and the entire criminal justice system need you to do what you can to encourage those who feel discouraged, those who don't feel like they have a friend to lean on, and those who want to give up. I also see several pastors in the courtroom. It is imperative that you step up your game; step up the work you have undertaken outside of your church walls. In most instances, those of us in these robes find no joy in sending away to prison thousands of our sons and daughters. But this is part of our job. We need each of you to help in steering our youth in the right direction—on the right side of the law.

I am grateful to my classmates from the Howard University School of Law who traveled here from New York and Philadelphia. Present here today are guests from five states, the District of Columbia, and ten counties in North Carolina. There are not enough words in the English vocabulary to adequately express how thankful I am for your sacrifice in making this a memorable occasion for my family and me.

I am about to conclude, but I suspect there are some of the lawyers among us here, especially those of you who practice criminal law, who may be wondering what kind of judge I will be when you appear before me. You may already be wondering, after your clients are arrested, whether I will keep them locked up pending trial or release them

Investiture Ceremony: Judge L. Webster taking oath of office as United States Magistrate Judge for Middle District of North Carolina, United States District Court, Greensboro, NC—December 14, 2024

with minimum conditions. I can only tell you that I believe in the rule of law and believe wholeheartedly in the Constitution of the United States and that of this great state of North Carolina. When you go downstairs for the reception shortly, there on the wall prominently displayed is a picture that includes a few lines from the preamble of the US Constitution at the top. There you will find one word that informs me of what I ought to be about and what I must diligently seek in each case as a federal judge. The word is found in the first clause of the preamble, describing why the founding fathers determined the Constitution was necessary. That word is "Justice." The first sentence says, "We the people of the United States, in order to form a more perfect union, establish justice...." I believe in justice and all that the word entails, including fairness and impartiality. As a student at Howard University, I visited the US Supreme Court, and there on the front entrance of that awe-inspiring building are the words "Equal Justice Under Law." I took an oath on November 7 and then again today publicly that I would administer justice without respect to persons and do equal right to the poor and to the rich, and that I would faithfully and impartially discharge and perform all my duties incumbent upon me as a United States magistrate judge under the Constitution and laws of the United States....

Whether our judicial system survives for another two-hundred-plus years depends in part upon me and all judges across this land who take the oath to administer justice fairly and impartially. In closing, you have my word that I will do just that every day that I am blessed to serve. This is my solemn pledge and promise to you and to all those who will appear before me.

Thank you for making this a memorable occasion. I will never forget all that this means to my family and me.

Memories of My Investiture as US Magistrate Judge

COURTROOM 1A

OURTROOM 1A

Excerpts from My Remarks at Swearing-In Ceremony as Administrative Law Judge

Old Capital Building, Raleigh, North Carolina

NOVEMBER 13, 2006

First, I want to say that I am so grateful to God for allowing me to be standing here today. I stand here not under my own power. I'm also standing on my mother's and father's shoulders and the shoulders of many others I will tell you about momentarily. I wish my father could be here today. I know that he would be so proud. To my friend of twenty-seven years, Justice Patricia Timmons-Goodson, other judges on the program, and other judges present, including the administrative law judges of the Office of Administrative Hearings, and to my family and friends, including some who have come from a long distance, I am truly grateful for your presence. I am not only grateful to many of you for being here today, but also for your support and encouragement in my journey over many years. I don't have the time today to talk about that journey—a journey that was sometimes filled with fear and anxiety—but I know that your prayers have made the difference and gave me the strength to keep on going.

I thank those who on short notice agreed to participate on this program. All of you are my friends, and the work you do as public servants is an inspiration to me. I encourage all present to give the next

Special Session to Administer
The Oath of Office to

Joe Louis Webster

Administrative Law Judge
Office of Administrative Hearings

Justice Patricia Timmons-Goodson, Presiding

November 13, 2006
4:30 p.m.
Old House Chamber
North Carolina State Capitol
Raleigh, North Carolina

Joe's first appearance as an Administration Law Judge Nov. 2006 Asheville, NC.

generation a chance to show the world that all our young folk are not hooked on drugs or in prison.

Today, I have here with me my family, including my mother, Bettie Ester Webster and most of my brothers and sisters. They have stood by me as I have tried to make a difference in my community and profession. To my wife, Diane, of twenty-six and a half years, who has stood by me even in the many lean and trying times, I want to say thank you for all you have done as a wife, friend and mother to our children. My three children, Briana, Camille, and Evan have brought great joy to our lives. A number of years ago as I was lamenting to a friend that I felt that I was doing so little to make a difference in my community and profession to help the poor and less fortunate. He responded, "Joe your greatest legacy and contribution to society might just be your children." As I have watched each of them grow in stature, maturity and accomplishment, I tend to agree with my friend.

I have taken the oath of office today knowing that I have much to learn, and that I will never know it all. You have my word that I will always be respectful of all those who come before me, find the facts as I am bound to do and do my best to apply the law fairly, impartially, with respect for all and without bias. I will do my part to live up to the true meaning of the principle of "equal justice under law," a constitutional mandate that still needs to be strived for in all parts of our judiciary. When my years of service are completed, I hope that it can be said that I was a just judge. In order to complete this goal, I will need your continued prayers for wisdom and courage, and that I might always maintain my integrity. Thank all of you again, and I wish you God's speed as you travel back to your homes.

Judge Joe L. Webster ceremony taking oath of office as Administrative Law Judge for State of North Carolina Office of Administrative Hearings and Remarks

Joe's children and Maggie Bryant

Experiencing Racism and Disrespect Firsthand

SEPTEMBER 20, 2022

Shortly after I moved into our then new home in Chapel Hill, North Carolina, in early July 2001, I parked my pickup truck down at the bottom of our driveway on Bayberry Drive. One morning I walked down to retrieve it and immediately noticed that it had been "egged." It was obvious someone had deliberately thrown eggs against it as eggshells were lying in the grass beside it, and the stain of egg yolk was on the body of the truck, The perpetrators of this hateful act may as well have placed a sign beside my vehicle: "Welcome to our all-white neighborhood. You are not welcome!" Days later I went to my mailbox to find the outer wooden exterior had been shattered to pieces. It was damaged to the extent that it could not be repaired. So, I removed the wooden portion that was hanging on to the metal interior. This was another sign that said your family is not welcome here.

Some eleven years after these two incidents occurred, in 2012, I was taking my frequent walks on my street a mile or so from our residence when a large dog charged toward me from its yard. It startled me greatly, and I feared for my safety. As usual I was walking with a golf club in my hand, so I used it to shoo the dog away to protect myself. The dog's owner, standing on his front porch, said nothing to his dog, but immediately started blasting me with hateful words. "What are you doing swinging that golf club toward my dog?" I immediately fired back at him. "Your dog was attacking me." He then said, "What are you doing walking in my yard?" I responded, "I was not walking in your yard; I was walking on the street. I never touched your yard." He then said, "Well, you were walking close to my yard. What are you doing in this neighborhood? You don't live here." I am sure by then my blood pressure had begun to boil. I engaged the man further. "What makes you think you are the only one that can afford to live here?" It occurred to me that this white man's real problem was bigotry and that he had a feeling of superiority or white privilege. My thoughts about this incident still resonate with me all these years later.

I chose not to immediately report either of these two earlier incidents other than to my wife. However, I not only told my wife about the incident involving the dog and its owner, but I told several friends, and spoke of it in a sermon I delivered at Oberlin Baptist Church in Raleigh. These incidents demonstrated to me that Chapel Hill was not completely that liberal stronghold in southern Orange County, North Carolina—that there were still some bigots in the community that could not stand to see persons of color living in a well-to-do neighborhood. And in the third incident, white privilege also reared its ugly head. Either way, upon reflection, I was reminded that being fair-skinned, being educated, and being a respected practicing attorney-at-law, former chairman of the North Carolina Board of Law Examiners, and in the latter incident, carrying the title of a state administrative law judge for the State of North Carolina at the time, did not shield me or my family from what happened in these incidents. Also, upon reflection, it comes to mind that I have suffered more such indignations as described herein as an adult professional than during my childhood during the first eighteen years of my life when Jim Crow was very much alive and well.

I have chosen not to linger on these incidents, nor to maintain anger or bitterness toward anyone who caused me discomfort at the time. While I don't linger on this and other such incidents, recently, during my Thanksgiving dinner with my wife and son, I related to my son something that happened in my present workplace in early 2019. It did not involve any of my fellow judges or others that I work with daily. The incident demonstrated the disrespect that whites often show toward persons of color who are in positions of power. As I shared with my son a bad experience that I had with one of the agencies that I deal with in my judicial capacity, I teared up amid the many people in the restaurant. It involved a situation where the disrespectful persons apparently consulted with many others except me, the only judge in the Durham Federal Court building. I recall vividly the day I received the written proposal and immediately voiced my disapproval. The authors of the report knew that I would have been opposed to what they were proposing, and they also knew their method of accomplishing their selfish goals was clandestine and disrespectful to me and my staff. During my youth, we had a name for such conduct, and it was called "dirty." That incident caused me to have as much anger and grief as anything that has happened to me during my forty-five-year legal career. It was more about disrespect than anything else. But I felt in my heart and mind that if I had been white, they would have afforded me due respect and discussed the matter with me rather than going about their plans behind my back.

Even more recently, I was attending a judges' conference at a resort in the southeastern part of the United States. Another black judge and I decided we would play golf during a break in the conference. Since I had not traveled with my golf clubs, I informed the concierge that I needed to rent golf clubs. Upon arriving at the club house, the treatment I received was troubling to me and smelled of prejudice. When I arrived at the clubhouse the attendant seemed to have problems finding our reservation, although the concierge told me the time, and the rate I would pay for the greens fee and golf club rental. I informed the host what I had been told, and one of the attendants said to me, "How did you get that rate? Are you staying here?" And then, after they found my reservation and I paid the fees, a young male attendant said to me, "You pick up the golf clubs out back. There will be fourteen clubs in the bag, and there must be fourteen clubs when you return them." As we walked away to begin our round of golf, I told my fellow judge, "If I didn't really want to play golf, I would have left from that clubhouse without playing." He responded to me, "You know that's one reason black folk have high blood pressure and other heart disease in greater numbers than whites—we have to put up with this kind of disrespect and anxiety all the time."

I try hard not to dwell on matters that are a daily occurrence with those of my race and other persons of low wealth daily. Rather I push forward toward the mark of my dual callings of law and ministry. I continue to seek justice while offering hope for those in and out of the courtroom by encouraging our youth, young men and women, not to give up despite life's struggles.

The welcome I received as one of the first to integrate my neighborhood in Chapel Hill, North Carolina. My truck was egged, and my mailbox was destroyed, July 2001.

An Inclusive System of Justice

"Reflections on Judicial Diversity," FMJA Bulletin

SEPTEMBER 2018

COURTESY OF THE FEDERAL MAGISTRATE JUDGES ASSOCIATION

Diversity on our courts, from our Small Claims courts to the Supreme Court of the United States, is critical to the administration of justice. An inclusive system of justice is paramount to dispensing justice. How can a judge dispense justice if he or she cannot at all relate to those who come before the court? I heard a pastor from the continent of Africa say one time that unless you have heard a person chewing his food then you cannot know him.

An inclusive system of justice is not possible without persons who have broad experiences, not only those who have practiced law in a wide variety of areas, but also those who might recognize injustice if he or she sees it. What a judge sees is shaped by his or her experiences from childhood to the time the oath of office is taken. If you have not seen poverty and its debilitating effect on one's physical and psychological well-being, or the judge cannot recognize injustice when the judge sees it, then that is a problem. If the judge hardly knows what the price of a gallon of milk or a gallon of gas is, then how can a judge mete out fair punishment to the mostly poor and desperate men and women who come before him or her. It is even more of a problem if a judge does not care to get close enough to people from all walks of life to hear them chew their food.

Race, gender, and disparate backgrounds are only a few of the categories that come to mind when considering what an inclusive system of justice looks like. Notwithstanding the race or gender of the judge, we need public servants who care about each person who comes before the courts; only then can one mete out justice. I have written that

> As judges, when these young men and women come before us, we must treat them with as much dignity and respect as we would the most respected person in society. And as judges, we must also seek to offer them hope as they go off to prison. I have found that to be respected, you must give respect, no matter what a person's station is in life.[35]

We need good stewards of our legal profession, including our judiciary. To be good stewards, there is no question that we need an inclusive system of justice.

35 Joe L. Webster, "Saving Our Profession, It's Up to Us," *Judicature* 101, no. 1 (Spring 2017), Duke University Law School, printed by the Duke Law Center for Judicial Studies.

Reflecting on Robes in the Schools

Miami Florida

APRIL 17, 2019

On April 17, 2019, I was fortunate to be one of the participants in the FMJA Diversity Committee outreach Robes in the Schools, which took place in conjunction with the FJC Magistrate Judges workshop in Miami, Florida. The program was organized with the assistance of the US Attorney's Office in Miami. Approximately 750 students from six high schools and ten magistrate judges participated in the program. Participating magistrate judges were Susan van Keulen, Northern District of California; Willie J. Epps Jr., Western District of Missouri; Lauren F. Louis, Southern District of Florida; Sashi H. Kewalramani, Central District of California; Andrew M. Edison, Southern District of Texas; Kandis A. Westmore, Northern District of California; Alka Sagar, Central District of California; William Duffin, Eastern District of Wisconsin; and Sarah Hays, Western District of Missouri.

My assigned school was Miami Edison High School, located in the Little Haiti community. The forum at Edison High School was cosponsored by a school club, Peace Ambassadors. Edison chose a topic of concern to them and many young persons across America: whether African Americans and other persons of color receive longer prison sentences than other races. Having reviewed the literature resulting from various studies, I admitted that the research illustrates that persons of color have historically received longer prison sentences than others, and that recently the federal government sought to address sentence disparities. One student asked me what I considered to be a profound question. I was asked how I felt about being part of an "unfair" system of justice. I explained that it is my opinion that more could and should be done to create a level playing field and that I personally try hard daily to assure that each person who comes before me has a fair and impartial hearing or trial. I also explained that through my public speaking and writings in legal publications, I try to encourage other judges and lawyers to do the same.

My audience at Edison was almost exclusively persons of color. As I sought to probe into how the students felt about our justice system, I asked for a show of hands as to how many of them agreed with the well-known phrase "If you do the crime, you ought to do the time." Not one hand was raised. Perhaps the response was influenced by peer pressure or other factors, including an audience that was inflicted by the ravages of decades of poverty, and a war on drugs that has left Little Haiti and many other communities of color with few male role models (and more suspicion than respect for law enforcement).

Amid the audience at Edison, despite the topic that illuminated concerns about unfairness in our system of justice, I personally observed a student body that contained many bright minds and I saw promise in many of them. I am confident that with more initiatives such as Robes in the Schools, and more arms placed around the sometimes forgotten and dispossessed, that hope will return to communities that have lost hope. Therefore, I left Edison encouraged.

Memories: North Carolina Association of Black Lawyers

OCTOBER 15, 2020; UPDATED JULY 2, 2024

COURTESY OF NCABL

I have many fond memories regarding my legal career, including my membership and active participation in the North Carolina Association of Black Lawyers (NCABL) during the first two decades of my legal career. I served on its Board of Governors and was a founding board member of the NCABL Land Loss Prevention Project, which was initially housed at the NC Central Law School.

I recall the first NCABL meeting I attended in October of 1979, only shortly after I passed the North Carolina bar exam. I believe that initial meeting took place at a hotel in the Raleigh/Durham area. In attendance was a large gathering of black lawyers from across the state. I do not recall all who were present that October weekend. However, among those who frequently attended the NCABL meetings were numerous well-respected pioneer lawyers of the day like Henry Frye, Sammie Chess Jr., Annie Brown Kennedy, Conrad Pearson, Floyd McKissick, Billy Marsh, Mickie and Eric Michaux, Charles V. Bell, T. T. Clayton, Buddy Malone, Julius Chambers, James Ferguson, Kenneth Lee, Earl Whitted, Harvey Beech, Herman Thompson, Frank W. Balance Jr., Ken Spaulding, and Herman Taylor. While he would not have considered himself a pioneer lawyer at the time, Professor Charles Daye of UNC–Chapel Hill School of Law (and volunteer executive secretary and editor for NCABL for twenty years) was always attended the NCABL meetings.

Many of these pioneer lawyer members of the NCABL have passed away, and I honor them today for allowing me and hundreds of others to stand on their shoulders. Among them are the late Buddy Malone, Conrad Pearson, Charles V. Bell, Floyd McKissick, Julius Chambers, Herman Thompson, Earl Whitted, Harvey Beech, J. Kenneth Lee, Elreta Melton Alexander, Herman Taylor, T. T. Clayton, Billy Marsh, Frank W. Balance Jr., Annie Brown Kennedy, and Charles Daye. They paved the way for me and generations of other black lawyers who came after them.

The NCABL membership met at least twice annually, once at the beach in the month of June and in the fall, usually in October. The fall meetings took place in cities across the state, quite often in the Raleigh/Durham area and, as I recall, occasionally in Fayetteville, Greensboro, Winston Salem, Asheville, and Charlotte. The NCABL meetings customarily began with a board meeting followed by a reception on Friday evening where we greeted one another and discussed events that had taken place in our lives since we had last been together. The Saturday agenda often included Continuing Legal Education (CLE) classes and a general body meeting. Saturday night's festivities concluded with a party filled with laughter, lemonade of varying proofs, and the latest dances of the time. I recall at least some meetings concluded on Sunday morning with a worship service.

On Friday and Saturday nights, numerous card games were played by NCABL members professing to be experts in the craft. While I was not one of those that participated in card games. I recall once being an eyewitness to a string of all-night card games in the hotel rooms of one of the members. I recall one memorable Friday night when fellow NCABL members Irving Joyner and James Williams were engaged in late-night card games. I have a vague recollection that Frank Balance was also involved in the card games at some point that night. The card games went on so long that I stretched out across the host's bed in my business suit and went to sleep. I woke up at 3 or 4 in the morning to loud laughter and observed that the card games were still being played. While I wanted to ask James whether he knew what time it was, I decided against that after observing how much fun they were having.

I returned to my nap, and when I woke up again, I noticed the sun rising. Both Irving Joyner and James Williams were still playing card games. I noticed James had taken off his shirt and it was lying on the card table. On our way to the car as we departed on Saturday morning, I asked James whether he had "lost his shirt in the card games." He responded, "No, but I almost did." We both thought that my question and his response was very funny and broke into laughter.

In later years a Sunday morning worship service was attended by those who mostly consumed zero-proof lemonade the night before.

These gatherings of black lawyers were much more than social gatherings. During the 1980s and 1990s the NCABL was one of the strongest organizations in the state. The governor of North Carolina often sought advice from the organization on whom to appoint to judicial vacancies. The NCABL board and its members often strategized on whether we should advocate a continuation of judicial elections or whether appointment by the governor or legislature would increase black judgeships across the state.

There were great opportunities for young lawyers to learn from the well-experienced senior lawyers, which was as important and beneficial as anything that took place at NCABL meetings. I recall one membership meeting in 1980 when I was sitting beside now-congressman G. K. Butterfield. He was practicing law at the time in Wilson, North Carolina. I had just hung my shingle to practice law in my hometown of Madison, and I was preparing to file my first civil lawsuit on behalf of a client who had been involved in a car accident. I told G.K. that since I had been in the criminal law clinic at Howard University, I had not learned how to prepare a civil complaint. G.K., without hesitation, said, "Give me your legal pad," and he began to draft the caption and body of the complaint. I will never forget how effortlessly G.K. wrote in that moment to assist me. This is just one example of how I personally stood on the shoulders of black lawyers during my early career. Even before I was licensed to practice law, while I was studying for the bar exam in the summer of 1979, I met one of the foremost leaders of the NCABL, Charles Daye on the campus of University of North Carolina's law school. I told him I was anxious about some of the North Carolina nuances in the law that I did not learn about at Howard's law school. One such nuance was the "Recent Possession Doctrine." [36] Professor Daye immediately explained it to me and compared it to other principles that he knew I had learned in my criminal law course at Howard. Years later I thanked him again for taking the time to tutor me when I first met him.

Other members of the NCABL blessed me with their great wisdom and advice. Another day of learning took place at an NCABL meeting in Greensboro in the mid-1980s at a time during which I had been heavily involved in a civil rights controversy that involved the firing of a black secretary by a recently hired school principal in my hometown's local school system. The black community was outraged about her firing. There had been a demonstration, television interviews, and newspaper coverage not only in my hometown, but in the Greensboro/Winston Salem area as well. There was no doubt that my mentor, then an associate justice on the NC Supreme Court, Henry Frye, had read or heard about my case. We greeted one another and briefly talked about my law practice. During our conversation he said, "Every controversy is not justiciable." I will never forget that moment and have told younger lawyers about the wise advice Justice Frye gave me that day.

I also recall the many years that the NCABL awarded a Lawyer of the Year Award. I recall some of its recipients and why they had earned this prestigious award, members such as Harvey and Harold Kennedy, and Terry Richardson. The association also

36 In North Carolina the doctrine of recent possession permits an inference of guilt based on a defendant's possession of stolen property recently after a larceny or breaking or entering. *State* v. Maines 301 N.C. 669 (1981)

annually presented a Community Service Award to a deserving member. I was fortunate to be the recipient of this award in 1986 for my community service work primarily in my hometown and county.

Like other bar associations, there came a time when the NCABL gained the ability to be an accredited sponsor of CLE programs and allowed participants to get state bar credits toward their annual requirements.

I also recall a period during the early 2000s when membership began to decline, or at least the regular meetings became more infrequent. Some said the retiring of Professor Daye from his dual roles as Executive Secretary and Editor for 20 years (1979–1999) took away some of the stability of the organization. Personally, I surmised that perhaps the younger generation had a few more opportunities with majority firms compared to those of us who had necessarily hung our own shingles or associated with others in small firms of the same race. I contemplated whether some progress in job opportunities may have caused the younger generations to feel they no longer needed to belong to an association of black lawyers.

Whatever the case, there was a period when the NCABL lost the appeal it once had. In recent years, an effort has been made to regain the strength of the organization, which is much needed, especially considering the degree of social injustice and social unrest that our country is facing today. I wholeheartedly commend the efforts of those who see the need for a revival of the once-great organization that meant so much to me during the early decades of my legal career. The June 28–29, 2024, gathering of the association in Wilmington, North Carolina, under the leadership of President Kimberly A. Moore was an outstanding example that mirrored the earlier glory days of the NCABL. The program was an excellent sterling example of the Continuing Legal Education programs sponsored by the NCABL going back more than thirty years. The 2024 Annual CLE conference was titled "Emerging Civil Rights Issues in the Twenty-First Century: Lawyering for a Cause in Black and Brown Communities." Indeed, this conference was an answer to the prayers of many that there would be a revival of the NCABL. I have no doubt that under the leadership of attorney Kimberly A. Moore and her board, regaining the past prominence of the NCABL is well underway.

Autograph of a Distinguished American, Rev. Dr. Pauli Murray

JANUARY 20, 2023

On April 21, 1978, I did not know that I was sitting among some of the most notable, distinguished persons who had ever graduated from or taught at Howard University as Howard celebrated the twenty-fifth anniversary of the establishment of the Phi Beta Kappa Chapter at the university in 1953. Included among those in attendance was Pauli Murray, a Howard University Law School graduate. I had been invited to this celebration because of my own induction into Phi Beta Kappa at Howard on April 30, 1976.

By the year of the twenty-fifth anniversary celebration, Pauli Murray had already established herself as a lawyer, and civil rights advocate for racial and feminist equality, labor rights, and author. In January 1977, she became the first African American female to become ordained as an Episcopal priest. Her biography *Proud Shoes* was first published some two decades earlier in 1956. I did know of these and other accomplishments at the time. I did not learn more about Pauli Murray until 1988 when I read an article about her in a book by Charles Kuralt, who covered her visit to the Chapel of the Cross Episcopal Church in Chapel Hill on February 13, 1977, for her first Eucharist. My wife had gifted me a copy of Kuralt's book to congratulate me on my passing the North Carolina bar exam in 1979. It was nine years later in 1988 when I revisited the book and immediately called the Episcopal Church to ask how I could contact Pauli Murray. I was heartbroken to learn that she had died a few years earlier. About that same time, as I perused one of my many family albums, I discovered that I had in fact met Pauli Murray as evidenced by the autograph attached to this writing. While I was pleased that I had this prized memento among my possessions, I was disappointed with myself that I had not sought out Pauli Murray while she was still walking among us.

I am so thankful that I had a brief encounter with Pauli Murray nearly a half century ago. Since that time, I have learned so much more about her courage and contributions to America. Because of Rev. Dr. Pauli Murray's courage and humility and that of many other pioneers of her generation, I have gained courage myself. I have also learned to remain humble as a catalyst to effect change in a divided nation still very much in need of healing and redirection. I have been afforded and blessed with the opportunity to walk among kings and queens and those like me from lowly beginnings from small communities that few not from those places have heard of. And for this I am grateful!

The Officers and Members
of
Gamma Chapter, District of Columbia
Phi Beta Kappa
request the honor of your company
at the
Installation and Initiation Ceremonies
to be held
Wednesday the eighth of April
Howard University Campus
Chapter Installation
The Browsing Room, Founders Library, at 5:30 p.m.
Dinner
Trustees Dining Room, Baldwin Hall, at 6:30 p.m.
Public Session
Rankin Memorial Chapel, at 8 p.m.

R.S.V.P.
The Secretary
Box 284
Howard University

Informal

JOE L. WEBSTER

TWENTY-FIFTH
ANNIVERSARY
April 21, 1978

Autograph of Rev. Dr. Pauli Murray and others at dinner for
Phi Beta Kappa celebrating 25th anniversary, April 21, 1978

The Naming of a Federal Courthouse

John Hervey Wheeler Courthouse Durham, North Carolina

OCTOBER 15, 2019

On October 15, 2019, It was my privilege and a blessing to preside at the ceremony to name the United States District Court for the Middle District of North Carolina in Durham, North Carolina. It was a glorious day, and the setting was held under a tent outside the building that houses the United States Post Office and the Federal Courtroom and chambers. My task was to bring the ceremony to order and announce the order of speakers. I took the liberty of thanking GSA representative Cynthia Edwards from Atlanta for her many hours of work coordinating the many details of the ceremony. Among those sitting on the dais was Congressman G. K. Butterfield, who I commended for having the insight to recognize the importance of the naming of this courthouse and for utilizing his legislative skills to champion the bill into law that made this day possible.

Among the others present on the stage that day were keynote speaker Vernon Jordan; Thomas Schroeder, Chief United States District Court Judge for the Middle District of North Carolina; Congressman David Price; Fourth Circuit Court of Appeals Judge James A. Wynn Jr.; and longtime state representative and state senator, Mickie Michaux. Among those in the audience were former chief justice Henry Frye of the North Carolina Supreme Court, as well as former justice Patricia Timmons Goodson of the North Carolina Supreme Court, United States District Court Judges for the Middle District Loretta Biggs and Norwood C. Tilley Jr., and retired Middle District Chief Judge James A. Beaty Jr. The Honorable Sammie Chess Jr., the first African American Superior Court Judge in North Carolina history and longtime friend of Vernon Jordan, was recognized among the many distinguished guests present. Local government officials were well represented, including former Durham mayor Bill Bell and Durham School Superintendent Dr. Pascal Mubenga. Former Durham City Council member, Eddie Davis had the honor of recognizing members of the Durham community who have contributed much to the community, including longtime member and former chair of the Durham Committee on the Affairs of Black People, Dr. Lavonia Allison.

The highlight of the occasion was the keynote address by Vernon Jordan. During the introduction of Mr. Jordan, Judge Wynn reminded the audience of a quote that has stuck with him over the years from Mr. Jordan: "When you stand on the shoulders of others, you ought to be reciprocal in living your life in a manner so that others can live and stand on yours." None of us present knew that Mr. Jordan would succumb in his

The naming of a federal courthouse: John Hervey Wheeler United States Courthouse, Durham, North Carolina, October 15, 2019 COURTESY OF SONNIE HARRIS

Judge Webster presiding at the naming of the John Hervy Wheeler United States Courthouse, Durham, NC and revealing of signage with name of courthouse, October 15, 2019

sleep not many months later on March 2, 2021, at age eighty-five. While he noticeably walked with a slow pace, when he took the podium, his voice and words were indeed powerful and steady, hewn from his long years of advocacy in the cause of civil rights after graduating from Howard University Law School some six decades earlier.

As Mr. Jordan began his speech, he thanked Congressman G. K. Butterfield for his devoted efforts to seek legislation for this momentous occasion. Mr. Jordan stated that John Hervey Wheeler was more than a name to him; he was a mentor, sponsor, idol, and someone he admired. John Hervey Wheeler was Mr. Jordan's dear friend. It was Mr. Jordan's hope that John Hervey Wheeler's life would not be in vain; rather, when people see his name, they would have a desire to learn about "his extraordinary life and career," including many of his great works in North Carolina—among those being president of Mechanics and Farmers Bank, NAACP lawyer, and civil rights advocate. Those in attendance that day were reminded that John Hervey Wheeler provided loans to blacks to purchase homes when other banks refused to loan to blacks. We were reminded that John Hervey Wheeler practiced law during a time where courthouses were not such friendly and "welcoming places" as "black men were assumed to be criminals not lawyers." As Mr. Jordan stated, John Hervey Wheeler "knew that the battle for freedom begins every morning and required every one of us." John Hervey Wheeler stayed dedicated to his works, including helping draft civil rights legislation of the 1960s. Mr. Jordan reminded the audience of one critical fact: "While John and his peers fought for equal rights, we're still fighting for equal recognition and equal representation to build a world where freedom of movement in all aspects of society is not just possible, but probable." By the end of Mr. Jordan's presentation, it was clear to all why we had gathered in large numbers that day. It was not to celebrate Mr. Jordan's presence as keynote speaker, nor the many other dignitaries present, but to celebrate the life and legacy of John Hervey Wheeler, whose contributions to Durham, our state, and nation so qualified his name to be forever prominently displayed and associated with the Federal Courthouse in Durham, North Carolina. Mr. Jordan left all of us with a charge to keep. It was to rededicate our courts and our ourselves to the commitment to justice that John Hervey Wheeler demonstrated daily in his life's work.[37]

37 Thanks to my career law clerk, Pedra D. Lee, for her contributions to this article.

Acceptance Speech at 2023 Bar Association Convention Legal Legends of Color Program

Wilmington, North Carolina

JUNE 22, 2023

I am honored to receive this award this evening. First, I want to thank the one that woke me up this morning, without whom I would be nothing. I'd be a "ship without a sail." I thank my wife and family members, friends and legal colleagues who have traveled from afar. I thank them not only for their sacrifices in traveling from distant places but also for their love, forgiveness, and patience with me as I have sought to make a difference in my dual callings of law and ministry. My wife, Diane, has been the "wind beneath my wings" for forty-three years.

NC Bar Association Legal Legends of Color Awards Recipient, NC Bar Association Convention, Wilmington, NC, June 22, 2023 COURTESY OF EFREN RENTERIA

This evening, I also think of my late mother, Bettie Ester Moore Webster, who told me she quit school in the tenth grade because she only had one good dress to wear to school. But she reminded me as I prepared to travel the three-hundred-plus miles to Washington, DC, and Howard University, that "If I put God first in my life and worked hard, someone would see me trying and someone would help me." What she prophesied for my life is still coming true today. Tonight, I also think of my late father, James Edward Webster, who had a "How come I can't?" attitude although he only went to the fourth grade in school. People called it being stubborn and hardheaded back in the day, but it is part of what allowed them to be successful parents to eight children and strong members of their community. He was strong willed or stubborn, as they used to say back in the day. I was like him a lot, but I'd like to think I am strong-willed or determined. I'm sure my wife would say I'm hardheaded.

I think that most of you present know what I stand for, but I'd like to make a few remarks that might especially encourage the younger lawyers present this evening. As I have tried to do in my career, you need to stand on the shoulders of those legends like the late Honorable Sammie Chess Jr., the late Julius Chambers, the late Annie Brown Kennedy, Henry Frye, and others who have received this award. Three of these named legends have passed on, but you still need to study their history and learn from them. You will learn that it takes courage to be an attorney. It takes courage to be a judge and one who is deeply respected in their communities, not because they drove nice automobiles or lived in big houses, but because of the content of their character. Their moral compasses were untainted. They have stood for truth, compassion for those less fortunate, and sought at all costs equal justice under law—and what is so important today: adherence to the rule of law. There is a need more than ever for you to stand up for the rule of law. It is also very important for you to adhere to your oath as an attorney, to "support and defend the Constitution of the United States against enemies both foreign and domestic." You will find in the history of Annie Brown Kennedy and Sammie Chess Jr., for example, that you can rise to the top of your profession by agitating the very system that you are a part of that still needs persuading to do the right thing.

Our nation is severely divided. You will also see in the lives of these two legal legends an effort to "bind up the nation's wounds," to use the words of President Abraham Lincoln. It seems the word "compromise" has been lost to the ages. It is lost in Congress, our states' legislatures, and among our neighbors.

I'm begging our young lawyers to do all you can to promote peace, harmony, and tolerance among the races, different cultures, genders, and other communities that feel marginalized and wounded by the actions of our state, nation, organizations, and others. It is only through getting to know and understand one another that the objective of reconciliation can be achieved.

I warn both young and older lawyers, to paraphrase a Bible verse, that you need to work while it's day, because when night comes, your steps will be shorter, your eyesight not as clear, your mind not as sharp, and your energy level not as strong. If you do this—if you work toward peace—then others will know by your actions that you love them, and that you see them as equals. I've been trying to do this in my court especially when I'm on criminal duty. I try to "dispense justice while offering hope" to the many mostly young African American males who come before me who seem to have lost all hope. Let's do all we can to promote hope in our communities. Thank you all again for coming to support all the honorees this evening.

Reflections on Going Back to School: An Unlikely Second Chance at Duke University Law School

NOVEMBER 27, 2023

On May 19, 2014, I joined nineteen distinguished judges from across the United States, Jamaica, and Germany as the second incoming class of the Master of Judicial Studies Program at Duke University Law School. My class was diverse, composed of an even number of males and females, state and federal judges, young and more senior judges. I was pleased that there was racial diversity among my classmates as well. The program required the completion of twenty-two credits over a span of four weeks during two consecutive spring sessions. There was much homework, composed of reading and writing assignments, final exams, and a thesis of high quality to complete the program. Both sessions were simply exhausting, but also simply amazing. It culminated with my graduation on May 14, 2016, at Cameron Indoor Stadium on the Duke University campus.

My journey to the Duke University Law School campus was interrupted by thirty-eight years of challenges, triumphs, and experiences that I would not exchange for any amount of money. Toward the end of my successful tenure as an undergraduate student

Duke University Law School Master's in Judicial Studies graduation, May 2016

at Howard University in 1976, Duke University became my first choice for law school. However, by early spring of 1976, a letter arrived at my 4752 Benning Road SE, Washington, DC, address from Duke University Law School, which indicated that my application for admission was denied.

I could have given up on law school but giving up had not been a part of my genetic makeup. Giving up was not in my DNA. I was blessed with a father and mother, James and Bettie Webster, who had been the epitome of hard work and perseverance for all my life. While the North Carolina law school's door remained closed to me, Howard University School of Law saw the promise in me, opened its doors, and welcomed me with a letter of admission. There is no doubt that I could not have attended a greater law school than Howard University to prepare me for the difficult work that I was to undertake in my hometown and surrounding rural communities of North Carolina. So I entered Howard's law school in mid-August of 1976. May 2024 represents forty-five years since my graduation in May 1979.

Now back to my reflections on going back to school. I had applied to the master's program at Duke on August 2, 2013, and I could not believe that only three business days later, on August 7, 2013, I received an email stating that I had been admitted into the master's program in judicial studies.

The courses at Duke Law were all challenging and caused me to ponder constitutional and other legal issues that I had given little thought to since my law school days at Howard. I had many discussions with my fellow classmates. During my first spring four-week session at Duke, my apartment roommate was Judge Michael Daly Hawkins, a senior judge on the Ninth Circuit Court of Appeals. While a member of my class, he was working on his Doctor of Juridical Science degree. Some years earlier he had received his master's in judicial studies at the University of Virginia Law School. In short, he is a legal scholar, simply brilliant, and very generous in sharing in his wealth of knowledge! In addition to being there to discuss the assignments, my roommate helped me focus on what I might do for my thesis. He knew of my love for history and so one day out of the blue he asked me, "Who was the first black superior court judge in North Carolina?" I replied, "The Honorable Sammie Chess Jr.," whom I had known for many years. My roommate said, "Why don't you write a biography on him for your thesis?" I called Judge Chess the same day, and he immediately said, "Yes." Both he and I became excited together about the project. Hundreds of hours were spent on my thesis, including many in-person interviews with Judge Chess at his home in Jamestown, North Carolina. Writing my thesis on Judge Chess was the highlight of my matriculation at Duke University Law School. Despite all the work to complete the thesis, it was a labor of love. Most importantly, the Honorable Sammie Chess Jr. loved the finished product and proudly shared it with many of his family and friends. During the second spring session, I was blessed to have as my roommate Judge Robert Morris, who serves on the Second District Court of Appeals in Florida. He is also a scholar and highly principled man, whom I am pleased to call my friend.

Upon learning of my matriculation at Duke, many lawyers and laypersons asked me whether I was in the program because I was seeking a promotion. Many of them had not heard of a sixty-year-old going back to school in the latter part of one's career. My reply was, "No, I am not seeking a promotion." I told them I was hoping to become a better judge, and most importantly, I told them, we all should be about a lifetime of learning. We are never too old to learn, and while our material things can be taken away from us, knowledge can never be taken away.

In addition to getting to know them well and learning with and from other judges from diverse backgrounds, one of the many highlights of the two four-week sessions was the two half-day classes spent with United States Supreme Court Justice Samuel Anthony Alito Jr. and Justice Antonin Scalia. During the first spring session, Justice Alito gave a lectured us. We all had the opportunity to stand with Justice Alito in a group and individual photo and talk with him personally as he joined us for refreshments after class. The second year of our on-campus studies brought United States Supreme Court Justice Antonin Scalia to our class. Somehow, I ended up sitting beside each of these justices at a social hour and lunch. Careful not to ask either of the justices about pending or even past decisions, I spoke to them about their children and family. We had no way of knowing that Justice Scalia would die unexpectedly in February 2016, only ten months after lecturing us at Duke University Law School. While my understanding and beliefs about how the constitution should be interpreted were different from Justice Alito and Scalia, I found both justices to be personable. Justice Scalia was a strong proponent that the United States Constitution should be interpreted as it was interpreted by the original drafters (originalism interpretation). I struggle to understand how one could reach that conclusion in as much as the original drafters believed it did not include black slaves as citizens let alone guarantee blacks or women the right to vote. My interpretation comes closer to the "Living Constitution" interpretation of the Constitution; that constitutional law should evolve in response to changing circumstances and values. Despite differences of opinions about constitutional interpretation, all of us are much better off when we can meet and learn from others who possess differing viewpoints, whatever the subject might be. While in the presence of Justice Alito and Scalia, I thought to myself about how blessed I have been to come such a long way from my home, the small farming community of Goodwill, outside the town of Madison in Rockingham County, North Carolina. While growing up I had never met a lawyer or judge, let alone a United States Supreme Court justice. Other professors in the Duke program were quite learned in their subject areas, and they challenged us and seemed to be appreciative of our challenging questions to them.

Prior to my first session at Duke, I had not remembered just how much of the development of the "law" in America involved cases and controversies concerning slaves. Several of our courses—American Constitutional Interpretation, Study of the Judiciary, and Judicial History—took us back to a time that caused me to feel the pain of my ancestors. To read and hear again that Jefferson and some other drafters of the Declaration of Independence owned slaves and died without freeing them caused me to have less respect for those founding fathers. After all, Jefferson and others were the same ones who proclaimed in the Declaration of Independence, "We hold these truths to be self-evident, that all men are created equal, that they are endowed by their Creator with certain unalienable Rights; that among these are Life, Liberty and the pursuit of Happiness." During one of our class discussions of the course materials on some of these cases, I told the class that years ago I had been doing some research on my African American ancestors, but at the time had little success. I later discussed my frustration with a family friend. The family friend, being familiar with genealogy research, said to me, "You were looking in the wrong place; you should have been looking in the livestock records." The common-law cases decided by judges and statutes passed by state legislatures early in American history made it very clear that slaves were "property" and they had no rights whatsoever.

Our classroom discussions in our American Constitutional Interpretation class were lively and sometimes controversial. Among those discussions was a dialogue about how the Affordable Care Act (ObamaCare) became so controversial and partisan. I took the position that President Obama's race was one of the factors that caused the ObamaCare legislation to be so controversial. As I recall, the Massachusetts Health Care plan supported by then Governor Mitt Romney, afforded much of the foundation of Obama Care. Others in the class disagreed with my opinion about race being a factor in the health care debate. Fortunately, the professor and at least one or two other classmates voiced their agreement with me. While engaged in such controversial discussions, the thought occurred to me why I had been blessed to be among the twenty selected students. I was the only black male in my class. I believe I was chosen so that I could raise important issues that no one else would raise, including issues surrounding race in America, both historically and presently.

Neither time nor space permits me to write about what it meant for me to have the opportunity to be a student and graduate from Duke University Law School, forty years after I first made application for and denied admission in 1976. It was a great opportunity and a great blessing to be granted a second chance to continue learning and growing along with other outstanding state and federal judges. I will always remember that experience and be grateful I received a second chance. And finally, it is highly unlikely I would have become a published author, as the requirement to write a thesis, lead me to publish a book about a great American. The title is *The Making and Measure of a Judge: Biography of the Honorable Sammie Chess Jr.*

What It Means in the Attorney Oath to "Support and Defend the Constitution of the United States against All Enemies Both Foreign and Domestic"

Remarks to Newly Admitted Attorneys

MAY 19, 2021

Congratulations to each of you, and I hope to see you in person practicing in the Middle District of North Carolina. There's one sentence in this attorney's admission oath that I wanted to say a few words about and have you to think about them. And that is the part that says, "To the best of your knowledge and ability you will support and defend the Constitution of the United States against all enemies foreign and domestic." So, I would ask that each of you give some thought to what that means in your lives and in your practices. And I think that to all of us it ought to mean something. These are important words in the oath, and they may mean something different to each of you. But it does require each of us who have sworn to it to do something, do something positive.

August will be the forty-second year since I first took the oath after passing the bar and graduating from the Howard University School of Law in 1979. And since then, I've often thought about this oath and what it means. And I wonder when we will do more, for example, to do something about the many hundreds and thousands of pro bono cases that are in both the state and the federal courts. I know that many of you have donated your time and maybe even money to this cause.

It has been eight and a half years since I've been with the federal court, but before that I worked with the Office of Administrative Hearings as an administrative law judge in Raleigh for six years. Often, I would look out in the audience and see a little old lady or little old man doing their best to represent themselves and maybe two assistant attorney generals on the other side. And I would always say to myself, *How could this possibly be a level playing field? How could justice somehow arise out a situation like this, where in many cases the person has never been to court a day in their lives, and they have no idea about what the rules of civil procedure are or what the rules of evidence are or just how to examine a witness?* And yet we often apply the same rules.

Is it time for us to consider a different kind of court for disputes where a person can't afford a lawyer? Many firms charge three hundred, four hundred, maybe even five hundred dollars an hour for legal services. Many people don't make much more than that to eat and pay their rent in a month's time. So, I just want you to be thinking about what we can do to fulfill our oath to support and defend the Constitution of the United States.

We've seen a lot that has gone on right before our eyes with the various cases we've had where police officers shoot unarmed persons. And I'll just tell you this story, and I've probably said more than most. But I have a thirty-one-year-old, six-foot-two son, brown in color, who told me when we were talking about some of what has been going on lately, "Dad, I don't even like to go outside now, because I feel like I could be killed any day."

Just think about that. Here I am a federal United States magistrate judge, and you hear that coming from someone that you love so much who is a manager at a well-known grocery store, who is doing well, who is married, who has two beautiful daughters. So we need to think about what kind of system of justice we need to have so that everybody will feel that they have a fair shot. I'm constantly thinking about this issue, and I know that people feel differently about it. I'm just asking you to consider what it means to support and defend the Constitution of the United States against enemies both foreign and domestic.

I could say more, but I've taken up enough of your time, and I look forward to seeing you all in person. I know that I can't discuss cases, and I'll always try to be fair and impartial, but if you ever have any thoughts about what I've just said, feel free to give me a call, especially if you're not involved in any case before me.

I appreciate all of you doing all you can to make our profession better. There's so much we need to do. For example, I don't think we as lawyers and judges have explained to the public the difference between being found not guilty beyond a reasonable doubt and being innocent. Some people think that they are one and the same. We've not adequately explained why it is very important that we still try to represent to the best of our ability even someone who tells you that they are guilty. People always ask, *How can you represent someone that you know is guilty?* That's a question that I've gotten many times over the last forty-two years. We have a much better chance of getting justice if there's a good lawyer on both sides of the aisle.

That's what I wanted to say to you. It certainly wasn't an attempt to offend anybody or cause you to think any way about it. But I love my profession, and I try to do what I can to make it better and fairer and more just to everyone who is affected by it. Have a great day.

CHAPTER EIGHT

Challenging Cases I Have Experienced as an Attorney, Judge, and Client

Prologue: Wisdom from Two Outstanding Judges

Below are among the more challenging cases I have been a part of during my legal career, as an attorney, judge, and client. As a judge, I have always tried to be fair and impartial in my treatment of both sides of the case, and always based my decision upon the facts and the law. In my human efforts to dispense justice fairly and impartially, I have erred from time to time. But like my late friend and mentor, the Honorable Sammie Chess Jr., "I have willingly accepted when an error has been brought to my attention, and if given the opportunity, have done what I could to correct the error. I try to be accurate and welcomed being corrected because in my error I might do injustice in some way." And, also, like Judge Chess, I also "believe that is why the system is tiered so you will have many eyes."[38]

(L–R) The Honorable Norwood Carlton Tilley Jr., the Honorable Sammie Chess Jr., and me

38 Webster, Making and Measure of a Judge, 112.

I don't know any judge who does not care about being reversed on appeal, including yours truly. One day I was having a conversation with the Honorable Norwood Calton Tilley Jr. about this very topic regarding a case that had met with disapproval from a higher court. Judge Tilley reminded me of an oft-cited truism: "that should you be affirmed, it doesn't mean you were right; should you be reversed, it doesn't mean you were wrong." Having considered this wisdom espoused by these two outstanding jurists, I felt relieved, especially since I knew I had done my best to make the right decision in the cases before me.

Many times, over the last eighteen years as a state administrative law judge and United States magistrate judge, I have wished that I had more time to study and ponder cases before ruling. However, because of heavy caseloads, there are time constraints in every case, and I simply do the best I can to make a fair and impartial decision guided by conscience, the facts, and the law. After doing that, I leave it up to the higher courts to correct any error. As for me, using these principles allows me to sleep well at night and feel good about my decisions, even if I am reversed by a higher judge or court.

Death on the Witness Stand

DECEMBER 17, 2022

In a cocaine conspiracy trial composed of multiple defendants that began in late July 1989 in the federal court in Winston Salem, North Carolina, one of the key government witnesses collapsed and died on the witness stand as she testified. Nearly a quarter-century later, memory has not dimmed. Nothing can erase my memory of the details of what took place on that ill-fated day. It was the most shocking event that I had ever witnessed in a courtroom during my legal career of forty-five years.

I vividly recall the day shortly after the lunch break that the United States marshal escorted Mrs. Mabel Cardwell of Durham, North Carolina, into court to testify. The legal teams for the multiple defendants had arrived back in court after lunch. These many years later I recall watching the elderly black lady as she entered the courtroom with the marshals. I thought to myself that that day may have been the very time she had ever been in a courtroom in her life. When court resumed, Mrs. Caldwell was called to the witness stand by the assistant United States Attorney, David Smith. Shortly after, she began to testify about her knowledge of packages being mailed to her home address by the post office. My memory was refreshed recently as I read the news coverage of this event. She signed for the packages delivered and that she did not know their contents. They were addressed to her godson, Stanley Nicholson. Her brief testimony also included a statement that he had told her there were Los Angeles jerseys in the packages. She also testified that she had not opened the packages and that she stored them in a closet in her home.

Not long into her examination by the assistant United States Attorney, Ms. Caldwell slumped forward. As reported in the news coverage of the trial, "Ms. Mabel Caldwell of Durham, took a deep breath, removed her glasses, and slumped forward in the witness chair."[39] My recollection after thirty-five years since the trial is that United States District Judge Richard Ervin asked someone to call 911. While we were awaiting the first responders, the marshals approached her limp body and removed her to the floor in front of the witness chair. I also recall that the jury was still in the courtroom, and at this point, one of the defense counsels reminded the judge that the jury was still present. Judge Ervin excused the jury to the jury room. Also, before the first responders arrived, my client, Donell Garrett, announced to Judge Ervin that there was a nurse

39 "In Drug Trial: Stalwart Churchwoman Dies in Witness Chair," Carolina Times, July 29, 1989.

in the courtroom. He said, "Come on up." Ironically my client's mother stood up and came forward to assist. It seemed to be a lifetime of waiting before the first responders arrived. Upon arrival, they also engaged in lifesaving measures, including cutting Mrs. Caldwell's blouse off and exposing her naked upper body. By then I suspect all knew she had expired, although Mrs. Caldwell was not pronounced deceased, and I wondered in the days that followed whether she had survived. However, as the first responders put Mrs. Caldwell on the gurney to remove her from the courtroom, I had moved toward the rear of the courtroom, and defense attorney Barry Stanback and I held open either side of the large doors as the first responders rolled Mrs. Caldwell's lifeless body from the courtroom. I couldn't help but notice Mrs. Caldwell's naked upper body exposed as she was rolled out of the courtroom. It was a very sad day.

As I recall the shocking memories of that day, it is my clear recollection that while efforts to revive Mrs. Caldwell were taking place, I approached the assistant US Attorney to attempt to provide comfort to him, having observed how distraught he was. My efforts were not met with the welcome that I had expected, and therefore I stepped back and made no further attempts to offer comfort. I was just as distraught as he was at the unexpected loss of this precious human being.

Shortly after the events had taken place, out of the presence of the jury, Judge Ervin inquired with the defense counsel and government how we desired to proceed, most likely thinking that defense would move for a mistrial in as much as the jury had witnessed at least some of the sudden and disturbing occurrence. As I recall, defense counsel requested a brief recess to consult with our clients. Upon our return to court, all defense counsel made a motion for a mistrial, which was granted. The thinking of defense counsel was that the jury would most likely be prejudiced by what they had observed and likely hold the witnesses' demise against our clients.

Of course, the death of one witness did not end the trial of the codefendants. My recollection is that a short time after the mistrial was declared, my co-counsel for our client brought a written motion into my office to share with me. It had been filed by the assistant United States Attorney trying the case. He moved the court to allow it to use the in-court testimony of the deceased witness in the new trial. I recall doing considerable legal research regarding the government's motion. Judge Norwood Carlton Tilley Jr. denied the government's motion because defense counsel had not been afforded the opportunity to cross-examine Mrs. Caldwell, presumably based upon defense arguments that it would violate the Confrontation Clause of the Sixth Amendment of the US Constitution.

I was assigned to conduct the opening statement in the new trial.[40] My co-counsel gave much thought to what strategy would be employed during the second trial. One of them, we believed, was to separate our client from the other four defendants. This even included separating our defense table from the others. Our strategy prevailed and after the testimony concluded, and closing arguments were made and the jury was charged, the jury deliberated, and our client was found not guilty. The not guilty verdict did not result in immediate release for our client since he had an additional, less serious charge pending. We successfully negotiated a plea deal for him on that charge, which resulted in a short term of imprisonment for him.

I will never forget the sad and unfortunate death of Mrs. Caldwell. Of course, I thought her death could have been avoided if she had not been used by her godson, Stanley Nicholson, to receive and store the alleged illegal drugs. However, one could never be certain of a different outcome should this seventy-four-year-old woman with health issues, as we learned of after her death, had not testified in this case. A quarter century after her death, I'm sure one could never convince her family that it was not the subpoena that caused her to travel in the company of US marshals the nearly ninety-minute ride from her home in Durham, North Carolina, and the trauma of testifying in a trial in a federal court in Winston Salem that prematurely took her precious life.

One can only wonder whether Mr. Nicholson thought of how he may have contributed to the death of his godmother, and whether Mrs. Caldwell's death was the responsibility of the others charged or convicted in this drug conspiracy. According to the newspaper coverage of this untimely death, the family was certain that Mrs. Caldwell did not know she would be traveling to Winston Salem, and that she thought she would be attending court in downtown Durham, which was just minutes away from her home. Mrs. Caldwell had left some liver thawing on the kitchen table. In a recent conversation with my co-counsel, Steve Bernholz, he recalled that Mrs. Caldwell did not want to come to court and therefore had to be subpoenaed. During my tenure as a judge, I have on several occasions repeated the events of this sad day in my life to the opposing contentious attorneys appearing before me to remind them that there are things far more important than the dispute they are seemingly almost coming to blows about, and that is the brevity and preciousness of life—and the certainty of death.

40 In the spring of 1994, I delivered a Continuing Legal Education program talk sponsored by Wake Forest University School of Law on "Opening Statements Revisited" using this case as an example.

Representing a Member of the Ku Klux Klan (KKK)

SEPTEMBER 11, 2023

No doubt the most stressful case I was ever involved with was for a defendant I was appointed to represent down in Chatham County in the late 1990s or early 2000s. The defendant was a member of the Ku Klux Klan. I had never knowingly met a member of the KKK before.

My abhorrence to the beliefs of this man was not as important as my belief that everyone charged with a crime should be entitled to a lawyer. I was sitting in the courtroom in Pittsboro, North Carolina, one morning waiting for my own case to be called. An assistant public defendant was standing before Judge Leon Stanback. The public defender, who was a black female, was making a motion to be allowed to withdraw from the case. I noticed a tall, lanky-looking, ponytailed man with tattoos standing beside her. Not paying close attention to all that was going on, I did hear Judge Stanback say he would grant the public defender's motion to withdraw. Judge Stanback then started looking around the court in the area where I was sitting alongside other attorneys. He said, "Mr. Webster, are you still on the court-appointed list?" I hesitated but finally said, "Yes, your Honor." Judge Stanback then said, "I believe I will appoint Mr. Webster to represent the defendant in this case." Before I could say anything else, the assistant public defender said, "Your honor, I do not believe it will do any good to appoint Mr. Webster." The judge said, "Why not?" and then asked the public defender and me to approach the bench. We did, and the public defender said, "Your honor, my client is a member of the Ku Klux Klan and that is why I needed to withdraw." Her client did not want a black attorney. Of course, Judge Stanback said, "If he cannot afford to hire his own lawyer, then he cannot pick and choose who I appoint to represent him." Judge Stanback then turned to me and asked whether that would give me any problems—the fact that the defendant was a member of the KKK.

Without mentioning publicly all I said at the bench, I agreed to accept the appointment. I did so because I had and still have a firm belief that everyone, no matter who they are or what they are charged with, is entitled to an attorney. That was the beginning of the most anxiety-filled criminal case I ever handled. While discussing my client's case in my office, on more than one occasion, the defendant issued threats to do bodily harm to the victims and other witnesses in the case. It was the only criminal case where I felt the need to consult with the state bar about whether I should consider withdrawing from the case. After meeting with my client several times in my office, I decided to have future meetings with him in the nearby courthouse. I thought to myself, *I have a wife and three children, and I do not want them to find me dead in some ditch out in the country between Pittsboro and Siler City.*

I tried to obtain the trust of my client. However, I never thought he ever thought about trusting me as a person or as his attorney. The prosecution offered a plea bargain requiring my client to serve a six-month active prison sentence. I made a chart with the most likely outcome should my client decline the plea offer and risk going to trial. He emphatically chose the latter, although we had little to work with. As I recall he even agreed that he would not testify in his own behalf. His estranged wife was one of the witnesses. He told me she was a "crackhead" and he was sure the prosecution would never find her or get her into court. However, they did locate her, and she came into court all dressed up and testified credibly as well as the other witnesses. I cross-examined the prosecution's witnesses as zealously as I could, attempting to score as many points with the jury as I could. I made as convincing a closing argument as I could with the "little" we had to work with. I thought, if we were lucky, perhaps the jury might return a verdict to a lesser-included offense, which would be misdemeanor conviction carrying a far less prison sentence. However, they found him guilty of all felony charges. While the jury was out deliberating the verdict, the bailiff overheard my client telling his brother what he planned to do to those that testified against him. Of course, that was brought to the attention of the assistant district attorney, who brought it to the presiding judge's attention during arguments at sentencing. The judge had the last words that day. "Bailiff, he's in your custody."

The judge did as I told my client that the judge would—give him every day he could do under the sentencing guidelines—and that was around eleven years as I recall. And on top of that, several weeks after the defendant was sentenced, I received a call from the assistant district attorney (ADA), informing me that the judge had erred in the sentence he gave. The ADA went on to tell me that the judge had not given the defendant enough time and that he would have to be brought back to court for resentencing. I thought my nightmare would never be over! When we returned to court for resentencing, sitting there in the holding cell was my client, and on the bench to conduct the resentencing hearing was the Honorable Gregory Weeks, an African American judge from Fayetteville. When I asked my client whether he knew why he had been brought back to court, he said, "No, why?" I said to him, "Because the judge didn't give you enough time." He began use every derogatory word in the English language. I am quite certain that by now my client was thinking that the criminal justice system had concocted a grand conspiracy to convict him because of his beliefs.

When all was said and done, I had zealously represented my client and tried to give him the best representation possible, including legal advice and counsel, while giving him the last word on whether he desired to plead guilty or not guilty and proceed to trial. He also had the last word on whether he wanted to take the stand to testify in his own behalf. He chose not to do so. In some ways it was a sad commentary on how a person's belief can cause them much harm, including a lengthy prison sentence. At least in America, in contrast with many countries around the world, one has the right to remain silent and to a jury trial to determine one's guilt beyond a reasonable doubt, which are two of the chief cornerstones of American democracy.

Presiding in Detention Hearings

2012–PRESENT

Some of the most gut-wrenching cases that I preside over as a US magistrate judge involve the mostly African American young men who are charged with serious felony offenses. After appearing before me usually a week earlier when I inform them of their right to remain silent; that they are not required to make any statements or answer any questions, and if they choose to do so, they should understand that their statements may be used against them; that they have a right to an attorney in their case, that they can hire their own, or if they can't afford one, they may request a court-appointed attorney. And if the government has made or makes a motion to detain them pending trial or further proceedings in their case, they have a right to a detention hearing. This hearing is usually about one week after their initial appearance. If they appear before me after having been indicted, I also inform them that they will be arraigned at the time of their next appearance. Last, I inform them that if they are not a US citizen, then they have the right for a law enforcement official or government agent to contact the consular officer of their country of nationality to report that they have been arrested. Of course, the detainees have the right to waive their right to a detention hearing.

The mostly young men appear before me in their jail attire, a red or orange jumpsuit, often looking disheveled and hopeless. During their detention hearing, they sit beside their attorney and listen to the sworn testimony being presented against them and evidence elicited on cross-examination by their attorney. Hearsay is admissible in detention hearings, and often the governmental agent is not the officer who had primary responsibility for investigating the case. After evidence by the government is presented, defense counsel is asked whether there is evidence for the defendant. If there is evidence, it is usually in the form of evidence from either a proposed third-party custodian such as parent (usually mother) or girlfriend. The purpose of such testimony is to hopefully convince the court that the person testifying is a suitable person in whose custody to place the defendant and that, while the evidence presented suggests the defendant may "be a danger to the community or a flight risk," the suitable third-party custodian, coupled with a monitoring device (if the court finds it necessary), would assure the safety of the community and defendant's appearance in court.

Often, I am unable to release a defendant because most have many convictions in their past of a serious nature, such as assaultive conduct, illegal gun possession, and gun violence—convictions resulting in long prison sentences. Also, they have often violated probations or other orders of the court, failed to appear in court, or otherwise shown disregard or lack of respect for the previous court orders.

The most difficult and gut-wrenching parts of these detention cases have sometimes caused me to go into my chamber, close the doors, and shed tears. I have shed tears not because I have ruled to detain or keep a defendant in jail pending trial but because I see before me the walking dead, those who seem to have lost all hope. Among the many sermons contained in this memoir is a sermon titled "Can These Bones Live?" I draw an analogy to those young men before me charged with serious crimes, and the valley of dry bones found in chapter 37 of the Old Testament Book of Ezekiel. Contained within the multitude of pretrial services (probation) reports are many examples of statements obtained by the probation officers who interview the detainees, or in court statements or other observations I have made that pierce my heart. Some are exemplary of the insanity of the mostly young men of this generation. Consider the following:

"My father never did anything for me. My mother had a lot of men in and out of her life. I know she loved me, but she didn't have time to spend with me. She had too many children."

Tears flowed down the cheeks of a handsome young man when he responded to my question in court about where his father lives. He said, "I don't know who my father is."

I've seen the following statement in the probation report more than any other: "I have no relationship with my father."

"My father is in prison."

"I dropped out of school in the 9th grade."

"Defendant has eight children by seven different mothers."

A defendant's record included numerous convictions of assaultive conduct, but he also had been assaulted numerous times himself. He had just been released from the hospital recovering from a gunshot wound to his scrotum.

My in-court observations include the fact that in eleven years as a federal magistrate judge, I have seen no more than a handful of fathers who appeared in court with their sons for consideration as third-party custodians.

Numerous detainees have appeared before me in court after having been administered Narcan to revive them, apparently not knowing they had been near death. They did not appear to be remorseful, or in any mental condition to want to change, to reverse their downward spiral toward imminent death.

I have been astonished with testimony in detention hearings that some defendants were "going live" (broadcasting a live video stream in real time) while committing crimes. Equally amazing are the number of young men in custody pending further proceedings and trial who make telephone calls from recorded jail lines to family or friends to discuss the facts related to their pending charges.

Most troubling of all my observations during criminal duty, however, is the overwhelming absence of fathers in the lives of black youth, from birth up to the time they appear before me in orange jumpsuits. The missing fathers, who often themselves are serving prison terms, or are in gangs which they joined to have a semblance of family, is glaring and truly disturbing. It is clear to me that most young defendants appearing before me that are facing very serious charges have not been taught right from wrong. It is not only young black males that suffer without working fathers in the home, but also young black females and the entire community. The dearth of working fathers as role models for their sons has been devastating in so many ways. Indeed "an idle mind is the devil's workshop!" The emotional strain on black female mothers and their daughters is undoubtedly shattering also. For years to come, America will pay a high price for its harsh prison sentences for its past and present sentences that amount to life in prison not only for the convicted persons, but for their families and the communities left desolate in their absence.

The Hepatitis C Case

2018

One of the challenging aspects of this case was that medical evidence was a big part of the overall evidence, which required the court to have some understanding of the testimony. One of the factors that influenced the court's decision was the plaintiff's medical expert's affidavit testimony and in court live testimony under oath that "effective treatment of [hepatitis C virus] involves treating patients well before the presence of cirrhosis and that the accuracy of the FibroSure testing mechanism was inconsistent."

While my decision was only a recommendation, which was in part confirmed by the district judge, I am of the belief that a thorough finding of facts supported by the law can lead to justice being afforded at the end of all appeals. The US Supreme Court eloquently summed up why it was important to rule in the manner I did in this case. In *Brown v. Plata,* the Supreme Court held that

> To incarcerate, society takes from prisoners the means to provide for their own needs. Prisoners are dependent on the State for food, clothing, and necessary medical care. A prison's failure to provide sustenance for inmates may actually produce physical torture or a lingering death. Just as prisoners may starve if not fed, he or she may suffer or die if not provided adequate medical care. A prison that deprives prisoners of basic sustenance, including adequate medical care, is incompatible with the concept of human dignity and has no place in organized society.
> (563 U.S. 493, 510–11, 2011) (INTERNAL QUOTATIONS AND CITATIONS OMITTED)

I recommended that a preliminary injunction that would enjoin the enforcement of the State of North Carolina's Department of Public Safety policy in effect at the time the lawsuit was filed. It denied medically necessary, lifesaving treatment to many in the prison population who suffer from one of the deadliest infectious diseases in the United States. I recommended that plaintiff's motion to certify a class be granted, and that the class be defined as "all current and future prisoners in DPS custody who have or will have chronic hepatitis C virus and have not been treated with direct-acting antiviral drugs." I further recommended that Lloyd Buffkin and Robert Parham be named as class representatives and that plaintiff's counsel be appointed as class counsel and plaintiff's motion for preliminary injunction be granted and that a preliminary injunction be granted ordering defendants to provide universal opt-out HCV screening to all persons who are or will be in DPS custody; cease denying direct-acting antiviral (DAA) treatment for the contraindications, other than patient refusal, set out in Step 4a of DPS Policy #CP7; and that plaintiffs and all members of their class with DAAs according to the current standard of medical care set out in the ASSLD/IDSA Guidance, regardless of an individual's fibrosis level.

The Alcoa Aluminum Case

2010–2012

Early proceedings in this case included Alcoa Power Generating Inc.; the North Carolina Department of Environmental and Natural Resources (DENR); Division of Water Quality, Stanley County, North Carolina; and Yadkin River Keepers.

Alcoa's fifty-year federal permit was expiring, and to get it renewed, they had to first obtain a water quality certification from the State of North Carolina. The most challenging aspect of this case was the fact that politics was a driving force. Sure, the various hearings, depending on their nature, brought well-respected lawyers from law firms from North Carolina, California, and Washington, DC. As I recall, Parker Poe Adams & Bernstein was representing Stanley County. A well-respected law firm in California was the main firm representing Alcoa, along with Hunton and Williams acting as local counsel. A special deputy attorney general and perhaps another attorney from the Attorney General's Office was representing the state, and a local attorney for Yadkin River Keepers, which opposed the petitioner's application to obtain a water quality certification, moved to intervene in the case, which I granted.

I recall that at least on two occasions, eight or nine lawyers were lined up at the respective parties' tables facing the court. Sure, some of the facts of the case were detailed, scientific in nature, and unfamiliar to me, especially those related to the water quality studies. I also recall that there were many evidentiary objections during the hearings that slowed the proceedings. And the quantity of legal briefings was voluminous and time consuming. However, the fact that remains in my memory is how political the case was from the very first hearing—which I recall was a preliminary injunction hearing.

I could not help but take notice that as I took the bench the first day for the hearing, the courtroom was unusually full of interested persons, and more attorneys than usual. Toward the rear of the court, I observed a well-dressed gentleman standing. After hearing the arguments of the attorneys of record, the well-dressed man rose to his feet and begin to speak without permission of the court. He just started speaking, and I was courteous to him, not knowing what he was about to say. He introduced himself and stated that he was there to represent the governor of North Carolina. The governor was not a party to the proceeding before me. The gentleman made a few other statements, whose purpose was obviously designed to assuage or gain the favor of the large Stanley County constituents present in the courtroom to oppose the petition for the water quality certification. I learned at some point that Alcoa used to be an employer of many

Stanley County residents, but Alcoa had closed much of its operations in the county with a resulting loss of jobs. The facts brought out later that at the time of the petition, Alcoa employed only a few residents in comparison to prior years and the residents felt that Alcoa was in Stanley County only to make money from the sale of electricity produced by its dams to residents.

Before the attorney representing the governor could complete his comments to the court, I stopped him and informed him that I had nothing before me that said the governor was a party to this action. I then requested counsel for the parties to the case to approach the bench for a sidebar. I recall looking squarely into the eyes of the main attorney for the state and saying, "I thought you said you were representing the state." He responded, "I am, your honor. I did not know he was coming." It seems I recall that I allowed the governor to file an amicus brief subsequent to the hearing.

A hearing of the contested case began some weeks after the initial proceedings in the case. I recall after many days of testimony the court and parties scheduled a "judge's view" of the Alcoa dams in Stanley County. Attorneys for the parties attended, and we got on a small boat with the attorneys and a representative of Alcoa to travel out to the facility that operated the dam. We went into the bowels of the dam to observe how it operated. It seems I recall that at some point in the proceeding, a stay was issued at the request of the parties.

As I recall, there came a time possibly in the late summer or early fall of 2012 that I informed the parties that I had been appointed to the position of US magistrate judge for the Middle District of North Carolina and would be resigning my position as administrative law judge. I read later that the case had made its way to the federal courts, where the state's new position was that the State of North Carolina owned the river and therefore Alcoa had no right to operate a dam on state-owned property. I learned later this position was not supported by the federal court. I also learned that the case was later settled.

During the period I was involved in the case, there was no doubt in my mind that the case was more about politics than the law or the facts of the case. And this complicated a final resolution of the case, and I'm sure increased the costs in time and resources expended to reach a final resolution. Notwithstanding the challenging nature of this case, acting as both judge and jury during my tenure in the case helped me become a better judge than I would be if I had not been selected to hear this complicated but important matter.

Barbara Fretwell v. Madison Mayodan Schools

1985–1986

Ms. Barbara Fretwell was a longtime secretary with the Madison-Mayodan School System, first as secretary for John W. Dillard, principal at Charles R. Drew High School, and later becoming secretary for another principal, Gail Collins. Ms. Collins fired Ms. Fretwell for allegations of unsatisfactory job performance. After twenty-five years of satisfactory job performance, no one in her community believed that could be true. In 1985, Ms. Fretwell came to me for representation, and I agreed to take her case.

We pursued Ms. Fretwell's appeal while seeking to resolve it before filing a lawsuit. The case became challenging because the black community knew Ms. Fretwell well and felt an injustice was taking place. The news media became interested in Ms. Fretwell's plight and reported on the case. As attorney, I was called upon to comment more than in any that case I had ever had previously. As I recall, a news conference was held in my office, and I traveled to a High Point news station for live coverage concerning my client's case. There being no effort by the school to resolve the case, a decision was made to hold a demonstration on February 17, 1986, from 8 a.m. to 5 p.m. so that the school could see Ms. Fretwell had broad support in the community. It was the first such demonstration in the nearly 170-year history of the founding of the Town of Madison. Reverend John Mendez, a civil rights advocate from Winston Salem agreed to speak at the rally. It was held in the front of the School Administrative Building. At the conclusion of his speech, participants, holding hands, sang "We Shall Overcome Some Day." The local paper reported on the demonstration and posted a photo of the participants walking the sidewalks and the leaders of the demonstration standing with arms clasped together in the traditional civil rights posture. It was a very peaceful demonstration and adhered to all Town of Madison requirements, including obtaining a demonstration permit. The demonstration included, in pertinent part, my statement to the audience:

> We are here today to say that the Christian and good people of this town will not stand by while our people are humiliated and treated unjustly in this school system and this town. We will not stand by while the future of our children becomes dimmer and dimmer in the town of Madison. We are here to demonstrate and tell the world that we will not commit the sin of silence anymore.

Further community support for Ms. Fretwell was demonstrated when a rally and fundraiser were held at the St. Stephens Methodist Church on April 25, 1986.

This case was very challenging because of my atypical advocacy and the involvement of the community that had an interest in the case and a commitment to obtaining justice for my client. I learned that it was important to make sure my client was on board with all the community was doing to help her, and she was. The case became very time consuming. During the time of my representing Ms. Fretwell, I was reminded of my mother's oft-stated advice to my family, as guided by the scriptures. She reminded us that there was a time and place for all things (ECCLESIASTES 3:1–11) and everything should be decent and in order (1 CORINTHIANS 14:40). In my representation of Ms. Fretwell, I tried to adhere to these principles, although I'm sure my opponent viewed my efforts as unnecessary and radical. The case was eventually settled. My client didn't get her job back, but my client and I felt it was in her interest and that of the community.

My mother, Bettie E. Webster, among the protestors

RALLY

AND

FUNDRAISER

On Behalf Of

Barbara B. Fretwell

FRIDAY, APRIL 25, 1986

7:30 pm

St. Stephens

United Methodist Church

Madison, North Carolina

PROGRAM

Opening Song	*Congregation*
Prayer	*Rev. Benjamin Mittman, Pastor, Goodwill Baptist Church, Madison, N. C.*
Welcome and Introduction of Mistress of Ceremonies	*Rev. Roger Hunter, Pastor, St. Stephens United Methodist Church and other churches in Madison Circuit*
Mistress of Ceremonies	*Ruth M. Wiley*
Solo	*Renee Lowe*
Introduction of Speaker	*Rev. Allandus Wright, Jr., Pastor, Mt. Sinai Baptist Church, Eden, N. C.*
Solo	*George Graves*
Speaker	*Rev. John Mendez, Pastor Emmanuel Baptist Church Winston-Salem, N. C.*
Song "We Shall Overcome"	*Congregation*
Call for Donations	*John W. Dillard*
Remarks	
Benediction	

Program Sponsored by the Committee for Fairness and Justice Jimmie Dalton, Treasurer, 319 Short Avenue, Madison, N. C. 27025

Rally and fundraiser program for Barbara Fretwell

Town of Green Level v. Alamance County

2003–2006

While serving as town attorney for the Town of Green Level, a majority-black town, as part of my general practice of law with my office located in Pittsboro, North Carolina, the town placed Alamance County on notice that it would enact an Extraterritorial Jurisdiction (ETJ) ordinance. I along with the town administrator visited the Alamance County manager's office to inform him of the town's plans. Shortly thereafter, the county sent a letter to the town that it had to obtain the county's approval to go forward with the town's ETJ plans. The town informed the county that it disagreed with the county's position. Thereafter, the town hired a surveyor to map the ETJ boundary and forthwith mailed notices to the affected residents of a town public hearing regarding the town's plan. As I recall, the county also noticed a hearing regarding its plans to enact an ordinance creating a Rural Community Zoning District, which if enacted would block the town's ETJ efforts. Because the county's notice requirements were shorter than the town's notice requirements, the county was able to schedule its required hearing before Green Level's ETJ hearing.

I was present at the county's hearing, which was full of county residents opposing Green Level's ETJ efforts. I could not believe what I was observing. It reminded me of what efforts at seeking integration of public schools and other public accommodations must have been like in the early days of the civil rights struggle. I overheard one man say he would rather be under any town other than Green Level. I did not hear any racial epithets, but I felt like it was possible because of the tone of the meeting. It was clear to me that the affected residents did not want ETJ because of the Town of Green Level being a majority-black town. The county voted to enact its new zoning ordinance. Thereafter the town also enacted its ETJ ordinance some days after the county enacted its ordinance.

In the early part of 2004, the town retained outside counsel and, along with me serving as co-counsel, filed a complaint against the County of Alamance. A hearing was held in the Superior Court of Alamance County, and after hearing testimony, the presiding judge ruled in the county's favor. Green Level filed a timely appeal, and in 2007, the North Carolina Court of Appeals unanimously ruled in Green Level's favor, finding that the county's denial of the ETJ was arbitrary and capricious. The North Carolina Supreme Court declined to hear the county's appeal, and the case was closed in July 2007.

This case was challenging in part because of its racial overtones. The town's council and all of its citizens knew why Green Level was being denied what nearly every other municipality had in Alamance County, including the Village of Alamance, which was smaller in population than Green Level. Moreover, it was sickening to realize how much money my client had to expend for representation, far exceeding one hundred thousand dollars, as I understand it. Upon reflection on this case, it saddens me today that race still plays a role in much of everyday life in America. When will it ever end?

A Lawsuit against My Hometown of Madison

1984

Up until the time of being denied a conditional use permit by the Town of Madison's Board of Adjustment, I had never felt so unfairly mistreated in my life. It hurts so much to be treated unfairly. I had stood for justice since opening my law practice in my hometown. I had represented many who could not afford a lawyer, conducted myself righteously, and tried to be an example for others. Yet that didn't seem to matter. I learned firsthand that there were still those in the world who didn't believe in fair treatment; there were those who didn't believe in justice.

Not only did the Board of Adjustment vote against me opening an office in the house my wife and I purchased at 215 Decatur Street, Madison, North Carolina, but the savings and loan located there turned down our application for a loan for $47,500. The purchase price of the house was $50,000. Perhaps agonizing and disheartening best describe how I felt at the time. Most in my hometown felt that I was being discriminated against because of my race by the power base of my hometown. It did feel that way, although I also felt the actions taken by the Board of Adjustment and the bank were simply unfair. After all, the house we had contracted to purchase was in an area of town where there was already a dentist's office across the street and down the street was a law office and a real estate agent's office. Of course, they were all white owned, so it was easy to wonder why I was being treated differently from those businesses.

As the only African American attorney in the history of my hometown, which had been founded in 1818, I knew that I had to fight this injustice—that the decision of the town could not stand. My thought was that if I could be treated so unfairly as an attorney who knows the law, then what chance would a poor person of color have to obtain justice? So, I made up my mind that regardless of the cost and no matter how long it took, I would fight this injustice. Recently I was reviewing my notes and documents from nearly four decades ago—my handwritten notes long since forgotten. The local savings and loan that denied us a loan later communicated to me and stated that if I got John and Mable Dillard and Charles and Helen Dalton to purchase the house with us and be on the mortgage loan, then they would finance the loan. Of course, they said, they would have to review their financial information also. Mr. John Dillard was the retired school principal of the former all-black Charles R. Drew High School. His wife, Dr. Mabel Dillard, was a retired professor at North Carolina A&T State University, and they had been longtime respected residents of the town of Madison. Charles Dalton and his wife, Helen, were also some of the most respected African American residents of Madison. Mr. Dalton was one of the few African Americans holding a supervisory position in one of the textile mills in town, and his wife worked in one of the textile company's offices in Madison. As far as I was concerned, the bank's offer was not an offer at all and was frankly insulting. It was also as hurtful as the town's decision to deny the conditional use permit. I learned that there was a black-owned bank in Greensboro. I applied there, and within a few days we had been approved for a mortgage loan without mention of co-owners or co-signers.[41]

At the time, I was renting my law office from Eugene Russell, whose law office was also in the same building that he owned. Gene, as I came to know him, was a Christian man exhibiting Christian principles in his daily walk. At the time, I recalled the well-known principle that "He who represents himself as a lawyer has a fool for a client." Therefore, I sought out an attorney to file a lawsuit on my behalf. Gene was indeed a real estate expert, and he agreed to represent me. I don't even recall whether he charged me a fee. If he did, it was very little. He timely filed a petition in Superior Court of Rockingham County. It was to my good fortune that the matter came before the Honorable Melzer "Pat" Morgan from Reidsville, North Carolina. He was known to rule fairly and justly. I had seen him in the Reidsville court many times as he represented his clients prior to becoming a judge. In all the decades that I have known him, I have never seen even one indication that he held any racial or other biases. After hearing the evidence and considering the arguments of counsel, Judge Morgan took the matter under advisement. Shortly thereafter, He ruled in my favor and remanded the case back to the Town of Madison for further proceedings. The headlines of the November 21, 1984, edition of the Madison Messenger read: Attorneys Permit: Judge Orders Board to Reconsider. In part, Judge Morgan's Order stated, "The Board of Adjustment may not deny Petitioner this conditional use in their unguided discretion, on the grounds that would adversely affect the public interest. Shortly after Judge Morgan's decision was rendered, the town settled the case, and a conditional use permit was granted, giving me the right to use the house we purchased as my law office.

I could not have accomplished this win without the help of many of my supporters in my hometown. Also, knowing the importance of this matter, people like my then–Masonic lodge brothers Billy Watkins, Early Moore, and others stepped up to the plate and assisted me financially. My parents and others helped me as they prayed for me daily. My wife, Diane, didn't give up on me, although I could see the toll that this matter was

41 In a recent conversation with my aunt Hazel Moore, I leaned, that years earlier, she and her husband, Early, had also been denied a home loan by a savings and loan bank in Madison. This was after having retained the services of a well-known local builder who presented the local savings and loan their application for new home construction with the house blueprints on land that they owned in town. The builder reported back to Early and Hazel that the officials of the institution denied the loan and stated, "There is not another black person in Madison that has a house that nice." This brought back the memory of the local savings and loan official asking me, "What if the town didn't approve my application to use the house as my law office?

taking on her. I tried to be strong, but in life sometimes you must shed tears. I'm glad that throughout this process I leaned on my Redeemer who woke me up this morning.

I have considered many times over the years whether my efforts were worth the struggle. I know that it was worth it, but the struggle for human dignity, respect, and fair treatment took much out of my wife and me. It was tiring, causing me many sleepless nights and tremendous stress. It was not as if my representation of clients or my responsibilities as husband and father could be placed on hold during our struggle to achieve justice. In some ways I never fully recovered the remaining time I practiced law in my hometown.

Two years after having a grand opening of my law office, I decided that I had experienced enough in my hometown. Therefore, I relocated to the state capital of Raleigh to begin work with the North Carolina Department of Justice, Attorney General's Office, as an associate attorney general. Four decades later, I'm still standing for equal justice and as an advocate for human dignity as an US magistrate judge for the Middle District of North Carolina. I try to make sure that those who come before me in criminal court know that I see them; that I understand their plight, even when I cannot release them from their prison cells pending trial. I try to encourage them not to give up on life; that their children need them as fathers to wrap their arms around them. After ten years now, I'm not certain I have reached one person, but I have tried. Observing one young man in tears standing before me in court, who said he had never met his father, I'm inclined to believe that my encouragement to him and others has not been in vain.

The subject of lawsuit in *Joe L. Webster v. Town of Madison* law office, fall 1984–November 1986

My first law office where I hung my shingle, 1980–1984

CHAPTER NINE

My Beloved Alma Mater, Howard University

Selected Writings from My Personal Blog, Makingadifferenceathowardu.blogspot.com

To the Class of 2014 and Future Classes: A Few Words of Advice from a Two-Time Graduate of Howard University

AUGUST 14, 2010

On or about August 15, 1972, I began my lifelong love affair with Howard University. My brother James drove me to Howard from rural North Carolina. I was too excited to be anxious about anything. I remember checking into Slowe Hall, my first visit to the "Yard," and the various social events that took place during freshman orientation week. I met many people from all walks of life, from all parts of the United States and the world. The girls were prettier than the ones I saw in the university bulletin I received in the mail. The smell of city life was all around me. Music was in the air. I heard the Last Poets, Gil Scott Heron, and others who put truth to music, and I liked that message. Practically everyone I met from up north used the slang word "solid," meaning there was solidarity or as an indication of agreement between two or more people. My platform shoes and afro hair style increased my height from six feet to six feet, four inches adorned in my bell bottom pants. I thought I was cool and had it going on. Howard University was the place for me, and I was happy that I turned down offers of admission to North Carolina A&T State University and the University of North Carolina at Chapel Hill, both great universities in my home state.

There was so much to see, do, and learn at Howard and in DC. Coming from the rural South, I hardly knew what a city block was. I had never ridden a city bus or hailed a cab. Nevertheless, I was fearless. I came to Howard with a deficient public-school education in some respects, and because of that, was required to take a remedial reading course. Sister Monica, a very petite nun, taught the course. Even now, I vividly recall the sight of her in full attire strolling across campus and how out of place she looked. But I also remember seeing Dr. Rayford W. Logan, who frequently walked across campus during his later years. At that time, I didn't know of his contributions to Howard, but later learned that he was an esteemed professor; author of *Howard University, The First Hundred Years, 1867–1967*; and one of the foremost African American scholars of the twentieth century. At the time, I did not know of Lucy Diggs Slowe, the namesake of my dorm and her contributions to the AKA sorority. History was all around me on the campus landmarks bearing their names: Frederick Douglass Hall, Locke, Drew, Carver, Wheatley, and Baldwin. And here I was, in a special place referred to as the "capstone" of Negro education.

I offer the following advice to the entering Class of 2014, those who are returning for another year, and future incoming classes:

- Be safe at all times. Don't let your youthful fearlessness cause you to take chances. There lurks danger in dark alleys and lighted streets as well.
- Stay focused. Don't let anything, including financial issues, deter you. I never forgot why I came to Howard, and you should not either. "A mind is a terrible thing to waste," an often-used motto by the United Negro College Fund. There is much to learn and for you to contribute to your classmates, the university, and the world. Drugs and alcohol will dim your focus and cause you to take your eyes off the prize.
- Take advantage of the many famous and not so famous who will visit Howard to tell you of their journey. Chose to attend a play at Ira Aldridge or a lecture on campus, every once in a while, rather than attending a party.
- Get to know, really know, your classmates and professors and do what you can to help your classmates. Some of my closest friends I have today are students and professors I met at Howard in the 1970s. Respect them and demand respect from them as well.
- Give your best in the classroom, and while matriculating at Howard, give the best of your service to the university and the DC community. There is much need there. It will pay dividends untold as you move through life.
- Finally, whatever your faith walk may be, attend chapel or a congregation of your choosing as often as your mind and body will allow you to get up after a late-night party or however you spend your Saturday nights. My own mother, now suffering with Alzheimer's disease, encouraged me greatly when I prepared to go off to Howard. She told me that if I worked hard and "put God first

in my life, then someone would see me trying and someone would help me." I didn't always follow her advice while at Howard, but I always remembered her words hewed out of the wisdom that comes from just living and her own faith walk. I've found her words to be just as true today as they were when she uttered them in August 1972.

Graduation photo, Howard University, May 8, 1976

Dressed for success as an undergraduate at Howard

From a required remedial reading class my freshman year in fall semester 1972 to Dr. James E. Cheek, Howard University president, congratulating me at the School of Liberal Arts Honors Program graduation ceremony, Spring 1976

Graduation Day, Howard University School of Law, May 12, 1979

Founders Library on the main campus. COURTESY OF CAMILLE J. WEBSTER

Lucy Diggs Slowe Hall, where I lived for three years as an undergraduate at Howard. COURTESY OF CAMILLE J. WEBSTER

Frederick Douglass Hall, where most of my political science major and history minor courses were held. COURTESY OF CAMILLE J. WEBSTER

Celebrating with son-in-law and grandson, 2023
Homecoming Weekend, "HU, You Know!"

On the law school campus, 2018

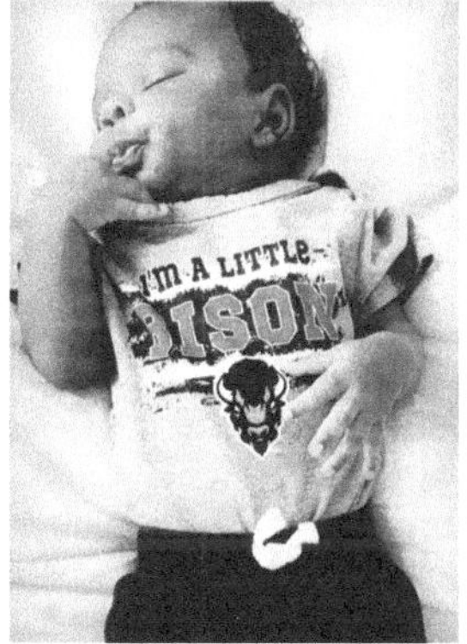

Future Bisons—Two of Joe's grandsons. Paraphrasing:
The Bible says train up a child in the way they shall go
and when they are old they won't depart from it.

Living History

AUGUST 3, 2008

For most, history resides on shelves, but for Howardites and the alums who attended a June 2007 meeting of the Howard University Alumni Association—Research Triangle Chapter, history is more than a book when it comes to a national treasure in the person of John Hope Franklin. Dr. Franklin, best known for his work *From Slavery to Freedom,* was the guest speaker during my last quarterly meeting as president of the chapter.

It was truly an honor for our chapter to host this former Howard University professor (1947–1956), United States historian, past president of the American Historical Association, Professor Emeritus of History at Duke University, and 1995 awardee of the nation's highest civilian honor: the Presidential Medal of Freedom.

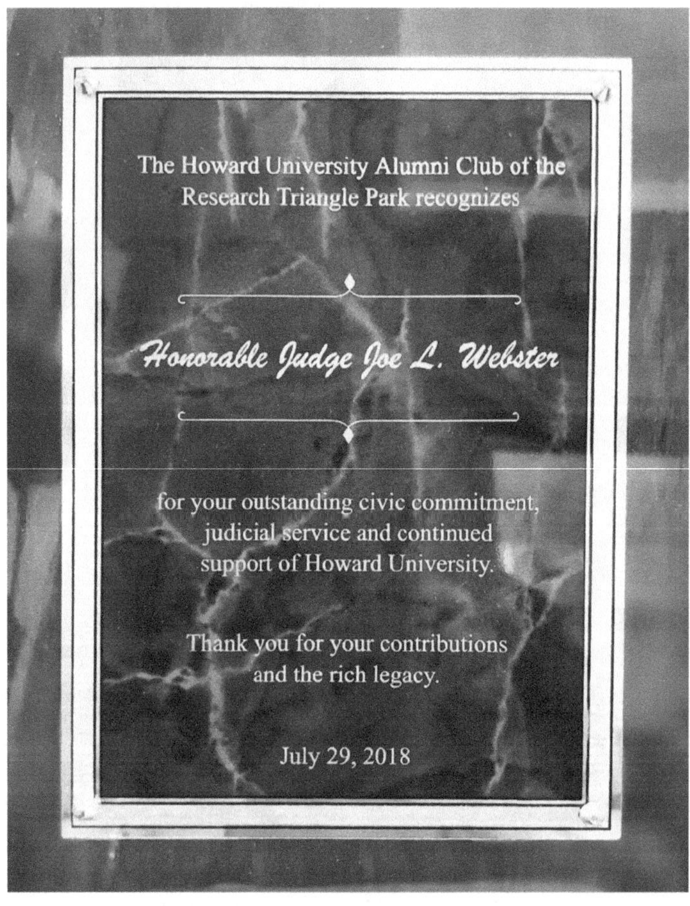

HBCUs in the Twenty-First Century

MARCH 31, 2008

Recently I read an article in the *Kansas City Star* about whether historically black colleges and universities remain relevant in the twenty-first century. I recall reading a similar article almost two decades ago and engaged in a debate about it with one of my legal colleagues. His argument was that since many of the HBCUs were inadequately funded, they should be closed. I was so angry that I couldn't think completely straight. He also stated that schools such as Howard University might remain open because of historical and cultural significance. Now that federal and state money is on the decline, this shortsighted debate has reared its ugly head once again. What in the world are those who entertain these thoughts thinking (or drinking)? Have they not heard, have they not witnessed, have they not given any thought to how HBCUs have transformed communities, cities, and countries? One need only read the bios of political candidates in a local newspaper. There's at least one HBCU candidate, and more than likely a graduate of Howard University, on the ballot. HBCUs have transformed a whole race, entire nations, as well as generations. Every HBCU graduate and others of goodwill should prepare to go to battle for the cause of continued full funding of HBCUs. HBCUs are as relevant today as they were when founded at the end of the Civil War. This country and this world have been and continue to be enriched by the impact of HBCU graduates, who carry not only a degree but, in the words of a Howard University Charter Day award recipient, a "commission to become a social engineer."

On March 13 of this year, I had the great honor to represent Howard University as the 2008 Alumni Achievement Recipient at the MEAC Basketball Tournament in Raleigh, North Carolina. As I stood at midcourt during the halftime ceremonies, I thought of what it all meant, and I thought mostly of my continuing obligation to make a difference to the local, regional, and global communities. As long as there is a breath of life in me, I will forever remain faithful to this calling, including fighting to keep Howard and other HBCUs open. Like you, I am a social engineer with a resounding and proud commitment to our past, present, and future.

Campus Security

MARCH 23, 2008

Three years ago, about this time of the year on a Sunday morning, I received a call from my daughter, then a freshman at Howard. I could tell she was full of anxiety. Before I could ask what was wrong, she said, "Richard and Cretia were robbed at gunpoint on campus." She described the ordeal, which happened on the side of Founders Library late at night. Richard and Cretia were talking when several men approached, pointed a gun at them, and demanded their money. Richard clerked in my law office the summer before, and I had met my daughter's friend Cretia, who had visited in our Chapel Hill home. So, I knew them well. It was as if my daughter or I had been robbed. What could I do? What should I do? After consoling my daughter, I resolved that I would call the university the next day to discuss the situation. What measures could the university take to protect its greatest treasure—its students, who sometimes don't use good judgment? I thought about how many times as a student, thirty years earlier, I walked from Slowe Hall to the yard for a party late at night. In fact, one time, while a friend and I were walking on Third Street on our way to a party, a man pointed a gun at us. The man appeared to be intoxicated and our instinct told us to run and hide behind cars parked along the street until the man passed by. Could an open campus such as Howard build a wall to prevent students from leaving and nonstudents or faculty from entering? Of course not. Could the university afford to hire enough security police to place an officer on every block of the campus from Sherman Avenue to North Capitol Street? Of course not. And then, what about Meridian Hill Hall, Sixteenth Street, and all the blocks in between? More officers, more walls? Of course not.

Security in and around Howard University, as well as campuses around the country, should be the number-one concern. Security should be the number-one topic on the agenda of every board meeting, meeting of the president, and other university officials 365 days of the year. University leaders must do everything within their power to protect the institutions' most precious resource: its students. Safety and security must be top priorities. And our students need to make safety a normal part of their campus routine. We preach this constantly to our daughter, who will graduate in May, and we pray for God's protection, knowing she will not always make the right choices, just like we didn't more than thirty years ago.

Miami Classic a Success!

OCTOBER 9, 2008

My recent visit to Miami, Florida, last month was a great opportunity to witness the Howard University Bison football team play the Savannah State Tigers football team in the first annual Miami Classic. The Bison, with twelve South Florida players on its roster, executed a well-prepared game plan to overpower Savannah State, 49-21. The game, crowd, and enthusiasm did not disappoint. Everything—including the wide-open offenses of both teams, the infectious energy of the cheerleading squads, the toe-stepping], foot-thumping drumbeats of the Savannah State and local high school bands, and the pride of the Bison Blue in the stands—rekindled fond memories.

This was the inaugural year of the Miami Classic and a great opportunity for Howard to showcase its South Florida talent. With some of the country's best gridiron football talent and hundreds of Howard alums who reside in the area, this event is a no-brainer. South Florida and the Classic is a perfect match. Despite the sparse stadium crowd, enthusiasm was at an all-time high. Therefore, I view this event as a success, for it cements a foundation for growth and leadership.

As I reflect on this weekend, I ponder the true meaning of success. Should we measure success by the size of a crowd in a stadium? One Howard University motto is "Leadership for America and the global community." If Howard is to continue to be a great beacon of hope, it must continue to reach out to places where the lights don't always shine so brightly. In my youth, many times my mother said that "charity begins at home and spreads abroad." Howard accomplished its leadership role by playing football against Savannah State in Miami, in a stadium not far from Liberty City, a community where riots and other evidence of despair have occurred.

There is talk that the Classic will continue in the future, perhaps in a larger stadium and against one of the conference teams from Florida. Let's hope that the Classic does, in fact, continue. With greater planning, publicity, and involvement of local high school coaches, community leaders, and die-hard fans, there is no doubt that this event will become an even greater success in the future. Maybe the Howard University Marching Band will accompany the team next year. Then it will really be Bison Showtime!

The Summer Wind Blows the Best and Brightest My Way!

AUGUST 12, 2008

This has been an incredible summer. Not only did we have another young Howard graduate (my daughter Camille) join the ranks of proud alumni committed to making a difference, but I, along with other members of the Howard University Alumni Club of the Research Triangle, had an extraordinary opportunity to meet a group of current Howard University students participating in a collaborative prostate cancer training program at the Duke University Prostate Center.

The students, twelve of them in fact, would spend ten weeks conducting important research on prostate cancer, the single most diagnosed non-skin cancer among African Americans and the second-leading cause of cancer death in African American men.

Joe attending 2023 Howard University Homecoming Parade with classmates Orlando Dixon and Clarence Pittman in the background

I first met the students at a dinner party hosted by the Honorable Bill Bell, mayor of Durham, NC, and a proud Howard alum. I met with them a few days later, hoping that, at the very least, I could ascertain their perspectives and concerns on the state of Howard University and, at the very most, just to be in the company of the best and brightest. I was not disappointed.

And when I thought it couldn't get any more impressive, on August 1, I attended the students' final presentations on their research. Never have I observed a more prepared, knowledgeable, confident, articulate, and poised group. They were outstanding. So outstanding, in fact, I witnessed many of the Duke professors nodding their heads in agreement with the students. One even commented to me, "You'd think that these students had already graduated from medical school." WOW!

These young men and women will climb great heights in their respective endeavors. They will change lives and they will change the world. They are the best and brightest, not only at Howard, but anywhere to be found. The summer wind blew them my way, and what a blessing it was to experience part of their journey.

POSTER COURTESY OF BRUCE DEPYSSLER

Howard University School of Law

JULY 12, 2024

During my teenage years, I had heard about Howard University's law school before I had heard about Howard University in general. Having grown up reading about the role Howard's law school played in the civil rights struggle was integral to my longing to attend the university. Thurgood Marshall's name was just one of those that I heard about before his appointment to the US Supreme Court in 1967. I had learned of his advocacy as a civil rights lawyer who became well known as one of the attorneys *in Brown v. Board of Education* and other cases brought to dismantle segregation in public schools and other public accommodations. I learned early in high school that Thurgood Marshall graduated from Howard University Law School, as did other legal luminaries such as Oliver Hill, Vernon Jordan, and Judge Damen Keith. In my native state of North Carolina, Howard Law School continues to produce advocates for equal justice under the law, such as three pioneers who made their mark in North Carolina from the Howard University Law School class of 1951: the late Honorable Richard Erwin, the late Representative Annie Brown Kennedy, and her husband, Harold L. Kennedy Jr., and more recent graduates, including my 1979 law school classmate the Honorable Loretta Copeland-Biggs. Judge Biggs is a US district court judge for the Middle District of North Carolina. On May 14, 2024, I had the great privilege of joining some noted scholars for a webinar sponsored by the American Bar Association in celebration of the seventieth anniversary of the *Brown v. Board of Education* decision, and its status in constitutional law and US society. The program was titled "*Brown v. Board* at 70: Is the Battle Over?" For my part on the program, I paid homage to some of the courageous lawyers who took on challenging cases to gain equal opportunity for African Americans using the Fourteenth Amendment's Equal Opportunity Clause as a weapon. Of course, many of the early pioneers were trained at Howard's law

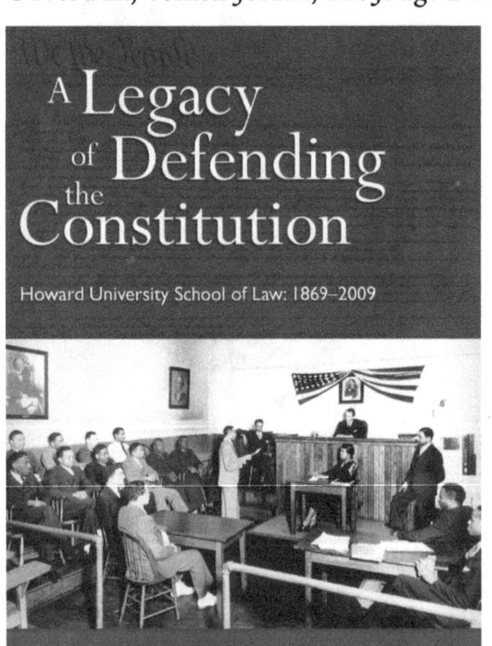

WITH PERMISSION OF HOWARD UNIVERSITY

school. I made the point that we need more courageous lawyers like those civil rights lawyers, who often worked for little or no pay.

While not a Howard Law graduate, Dean Charles Hamilton Houston provided leadership for the law school at a crucial period in the civil rights struggle. Howard students were groomed to be "social engineers." He once said to his Howard Law students that "a lawyer is either a social engineer or a parasite on society." Thurgood Marshall and many other eminent and even not-so-well-known Howard Law graduates took up this mantle of becoming zealous advocates for eradicating the injustices of inequality and racial discrimination that had long been a terrible stain on American society. For all its existence, my alma mater truly does have a legacy of defending the Constitution, and I'm confident it will continue to do so in the years to come.

Lasting Memories

There have been many memorable occasions both as a student and the many times I have returned to my alma mater during Homecoming Weekend and for other gatherings. As a student, one day during my last year of law school in 1978, one weekend in 1983, and my thirtieth law school reunion in 2009 still rank high among the many memorable moments I will never forget. I have often reminisced about the installation ceremony of former civil rights attorney Wiley Branton as the dean of the law school, and dedication of the newly renovated Moot Courtroom that took place in November 1978. How could I ever forget? US Supreme Court Justice Thurgood Marshall gave the keynote address, and afterward I met him at a reception in the cafeteria. The Chief Justice of the Supreme Court, Warren Earl Burger, was present, as was Sixth Circuit US Court of Appeals Judge Damon Keith, who also spoke.

The twenty-fifth class reunion of the law school class of 1983 activities on Sunday morning will also be a memorable occasion. I had been in Washington for Howard's Homecoming and learned that my friend and mentor US District Court Judge Alexander Williams Jr. would be the guest speaker on Sunday morning. His powerful sermon came from the sixth chapter of the Book of Micah, verse 8: "And what does the Lord require of thee, but to do justly and love mercy and to walk humbly with thy God?" Judge Williams exhorted and challenged those present to do these three things so that we could stay grounded in our professions and in our everyday lives. If his message was not enough to encourage those present, the Howard University Law School Gospel Choir sang a stirring rendition of "What If God Is Not Happy with Our Praise?" and other songs that spoke to our hearts, spirits, and even our souls. After our souls were fed, Dean Kurt Schmoke took care of our physical needs with a lavish lunch in the president's suite of the law school.

My thirtieth-class reunion in October 2009 brought many of my classmates back to the law school. I am thankful I was one of them. It was held in conjunction with the 140th anniversary of the founding of the law school in 1869. I had not seen most of my classmates since our graduation in 1979. I was asked to write and read a poem about our experience as students. It was titled "A Tribute." I named most of our law school professors and recalled some of the courses and exams, including one professor's six-hour final exam in Section 2. Remembering one evidence professor's frequent statement about someone "drinking muddy water and barking at the moon" brought laughter to the gathering on the Saturday agenda. A statement closing out our Sunday morning worship service was made by our class secretary, Joy West, who was responsible for bringing us together for our thirtieth and every reunion we have had since our graduation.

We all recognized how instrumental our professors have been in our careers. They not only taught us the law, but more importantly, they taught us to be advocates for justice, no matter what path we traveled in the legal profession. "Equal Justice Under Law" was a concept deeply ingrained in each of us, and it is the standard that has guided me throughout my legal career in private practice, my public service as a legal aid advocate, administrative law judge for the State of North Carolina, and my present position as US magistrate judge for the Middle District of North Carolina. Throughout the reunion activities, reunion chair Joy West reminded us that "Howard University Law School didn't graduate any wimps, and that we must advocate for justice throughout society without fear of losing our positions." On the last day of the reunion, Joy reminded us that "prior generations of Howard Law graduates not only risked their positions but their lives as well."

Joy West leading Howard University Class of 1979 Memorial Service for our deceased classmates

The Legacy of Defending the Constitution Continues

The twenty-first century has brought new and even greater challenges for Howard Law and all law school graduates to defend the Constitution. Indeed, the Constitution, our nation's democracy, and the rule of law are under attack. There is no better example of this attack than the January 6, 2021, mob attack on the US Capitol seeking to overthrow the November 2020 national election for president. Even the social norms that have been the bedrock of civilized nations, such as truth, respect for differing opinions, and the dignity of each human being, are also being challenged.

Lest Howard Law alumni and other law school graduates who are licensed to practice law or preside as judges need to be reminded, we take an oath "to support and defend the Constitution of the United States against all enemies, both foreign and domestic." Throughout our nation's history, lawyers have played a crucial role in securing the "life, liberty and pursuit of happiness" declared in the Declaration of Independence, and that the Constitution guarantees for all. The preamble to the US Constitution is clear as to why it was established: "We the people of the United States, in Order to form a more perfect Union, establish Justice, insure domestic Tranquility, provide for the common defense, promote the general Welfare, and secure the Blessings of Liberty to ourselves and our Posterity, do ordain and establish the Constitution of the United States." And now, we find that many seek to degrade the important role attorneys and judges play in our democracy, including that of breathing life into the four words displayed prominently on the side of the US Supreme Court building: "Equal Justice Under Law." No group of professionals is better suited to "establish justice" than those trained in the law, including ensuring that the principle that "no one is above the law" is faithfully adhered to.

Judges understand their oath to remain impartial in all cases before them. I suspect many choose not to take a position on anything outside the court that is controversial, for fear of causing litigants to believe that the judge may be prejudiced against them. Clearly, judges should not get involved in political campaigns. However, when the Constitution and rule of law is being attacked, it seems to me that our oath requires judges and even more so private lawyers to get involved individually and through their state and federal bar associations. Again, lawyers' and judges' oaths require us to "support and defend the Constitution of the United States against all enemies, foreign and domestic." Numerous times during my career, I have spoken on the subject "The Sin of Silence." I frequently tell lawyers coming before me to be administered the oath to be able to practice law in the Middle District of North Carolina that this oath requires lawyers and I also believe it requires judges to take some action. Staying clear of politics by federal judges is mandated by our Code of Judicial Conduct and should be adhered to. However, not every issue in society is political. One's labeling of a particular issue as political doesn't make it so. Moreover, the Commentary to Canon 4b of the 1990 Model Code of Judicial Conduct states as follows:

> As a judicial officer and person specially learned in the law, a judge is in a unique position to contribute to the improvement of the law,

> the legal system, and the administration of justice, including revision of substantive and procedural law and improvement of criminal and juvenile justice. To the extent that time permits, a judge is encouraged to do so, either independently or through a bar association, judicial conference or other organization dedicated to the improvement of the law.

Judges are also in a unique position to enhance respect for our system of justice by the people of our nation, but they are also in a great position to do great harm to our system of justice and our nation. Those judges who rule not based upon the facts and law applicable to each case before them offer a prime example of my assertion. There have been far too many cases where it appears that wealthy persons who are able to hire the most prominent attorneys that money can buy, and who can appeal multiple times to the highest court in the land and thereby delay final judgment, give the appearance that justice is bought. Bought justice is not justice at all, and those in the legal profession should seek to eradicate this disparity in the availability of justice for all. One of the most celebrated trial judges in American history, Judge Learned Hand, is commonly cited as saying, "If we are to keep democracy, there must be a commandment: Thou shalt not ration justice." Access to justice by those who cannot afford an attorney is an imperative if our democracy is to survive as we know it.

As I move closer to the conclusion of my long career in the law—where I have sought to make a difference in my community, including my profession—I am hopeful that there will be a multitude of voices of reason, righteous purpose, and courage to stand without fear of losing their positions, treasure, or other "things that perish," to use the words of Presidential Medal of Freedom awardee the late Rev. Dr. Gardner C. Taylor. After all, those who trained at Howard Law School in the early years of its existence did not do so for fame or fortune. They often put their lives on the line in the battle to defend the Constitution, particularly the battle for equal rights for all, including those who could not afford their services.

On the anniversary of the sixtieth anniversary of the passing of the Civil Rights Act of 1964 commemorated in Chapel Hill, North Carolina on July 2, 2024, I heard esteemed lawyer James Ferguson recounting the early days of the law firm where he was an early partner along with civil rights attorney Julius LeVonne Chambers and Adam Stein. Paraphrasing, Ferguson said Chambers considered every case that came through the door to be a civil rights case. He felt this way because Chambers had seen his father suffer from being unable to find a lawyer to represent him. Finding a way to provide an attorney for people who can't afford one is perhaps the greatest deficiency in our legal landscape today. If we as the justice bearers do not solve this problem, our Constitution will indeed be in great jeopardy, because as we have seen in the past and see clearly before our eyes being televised today, justice delayed often leads to justice denied. And the public's respect for our system of justice will continue to decline because it works much better for the rich and powerful. This remains our clarion call and our charge to keep.

The Celebration of the 140th Anniversary of the founding of Howard University School Law honoring the Honorable Annie Brown Kennedy, Winston Salem, NC. (L) Co-Chair, the Honorable Joe L. Webster, Annie Brown Kennedy and Howard Univ. Law Dean Kurt Schmoke with Honoree Annie Brown Kennedy and (R) Webster, The Honorable Co-Chair Loretta Copeland Biggs and Dean Schmoke.

The dean of Howard University Law School, Danielle Holley, at Law School Homecoming Reception 2016

CHAPTER TEN

Joe's Book of Poetry

1973–2005

This publication of my poetry is dedicated to my beloved parents, who I owe so much for what I am; to my wife of twenty-five years, who has taught me the meaning of love and patience; and to my three children, who keep my spirits up and who allow me to see the best of me and the worst of me daily. APRIL 17, 2005

My Birthplace

The trees and flowers are beautiful there
For man has not yet exiled them from the earth
And life is given by breathing the fresh air
For nature is nature in my place of birth—
The warm dust accumulates from time to time
But a cool rain quenches the earth's thirst
And the outdoorsmen, who curse it, don't really mind
And the newly born calf bellows as she is being nursed
Loneliness sometimes creeps upon the weary soul
But they can lie down and embrace the earth
Or gossip of the winter and the bitter cold
And thank God every day for his beautiful place of birth.

APRIL 1973

Follow Someone Who Is Good

Hear the voices of someone speaking little boy
For the voice may be truth
Hear the words, their meaning behold

Watch the actions of someone my child
For the person may be wise and old
Watch the direction someone walks
For he may lead the riches untold
Follow in the footsteps of someone my lad
For he may be honest and fair
Follow someone my friend
—Only if he is good.

APRIL 1973

To Help Someone

If I can only help someone
Someone in need of something to eat
Or someone who needs an errand to be run
Or help an old lady get onto her feet
I will have accomplished my dream
If I can only risk my life
By helping a drowning infant from a swift stream
Or people of a country in war and strife
I want to help those who are less fortunate than me
Or help a wounded bird fly once more
Or hear someone call when no one else seems to hear his plea
Or allowing a rain-soaked stranger to enter my door
If I can only help someone
To have a little pleasure once in a while
Or help a crippled child have some fun
I want to help someone run their last mile.

APRIL 1973

Try Being Yourself

Just once in a while try being yourself
When all around you are playing their role
When everyone else is going to the right—you go to the left
Try standing up for right and be bold

And when the situation arises try telling the truth
You may be hurt by your word at first
But eventually all will go on smooth
And when others drink wine try drinking water for the thirst
Just try being yourself for this is the way
And don't always conform if it is not you
Always be consistent and don't sway
Be yourself and others will know that you are true.

1973

Not Tomorrow, Not the Next, but Today

If I can only be your friend
To talk with you and counsel your whims
And you talk with me and counsel mine
Or if we could voyage to some distant spot
Where no one could discern our whispering voices
For we are together as one; hopefully forever
But it cannot be thus just now
The causes are sufficient though
And true friendship was a trait of ours
For we could hold each other's hand
And blot out the world of pain and sorrow.
Not tomorrow, not the next, but today.

APRIL 1973

Let's Fly Away

Someday we'll all fly away into the mystical beyond.
Beyond the grasp of the greatest reach into the
past and future.
Into the tranquility of one's inner self.
Beyond the twinkle of the brightest star.
We'll all create within ourselves a new dimension.
That dimension will overshadow hate and sorrow
and transgression.

That dimension will avail itself like a cloak
on a rain-soaked tomorrow.
There'll be time for meditation, for jubilation and devotion.
Someday we'll all fly away from this time and place.
Away, so far away that mortal man can't comprehend
Beyond superficial love and all degrees thereof
Into the twilight of an invigorating understanding of
The essence of the true brotherhood and sisterhood of man.
We'll all rejoice that we shared our time and few skills with the unfortunate
And we all walked as one when it was much
easier to walk another way.
And sought to understand to the fullest extent that all
individuals are as different as they are alike.
And wept and prayed that our brothers and sisters
would too understand.
Oh yes, let us all fly away one day.
And leave a small part of ourselves here, there,
and in all places.
Let's fly away utilizing our righteous wings.
The flight may indeed be as quiet as the flutter
of the smallest butterfly.
For we will have left our indelible footsteps
at this place and time.
For we will have succeeded even if we failed.
Oh yes, let's fly away, let's glide quickly into a new dimension,
and into a new level of love.
Let's take with us all others who somehow
saw our good.
Let's fly away into the heavens, into ubiquity,
And into all places at the same time.

APRIL 28, 1976

The Capital

On the grounds of the Monument, tall and strong
D.C., chocolate city, the capital became my home.
Surrounded by concrete in the form of fortresses
And perpendicular streets
On the fringes of the Big House, white as snow, poverty abounds,
Visible to some and invisible to fewer still
Cause tinted windows and bullet-proof windows bring forth
a mirage that illuminates only the majestic
On the banks of the Potomac, wide and long
I heard the sonic booms
Evidencing more modernity amidst the rest
While commuters crawl amongst the sights ahead.
While others are in awe for the very first time
On the top of a hill, like the capstone that it is I grew deeper
into manhood
Life became living, great indeed
Yearning and learning about life and academia
Heaven visited earth for those short years
On the fringes of the Park, Rock Creek that is, Prayer changed things
It gave us hope and confidence while those cruel days
And nights of study had shaken us and transformed us from young
men to old men both physically and mentally
All in search of manifest destiny
In the Courts of Justice
I saw just us
Being herded like cattle to and fro
From the jail cells back to the jail cells
While other races determined our destiny
Are we the only perpetrators of criminal activity? In the gems
of reality I often shook my head
Following those walking among the living who were dead
No hope could be discerned from anguished Black faces
No concept of time was traceable
In front of the Capitol they lay.

APRIL 1979

Commemoration of Our Love

On this night I dedicate my love to you
Forever to be committed and true
To console you when you are distressed
To comfort you when you are at rest
On this night when God stares down from above
And listens to these words, these words of love
Of promise and hope, and trust
To exist forever, until we return to dust
On this night, on February the first
These months of your tender love have quenched my thirst
And so my single days are drawing near
But I'm so happy I could shed a tear
On this night, with you in my view
I tell you that all of my love will go to you
Throughout the coming days and months and years
Even in the presence of family and peers
On this night, so exciting and real I have so much life, so much zeal
That with this ring I manifest my love
And give it to you to forever keep and wear
And commemorate our dedication to each other.

FEBRUARY 1, 1980

"Your Faith Has Made Thee Whole"

A blind man said to God, if I had the courage of Bea, truly I would be able to see.
A sinful man said to God, if I had the courage of Bea, truly I would serve thee.
A lame man said to God, if I had the courage of Bea, truly I would walk with thee.
A deaf man said to God, if I had the courage of Bea, truly I would hear thee.
A man who could not talk wrote on a piece of paper to God, if I had the courage of Bea, the power to speak you would grant me.
A faithless man said to God, if I had the courage of Bea, truly I would call upon you and immediately I could move the largest tree.
And God replied to all six, "Your faith has made thee whole."

DECEMBER 6, 1983

[A short visit with Mrs. Beatrice ("Bea") Price as she fought terminal cancer inspired me to write this poem.]

I Watched Her

I watched her as newborn
Curly dark hair, my firstborn child
Dimples, I'd always wanted someone to love with dimples
Pretty smooth skin
I watched her as a toddler
Pretty brown eyes
Plump with two teeth
Hanging onto me for dear life I was her God
I watched her begin to talk Dad a, Dad a,
And a big smile appeared on my face
I watched her go off to Big Mama's, a nursery
Only for her
Gladly to receive lots of hugs, kisses, food.
Juice, whatever she wanted
I watched her go off to school
She was bright and a quick learned, talented
She could draw like her mother
She loved to read
I watched her and I watched her
She grew taller and stronger
More beautiful in her tutu and tap dance attire with a little
black hat—with makeup and all—simply beautiful!
I watched her learn to play piano, good, real good.
And the teachers all say she is a joy to have in their class; that
she will be an orator one day.
I agree.
She is a joy just to have
And I thank God everyday as I watch her.

FEBRUARY 2, 1992

To My Valentine

Will you be mine this special day
Will you hold me and love me in a special way
Will you think about the many special days already past
And with me pray that the wonderful memories will always last

Will you hold my hand in times of strife
And forever be my beautiful wife
Will you continue to teach our children how to love everyone
And share with those less fortunate in the rain or sun
And with the world will you continue to share your enthusiasm and love
And always remember that all we have comes from those above
Will you always remember how much I love you
And to you, no matter what, I will always be true
Will you never forget the vows we said
On that special day we were wed
I cannot say what the future may hold
But there is one thing for certain I do know
That our relationship is more precious than gold
There is not enough time to say just how I feel
But I do know the love we have for each other is real
And that on this Valentine Day and every day
I will do my best to honor the vows I made on that very special day
thirteen years ago this May.

FEBRUARY 14, 1993

The Law

What's this thing they call the law
That makes many stand in awe
Is it what we lawyers thought it would be
Or is it today what we really see
Is this a profession, business, or just a job
Where we represent those who rape, murder, or rob
Where has all the honor gone
Too many lawyers taking trust funds
And doing other wrongs
Who's that judge all dressed in black
And those faceless persons going to prison and back
They say innocent until proven guilty
But is that truly reality
Who am I after taking that oath to do my best

As I represent the guilty as well as the rest
Where oh where may justice be found
Is it real or is it just a sound
Do you have a job, the judge said
And the faceless defendant replied, Judge I don't even have a bed
The judge scowled, can you pay restitution.
But the defendant who had lost all respect could
Only think of revolution
Why does justice take so long
Is it because it is also wrong
Do the rich really get a fairer shake
While no one thinks the poor have anything at stake
Did the lawyer really object
Or did he simply forget
Did he file that answer on time
Or did that task merely escape his mind
Who are those guys all dressed the same
They're corporate lawyers; they know their game
That's not pollution coming from those pipes they said
As they cleared their throats and as their eyes turned red
He will come back to court if allowed out on bond
And in disbelief the judge acted as if he was really stunned
The deed wasn't recorded as it should have been
And the lawyer refused to take the blame for such a cardinal sin
So what is this thing they call the law
That makes many stand in awe.

FEBRUARY 14, 1993

Thurgood Marshall, What a Man

What a man he was
Doing good for all men
What a lawyer he was
Advocating for the disenfranchised
What a shining example he was
Arguing for equality for everyone

What a judge he was
Applying righteous principles
What a statesman he was
The pride of Howard University
What a patriot he was
Strived to make America a better land
What courage he had
Even when others were afraid
What a hero he was
To all who felt hopeless and downtrodden
What a giant he was
In the annals of jurisprudence.
What a man, what a man
His works will live forever
What a man, what a man,
America is indebted to him forever.

MARCH 11, 1993

Give a Helping Hand

He ain't heavy someone once said
He just gave up and needs a helping hand
He was once proud and full of joy
He visited the sick and shared with the homeless too
But life ain't fair someone did say
Was it just one tragedy, or two, or some unforeseen
circumstance that has not happened to me or you
He used to be respected and revered throughout the land
But now he has lost hope and gone astray
No more faith in judgment day
But he ain't heavy someone once said
Reach down and give a helping hand while you can
For this mighty height we have reached
Is only temporary and we must come down
So, reach out and touch those who are stuck in the ditch,
Or those whose hands are withered with age,
Or those whose health is no longer good

Reach out and share a gift more precious than gold
Give a little of yourself to others less fortunate.
For this mighty height we have reached
Is only temporary and we must come down.

APRIL 24, 1993

Quiet Beauty

My second born child, my little girl
As beautiful as anyone in the whole wide world
Quiet as a whisper
And gentle like a lamb
Patient like Job and smart as can be
As the whole world can see
Beautiful smooth skin
And a gorgeous inviting grin
Humble like the lamb of God
Physically made in the image of her earthly father·
Lovable like a cuddly bear
Sometimes I look at her and just stare
For she is wonderful to behold
As she quietly without words grows into ladyhood
I cannot thank God enough
For giving me this quiet, beautiful girl
Truly a gift from above
Someone for the whole world to cherish and love.

DECEMBER 13, 1994

It's a Boy

It's a boy, the doctor said
As I jumped for joy beside my wife's bed
A long slender little boy with big hands
I must have been the happiest Dad in the land
He was healthy and we thanked God
For this precious gift of life
I have a son, I told everyone with pride
A little Joe they said with a smile

Can't wait till he grows up so we can play ball
I just knew one day he'd be tall
He likes to run and laugh and play
From early morning till late in the day
Full of energy and strong too
Sometimes I have to say, boy, I'm going to get you
Such a handsome little man
Still got those big big hands
It's a boy the doctor said
As I jumped for joy beside my wife's bed
Thankful over and over and over again
For being given a handsome little man.

JULY 1, 1995

To Get to the Promised Land

Going through Nineveh to get to the Promised Land
Much hardship and turmoil
Many mountains to climb and valleys to go down
Much sickness and pain and heartaches to spare
Going through Nineveh to get to the Promised Land
Many enemies to love
and crosses to bear
Much hatred and bitterness along the way
Many stones to turn
and boulders in your way
Going through Nineveh to get to the Promised Land
Many invisible paths
And unchartered wilderness
Many rivers to wade and deserts without water
Much disagreement and fighting and tribulation in the air
Going through Nineveh to get to the Promised Land
Much sorrow and dying
and tears, many tears along the way
Many bitter pills to swallow
But joy in the morning
Eternal life is coming my way.

AUGUST 16, 1996

Where Have All the Brothers Gone

Where have all the brothers gone
They have gone astray
Head all bad, not thinking straight
All dressed in bright colored jump suits and locked away
Where have all the brothers gone
They have gone astray
Many have lost hope
Got no respect for self and even less for others
Freedom ancestors fought and died for, is not now revered
And life itself, once sacrosanct, has little meaning
Where have all the brothers gone
Too few trying to find them
Too selfish and busy to care
That their brothers have gone away
But hopefully not to stay.

DECEMBER 4, 1996

Blessed

How blessed I am
Alive this day!
Can walk and run and even play
How blessed I am
Can speak and see
And have feelings of glee
How blessed I am
Can think for myself
And remember when to go to the right
rather than the left
How blessed I am
To have family and friends
And a job with losses and wins
How blessed I am
To be in the bosom of God
With all of his blessings and spiritual rod

How blessed I am
From morning to night
He cares for me even when I am not right
How blessed I am
I can recognize his love
and that all good things come from above
How blessed I am!

FEBRUARY 20, 1998

Who Will Carry the Load?

Who will carry the load
Will it be you or me, or some stranger
Who will teach those who seemingly are unteachable
Or care for the mentally ill who seemingly are unreachable
Who will carry the load
Will it be you or me, or someone from another land
Who will spread the word of what our ancestors stood for
Who will go for us when our eyesight grows dim and our footsteps smaller
Who will carry the load
Will it be you or me, cousin Jim or Mary, or someone not kin
Who will say love is the answer or remember to pray when all else fails
Who will keep going when even your very soul is weary
Who will carry the load
Will it be you or me, or the one others said is no good
Who will say work and stay together children and don't fight
And that together we stand and divided we fall
Who will carry the load
Will it be you or me, or someone from another family
Who will remember the great invitation
To come unto Him all ye that labor and are heavy laden and He
Will give you rest; that his yoke is easy and His burden is light
Who will carry the load
Will it be you or me or someone who gave up in the past
Who will sing the song fight on till victory is won

And know in your heart that you've done your part to keep
the family together
And its cherished goals at heart.

JULY 30, 1998

Death Bed

As I entered the nurse's station, a nurse said Chaplain
The patient in Room 16 has terminal cancer
He's having a rough time and no family has come by to see him
He's expected to die soon
Oh God I thought to myself, who am I to be called to this test
Is he married, any children I said
No, the nurse said, apparently, he doesn't even have a friend.
I'll go by and see him I said with anticipation.
Mr. Smith, I called out amidst moans and groans of a man in distress
I'm in so much pain; I'm ready to go home to be with my Lord
I'm so sorry you're going through all this I said as I reached
out for his hand
And I looked around and saw a frail and battered image of his former self
Is there anything I can do for you I said as my heart began to sink
No, he sighed, they say I don't have long to live
Sweat popped onto my face as my heart sank even more pondering
what I could give
Instinctively words of my mother, I said, the doctors
don't know it all
Only God determines our time and place.
My mouth is so dry I barely heard and I saw lips cracked and neglected
Can you have anything to drink as I glanced at the NPO sign above his bed?
What about some ice chips I said
Yes, he acknowledged with a slight nod of the head
I'll go see the nurse so I rushed out of the room
I thought surely they wouldn't deny just a little comfort to a man
so full of gloom
I found the nurse, but it was obvious she was too busy to put
Mr. Smith first.

Minutes later the nurse rushed into the room and sat a cup of ice chips onto the bed
But she immediately left without hardly saying a word
Mr. Smith didn't have the strength to hold the cup of ice for himself
What a shame I fumed to myself
That nurse was too busy to give Mr. Smith a spoon of ice, such a simple thing
Where have we gone in our health care system I thought
When we cannot spare a moment for those that are dying.
Would you like to have prayer I said to Mr. Smith
Yes, he crackled and slowly reached out for my hand
I could feel God's presence even though Mr. Smith lay dying
God thank you for being with us in this hospital room
In times like these, I admit that I don't know all that I should
ask I feel so inadequate, but I know that you are able
That before the earth was formed you were present
You said blessed are they that mourn for they shall be comforted
God, we ask your blessings upon Mr. Smith
Give him peace and let him know that you are a friend to the friendless
God grant him joy even in this hospital room
Please Lord Mr. Smith whispered in response
And my voice began to crackle as tears began to flow
God, we know you are able as suffering overwhelms and consumes Mr. Smith
We know that you are able to bring peace in the valley and joy even in our pain
So be with Mr. Smith in his hospital bed and allow him to feel your presence. A-men.
Thank you Chaplain, Mr. Smith whispered to me
You're welcome I said as my hand continued to cling to his
I'll come back to see you soon, as I wondered if I would have the chance
And wondered whether this was indeed Mr. Smith's deathbed.

NOVEMBER 3, 2001

[Inspiration for this poem came from my experience as a chaplain intern at the University of North Carolina–Chapel Hill Hospital from August 22 to December 7, 2001.]

War or Peace

Shall there be war or peace?
War and rumors of wars have been foretold
On the homeland and on distant shores
God bless America our leaders said with a certain disdain
As bombs dropped and killed the enemy as well as the innocent
There can never be any peace until God is at the conference table
One soul singer once said as he mourned the dead
But the leaders seemed to proclaim, but before He arrives, let's fight some more
To finish the job unfinished on foreign soil
Peace is a state of mind, not the absence of war the leaders thought to themselves
One day there will be peace in the valley and war no more
Antietam, Gettysburg, Normandy, Vietnam, Afghanistan, and Ivory Coast
Death and destruction across the land
War talks tough and wins votes
But peace is strength, of mind, body and soul
There are no victors in war, and peace should be sought at all costs
God bless America and Afghanistan and Iraq and Israel and Palestine and all the rest.

OCTOBER 2, 2002

Remembering Twenty-Five Years and More

She had a little pink skirt and vest on when I met her on June 26, 1979.
Love at first sight, pleasing to my eyes, I just knew one day she would be mine.
She was eating lunch alone in McDonald's at University Mall in Chapel Hill.
Yep, that's where I found my thrill.
As I stood in line waiting to get my lunch, I vowed to myself.
I'm going to meet her; I was just hoping she wouldn't have left.
Courage was what I needed to approach this beautiful lady so true.
As I approached her table, words did come out of my mouth, may I join you.
Yes, she said, and my heart began to pound.
Her voice was not so southern; it was just a sweet sweet sound.
She had recently broken up with someone she said to me.

Man, I thought, what a blessing for me as far as I could see.
She was one of fifteen children and I one of eight.
Grew up on a farm and so did I; many things in common; I immediately began to think about asking her for a date.
We exchanged telephone numbers, and I didn't waste any time. I just knew that one day she would be all mine.
Those first few weeks we moved fast indeed.
As I studied for the Bar Exam, she brought me lunch one day seeing I was in much need.
Within two months, I asked her will you marry me, even though I didn't have any money to buy her a ring.
She said yes, even though I couldn't give her anything.
In early February I gave her a ring, and a date for matrimony we had already set.
It would be at Duke Gardens on May 3, 1980; got that first ring by going into debt.
A beautiful sunny day in the Gardens made sunnier by the glow she carried.
It didn't matter that we didn't have much money; we had all we needed, because we were getting married.
Since that beautiful day twenty-five years ago all filled with joy, there have been many days we could have said we've had enough.
You know marriage sometimes is really tough.
But all and all, so blessed we've been.
From our own good health and that of our children.
After all these years, there's still something captivating about my bride.
She's kept her vow and has always been right by my side.
She's put up with my stubborn trait.
And has never once shown any hate.
She's been patient, when many would have said, "Negro, please," I'm about to leave.
She stayed right there for twenty-five years and I'm so thankful, to me she did cleave.
I don't know where I would be without her love.
I'm so thankful to the master of the universe for this gift from above.
She gave me three precious little ones.
I was blessed to be by her side when all three were born.
She has demonstrated so much love and forgave and forgave.

Even when I was bad and the children wouldn't behave.
I could go on with praises to the center of these twenty-five years.
Her name is Diane; thank God; the time for her to come home from work is almost near.
I can't wait to behold her again and again.
And thank her for helping make me a man.

APRIL 15, 2005

Praise the Lord!

Praise the Lord Church
See what the Lord has done
Praise the Lord everybody
For allowing us to see a new mom
Praise the Lord for his many blessings
We woke up to see the rising of the sun
Praise the Lord for his unconditional love
For a new day has begun
Praise the Lord over and over again
For in a manger a savior of the world was born
Praise the Lord for healing our bodies and minds
And for allowing us to get up and run on
Praise the Lord for sickness and good health
And for allowing us to see that even death is not a thorn
Praise the Lord for his truth endures
And for the blood sacrificed by this son
Praise the Lord everybody for he did rise
Hallelujah, for we too can overcome!

APRIL 17, 2005

CHAPTER ELEVEN

The Mentors or Those Who Have Inspired Me

Beginning September 2022

"Please keep your chin up, count your blessings, and never forget that He knows best."

COACH JOHN WOODEN, 1971
October 14, 1910–June 4, 2010

I'm sure one day someone will wonder how a coach who lived and worked nearly three thousand miles away could become a mentor or inspire a seventeen-year-old teenager. I had just completed the basketball season of my junior year at Madison-Mayodan Senior High School. It had not been a good year for me. My attitude was not good. In hindsight I was immature and had a very selfish attitude, not at all team oriented. Once I was asked to substitute in a game with less than a minute left. I refused to go in. In hindsight, the coach should have called me in and told me that if I didn't improve my attitude, he would kick me off the team. He would have been right to do so. However, at the time I felt I had worked hard and earned a right to be getting more playing time. Selfishly I felt I had much more talent than several of my teammates who had earned the respect of Coach Myers, yet I was relegated mostly to the "pine," as we referred to the bench back then. I was mostly a benchwarmer, and I hated that. In fact, I quit the team at least once. On one occasion I came back to the team and sat on the sidelines to watch my team practice. On that occasion, Coach Meyers approached me and asked me when I would return to the team. I came back the next day on the court in my practice attire. I'm so glad Coach Meyers didn't give up on me and I didn't give up on myself. For as the scripture says, "Weeping may endure for a night, but joy cometh in the morning." The very next season, my senior year, as a starting wing guard, my team won twenty-seven consecutive games before losing the semifinal game in the state tournament.

But it was at the end of the basketball season my junior year, feeling frustrated and feeling like I had no one to talk to, that I sent a letter to Coach John Wooden, one of the greatest basketball coaches in the history of the game. It caught my eye that Coach Wooden had recruited a North Carolina player from the small town of Franklinton, North Carolina, Henry Bibby. He was their starting point guard, a great passer and outside shooter who ran his very talented team with precision. I watched the mighty Bruins on our family's black-and-white television during the times they played on national television during the regular season and the NCAA tournaments. They were most often the number-one seed and picked to win another national title. I watched Henry Bibby carefully and sought to play like him. I even shot my foul shots to the right of the foul line rather than at the center of it. So, I wrote Coach Wooden a letter requesting him to let Henry Bibby know I wanted him to write me. Rather than receiving a letter from Henry Bibby, Coach Wooden mailed me a handwritten letter with a photo of Henry Bibby. While I never heard from Henry Bibby, I have possessed Coach Wooden's letter among my prized possessions for over fifty years. Among the lines of that letter were the words

> Please keep your chin up, count your blessings, and never forget that He knows best.

It took several years for me to realize that the "He" Coach Wooden was referring to was God, one in whom Coach Wooden placed his trust. Many years later after his retirement, and years after I began to practice law, I wrote Coach Wooden again. He responded back to me on July 4 of that year. I had informed him how I had been blessed with success in my personal and professional life. The first lines of this response were,

> There can be no greater joy than to know that something you have said or done has been of help to another, especially when it was done with no thought of something in return.

And even later after that, I wrote Coach Wooden yet a third time. This time, I was writing him for advice about two of Diane's and my three children, Camille and Evan. Both were very good basketball players with promising college futures, but both had decided to give up playing basketball for their own reasons. So, I wrote Coach Wooden asking what I should say to them as their father. He gave me good advice about this inquiry also. Coach Wooden first stated that

> There was no way that he could offer me any meaningful advice regarding my children without knowing them personally.

However, he went on to remind me that

> Parenting is the most important profession of all, and it is most essential in their early formative years. Our youth must be led, supported, and directed, but never driven.

What great universal advice on parenting! While I never got the opportunity to meet Coach Wooden in person, his sound advice to me over the years has been invaluable. Coach John Wooden was a mentor who inspired me not at all because he, during his last twelve years of coaching at UCLA, won ten NCAA Championships, but it was because he freely gave me his wise advice and found time for me despite his busy schedule. I did have the occasion to sit in the bleachers at Pauley Pavilion on the Westwood Campus of UCLA in early July 1978, having been taken there by my best friend from Howard University Law School, Wayne Mason. I once wanted to attend UCLA. However, I felt it was too far from the farm where I lived outside my little hometown of Madison, North Carolina. Therefore, I directed my efforts to a place far more suited and attainable, which was only three hundred miles from home, Howard University. God had truly ordered my steps and my paths, and I'm so glad I walked therein.

My Spiritual Father: Rev. Dr. Elliott James Mason Sr.

JANUARY 13, 1922–MARCH 23, 2010

"I Can Do All Things through Christ That Strengthens Me"

PHILIPPIANS 4:13

On April 8, 1997, I talked with Rev. Dr. Elliott Mason Sr. about how I had always felt my work as a lawyer was a form of ministry. I told him that many, especially other preachers who heard me speak, have said to me that "I had missed my calling." Dr. Mason told me that no matter what others say about what my spiritual gifts are, my gift as a lawyer is just as important as their gift in traditional pastoral ministry. He told me that what I was doing as a practicing lawyer was just as important a "ministry calling" as those who were pastors or preachers. Dr. Mason referred to me to 1 Corinthians, chapter 12. He said that God might call me to another "traditional ministry" later. He said that others only think of pastoral work as traditional ministry. Dr. Mason gave me an example to illustrate his point by referring to his postretirement pastoral ministry. He said that when he left the pastorate of Trinity, people were viewing it as a traditional retirement, but he knew that the prayer and counseling ministry that he and his wife engaged in is just as important as any other ministry or maybe the most important ministry in his life.

I would periodically reach out to Dr. Mason, and he would reach out to me through a telephone call or letter. He sent me a letter as I was preparing to take the final exams my first year at Howard Law School. The entirety of the letter was these words quoting from Philippians 4:13: "I can do all things through Christ who strengthens me." Dr. Mason always gave me sound advice. He and his wife, Gerry Mason, shared that they were very proud of me. It's been nearly ten years since Dr. Mason passed on March 23, 2010, but I still miss him and his wife, who I was blessed to visit with not that long prior to her death.

In late January 2001, at Walker Memorial Baptist Church in Washington, DC, I selected St. John, chapter 3, verses 1 to 6, and Ephesians, chapter 4, verses 21 to 24). I chose to preach on the subject "A New Heart for a New Year." In that sermon I quoted Dr. Mason as I had called him to ask what it meant to "be born again." In John, chapter 3 verse 3, Jesus told Nicodemus that except a man be born again, he cannot see the kingdom of God. Dr. Mason told me,

> Being born again is the result of the total surrender and submission of one's heart to our Lord and Savior Jesus Christ, and it involves the confession of that belief with our mouths.

Dr. Mason is the kind of extraordinary individual who you continue to learn from even after that person has passed on. As many times as I had spoken to him at length, I do not recall him telling me about the dream he once had that changed his life. From his obituary I learned that the dream came when Dr. Mason was in his early fifties. In 1975, Dr. Mason experienced an unusual and unexpected encounter with God. Everything seemed to be going well in his life: his ministry was highly effective, and the church (Trinity Baptist Church of Los Angeles) was thriving, his marriage was fulfilling and happy, and his children were well grounded and advancing educationally. He was highly regarded in religious circles around the country as a scholarly yet extremely spiritual pastor with an exceptionally gracious and humble spirit. He pondered these blessings with thanksgiving and praise, but soon thereafter God confronted him in a way that would forever change his life.

One night Dr. Mason had a dream that he was standing on the roof of a school bus filled with preachers and religious leaders. The bus was speeding out of control and headed straight toward a deep lake. He was bound for certain death. In this dream he had to make a split-second decision to either jump off or drown with the others in the lake ... then he awaked. Over the following months God slowly and lovingly revealed the meaning of this dream to Elliott:

> Elliott, you're no better than those other preachers and religious leaders on the bus. Many of the seemingly wonderful things that you do for me are merely the product of your own good intentions and self-effort; they are not generated by the leading of my Holy Spirit. Many of your good deeds are diminished in significance because they do not originate with me. You have often confused your vast knowledge of me with really knowing me, and this knowledge, instead of drawing you closer to me, has instead insulated you from experiencing the full power of my Spirit. However, if you will allow me to expose your defects, over time I will begin to teach you how to abide in me, walk in my spirit and ultimately fulfill my purpose for your life.

Dr. Mason's humility, willingness to allow God to order his steps, and his love for humankind will always remain with me. I feel so blessed to have crossed paths with him and his beloved wife, Geraldine, and their children, especially their son, Wayne Mason, who was my best friend in law school and best man in my wedding.

Dr. John Hope Franklin

JANUARY 2, 1915–MARCH 25, 2009

> When we also learn that this country and the western world have no monopoly of goodness and truth or of skills and scholarship, we begin to appreciate the ingredients that are indispensable to making a better world. In a life of learning, that is, perhaps, the greatest lesson of all. —DR. JOHN HOPE FRANKLIN

It was my great pleasure to get to know Dr. John Hope Franklin. I visited in his home in Durham on several occasions. One of my former interns in my Pittsboro law office, Jason Groves, took me to Dr. Franklin's home. Jason, the grandson of the late Dean Harry Groves, former dean of the North Carolina Central School of Law, was residing with Dr. Franklin at the time. I once took my son, Evan, to meet him. On two occasions Dr. Franklin treated me to lunch at the club he belonged to located on the top floor of the University Tower in Durham, North Carolina.

Prior to meeting Dr. Franklin, I had read much about him and about some of his published books, including *From Slavery to Freedom*. He was unsurpassed in his scholarship on African American history.

I had several conversations with him that remain in my memory years after they occurred. He told me of his experiences at my alma mater, Howard University (1947–1956), where he taught after leaving North Carolina College for Negroes (1943–1947) now North Carolina Central University. Dr. Franklin told me that at the time Howard University was the zenith of higher education for African American professors—that you could not teach at any university higher ranked than Howard.

Dr. Franklin vividly recalled to me that he was standing in line for his paycheck at Howard University (as was the custom while Dr. Franklin taught at Howard) only to be told when he reached the front of the line by the disbursing employee that he did not have a check for him. Dr. Franklin said he told the employee, "If Howard doesn't have a check for me by the end of that day, that he would return to Oklahoma and sit down on the front porch." They found his check before the end of that day. Dr. Franklin later told me that the then-president, Dr. Mordecai Wyatt Johnson, called him into his office regarding a rumor that he had heard that Franklin would be leaving Howard to become head of the History Department at Brooklyn College. As I recall, Dr. Franklin told me that he told Dr. Johnson that it was not a rumor and that he would soon be leaving Howard.

There came a time when Dr. Franklin's wife, Aurelia Whittington Franklin became ill with Alzheimer's disease, which became progressively worse over time. She lost the ability to care for herself and lost the ability to read. Franklin expressed to me that his wife had been an avid reader all her life. He also recalled that one day he learned that she had gotten lost as she was driving her car a short distance from their Durham residence. When he arrived home, she was lying on the bed. As I recall, Dr. Franklin said that the police had escorted her home. Eventually she was placed in a care facility in Chapel Hill and her health steadily declined.

The last time I had lunch with Dr. Franklin, I asked him how his wife was doing. He told me she had passed. I said something to effect that I was very sorry, and I had not heard of her death or about funeral arrangements. He responded that there had not been a funeral and he had not made a big deal of her death. I asked Dr. Franklin what he remembered most about his wife. He said, "She was longsuffering." At the time and years later, I know that is quite a tribute for one to be longsuffering. I did not ask Dr. Franklin to elaborate, but my mind caused me to think of the many long days and nights he had been away from home as he did the tedious work of researching material for his book *From Slavery to Freedom* and his many other publications.

I once asked Dr. Franklin whether he had met preeminent, sociologist, historian, and Pan-African Civil Rights activist, Dr. W. E. B. DuBois? Dr. Franklin responded that he happened to be in the same location with him once and saw him sitting at a table looking down at whatever he was reading. He approached Dr. Du Bois, introduced himself, and informed Dr. Du Bois that he had gotten his doctorate degree from Harvard. Dr. Franklin said that his conversation was very brief and recalled that Dr. Du Bois never looked up while he was talking to him. Ever since I had that conversation with Dr. Franklin, I have sought to look persons in the eye when they are talking to me and give them the attention they deserve, no matter what their station is in life.

I feel so blessed to have crossed paths with and shaken the hand of such an internationally known and consequential human being as Dr. John Hope Franklin.

[Postscript: On December 6, 2017, I had the great privilege of giving a talk about my book *The Making and Measure of a Judge: Biography of the Honorable Sammie Chess Jr.* at the John Hope Franklin Center for Interdisciplinary and International Studies (JHFC) at Duke University.]

The Honorable Chief Justice Henry E. Frye

> Everybody can't be a great speaker. Everybody can't lead a great movement. But everybody can do something.

Sometime prior to graduating from law school, I had heard about the Honorable Henry Frye. I knew he was someone who I must meet to get his perspective on hanging my shingle in my hometown of Madison after graduating and passing the bar exam. As I recall I met him at his downtown Greensboro office on a Saturday morning. Upon arrival I sat down in the lobby outside his office. I could see him busily conversing with someone on the telephone. After completing his call, he welcomed me into his office.

Too many years have passed for me to recall the specifics of our conversation. However, I do know that I departed very happy that I had the opportunity to meet this man, who had already established himself as a pioneer and respected leader of his community and state. As I had learned in 1968, Justice Frye became the first African American to serve in the North Carolina General Assembly in the twentieth century and later served in the North Carolina Senate. In 1983 he was appointed as an associate justice of the NC Supreme Court, and in 1999 he became the Court's chief justice, the first African American to hold that title. These are but a few of his accomplishments.

What I did not know until much later after I first met Justice Frye was that he too had suffered indignities in his life, including being subjected to a written test, which he failed, to become a registered voter in his hometown of Ellerbe, North Carolina. This motivated him to attend law school so that others would not have to suffer this same humiliation.

After first meeting Justice Frye, I frequently saw him again at NCABL and other Bar Association meetings early in my law career. He was always cordial and afforded me great respect. I latched on to his every spoken word as I knew I could learn from his great wisdom, including advice he gave me about cases I was handling. I am blessed to have gotten to know his wife, Shirley Frye, who is an esteemed and accomplished public servant in her own right.

After getting burned out in my hometown, I closed my office and my family moved to Raleigh for an associate attorney general position with the North Carolina Department of Justice. Later I served as deputy director of Legal Services of North Carolina there. I'd see Justice Frye frequently during this period. I'd often seek out his advice. I was not happy with either of those positions, the latter mostly because it was administrative in nature and not the in-court legal advocacy that made me feel good about my work. So, while serving as deputy director of Legal Services of North Carolina, I said to him, "When are you going to help me find a job?" His immediate response was, "You have a job!" In those four words, Justice Frye taught me yet another valuable lesson that came through very clearly without him having to say more. I took those four words to mean, be thankful for the job God has given you. It may not be your dream job, but it was coveted by many; it was a regular paycheck and keep on doing the best you can in that position until something more to your liking comes to you.

Many years passed after the mid-1990s. I sought out appointment to the North Carolina Court of Appeals, sought an appointment to fill a vacancy as US magistrate judge in 2009, and actively sought other positions that came to my attention. In 2012 another federal magistrate judge position came open in the Middle District. I applied for it and was selected. I was sworn in on November 7, 2012. Shortly thereafter I had breakfast with Justice Frye. He gave me more advice. He said I should not accept any gratuities or gifts from anyone. I knew that I would have to avoid even the appearance of impropriety. I knew that I had to be impartial to all who appeared before me or had a case that I had to rule upon. If I accepted anything of value from anyone who had a case before me then someone may call into question my ability to be unbiased and impartial.

Besides being able to go to Justice Frye for advice, he afforded me the opportunity to spend time with him on the golf course. Even though he was a little more than twenty years my senior, he remained a better golfer than me when he was eighty-five years old. Justice Frye and I have a lot in common: we both grew up in rural North Carolina and know what tobacco gum is and what it's like to use an outdoor toilet. We are both persons of faith, and both believe strongly in public and community service. And lastly, both Justice Frye and I have wonderful, longsuffering wives who have sacrificed much during our long marriages, and we have been blessed with good health and with children and grandchildren.

My Wife, Diane Ramsey Webster

> Upon me mentioning that someone had been rude to me, my wife, Diane, gave me an early lesson about grace and forgiveness. She said, "The person must have been having a bad day." (1980)

In the spring of 2023, I was nominated for the Legal Legends of Color Award by the North Carolina Bar Association's Minority in the Profession Committee. Nominees were asked to address the following question: "As you reflect on your life's journey so far, who has been your greatest inspiration and why?" I responded as follows:

"My wife of forty-three years, Diane Ramsey Webster, has been my greatest inspiration. I have had many mentors on my life's journey; however, no one has inspired me like Diane."

Long ago I hung my shingle to practice law, at a time when I was motivated by my parents' upbringing and an old professor at Howard University. Upon learning that I planned to return to my native state to practice law, he reminded me that I may as well stay in DC if I was not going back to North Carolina to make a difference. It was Diane who put aside her own career dreams to support me and our three children. Three months after we got married, we moved to my home in rural Rockingham County, where Diane had never been before. When I set out to make a difference by trying to level the playing field in and out of courtrooms, Diane was "the wind beneath my sails." She sacrificed her own career to help me represent those who were all too often financially unable to pay me a reasonable fee. It was at a time when I took on clients and causes that no other lawyer would accept. It was at a time when I spearheaded my hometown of Madison's first civil rights demonstration to protest an African American woman's wrongful firing. Later I had to resign my position as deputy director of Legal Services of North Carolina to seek a state district court judgeship. While I'm sure Diane thought about whether I had lost my mind, since we then had three young children to raise, she stood by me. And even later when the Honorable Leon Stanback appointed me to represent a member of the Ku Klux Klan who had been criminally charged in Pittsboro, North Carolina, and after hearing me voice some concern about my safety and perhaps that of my family, Diane stood fast and continued to inspire me.

Throughout my career I've sat on numerous boards and committees, and in the late 1990s when I accepted a higher call to gospel ministry, I'm sure Diane thought that my life of service to others was too much to bear. Whatever her thoughts, she remained faithful and an inspiration to me. It was Diane who made sure the children were fed and bountifully nourished, and she made sure that our children and children of our neighbors got to soccer and other school and church activities on time. It was Diane who sacrificed her own career to devote five years of her life as a secretary to my law practice as the first African American attorney in the then two-hundred-year history of my hometown. It was Diane who encouraged me when I filed a lawsuit against my hometown for denying me a permit to operate a law office on a street where white lawyers and other professionals had previously located. It was my wife whose presence encouraged me when a local savings and loan denied us a loan to purchase the property for law office use, causing us to seek loan approval by a black-owned bank in Greensboro. Of all those who have inspired me, Diane stands tall above the rest.

The Honorable J. Michelle Childs, US Court of Appeals for the DC Circuit

JUNE 1, 2024

Serve people, not just professional accomplishments. Step into your role for your community, your clients, your environment, and your nation.

From the May 2022 convocation speech at Duke University Law School

When I met Michelle in mid-May of 2014, we were classmates in the Master of Judicial Studies Program at Duke University School of Law. She met everyone with the same smile that she carries eight years later. She was a US district court judge for the District of South Carolina at the time, but one who all knew would be elevated in the not-too-distant future. She had all the characteristics of a great judge that even those who held a different judicial philosophy would appreciate.

During my thesis research on the late Honorable Sammie Chess Jr., a native of South Carolina, when I traveled to Allendale, South Carolina, and adjoining Barnwell County, Michelle offered me a place to lay my head in her spacious home in Columbia, South Carolina. We went to dinner with one of her neighbors. I was made to feel very welcome during my stopover in Columbia. Recently, two of my golfing buddies from Howard University joined me in Columbia for golf, and we were blessed to be in Michelle and another judge's company for dinner. Once again Michelle's hospitality shined brightly. In 2016, I asked Michelle to be one of those who endorsed my book; her blurb along with two others is forever displayed on the back cover of *The Making and Measure of a Judge: Biography of the Honorable Sammie Chess Jr.* She could have easily said no to my request for fear that somehow something within the book would have caused the appointing powers that be to attribute to her the many truths within the book. Michelle is one of those who have inspired me because she has the courage required to be a judge.

It came as no surprise that Michelle would be considered for appointment to the highest court in the United States, the Supreme Court. I let her know that I was praying for her during the long process of being considered for that High Court and eventually the DC Circuit Court of Appeals. I am so grateful to her for allowing me to be one of those allowed in her life at a time of great scrutiny when caution was very much needed. In the end, Judge Childs's strength of character prevailed, and I was elated to be invited and to attend her investiture in November 2022. It was truly a memorable occasion, not only because two justices of the US Supreme Court were present, but even more so because of the throng of family, friends, and well-wishers who attended from her native state as well as members of Congress. Michelle's remarks were amazing and heartfelt. They brought tears to many eyes, including her own. That evening, I received the following texts from my two daughters. My daughter Camille, an attorney, texted,

> I listened to the Investiture of Judge Childs of the Court of Appeals for the DC Circuit, and it was so amazing. To see her sworn in by another amazing black woman Justice Brown Jackson was so beautiful. It kind of made all of trauma from work today go away. At least temporarily.

My other daughter, Briana, texted, "It was so beautiful! So proud of her and glad to sort of know her, through dad."

So, the significance of Michelle's appointment to the DC Circuit rises far above her elevation to that court. I'm certain that my two daughters along with thousands of others were encouraged to believe that they too can achieve such high accomplishment with faith, family support, and hard work. This is one of the many reasons why I consider the Honorable J. Michelle Childs to be one of those I have selected to be one of my mentors or those who have inspired me.

The Honorable Sammie Chess Jr.

MARCH 28, 1934–JULY 23, 2022

> What shall it profit a man, if he shall gain the whole world and lose his own soul? —MARK 8:36, KJV

The Honorable Sammie Chess Jr. was one of my closest mentors and friends. He had just celebrated his eighty-sixth birthday on March 28, 2020, and I called him up to tell him Happy Birthday. I had sent him a computer-generated birthday card, which he acknowledged receiving. The day before I had sent a reminder of his birthday to my mentors and friends Henry and Shirley Frye, Julius Mann, Pat Timmons-Goodson, and a few others. While Judge Chess had told me earlier that his birthday would not be a big deal, I wanted that day to be special for him. I thought he would appreciate receiving well wishes on his birthday from old friends, and that would make him happy.

None of the birthday wishes could compare with the many accolades Judge Chess had earned over a long career of service to humankind. His service would not have been possible without the Lord God in whom he undoubtedly placed his faith; the courage that he was blessed to have; a purpose for living that he took hold of after being encouraged by his high school principal, Samuel E. Burford, and the many lessons learned especially from his father, Sammie Chess Sr., and his grandmother Ella Baxter Chess. He learned those lessons well and has passed them down to the generations that have followed him. Much of what I describe here is covered in the biography I was blessed to publish in February 2017 on the life of Judge Chess, *The Making and Measure of a Judge: Biography of the Honorable Sammie Chess Jr.*, published by Chapel Hill Press. I have gifted many books to friends and those I didn't know well because I want others to get to know this great man as I have.

My appreciation for my mentor and friend Judge Chess grew immensely over the many hours I spent with him in person and by telephone during my research and writing of his biography. I learned that through his imperfection, God hewed out a model for Christian living, and service especially to those on the front lines of the civil rights struggle—those charged with serious crimes by carnal and depraved hearts and minds, and those in need of an encouraging word. For Judge Chess's complete dedication to others, I love him greatly.

I am so grateful that God made it possible for me to get to know well Sammie Chess Jr., and I pray that we will have many more days to fellowship together.

Postscript

Early Saturday morning, July 23, 2023, I received a telephone call. Excitedly, I answered the call because my mentor and friend Judge Sammie Chess Jr.'s name appeared on my phone. My excitement quickly vanished as it was his wife's voice on the line. She told me that Judge Chess had passed in his sleep overnight. My heart raced with sadness, grief, sorrow, and all the other emotions that accommodate the loss that I felt. She told me she found him lying there already cool to the touch. Our conversation was brief, and I hurried inside to inform my wife of this news.

I reflected on Judge Chess the remainder of the day, including our long friendship, what he meant to me, and the many hours I spent with him regarding the biography I wrote and published. I thought about the many times I had considered that his health was declining and that one day I would likely face his passing. One can never be fully prepared for the death of one whom you love so much. Without mentioning to him what I was thinking about his declining health and where it might end, I told him several times that I would begin calling him at least twice weekly. He responded, "That would be good." I think he knew that the time of his departure was near. He had shared with me not too long before that conversation, that he had fallen in the bathtub and could not get out on his own. He shared his health with very few people, and in this case, not even his daughters. I was honored that he thought me to be close enough to share this information.

Within a day or two after his wife had called to inform me of the death of Judge Chess, I visited her in their home. She told me she wanted me to write his history for the program and to do the eulogy at his funeral to be held in High Point by the end of the week if possible. I promptly said yes to these requests and, with a sense of great privilege and honor, preached Judge Chess's eulogy at the St. Stephen Metropolitan AME Zion Church on July 30, 2022. The title of my eulogy was "Fighting the Good Fight: He Chose the Road That Leads to Calvary." It was not difficult for me to eulogize such a great man. I had spoken of this great man on numerous occasions at book talks, including at the Dr. John Hope Franklin Center at Duke University. I pointed to many quotes from his biography, including one of Judge Chess's favorite scriptures: "What shall it profit a man to gain the whole world and lose his soul?" (MARK 8:36). I have great confidence that Judge Chess did not lose his soul.

Attorney Annie Brown Kennedy

"A True Public Servant"

OCTOBER 13, 1924–JANUARY 17, 2023

The Honorable Annie Brown Kennedy was one of the early African American female attorneys to practice law in North Carolina, becoming only the second black female to receive a law license to practice in the state. She was an example of great courage as she represented clients in courts that had seldom seen a black female attorney. Her service to the state of North Carolina as a civil rights lawyer included winning in 1957 at the district court level and Fourth Circuit Court of Appeals the case of *Simpkins v. City of Greensboro,* only three years after beginning her law practice. This case desegregated the Greensboro city-owned golf courses. As the first black woman to serve in the General Assembly in 1979, I'm certain she carried the weight of being a woman and being a person of color.

In 2009, my classmate the Honorable Loretta Copeland Biggs and I cochaired efforts to honor Annie Brown Kennedy as a part of the 140th anniversary of the founding of the Howard University School of Law. At the event held in Winston Salem, I listened to The Honorable Annie Brown Kennedy's remarks, which included vivid comments about one of her first trials in the courts of Winston Salem. My only regret is that I did not get to know her better. But in the little that I leaned about her, I found her to be dignified, respectful, and courageous. She was a trailblazer—one whose shoulders were broad enough to carry me and many other attorneys of color—as an exemplary lawyer and person who sought not self-publicity or gain but to better her community in many ways. One of her and her husband's great contributions was in the form of three sons, two of them identical twins, Harold and Harvey Kennedy. For over forty years they have been trailblazers themselves, in sexual harassment cases and other civil cases that many other trial attorneys would not have accepted for representation.

It is for these reasons and more that I include the Honorable Annie Brown Kennedy as one of my mentors or those who have inspired me.

My Career Law Clerk, Pedra Denise Lee

> Never stop being who God called you to be.... The world is a better place because of your courageous spirit. —JUNE 2016
>
> I need some grace myself, that's why I try not to judge others. —APRIL 2021

The English vocabulary is not sufficient to describe the inspiration that my career law clerk, Pedra Denise Lee, has graced me with her presence over the last dozen years. I have been richly blessed to observe her immense talent daily, and it has been my privilege to be in her midst. Below are some of her outstanding personal characteristics:

- Grounded
- Full of grace but admits her humanness, including her faults, and openly admits that she needs some grace herself, which is why she tries hard not to judge others
- Patient with others, especially me
- Intelligence
- Wise and mature well beyond her years
- Forgiving
- Dedicated to her family, church, community, and work
- Humble
- Trustworthy
- Committed and loyal; she has served with me for twelve years as of December 2024
- Hard work ethic
- Student of the law extraordinaire
- Teacher extraordinaire; she could teach at any law school in the country
- Legal writer extraordinaire
- Legal researcher extraordinaire
- Excellent in most things related to information technology (IT)
- Loved by all throughout the Middle District of North Carolina and beyond and all who get to know her

I asked Pedra to describe some things that were important to her in life. She said,

> Three things of great importance to me on my journey and in my

> next chapter: 1. God's direct assignment for me, His plans for me as I'm a strong believer in Jeremiah 29:11. 2. An environment where I can have great impact, not about "visibility" but working with others to make a difference. 3. Money: God has been good to me so I don't worry about the money; it will take care of itself.

Pedra Denise Lee is simply an extraordinary human being who has prolonged my career. For that and more I am truly and forever grateful!

Attorney Walter Foil Brinkley Jr.

JUNE 22, 1926–APRIL 6, 2015

> I have served with Joe Webster for several years on the North Carolina Board of Law Examiners and I feel Joe is a lawyer of the highest integrity whose knowledge of the law and keen sense of justice qualify him admirably for service as judge.
>
> FROM JOE'S 1994 DISTRICT COURT CAMPAIGN

I first met the late Walter F. Brinkley Jr. in October 1989 during my first day of service as a board member on the North Carolina Board of Law Examiners. He had already been serving on that distinguished board for a long period of time. Also, by then, as I would learn, he was one of the most well-rounded and respected lawyers in the state of North Carolina. He was a partner in a Lexington, North Carolina law firm. Prior to law school, Walter Brinkley had served in the US Navy during World War II and the Korean War. He never spoke of that service to me, and I am not surprised because there was no boast about him. He was a recipient of the coveted John J. Parker Award by the North Carolina Bar Association. Walter Brinkley also served as president of the North Carolina Bar Association and was one of the bar leaders who advocated for a statewide legal services program to represent those in civil cases who could not afford an attorney.

Walter Brinkley was a mentor and great friend of mine. He came to be that while we served together on the Board of Law Examiners, particularly on the Drafting Committee. As chair of that committee and as chair of the entire board, he led with respect and obvious command of each subject area that would be tested on the bar exam. While I never knew him to practice criminal law, I saw that his knowledge of even that area of the law surpassed my own knowledge, even though I had practiced criminal law considerably from the beginning of my law practice soon after becoming a member of the state bar.

I have told many people that Walter Brinkley was like a second father to me. During our long Board of Law Examiners' grading sessions, we took long walks and talked. I asked his advice on many subjects, and he took the time to listen to me on whatever subjects I wanted to discuss, and then give me his advice. His wisdom compares with that of my late friend the Honorable Sammie Chess Jr., one of the wisest individuals I have ever known.

Walter Brinkley truly can be characterized as a "citizen lawyer." His reputation was untarnished, a man of utmost integrity and respect in every manner. An added joy of knowing Walter Brinkley was getting to know his wife, Helen, who was a phenomenal person. I still recall her smile to this day.

I can think of no one who epitomized the citizen lawyer title in North Carolina more than Walter Brinkley. His natural body died some eight years ago, but his memory will live on for as long as those who knew him continue to call his name. Years after his death I still often think of him and what he meant to me, and I will continue to call his name. Indeed, he was both a mentor and one who inspired me greatly. I miss him so much!

The Honorable Chief Judge Linda Mace McGee

> Joe Webster will bring to our courts the very best in integrity, dedication, sensitivity and legal ability. He is a person who deals with the important issues we now face in a reasoned and caring manner. The issues are not just catch phrases to him but are challenges he thinks through carefully in reaching his decisions. Then he moves forward with his decisions to turn them into actions that help others.
>
> FROM JOE'S 1994 DISTRICT COURT CAMPAIGN

I first met the Honorable Mace McGee during our board membership on the NC Board of Law Examiners in 1989. As I recall, she was still practicing law at the time with a firm up in Boone, North Carolina. I immediately found her to be kind, cordial, professional, and obviously brought up by good parents in rural Western North Carolina.

I recall attending Judge McGee's investiture after she was appointed to the North Carolina Court of Appeals by then-governor Jim Hunt. As we proceeded through the receiving line to congratulate her, I vividly recall telling Governor Hunt why I thought she was the best possible choice for the appointment. What I told him had more to do with the fact that Judge McGee was not "political" in nature and was deserving because of her commitment and dedication to her faith, family, and profession. Based upon my experience with her on the North Carolina Board of Law Examiners, I knew that she was a student of the law and that she had sound judgment and an outstanding judicial demeanor. She treated each candidate before the board with dignity and respect.

I was so blessed to get to know Judge McGee and would not hesitate to tell my attorney daughter and any other member of the legal bar—or any other profession for that matter—that they should follow in her footsteps.

Serving as Board of Law Examiners members together, I miss the days we spent during long character and fitness hearings and bar exam gradings. We also spent time with our children at long dinners during the summer bar exam gradings and had many occasions to laugh as we saw our children grow right before our eyes. We knew how blessed we were to be a part of a special group of attorneys from across the state of North Carolina. Since the days as board members on the Board of Law Examiners, our paths have often crossed at bar-related and other occasions. I visited and observed Judge McGee for at least one oral argument. She was dignified yet modest and professional in her approach to the cases and attorneys who argued their cases before her. She was a shining example of a judge who unquestionably garnered the utmost respect of her fellow judges, attorneys, and public in general. Her rulings have been well thought out and well written, evidencing her great understanding of the facts of the case and respect for the law.

I am so blessed to have had the Honorable Linda Mace McGee as a role model for me. I called upon her for recommendations for the numerous appointments I have sought to the judiciary and other positions during my career. I regret the delay in telling the world and, more importantly, Linda what's been on my heart for over three decades. May God continue to bless her for years to come.

My Father, James E. 'Tom' Webster

"How Come I Can't?"

JULY 3, 1925–MARCH 29, 2003

My dad, who succumbed to cancer at age seventy-seven, was a hard-working man, husband, and father of eight children. He was one of fourteen children born to Fred and Annie Webster and lived in the Goodwill or nearby area all his life. I hear from my mom that he did move up to Washington, DC, for a short while prior to marriage and returned with a "conk" hairstyle, which entailed having one's hair chemically straightened. She said he looked like a po' white man when he returned home. The implication was that he didn't get much to eat in the big city. Dad never mentioned one word to me about the days he spent in Washington, DC. Because he never breathed one word about his sojourn in the nation's capital, I don't know whether he intended to live there or perhaps just went there to visit his cousin James Brown, also from the Goodwill community where they grew up. It is ironic that my choice for college and law school was Howard University in the nation's capital, and that DC is the home to my two daughters and their families for nearly two decades.

My father was a Christian man, who undoubtedly believed in God. The entire family attending church on Sunday morning was not an option, no matter what time you came in from partying on Saturday night. My father, like many Websters, had a stubborn streak and temper that he had to work on. I consider my dad to be someone who inspired me because he went to work every day he was supposed to work and came home from work every evening most often in time for family dinner. In that sense he was a perfect role model. I believe from my heart that he was completely faithful to my mother for their entire marriage—some fifty-seven years, although they fussed about many things, most of them unimportant. Dad came home from a hard day of work driving a brick truck, and as he came through the living room where we sat watching television, he would thump our heads, one at a time. My father was from the generation of men that seldom if ever would tell their children that they loved them. I don't recall my father ever hugging me or kissing me. But thumping our heads when got home from work was his way of showing his love and affection for us. But I have no doubt that he loved us. I could see in the photos of our family that he was proud of us and loved us.

My dad proudly told many of his acquaintances that "My son Joe is a lawyer and a preacher." That was his way of saying how proud he was of me. I doubt he ever thought about that one day his son would become a judge. Around the house, he was mostly quiet and reserved. Until I had my own children, it seems we didn't have too much in common and little conversation took place between us. When I returned to my hometown to practice law, I attended my home church, Goodwill Baptist Church. My dad got very frustrated with what he perceived to be wrongdoing or improper actions on the part of the pastor, especially if he did not consult with the deacons first. As soon as I arrived at my parents' home for dinner after church, he'd say, "The pastor said or did such-and-such. Boy, is there any book on that?" He meant is there any Bible scripture or other support to be found that would support what the pastor did or said. My dad believed strongly that we should do what is right and not wrong. He knew the difference for sure. All those in my community who didn't stand with him as he tried to make his point to the pastor now know that my father was completely right. Having quit school in the fourth grade, he didn't know how to express himself as he could have if he had been more educated. But he was educated in life. You had to be hard working and smart to be able to raise and support a wife and eight children and buy a ninety-eight-acre farm in 1966. He also bought a new car and other late-model vehicles that were very clean. My great uncle Early Moore said of my dad, "If you bought a Coke, Tom could buy one." This was Early's way of saying my father was not one who sought handouts but was a hardworking, independent man. Early told me my father quit school to go to work in the fields. The early family photos of my father, mother, and their children, all dressed in suits and neckties, demonstrated that they had achieved a certain amount of financial success. I can see in those photos the pride that my parents had in their children.

Last I visited Dad was in his hospital bed as he suffered with terminal cancer. He began to cry as I spoke with him about how hard he had to work to support his family. He was six feet, two inches tall and got every ounce of energy out of his slender build. As a result, my dad and mom's faith and hard work allowed my family to move out of poverty in one generation and inspired my siblings and me to "make something" out of ourselves. Dad overcame many obstacles to raise his eight children in a comfortable home. This is also why I included my father among those who have inspired me.

My Mother, Bettie Ester Moore Webster

OCTOBER 10, 1929–SEPTEMBER 16, 2013

> Joe, if you put God first in your life and work hard, someone will see you trying, and someone will help you. —AUGUST 15, 1972

From early in my life, perhaps as early as when I was four years old, I remember that my mother was my protector, comforter, and encourager. She was there when I was sick or had gotten hurt, although she administered corporal punishment if my injuries resulted from me being disobedient or doing something that she had told me not to do. I know that it was out of love.

My mother was there when I was upset with my father for cutting my hair too close, causing tears to flow down my cheek. I recall my dad saying, "What's wrong with you, boy?" as I sat in the bar-type stool as he cut my hair during my youth. Of course, I didn't have the courage to tell my dad that I was upset that he was cutting my hair too short. Immediately after my haircut, I would run to my mother with tears. She would say, "Joe, your hair will grow back." While I'm sure it made me feel better, it did nothing to lessen my embarrassment I felt in the early school grades. During my early school grades, my mother let me stay out of school when I didn't feel well. My mother was a stay-at-home mom during the first years of my life and that provided much comfort to me and my siblings. My mom was not too hard on my younger brother and I during the bedwetting days of our youth.

My mother's meals were delicious and nutritious. She was an excellent cook. My favorite meal took place after church on Sundays. My mother had caught one or more of what we would call today "free-range chickens" roaming freely in our backyard. Early in life I observed her ringing the necks of the chickens and preparing them for dinner. The fried chicken, gravy, and fresh vegetables such as stewed corn, potatoes, fresh tomatoes from the garden in the spring and summer months and canned or frozen vegetables throughout the winter, and freshly made biscuits or corn bread made for some memorable meals. I recall some members of the community coming by while we were eating dinner and my parents would say, "Join us, you are welcome; We got plenty, such as it is." It may be that we only had fatback pork as our entrée, but we had plenty, such as it was, and were willing to share it with others in the community.

My mother read from the Bible frequently and taught Sunday school for many years. She was a true missionary and visited the sick and shut-ins and elderly of our community.

In her latter years, she prepared the Communion for the first Sunday of each month. She quoted scripture to our family seemingly daily to the point that my father would say that someone should give my mom a license to preach.

My mother, like most of her generation, never received a high school diploma. She married at age sixteen and had her first child, a son, at age seventeen, and another son at age nineteen, and another son two years after that. I came along three years later, and another son two years after that, by the age of twenty-six, my mother had five sons, ages one to nine—stairsteps, for sure. But she wasn't finished. Three more siblings, a daughter, son, and then another daughter, completed the family of eight children. As I observe my three grandsons by two daughters and two daughters by our son, and what hardship my three children endure, I know how difficult it must have been for my mother to be the primary caretaker of those first five boys. She loved and was so proud of her children. In fact, she thought they were next to perfect, although we were not by a long shot.

Even after I became an adult and entered college, I recall the many letters I received from my mother with thirty-dollar and forty-dollar money orders enclosed. They seemed to arrive in time for the weekend. I once sent her a letter informing her that I would one day repay her. As the years passed and I had a family to support, I knew that I would never be able to repay her for all she and my dad had done for me. More than anything else, she prayed for my siblings and me daily and expected nothing in return.

My mother was very supportive of my work as an attorney and had begun to decline in health with Alzheimer's disease by the time I was appointed as an administrative law judge in 2006. She attended my investiture. However, six years later, her health had declined even further, and she had entered a nursing home facility when I was appointed as a US magistrate judge. Her health would not permit her to attend my investiture ceremony.

For these reasons and many more, I count my mother as one of the most important of those who have inspired me in my life.

Reverend Dr. James A. Webster

APRIL 28, 1947–MAY 23, 2023

> From Acts 7:58 where Saul held the cloaks of the ones who stoned Stephen to death. James preached from the subject "Don't Be Caught Holding the Devil's Coat."

My earliest memory of my oldest brother was that he was a tall, handsome preteenager with walnut-colored skin. He was, in the image of our father, growing into the six feet, two inches in height he would become during his high school years. His hair was much straighter than my own, and as was the practice of the day, a stocking cap and a little Murry's hair product, produced enviable waves in his hair. I recall attempting to do the same with my own hair without success. My hair was too course, and a stocking cap and Murray's Superior Hair Dressing Pomade in the orange container, nor anything else I did, produced the desired result.

James played on the Charles Drew High School basketball team, although I have no memory of seeing him perform on the team. It may have been because he graduated in 1965, when I was in the fifth grade and didn't attend afterschool athletic events. James was also a school bus driver at some point during his latter high school years. It seems like I remember him stating that he earned thirty dollars per month, but I'm not certain of this fact. I'm sure this responsibility allowed him to grow into manhood quickly. In addition, my father required the help of him and my older brother John in loading pulpwood and firewood as part of the numerous side jobs our dad held to support a family of eight children.

By the time I graduated from high school in 1972, my brother had gotten married to Brenda Elaine Dalton at the early age of twenty, served four years in the Air Force amid the Vietnam War, and purchased a house in Greensboro. He later built a house on our parents' farm in the Goodwill community.

My brother was full of humor, especially when he was among relatives and close friends. That character trait caused him to be a magnet, drawing many to desire to be in his presence. On occasion, if I happened to be in the audience, James often humorously told the audience from the pulpit that he had driven me to Washington, DC, to enroll at Howard University and that if he hadn't done that, I wouldn't have attended college and become a lawyer. I could never refute the fact of his driving me there, but I would have gotten there if I had to walk because of my determination. This was only one of the many examples of humor James frequently displayed to those who got to know him well.

I recall vividly on one occasion nearly thirty years ago I purchased a 1970s model rusty green Chevrolet Nova from one of my fellow attorneys in the law firm where we worked in Chapel Hill. It passed inspection, and I washed and polished it with the best polish I could find to bring out the color and make it look a little better. Well, one day I drove it to my hometown to visit my parents. I pulled into the driveway and parked, went inside, and visited with my parents. James came by, greeted me, and said, "Is that you?" as he pointed toward my car. I responded yes. He then said, "You just about walking." James always kept very clean late-model vehicles in his yard, and I'm sure he was thinking that I must not be doing well financially as a practicing attorney.

On another occasion, during my family's preparation to attend our mother's funeral in September 2013, we had gathered at my sister Kathy's home just up the road from Goodwill Baptist Church. While we were awaiting the arrival of the funeral home members to transport the family to the church, I noticed my nephew Tim was no longer in the room where most of us had gathered. He had arrived from his home in Johannesburg, South Africa. Tim was attired in his more traditional European–South African shorter-style suit coat. Not seeing Tim in the room for a short period of time, I asked James, where was Tim? James, without hesitating, responded, "Probably gone to try to find the rest of his suit." This was just another indication of how conservative-minded James was. Recently Tim told me he measured James once to have him a suit tailored. Tim recalls James telling him, "Just don't make mine like you make your own suits." That was James Arthur Webster, and all those who knew him miss his humor.

My greatest momentous memory of my brother took place during the summer of 1975 when he, after receiving his calling, preached his initial sermon at Goodwill Baptist Church. I do not recall his text, but I vividly recall his stirring proclamation from Matthew 6:25–33, wherein James said, "Look at the birds of the air, they neither sow nor reap nor gather into barns, and yet your heavenly father feeds them." Forty-eight years later, on August 12, 2023, I found myself proclaiming as invited guest preacher from the Goodwill Baptist Church pulpit the same truth: that if God feeds the birds, then surely, surely, He will provide for us. But perhaps the greatest sermon I heard James preach was the eulogy of our cousin Regina Johnson Mahatha Brooks. It was moving and powerful! Also ranking high on the list of the many sermons I heard James preach was the very relevant and timely one he preached at Goodwill Baptist Church on July 14, 2018, for the twentieth anniversary service of my own initial sermon. On that occasion, James's text came from Luke 17:11–19, wherein he compared my returning to Goodwill to give thanks on my 20th anniversary to the one of the ten lepers healed by Jesus who returned to thank him for healing him. My best law school friend, Wayne Mason from Los Angeles, reminded me in recent years that he recalls attending a church service in which my brother took his text from Acts 7:58 where Saul held the cloaks of the ones who stoned Stephen to death. My classmate said some forty-five years later he still remembered his subject: "Don't Be Caught Holding the Devil's Coat."

In my youth and adult life, I observed that James was human like the rest of us. He had flaws sometimes unbecoming of a Christian, but he was, without a doubt, saved by grace. There was no doubt that he had been like Jesus in Luke 4:18: that the spirit of the Lord was upon him, and James had been anointed to preach the gospel to the poor, had been sent to heal the brokenhearted, to preach deliverance to the captives, recovery of sight to the blind, to set at liberty those who are bruised...."

So when James's mortal body was ready to be offered, when the time of his departure was at hand, when he knew that he would not be getting well; when he no longer had the energy or will to fight, when he knew that he had already fought a good fight and finished his course, when the assignment that he had faithfully carried for nearly forty-eight years in ministry was clear in his mind, when James was ready, it was then on May 23, 2023, that he transitioned and went home to be with the Lord. Less than forty-eight hours earlier I had been afforded the privilege of sitting with him while his wife, Brenda and son, Derrick attended his thirty-ninth pastoral anniversary at Oak Ridge First Baptist Church. James had just gotten out of the hospital the day before his anniversary and was far too weak to attend. As he sat in his favorite chair, he drifted in and out of sleep with his oxygen mask in place. I sensed that my brother was not getting any better, but I had no idea that he was so close to death. We talked periodically, but only when he wanted to talk. James found the energy to rise from his chair and visit the restroom.

I wished that I had known what else to say to comfort and encourage him, but I did not know what I could say that would have mattered. I sensed that he knew his time for departure was near, and that he was not desirous of fighting any longer. I read in his obituary that he had stated,

> If he could leave a legacy, it would be that he lived his life with integrity and his due reward would be found in Matthew 25:21, "His Lord said unto him, well done, thou good and faithful servant: thou hast been faithful over a few things, I will make thee ruler over many things. Enter thou unto the joy of the Lord."

James inspired me with his commitment to his calling; his humble but strong leadership abilities were evident and unmatched and on par with the powerful and inspiring preaching revealed by and through the Holy Spirit each time he preached. The Spirit got a hold of him each time James brought the word—thousands of sermons over nearly half a century that had been placed on his heart to deliver to the congregation. Many pastors-preachers must have envied the Spirit that resembled a drunk man in the pulpit toward the end of his sermons brought on by the Holy Spirit, the I am, the Lily of the Valley, the Bright and Morning Star, the Chief Cornerstone, the Word, the Light, the Son of Man, the Righteous Lamb of God, the Good Shepherd, the Savior of the World, the Redeemer, Bread of Life, Only Begotten Son, Prince of Peace, Son of God, and the Alpha and the Omega. Hallelujah!

James left a legacy that will live long after his earthly death. I'm comforted in the word that makes it clear in Philippians 1:21–26 (KJV): "For to me to live is Christ, and to die is gain." And Job in 14:14 poses a question that I believe he knew the answer to: "If a man dies, shall he live again?" And John 3:16 (NKJV) makes James's fate even clearer: "For God so loved the world that he gave his only begotten son, that whosoever believes in him should not perish but have everlasting life." James was saved by grace, and that is all that is important.

The Honorable Alexander Williams Jr.

FEBRUARY 20, 2020

Some are called. Some are sent. Some came anyway.

I met Alexander Willams Jr. when I was a 3rd year student at Howard University School of Law. He was one of my professors. I don't even recall what course he taught me. However, he taught well. He was voted "teacher of the year" his first year of teaching at Howard. We became life-long friends. We have visited each other in our respective homes, and we have gotten to know each other's wives and children. We have a lot in common. We are avid supporters of Howard University and its athletic teams. Both of us are persons of faith who became ordained ministers, and members of the federal judiciary. Alex was appointed by President Clinton as an Article III U.S. District Court Judge for the District of Maryland. I later became a U.S. Magistrate Judge for the Middle District of North Carolina.

Alex's resume is outstanding, and he has earned all the accolades bestowed upon him. But mostly he has been my friend, confidant, supporter, and encourager. He is one of my mentors. Alex never questioned my many attempts to obtain promotions. He always wrote letters of recommendations for me upon request. Alex has even taken the time to mentor and recommend my daughter Camille for employment when she entered the legal profession.

As fellow ministers of the gospel, I credit Alex for giving me the confidence to know that God even calls lawyers to preach God's word. Alex has humor. He was on my Initial Service program in July 1998. When his turn to speak came, he said, "Some are called. Some are sent. Some came anyway." He then turned around in the pulpit and looked squarely at me. Of course, the audience broke into laughter. Alex also traveled from his home in Maryland to my home in Chapel Hill and then on to Yadkinville, North Carolina. He and I had been invited to speak at my cousin, Reverend James Moore's church. Fortunately, I was selected to preach at the 11 a.m. service. In between the 11 a.m. and 3 p.m. services, the congregation served the largest country feast neither Alex nor I had ever seen. Fat back meat, fried chicken, greens, deserts and much more; there was nothing missing. We ate so much that Alex and I had to loosen our belts. During Alex's turn at the podium, he told the congregation that I had engaged in a conspiracy with the pastor to allow me to preach first, knowing there would be a feast after the first service.

Nevertheless, Alex preached the word. When Reverend Moore sees me, he still asks me about that preacher judge from Maryland.

I am grateful to Alex for being patient with me as I have grown into whatever I have become. I am also grateful for his friendship and the love he has shown for me for over four decades. He has contributed mightily to my life, and I will never forget him.

Frances Glenn Ramsey: Leaving a Committed Life Behind

APRIL 20, 1921–JANUARY 8, 1987

> Joe, sometimes I have gone to the cupboard and the cupboard would be bare, but there was always food on the table.

In one of his last sermons two months prior to his death, Dr. Martin Luther King Jr. reflected upon his own mortality and what others should say at his funeral. In short, he wanted to be remembered for having lived a life of commitment.

As I think about Dr. King's words, I ponder the thought of my own legacy. I have come to understand and appreciate that leaving a committed life behind comes in many forms. One doesn't have to be so famous that others can Google you and your accomplishments will appear on your computer. Twenty-two years ago, my mother-in-law, Frances Glenn Ramsey, also left a committed life behind even though she never graduated from high school.

Mrs. Ramsey was born and raised and lived most of her life in North Carolina's rural communities, off the beaten path, down the road, in the country in areas like Person County's community called Shake Rag. After the Great Depression of the twentieth century ended, Mrs. Ramsey gave birth to fifteen children, fourteen of whom survived her. She lived a simple yet fulfilling life without the comforts of running water or emerging technologies. Mrs. Ramsey seldom traveled far from the places she called home. She never even owned a car.

Joe's mother-in-law
Frances Glenn Ramsey

Frances Glenn Ramsey left a committed life behind by leaving a legacy of sharing the little that she had in material things with others in the community. I hear that she allowed the wayward friends of her sons to stay in her home for long visits, and she treated them like her own children. She was an excellent cook and had a wonderful sense of humor and a contagious laugh. On one occasion, after resolving that I was an ordinary person without much money, she told me that growing up she used to think all preachers and lawyers were rich, but "I can see that my coattails are just as long as yours." She followed this comment with her trademark laugh, which caused her whole body to shake. On her deathbed as she lay dying of cancer, she asked my wife, Diane, to go in the kitchen and make me a plate of food. She was always looking out for others. Once I asked Mrs. Ramsey how she and her husband were able to feed all her children. Her husband had a stroke when my wife was a teenager. She said, "Joe, I have gone to the cupboard and the cupboard would be bare, but there was always food on the table."

I know now that you can't feed fifteen children without great faith. I know now that neither a map nor a Google search will reveal the significance of a life deeply rooted in love, compassion, culture, tradition, and history. I thank God for placing Frances Glenn Ramsey in my life so that I could learn how to leave a committed life behind. What kind of life do you want to leave behind?

Addie Mae Collins, Denise McNair, Carol Robertson, Cynthia Wesley, and Sarah Collins

SUNSET, SEPTEMBER 15, 1963

They aren't dead as long as we continue to call their names.

Addie Mae Collins, Denise McNair, Carol Robertson, and Cynthia Wesley were the four little black girls killed by racists in 1963 when they set off a bomb in the Sixteenth Street Baptist Church in Birmingham, Alabama. Until recently I had not recalled that Addie Collins's sister, Sarah Collins, had survived but lost her right eye in the bomb blast. Since the writing of the Honorable Sammie Chess Jr.'s biography, which was published in 2017, I have stated on several occasions that my only regret was that while I mentioned the four little black girls in the biography, I did not call their names. I did not even mention the fact there was a fifth little girl who suffered serious injury, let alone call her name. Having recently read about her being a victim in the bombing, I wondered to myself whether she had wished that she had died with the others, as losing an eye at any age is a devastating blow that can affect one's self-worth and self-esteem for life. I also have read that sometimes surviving victims wonder why they survive and not the others.

While I can only imagine how devastated the families of these little souls who lost their lives and the one who lost her eye must have felt, like Judge Chess as stated in his biography, somehow, I can still feel their deep anguish. Thinking about them sixty-one years later, and the many others who lost their lives, bore the brute force of water cannons, rocks, and insults hurled at those courageous enough to be on the front lines of the civil rights struggle, so that I and all others might have a chance of equal treatment and equal human dignity, I am truly grateful for their sacrifice. That is why I list these five precious little girls among my numerous heroes and those who inspired me during my life's journey. They, more than any of the others listed in this chapter, suffered the most: serious injury or a loss of life at an early age.

CHAPTER TWELVE

Legacy

I hope others will remember me as a person who was grounded in faith, family, and a strong commitment to serve others in all aspects of my life. I would like to be remembered as a person of calm purpose, but nevertheless, an unmistakable person of faith crying in the wilderness for equal justice under law, respect for human dignity, and reconciliation among all people.

ABOUT THE AUTHOR

On the steps of the United States Supreme Court after listening to an Oral Argument November 5, 2019

Joe L. Webster is a native of North Carolina, one of eight children born to James E. and Bettie E. Webster in Rockingham County. Joe graduated from Howard University (B.A.), 1976, Howard University School of Law (J.D.) 1979, and Duke University School of Law (LLM), 2016. He has served with Legal Services of North Carolina, engaged in the general practice of law for nearly 20 years, Chair of the North Carolina Board of Law Examiners, and served as Adjunct Professor of Law at the Norman Adrian Wiggins School of Law at Campbell University. Joe also served as Administrative Law Judge in the State of North Carolina Office of Administrative Hearings, and since 2012, has served as United States Magistrate Judge for the Middle District of North Carolina. Joe was ordained by the Goodwill Baptist Church and the High Point Educational and Missionary Baptist Association in 2001 and served as Associate Minister, Oberlin Baptitst Church in Raleigh, NC (2012–2024). He has received many recognitions, including being honored by his alma mater by induction into the Howard University Alumni Club of the Research Triangle Park Hall of Fame, and acknowledgement by the North Carolina Bar Association with its 2nd Pro Bono Service Award in 1985, and the Legal Legends of Color Award in 2023. Joe has been married to Diane Ramsey Webster for 44 years, and they are the proud parents of three children and seven grandchildren.

BENEDICTION

Finally, brothers and sisters; rejoice! Strive for full restoration, encourage one another, be of one mind, live in peace. And the God of love and peace will be with you. 2 CORINTHIANS 13:11 (NIV)

My wife, Diane, and I were relaxing as we observed a beautiful sunset over Jordan Lake, near Pittsboro, NC, 2023